GOVERNING GLOBAL BIODIVERSITY

Global Environmental
Governance Series

Series Editors: John J. Kirton and Konrad von Moltke

Global Environmental Governance addresses the new generation of twenty-first century environmental problems and the challenges they pose for management and governance at the local, national, and global levels. Centred on the relationships among environmental change, economic forces, and political governance, the series explores the role of international institutions and instruments, national and sub-federal governments, private sector firms, scientists, and civil society, and provides a comprehensive body of progressive analyses on one of the world's most contentious international issues.

Also in the series

Agricultural Policy Reform
Politics and process in the EU and US in the 1990s
H. Wayne Moyer and Tim Josling
ISBN 0 7546 3050 1

International Equity and Global Environmental Politics:
Power and principles in US foreign policy
Paul G. Harris
ISBN 0 7546 1735 1

Linking Trade, Environment, and Social Cohesion:
NAFTA experiences, global challenges
John J. Kirton and Virginia W. Maclaren
ISBN 0 7546 1934 6

Governing Global Biodiversity

The evolution and implementation of the
Convention on Biological Diversity

Edited by
Philippe G. Le Prestre

ASHGATE

Published by
Ashgate Publishing Limited
Gower House
Croft Road
Aldershot
Hampshire GU11 3HR
England

Ashgate Publishing Company
Suite 420
101 Cherry Street
Burlington, VT 05401-4405 USA

Ashgate website: http://www.ashgate.com

British Library Cataloguing in Publication Data
Governing global biodiversity : the evolution and
    implementation of the Convention on Biological Diversity. -
    (Global environmental governance)
    1. Biological diversity conservation 2. International
    cooperation 3. International obligations
    1. Le Prestre, Philippe G.
    333.9'516

Library of Congress Cataloging-in-Publication Data
Governing global biodiversity : the evolution and implementation of the convention on
biological diversity / edited by Philippe G. Le Prestre.
        p.cm. -- (Global environmental governance)
    Includes bibliographical references (p.).
    ISBN 0-7546-1744-0 (alk. paper)
    1. Biological diversity conservation. 2. Biological diversity conservation--Government
policy. I. Le Prestre, Philippe G. II. Series.

QH75 .G65 2002
333.95--dc21

                                                                        2002071162
ISBN 0 7546 1744 0

Printed in Great Britain by Antony Rowe Ltd, Chippenham, Wiltshire

Contents

List of Figures

List of Tables

List of Boxes

List of Contributors

François Blais
François Blais teaches political philosophy at Université Laval (Quebec). He is the author of *Un revenu garanti pour tous: Introduction aux principes de l'allocation universelle* (Montreal, Boréal, 2001; English translation, Toronto, James Lorimer, 2002). He has also published a number of articles on environmental and social justice.

Louis Guay
Louis Guay is a professor in the Department of Sociology at Université Laval (Quebec). He has taught and researched on environmental problems, with special emphasis on science and politics in environmental policy-making and on the social construction of ecological problems. He also holds the UNESCO-Université Laval chair on sustainable development.

Paule Halley
Paule Halley is an assistant professor in the Faculty of Law at Université Laval (Quebec). She is an attorney and holds a JD. She has authored several publications and conference papers, including *Le régime pénal québécois de lutte contre la pollution* (Cowansville, Yvon Blais, 1997) and *Le droit pénal de l'environnement: L'interdiction de polluer* (Cowansville, Yvon Blais, 2001). Her research interests revolve around environmental law and new modes of regulation.

Marc Hufty
Marc Hufty is associate professor of political science at the Graduate Institute of Development Studies, University of Geneva, where he leads the Research Group on Environment and Governance. He has lectured in Madagascar, Chile, Peru, and South Africa. He has been conducting research on the North-South aspects of the political economy of biodiversity since 1993. Among his latest publications is "La gouvernance internationale de la biodiversité" (*Etudes internationales*, vol. 32, no. 1, 2001, pp. 5-29).

Jane Hutton
Jane Hutton is currently studying ecology, design, and urban issues in the landscape architecture programme at the University of Toronto. Previously, she studied biology and environmental studies at McGill University and worked with Catherine Potvin, studying traditional plant use in Ipeti, Panama.

Philippe G. Le Prestre
Philippe Le Prestre is professor of political science in the Department of Political Science and at the Institut des sciences de l'environnement (ISE) of the Université du Québec à Montréal where he specializes in international environmental politics and foreign policy analysis and heads the Global Ecopolitics Observatory. Between

1995 and 1999, he chaired the Environmental Studies Section of the International Studies Association. He is the author of *Ecopolitique internationale* (1997) and *The World Bank and the Environmental Challenge* (1989) and edited *Protecting the Ozone Layer* (1998) and other books on foreign policy.

Désirée M. McGraw
Désirée M. McGraw works as a consultant, researcher, and speaker in the field of international environmental negotiations and communications. She currently lectures on globalization and governance at McGill University and serves as the environmental expert for the G-8 Research Group based at the University of Toronto's Munk Centre for International Studies. She has followed the Biodiversity Convention both as a reporter for the *Earth Negotiations Bulletin* (1993-1997) and as an advisor to the Government of Canada (1997-2001). The CBD also served as the case study for her doctoral research at the London School of Economics and Political Science.

Frank Muttenzer
A graduate of the University of Basel Faculty of Law, Frank Muttenzer also studied comparative law and the sociology of law in Brussels before turning to social sciences at the Geneva Institut universitaire d'études du développement. He has worked on international law pertaining to indigenous populations. His PhD research focuses on legal policy in Africa with a particular focus on environmental problems in Madagascar.

Geneviève Patenaude
Geneviève Patenaude is a PhD student at the Environmental Change Institute, University of Oxford. Her current research interests include forest ecology, conservation, and issues pertaining to forestry in international policy (notably in relation to the Kyoto Protocol).

Catherine Potvin
Catherine Potvin is associate professor in the Department of Biology, McGill University, and director of the McGill-Smithsonian Tropical Research Institute Neotropical Environment Option. She was trained as a botanist at Duke University, where her initial research interest centred on global warming. Development of an undergraduate course in conservation biology took her to Panama, where she started working with the Embera people in 1994.

François Pythoud
François Pythoud is senior scientific adviser at the Swiss Agency for the Environment, Forests and Landscape. A plant biologist by training, he holds a PhD in science and has worked on biotechnology and biosafety-related issues since 1990. He has been closely involved in all the biosafety talks within the Convention on Biological Diversity since 1995 and headed the Swiss delegation to the

Biosafety Working Group from 1996 to 1999. He was spokesperson for the Compromise Group during the Cartagena EXCOP meeting in 1999, chair of the Commodities Contact Group, and co-chair of the scope and trade-related issues contact groups during the final round of negotiations of the Cartagena Protocol in January 2000 in Montreal. He now serves on the bureau of the Intergovernmental Committee for the Cartagena Protocol.

Geneviève Reed

Trained in communications and political science, Geneviève Reed is a graduate of the Department of Political Science of the Université du Québec à Montréal where she undertook research and wrote her thesis on the Clearing-house Mechanism of the Biodiversity Convention. She was also the founding editor of *Objectif Terre* (1998-2000).

Jean-Pierre Revéret

Trained in development economics and ecology, Jean-Pierre Revéret is a professor in the Department of Biology and at the Institut des sciences de l'environnement (ISE) of the Université du Québec à Montréal. He was the first director of the ISE, head of the Department of Environmental Management at the Université Senghor (Alexandria, Egypt), and deputy director of Geneva's Académie internationale de l'environnement. He has acted as an expert with UNESCO, UNCTAD, UNCED, the World Bank, and the Canadian International Development Agency. His research interests include the economics and management of natural resources as well as environmental impact assessments about which he has widely published.

Urs P. Thomas

Urs P. Thomas is a research associate at the University of Geneva's Department of Public International Law. His research area pertains to the trade-environment interface, more specifically biodiversity, agribusiness and North-South relations, and the legal and organizational aspects of the relationship between the CBD, FAO, WTO, and WIPO. He holds a PhD in political science from the Université du Québec à Montréal, has taught at universities in Montreal and Ottawa, and has served as a consultant for the Swiss government.

Alain Webster

Alain Webster holds a MSc in biology and has pursued advanced studies in economics. He has taught environmental economics for more than a decade at the Université du Québec à Montréal and at the University of Sherbrooke (Quebec). His areas of expertise include biodiversity, climate change, and environmental accounting. He is a special assistant to the president of the University of Sherbrooke and a member of the Global Ecopolitics Observatory.

Amanda Wolf

Amanda Wolf is senior lecturer in public policy at Victoria University, Wellington, New Zealand. Her current research interests include fairness analysis in public policy, food labelling policy, and the "right to know". She is the author of *Quotas in International Environmental Agreements* and articles on food policy, informed consent, and fairness in environmental negotiations.

Acknowledgements

In addition to those mentioned by individual authors, many intellectual and other debts were incurred in the process of producing this book. First of all, we are indebted to the biologists who have long sought to raise awareness of the importance of biodiversity and warn about its fate, and to people like Calestous Juma and Arthur Campeau, who have insisted that the Biodiversity Convention is not merely about biodiversity but also an important tool for changing relations between humanity and nature and within societies themselves, all of which are dependent on healthy ecosystems. We are also indebted to the many national and international officials as well as private citizens who participated in the negotiation and implementation of the regime – for their readiness to share their experience and ideas. We hope that they will find our efforts worthwhile. Production of the book also relied on the labour of many assistants, such as Edouard Buffière, Florence Fitoussi, Marie-Hélène Laurence, Jena Webb, and above all, Julie Crowley, who not only compiled the annexes but was also responsible for the production of the final manuscript and made key additional contributions.

This book was originally conceived as part of a team project on the Biodiversity Convention under the leadership of Marie-Hélène Parizeau, funded by the Social Sciences and Humanities Research Council of Canada (SSHRC), which supported research for chapters 4, 7, 8, 11, and 12 and covered part of the associated production and translation costs as well. SSHRC individual grants also supported work for chapters 3, 4, and 10. The Aid to Publications Committee and the Faculty of Political Science and Law of the Université du Québec à Montréal (UQAM) provided welcome financial support for the revision and production of the final manuscript. UQAM and its Institut des sciences de l'environnement also provided key support for a meeting in May 2001 that helped several authors present and refine their ideas, while the Biodiversity Convention Office of Environment Canada was instrumental in enabling Philippe Le Prestre to share and discuss the thesis of the book and identify further contributors at a meeting at the Institut universitaire d'études du développement (IUED) in Geneva in March 2001.

We are grateful to John Herity, head of the Biodiversity Convention Office of Environment Canada, and to Léopold Gaudreau, director of the Bureau de la conservation du patrimoine écologique of Quebec's Ministry of the Environment for their support over the years. We are also indebted to our anonymous reviewers for having taken the time to assess the manuscript carefully. Their thoughtful suggestions significantly helped to improve the final product. Last but not least, the gentle, firm, yet understanding prodding and support of John Kirton and Madeline Koch gave a crucial impetus to the endeavour and helped to see it through to completion.

List of Abbreviations

ABS	Access and benefit-sharing
ACTS	African Center for Technology Studies
AIA	Advance informed agreement
AIDS	Acquired immuno-deficiency syndrome
ANAE	Association nationale d'action environmentale
ANGAP	Association nationale de gestion des aires protégées
ASSINSEL	International Association of Plant Breeders
BCH	Biosafety Clearing-House
BDCP	Bioresources Development and Conservation Programme
BP	Cartagena Protocol on Biosafety (or Biosafety Protocol)
BSE	Bovine spongiform encephalopathy
CBD	Convention on Biological Diversity
CCD	Convention to Combat Desertification
CCME	Canadian Council of Ministers of the Environment
CEL	Commission on Environmental Law
CEPA	Canadian Environmental Protection Act
CFC	Chlorofluorocarbon
CFE	Comité du fonds pour l'environnement (Madagascar)
CGIAR	Consultative Group on International Agricultural Research
CGRFA	Commission on Genetic Resources for Food and Agriculture
CGS	Convention governance system
CHM	Clearing-house Mechanism (CBD)
CHM	Common Heritage of Mankind
CITES	Convention on International Trade in Endangered Species of Wild Fauna and Flora
CMS	Convention on Migratory Species of Wild Animals
COP	Conference of the Parties
CSD	Commission on Sustainable Development
CTE	Committee on Trade and Environment (WTO)
DNA	Desoxyribonucleic acid
DSB	Dispute settlement body
DSU	Dispute Settlement Understanding
ELC	Environmental Law Centre
ENGO	Environmental non-governmental organization
ESFUM	Écosystèmes forestiers à usages multiples (Madagascar)
ETC group	Action Group on Erosion, Technology, and Concentration (formerly RAFI)
EU	European Union
EXCOP	Extraordinary Meeting of the Conference of the Parties
FAO	Food and Agriculture Organization
FCE	Funding Committee for the Environment

FFP	Feed, food or processing
GATT	General Agreement on Tariffs and Trade
G-7	Group of 7 Nations
G-8	Group of 8 Nations
G-77	Group of 77 Nations
GBF	Global Biodiversity Forum
GECP	Global Environmental Change Programme
GEF	Global Environment Facility
Gelose	Gestion locale sécurisée
GEO	Global Environmental Organization
GIC	Global Industry Coalition
GISP	Global Invasive Species Programme
GM	Genetically modified
GMO	Genetically modified organism
GRAIN	Genetic Resources Action International
GRULAC	Latin American and Caribbean Group of Countries
GTI	Global Taxonomy Initiative
HCFC	Hexachlorofluorocarbon
HFC	Hydrofluorocarbon
IAC	Informal Advisory Committee
IATP	Institute for Agriculture and Trade Policy
IBES	International Bank for Ecological Settlements
ICCBD	Intergovernmental Committee for the Convention on Biological Diversity
ICCP	Intergovernmental Committee for the Cartagena Protocol on Biosafety
ICDP	Integrated Conservation and Development Projects
ICEL	International Council of Environmental Law
ICGEC	International Center for Genetic Engineering and Biotechnology
ICRI	International Coral Reef Initiative
IGO	Intergovernmental organization
IIFB	International Indigenous Forum on Biodiversity
IMF	International Monetary Fund
INBio	Instituto Nacional de Biodiversidad (Costa Rica)
INC	Intergovernmental Negotiating Committee
IOC	Intergovernmental Oceanographic Commission (UNESCO)
IP	Indigenous peoples
IPCC	Intergovernmental Panel on Climate Change
IPPC	International Plant Protection Convention
IPR	Intellectual property rights
ISOC	Inter-Sessional Meeting on the Operations of the Convention
IT	International Treaty on Plant Genetic Resources for Food and Agriculture
ITTA	International Tropical Timber Agreement

ITTO	International Tropical Timber Organization
IU	International Undertaking on Plant Genetic Resources for Food and Agriculture
IUCG	International Undertaking Intersessional Contact Group
IUCN	World Conservation Union
IWC	International Whaling Commission
JUSCANZ	Japan, US, Canada, Australia, New Zealand
JWP	Joint work programme
LMOs	Living modified organisms
LMO-FFPs	Living modified organism designated for use in feed, food, or processing
LRTAP	Long-range transboundary air pollution
MEA	Multilareral Environmental Agreement
MOP	Meeting of the Parties
MOC	Memoranda of co-operation
MOU	Memoranda of understanding
MS	Multilateral system (IU)
MSP	Meeting on the Strategic Plan
NCE	Networks of Centres of Excellence
NCI	National Cancer Institute
NFP	National focal point
NGO	Non-governmental organization
NICT	New information and communications technology
NRP	Norms, rules and procedures
NWFP	Non-wood forest product
OECD	Organization for Economic Cooperation and Development
OGEF	Organized global ecopolitical force
ONE	Office national de l'environnement (Madagascar)
PAE	Plan d'action environnemental (Madagascar)
PAGE	Pilot Assessment of Global Ecosystems
PBR	Plant breeders' rights
PCDI	Projets de conservation et de développement integrés (Madagascar)
PE 1	Plan Environnemental 1
PGR	Plant genetic resources
PIC	Prior informed consent
PNI	Pro-Natura International
POPs	Persistent organic pollutants
RAFI	Rural Advancement Foundation International (until 2001; now ETC Group)
SBSTA	Subsidiary Body for Scientific and Technological Advice (UNFCCC)
SBSTTA	Subsidiary Body for Scientific, Technical and Technological Advice (CBD)
SCBD	Secretariat of the CBD

SCCD	Secretariat of the UNCCD
SIR	Systems of implementation review
SPS	Agreement on the Application of Sanitary and Phytosanitary Measures (WTO)
STAP	Scientific and Technical Advisory Panel
STC	Science and Technological Committee (UNCCD)
TBT	Technical barriers to trade
TEK	Traditional ecological knowledge
TEV	Total economic value
TIP	Traditional intellectual property rights
TRIPs	Trade-related aspects of intellectual property rights
TRR	Traditional resource rights
TK	Traditional knowledge
UK	United Kingdom
UN	United Nations
UNCCD	United Nations Conference to Combat Desertification
UNCED	United Nations Conference on Environment and Development
UNCHE	United Nations Conference on the Human Environment
UNCLOS	United Nations Convention on the Law of the Sea
UNCTAD	United Nations Conference on Trade and Development
UNDP	United Nations Development Programme
UNEP	United Nations Environment Programme
UNESCO	United Nations Educational, Scientific and Cultural Organization
UNFCCC	United Nations Framework Convention on Climate Change
UNGA	United Nations General Assembly
UNIDO	United Nations Industrial Development Organization
UNON	United Nations office at Nairobi
UNU	UN University
UPOV	International Union for the Protection of New Varieties of Plants
US	United States
USAID	United States Agency for International Development
WB	World Bank
WCED	World Commission on Environment and Development
WCMC	World Conservation Monitoring Centre
WEO	World Environment Organization
WGABS	Ad Hoc Open-Ended Working Group on Acces and Benefit-Sharing
WG I	Working Group I
WG II	Working Group II
WG8J	Ad Hoc Open-Ended Working Group on Article 8(j) and Related Provisions
WHO	World Health Organization
WHC	World Heritage Convention
WIPO	World Intellectual Property Organization

WRI	World Resources Institute
WTO	World Trade Organization
WWF	Worldwide Fund for Nature

Instinctively, intuitively, perhaps the loudening whisper of a survival instinct within many of us is a deepening, more or less articulate sense that our own survival as a species depends on the co-existance of others.
Arthur Campeau

This book is dedicated to the memory of the late Ambassador Arthur Campeau, Canada's first ambassador for the environment and sustainable development, whose faith in the capacity and responsibility of the human community to address threats to the global environment, notably the biodiversity of the Earth, has inspired all who have had the privilege of knowing him and working at his side.

Introduction

The Emergence of Biodiversity Governance

Philippe G. Le Prestre

In 2000 the US National Intelligence Council boldly predicted that by 2015 "[o]ther agreements, such as the Convention on Biodiversity, will fall short in meeting their objectives".[1] Discounting that the US is apt to belittle agreements it has refused to join (and even worked to undermine during the negotiations), predictions about the success of the Convention on Biological Diversity (CBD) are indeed largely pessimistic. Reports continually suggest that the race to protect ecosystems is being lost, while new threats keep appearing. Existing agreements, which reflect the very complexity of the environment-politics nexus, are considered too unwieldy and ineffectual even to begin to stabilize a dramatic trend that seems to go irrevocably downwards.

The preservation of species and ecosystems lies at the core of the environmental movement and of the earliest attempts to protect them. These concerns have led to numerous agreements, yet species and ecosystems have continued to vanish. Adopted on 22 May 1992 in Nairobi and formally opened for signature on 5 June 1992 at the UN Conference on Environment and Development (UNCED, or Rio Earth Summit), the CBD entered into force in December 1993. With its sister conventions on climate change and desertification, the CBD is one of the three main global sustainable development conventions, either signed (climate) or conceived (desertification) at UNCED.[2] But the scope of the CBD is much larger and its social and political impact arguably more profound than either of the other two conventions.

Conceived initially as a means of putting some order into disparate agreements regarding the protection of wildlife, the CBD quickly moved beyond this narrow concern. It addresses issues that range from ecosystems protection to the exploitation of genetic resources, from conservation to justice, from commerce to scientific knowledge, from the allocation of rights to the imposition of responsibilities. It is, therefore, criss-crossed by widely differing political dynamics. Indeed, its three goals of conservation, sustainable use, and benefit-sharing make it perhaps the first true sustainable development convention.

The year 2002 marks the tenth anniversary of the signing of the CBD, at which time the UN system will have completed a review of the implementation of the Rio agreements, notably Agenda 21 and the conventions associated with Rio. Ten years after its adoption, how can we assess the difference that the CBD has made, if any? Are we witnessing the gradual emergence of new patterns of relations between societies and nature?

To ascertain the existence of a new, if incipient, biodiversity order, one would have to examine the entire set of key international agreements that pertain to species and ecosystem conservation. This book is both more limited and broader in scope. More limited because we focus solely on the CBD as representative of that incipient order since it was primarily intended to put some order into this constellation of efforts and serve as the focus of a new international endeavour to co-ordinate these efforts and promote further co-operation in light of the evolving normative concerns of the international community in that area. Broader because the CBD is not just a conservation convention in that it also touches on the core of contemporary international issues, notably development and trade.

Whether ten years is sufficient for a first assessment really depends on what one wants to know. Ten years is indeed a short period on which to base an evaluation of the CBD's normative impacts on state behaviour or determine whether it has improved the state of ecosystems and people's quality of life. But it is long enough for us to assess the state of implementation and whether the CBD is redirecting behaviour toward meeting its goals. That is, to what extent does it foster the dynamics that are necessary (but not sufficient) for change to occur? In short, to what extent has it contributed to changing the rules of the game?

In the eyes of many observers, the CBD stands out as emblematic of the fate of international agreements, their complexity, the obstacles they face, the dashed hopes and paths not taken, and the nature of contemporary international environmental politics, where new issues (intellectual property rights, community rights) mix with old ones (familiar trade-offs between social and natural welfare). Given the wide range of issues encompassed by the CBD and its myriad connections with other environmental and political problems, how these trade-offs and complex questions are addressed will have a profound impact not only on the biodiversity of the world but on humanity's capacity to reconcile its various aspirations and halt the destructive path upon which it is set.

Consequently, this study presents various aspects of the implementation of the CBD and analyses its potential normative and behavioural impacts, that is, its effectiveness. In essence, the study traces the contours of an emergent global order and in so doing illuminates many facets of today's international environmental *problématique*. The study confronts four basic questions:

- How has the CBD evolved since its adoption in 1992?
- What obstacles and opportunities have arisen in the course of its implementation and how have they been handled?
- To what extent have the implementation and evolution of the Convention strengthened certain prerequisites to the effectiveness of an environmental regime? and

- To what extent are the Convention, its implementation, and its evolution changing relations among societies? Have they facilitated the emergence of new norms and modified the distribution of power among relevant domestic and international stakeholders?

Our goal is not to ascertain the extent of biodiversity loss and the impact of its degradation. Rather, we start from the premise that governments and other groups have concluded that such a threat exists, even though the exact magnitude, the underlying causes of biodiversity loss, and the nature of its impact, may be subject to debate.[3] Several international assessments, some initiated within the CBD and others independently of it, such as the Pilot Assessment of Global Ecosystems (PAGE), the Millennium Ecosystem Assessment, and the Global Taxonomy Initiative, are currently underway.[4] Nor does this study attempt to assess the success of the CBD in solving the problem of biodiversity loss as it was designed to do. First, as mentioned above, it is too early to tell. Second, the objectives of the Convention are not fixed but dynamic; they represent trends that the international community should promote and moving targets toward which it should strive. Third, the Convention above all institutes a *process* for handling issues linked to the conservation of biodiversity. Therefore, rather than attempting to assess whether it has actually helped to improve matters in the field, it seems more fruitful at this stage to inquire whether and to what extent the CBD is creating the *conditions* that will strengthen its ability to fulfil the three goals of conservation, sustainable use, and benefit-sharing in the future.

With this in mind, we have organized the book roughly around two main objectives:

Emergence and evolution The first objective is to tell the story of the emergence and evolution of the Convention and present various aspects of the biodiversity regime. Chapter 1 by McGraw and chapter 2 by Pythoud and Thomas examine the genesis and negotiation of the CBD and of the Cartagena Protocol on Biosafety respectively. They make it clear implementation issues can both be traced to the negotiation process and determine its success. These accounts are complemented by additional data in Annex 2 which provide factual information on the evolution and various dimensions of the regime. The reader, however, will not find a detailed and comprehensive account of the steps taken at the international and national levels to address specific biodiversity issues, such as coastal and marine ecosystems, agro-biodiversity, access, and benefit-sharing. This is not an official history of the Convention. However, various chapters raise general issues associated with implementation and provide more specific information on a particular topic.

Of greater concern is the operation of the Convention and the extent to which it is setting the stage for new modes of biodiversity governance. This is the specific topic of chapter 4, which describes the nature of the institutions created by the regime, their potential, and some of the constraints under which they operate and which they have tried to overcome. Transparency, for example, which Reed examines in chapter 5, has been singled out as a key ingredient of successful regimes. It lies at the core of the Convention through the development of what are called "clearing-house mechanisms" (CHMs). By studying the implementation of CHMs, we can gain new insights into the obstacles that the CBD faces, the complexity of the issues it must address, and the prospect for resolving them. In chapter 6, Wolf examines another implementation tool, advance informed agreements, a procedure that is central to the implementation of the Cartagena Protocol on Biosafety and a promising tool for reconciling commercial, environmental, and human rights, provided Parties are able to resolve several difficulties associated with the meaning and operationalization of the concept.

Management Secondly, the book reviews a number of challenges and issues related to the management of biodiversity. Some authors look into the normative and political changes that the regime fosters. How is the CBD changing norms and rules that govern relations among groups? That is, to what extent is it – or is it not – helping to build a new international order? In this context, Blais (in chapter 7) examines the dimensions and difficulties of the operationalization of the CBD's third objective: sharing the benefits associated with the exploitation of genetic resources. Potvin and her colleagues (chapter 8) examine the relationship between scientific and traditional knowledge relevant to biodiversity conservation and the issues surrounding their respective identification, use, and legitimacy. This issue raises the question of how the regime can harmonize the desire to ground action in "western" science (the taxonomy initiative, discussions on indicators and the ecosystem approach, and the definition of what constitutes a "threat" to biodiversity are prominent examples of this desire) with the requirement to protect *in situ* biodiversity through the protection of traditional knowledge and biodiversity management and attendant benefits. The issue of harmonization is also addressed by Thomas in chapter 9, which focuses on a specific, important, and extremely complex aspect of the operation of the Convention – its relationship with commercially-oriented agreements and regimes, in particular the WTO and the former Undertaking on Plant Genetic Resources (now the International Treaty on Plant Genetic Resources for Food and Agriculture, concluded in November 2001).

Various contributions to the book, therefore, help to probe the role and evolution of elements associated with regime effectiveness and the challenges they present. These elements include the operation of the regime (chapters 1 and 4), the nature, availability, and use of information (chapter 5), the role of scientific knowledge (chapter 10 by Guay, in addition to chapter 8), the use of economic instruments, and the thorny issue of how to place a "value" on biodiversity (chapter 11 by Revéret and Webster). These factors affect the capacity of the regime to deliver benefits to members, ascertain progress toward its fundamental objectives, and adapt to an evolving scientific and political environment.

In this context, the national level remains the most challenging of all, because not only is the biodiversity issue, a "world-wide" problem (experienced by all countries but resolved in a way that is largely national) rather than a "global" problem (affecting all countries indiscriminately and resolved on a largely global scale), but the Convention reaffirms and even expands national sovereignty over natural resources and the right of states to choose the policies that they deem most appropriate. This volume examines the weight of domestic issues through two crucial cases. In chapter 12, Halley looks into the issues surrounding the domestic implementation of the CBD and some of its concepts in Canada, a country that has contributed significantly to knowledge-building in that area. Canada was a leader during the CBD negotiations, has pursued an active international role since then, and hosts the CBD Secretariat. The other case, by Hufty and Muttenzer (chapter 13), examines the constraints that a poor country (Madagascar) still faces even though it has long benefited from the international community's deep concern for preserving its unique fauna and flora.

As chapter 3 explains, the CBD aims to institute a *regime*, that is, a set of norms, rules, and procedures that structure the behaviour and relations of international actors so as to reduce the uncertainties they face and facilitate the pursuit of a common goal. A regime is not just a legal text; it also embodies practices and dynamics. It defines the rights as well as the responsibilities of national and international actors – international organizations, states, non-governmental organizations, indigenous peoples' organizations, industry, local communities – in very diverse areas all concerned with the living.

The elements of such a new order include (i) new relationships between societies and nature, (ii) the distribution of rights and responsibilities between developed and developing countries, among international organizations, and between the state and civil society, (iii) a redistribution of costs and benefits arising out of the use of biodiversity, and (iv) norms that define new expectations, behaviours, and the evaluation of the actions of relevant actors. The definition of a new order remains virtual, the subject of complex political games. Some factors promote its development while others impede it. Thus, rather than examining the main elements of the CBD (the conservation of various ecosystems, the development of new conceptual tools, etc.), this book adopts a specific level of analysis that looks into the normative and political changes that the regime fosters and examines several key determinants of effectiveness, which are also identified in chapter 3.

This approach has two distinct advantages: it removes us from the day-to-day vagaries of policy discussions and implementations, and it makes it easier to draw lessons or hypotheses that can be applied to other global regimes, such as climate change and desertification. This approach also reflects a desire to adopt various disciplinary perspectives. The new order is the product not only of civil servants, lawyers, and political scientists but also of scientists, indigenous and local communities, NGOs, industry, economists, and philosophers. Individually, each author illuminates particular aspects of the biodiversity *problématique* and advances concerns and understandings specific to his or her disciplinary perspective. Collectively, their approach leads to an integrated whole that gives a normative, legal, political, scientific, economic, and social basis to the emerging order.

International politics around multiple centres of power has become the defining characteristic of contemporary international relations, characterized by rising uncertainties, interdependence, multiple actors, competing legitimacies, transnational relations, and regarding the nature of the problems, the solutions, and the consequences of one's actions. In this context, protecting biodiversity effectively while ensuring fairness and promoting sustainable development poses profound challenges. As the Global Environmental Change Programme report (1999) points out, "There are great opportunities for more open, legitimate and flexible governance, but there are also dangers that expectations are not met". This is what this book will attempt to trace: is the CBD regime providing the tools and helping to build the conditions that will enable stakeholders to address these challenges and, in so doing, contributing to a new form of governance of the natural world?

Notes

The author would like to thank J-P. Le Danff and D. M. McGraw for helpful comments.

[1] US National Intelligence Council (2000*), Global Trends 2015: A Dialogue about the Future with Nongovernment Experts,* NIC2000-02 Letter from the Director of Central Intelligence.

[2] Although negotiated after Rio, the United Nations Convention to Combat Desertification (UNCCD) is usually considered part of the Rio process, for the call for its negotiation underlay some of the bargaining that took place between the North and the South at that time. It was signed in 1994 (June 17) and came into force in 1996 (December 26).

[3] On the magnitude, readers are referred to a variety of studies, mostly from scientists attempting to ring the alarm bell. See, for example: Gaston (2000); Purvis and Hector (2000); Cracraft and Grifo (1999); MacPhee (1999); Heywood (1995); Wilson (1993). Useful web sites include: www.sp2000.org (species list), www.gisbau.uniroma1.it (geographical range of species), www.wcmc.org.uk (conservation status), http://eteweb.lscf.ucsb.edu (bibliographies) (from Purvis and Hector, 2000).

[4] The Pilot Assessment of Global Ecosystems (PAGE) was launched in 1999 by the World Resources Institute (WRI), UNDP, UNEP, and the World Bank, with the support of the FAO and the World Conservation Monitoring Centre (WCMC). Its conclusions were published in 2000. The main purpose of the Millenium Ecosystem Assessment is to improve the management of ecosystems and our understanding of their contribution to human development through the identification of the state of knowledge on the goods and services they provide. The first assessment will cover the period 2000-2003. The Global Taxonomy Initiative (GTI) was launched after the realization that serious gaps in taxonomic knowledge, and a shortage of taxonomists and qualified collection specialists affected the capacity to conserve and manage global biodiversity. The GTI aims to promote the examination of taxonomic obstacles to data collection and the development of knowledge. The establishment of a Global Biodiversity Information Facility was proposed by the OECD in 1999. Other established programmes and organizations that compile and maintain biological information resources include the World Conservation Monitoring Centre, DIVERSITAS, Species 2000, and the Integrated Taxonomic Information System of the United States. The impacts of biodiversity loss have also led to numerous studies and much speculation. See, for example: Chapin, Zavaleta et al. (2000); Tilman (2000).

Chapter 1

The Story of the Biodiversity Convention: From Negotiation to Implementation

Désirée M. McGraw

Introduction

The UN-sponsored series of world summits throughout the 1990s was an important innovation in global governance. The first of these, the 1992 UN Conference on Environment and Development (UNCED) or Rio Earth Summit, provided an unprecedented forum for focusing worldwide attention and action on sustainable development. As the largest gathering of heads of state and government in human history, UNCED also served as a crucial incentive for concluding two treaties: the Convention on Biological Diversity (CBD) and the UN Framework Convention on Climate Change (UNFCCC). At the Rio Earth Summit, a record 157 countries signed the Convention on Biological Diversity. Following ratification by the requisite number of countries, the CBD entered into force in December 1993.[1]

What is most striking about the CBD is that it reflects concessions secured by developing countries that they had been unable to obtain in other multilateral negotiations, whether on trade, security, or even other environmental issues such as climate change. Throughout the course of negotiating the CBD, the bargaining position of developing countries was significantly enhanced by their possession of a preponderance of the assets under negotiation. As the collective repository of four-fifths of the world's biodiversity,[2] developing countries successfully secured sovereign rights over the biological resources within their respective borders and can now better control the terms of access to these assets.

As a result, attempts by powerful state and non-state actors to create a convention aimed solely at *conserving* biodiversity were thwarted. The CBD goes beyond environmental preservation and provides for the sharing – with communities and countries of origin – of benefits arising from the *use* of genetic resources.[3] The enormous revenue derived from these resources – the raw material for multinational, multi-billion-dollar (US) industries in agriculture, biotechnology, and pharmaceuticals[4] – raises the issue of who owns, controls, and profits from the genetic information stored in species. Because the CBD addresses these economic issues, it is far more than an environmental treaty. Its cutting-edge approach to conservation has implications for intellectual property rights, trade, technology, human health, and culture.[5] Indeed, international lawyers have characterized the CBD as one of a new generation of international legal instruments that seek to reconcile the development imperatives of the South with the environmental exigencies of the North (Tinker, 1995). How did this new global treaty emerge and how has it evolved?

Ten years after the CBD's adoption, the present chapter explores these questions by providing an overview of the Convention's origins and key factors in its negotiation. It then examines the implications of this history, as well as the Convention's core characteristics, for the CBD's current implementation and overall operational effectiveness.

Such considerations are key to current high-level deliberations aimed at improving the effectiveness of multilateral environmental agreements (MEAs)[6], which provide the legal backbone of international environmental governance – a key agenda item for the World Summit on Sustainable Development (WSSD) scheduled for August/September 2002 in Johannesburg.[7]

Origins of the CBD

Unlike its sister agreements on climate change and desertification, the CBD entered a legal field crowded with agreements addressing at least its first objective of biodiversity conservation. (A later section will examine the CBD's overlap with agreements relating to its two other objectives, sustainable use and benefit-sharing.)

As an elaboration of the question posed above regarding the CBD's emergence, Swanson (1999, p. 283) asks, "Why is there a global convention on biological diversity when there is no global resource by this name?" Arguing that the essential rationale for the CBD is the centralized management of land use planning, Swanson (1999, pp.281-305) details six main movements that contributed to the Convention's development: the parks and protected areas movement (addressed below), the debt-for-nature movement, the environmental fund movement, the sustainable utilization movement, the farmers' rights movement, and the bioprospecting movement. While an account of all these movements is beyond the scope of this chapter, their confluence resulted in the unique combination of objectives encompassed by the CBD.

1950s-1970s: The Use of International Law for Biodiversity Conservation

Although the first environmental treaties of the 19th century pertained to conservation of an economic resource, information about and sensitization to the complex issues of biodiversity have increased dramatically throughout the 20th century. Consequently, the period from 1950 onward was marked by a growing interest within the international community in the use of law as an approach to the conservation of biodiversity.[8]

There are at present over 300 multilateral agreements for the protection of the environment, or MEAs. Of these, approximately 30 per cent address biodiversity either in full or in part. Most are aimed at protecting specific species and sites as well as regulating particular activities. In addition, while the majority of biodiversity-related MEAs are regional in scope,[9] several are global (listed in Box 1.1).

Box 1.1 Global Agreements related to Biodiversity

International legal instruments that are concerned with wider environmental issues but address at least one aspect of biodiversity:

- The Convention on the High Seas (Geneva: 29 April 1958).
- The Convention for the Conservation of Antarctic Seals (London: 1 June 1972).
- The Convention concerning the Protection of World Cultural and Natural Heritage (Paris: 23 November 1972).
- The Convention on the Conservation of Migratory Species of Wild Animals (CMS) (Bonn: 23 June 1979).
- The United Nations Convention on the Law of the Sea (UNCLOS) (Montego Bay: 10 December 1982).
- The International Tropical Timber Agreement (ITTA) (Geneva: 18 November 1983).[10]

International legal agreements that deal squarely with the conservation and management of the flora, fauna and habitat:

- The Convention Relative to the Preservation of Fauna and Flora in their Natural State (London: 8 November 1933).
- The International Convention for the Regulation of Whaling (Washington DC: 2 December 1946).
- The International Convention for the Protection of Birds (Paris Convention) (Paris: 18 October 1950).
- The International Plant Protection Convention (IPPC) (Rome: 6 December 1951).
- The Convention on Fishing and Conservation of the Living Resources of the High Seas (Geneva: 28 April 1958).
- The Convention on Wetlands of International Importance, Especially as Waterfowl Habitat (Ramsar Convention) (Ramsar: 2 February 1971).
- The Convention on International Trade in Endangered Species of Wild Fauna and Flora (CITES) (Washington DC: 3 March 1973).

Among these agreements, the World Conservation Union (IUCN) identifies four major global conventions based on the criteria of "recency" and relevancy (see

Glowka, 1993). These conventions are: the Convention on International Trade in Endangered Species of Wild Fauna and Flora (CITES); the Convention on the Conservation of Migratory Species of Wild Animals (CMS); the Convention on Wetlands of International Importance, Especially as Waterfowl Habitat (Ramsar Convention); and the Convention concerning the Protection of World Cultural and Natural Heritage (Paris Convention). While the first two are aimed at specific activities (CITES) or species (CMS), the latter two focus on specific sites (Paris) or habitats (Ramsar). Lyster (1985) also singles out these four treaties in his renowned book, *International Wildlife Law*, and Bilderbeek (1992) cites them as "positive sources of international law" on biodiversity. Each of these treaties took from two to four years to enter into force (in contrast to the CBD's 18 months), and the number of Parties range from 30 to 100 (in contrast to the CBD's near-universal membership).

1980s: Conceptualization of a Biodiversity Convention

In 1981 the 15th IUCN General Assembly (held in Christchurch, New Zealand) adopted a resolution presented by the International Council of Environmental Law (ICEL), which requested that the IUCN Secretariat analyse:

> the technical, legal, economic and financial matters relating to the conservation, accessibility and use of these [biological] resources with a view to providing the basis for an international arrangement and rules to implement it. (de Klemm 1982, p. 120).

The following year, at the IUCN Third World Congress on National Parks and Protected Areas (held in Bali, Indonesia, in October 1982), the lawyers from its Commission on Environmental Law (CEL) initiated a more comprehensive way to view genetic resources management. They called for the extension of protected-area principles to land outside protected areas and proposed a world treaty to protect wild genetic resources for the future. The congress invited the IUCN to investigate the "possible development of international instruments to regulate the commercial exploitation of wild genetic resources".

In 1985 the 16th IUCN General Assembly adopted Resolution 16/24, which served as the basis for a preliminary draft global agreement. The resolution enumerated several principles to guide the drafters, including: the role of genetic resources in maintaining ecological diversity; access to genetic resources; state responsibility towards genetic resource conservation; national legislation; financial resources and commercial use (de Klemm 1985, p. 123).

On the basis of these principles, the IUCN Environmental Law Centre (ELC) started preparing a first draft of a convention that was later submitted to the IUCN Council. The drafting continued with ELC drawing on the extensive expertise of members of the several IUCN commissions, in particular the CEL. As a draft convention was circulated to governments and NGOs (such as Norway and the Worldwide Fund for Nature, respectively) for comments, the UN Environment Programme (UNEP) as well as several states became increasingly interested in the idea of a global biodiversity convention (interview with Burhenne-Guilmin, 1996).

1987-1992: Negotiation of a Biodiversity Convention

The CBD was formally negotiated over the course of ten intergovernmental meetings held between November 1988 and May 1992. This three-and-a-half-year period can be separated into two phases:

- The first phase consisted of three meetings of UNEP-designated national experts on biodiversity (formally entitled the Ad Hoc Group of Experts on Biological Diversity) as well as two meetings of a slightly expanded version of the previous group (the Ad Hoc Group of Legal and Technical Experts on Biological Diversity).
- The second phase comprised five meetings of the formally constituted Intergovernmental Negotiating Committee (INC) for a Convention on Biological Diversity.

Pre-negotiations: issue-framing and agenda-setting   In 1987 UNEP's *Global Environment Perspective to the Year 2000* and *Our Common Future*, the report of the World Commission on Environment and Development (WCED), highlighted the new challenge facing the conservation and sustainable use of biological diversity. Among other issues, the latter publication underscored the economic importance of biodiversity, which it described as a "common heritage," and proposed a "Species Protection Convention" to be accompanied by appropriate funding arrangements (WCED, 1987).

In June of that same year, the United States formally sponsored a resolution within the Governing Council of UNEP for an all-encompassing convention on the conservation of species. Indeed, the conservation of biological diversity has constituted one of the main activities undertaken by UNEP since its inception in 1972. The Action Plan on Programme Development and Priorities, adopted in 1973 at the first session of UNEP's Governing Council, identified the "conservation of nature, wildlife and genetic resources" as a priority area.

It has been argued that the US was motivated by "a growing frustration with the sectoral approach taken by many international conservation agreements" and wanted to foster "a comprehensive, global approach to species and ecosystem conservation".[11] However, others have described American efforts as more self-serving: the US sought to create a global convention on parks and reserves modeled after its domestic Endangered Species Act (interview with Savage, 1996). Nevertheless, as we shall see, American domestic concerns were quickly supplemented – and to some extent supplanted – by international concerns for equity and economic development. It is noteworthy that the treaty's original state sponsor ultimately became its most vocal opponent. This evolution was not so much due to a change in the American position; rather, it reflected the CBD's own evolution from a traditional conservation convention to one with broader implications for the economy and other key areas of national interest.

While some delegations supported the idea of an umbrella convention, others favoured efforts underway within the IUCN to draft a global convention on *in situ* conservation of flora and fauna. In 1988 the 17th IUCN General Assembly held in San José, Costa Rica, noted these obstacles to an umbrella convention and amended its draft convention accordingly. In addition, the Governing Council of UNEP called for formal support of the IUCN's efforts toward developing "a convention for the preservation of biological diversity".[12]

Pursuant to this decision, then-Executive Director of UNEP, Mostafa Tolba, convened a two-day meeting of a Senior Advisory Panel of Experts on Biological Diversity in September 1988. This panel of scientific, technical, and legal experts from 25 countries was appointed by the Executive Director of UNEP himself (interview with Tolba, 2000). Their mandate was to examine the possibility of establishing an international legal instrument on the conservation of biodiversity. The panel's principal recommendation was to establish an Ad Hoc Group of Experts on Biological Diversity with a view to harmonizing the existing global conventions related to biological diversity. The Group of Experts met in Geneva for three sessions in 1988 and 1990 (see Annex 1 for a detailed chronology of the CBD negotiations).

At its first meeting, the group adopted a series of recommendations with regard to rationalizing, strengthening, and co-ordinating efforts within the existing framework of global nature protection conventions (UNEP/BioDiv.1/Inf.2).[13] Citing "numerous practical, political and legal obstacles" to an umbrella convention, the group did not ultimately support the harmonization of existing conventions. However, it did recommend the creation of a new international binding instrument on biodiversity. Moreover, the group established a Sub-Working Group on Biotechnology, which met only once, November 1990 in Nairobi.[14]

Despite its limited mandate, the group touched on many of the problems that would later become the substantive issues throughout the negotiation phase, such as: links between biodiversity conservation and development; financial resources; transfer of technology; access to genetic resources; and indigenous peoples. Regarding genetic resources, for example, developing countries sent strong signals that they could not accept that these genetic resources be considered the "common heritage of mankind" but rather affirmed national sovereignty over them.[15] This position prevailed throughout the negotiation process, and the more benign term "common concern" is employed in the CBD. Given the issues outlined above, it was clear from the beginning that the proposed biodiversity convention would not be a traditional conservation treaty. Indeed, these issues remained key throughout the negotiation of the CBD.

On the basis of the third and final report of the Ad Hoc Group of Experts on Biological Diversity, the Executive Director was instructed to convene another intergovernmental group with a mandate to negotiate an international legal instrument, "possibly in the form of a framework convention," for the conservation of biological diversity with the aim of having the proposed convention "ready for adoption as soon as possible".[16] Executive Director Mostafa Tolba, under pressure from both Governing Council Decision 15/34 and a shortage of funds, was criticized for "trying to force" the group to proceed to the negotiation stage at the next session despite protests regarding lack of preparedness (Koester 1995, p. 7). Resolution of this matter combined elements of both the Executive Director's and the group's positions: a change of status and title for the group but no formal negotiating mandate. A decision was made to convene a meeting of technical and legal experts to "consider the content of detailed draft elements in preparation for the actual negotiation of draft articles".[17]

Thus, a second expert group, named the Ad Hoc Group of Legal and Technical Experts on Biological Diversity,[18] then met for two sessions in Nairobi in November 1990 and February 1991. At its third session, held June-July 1991 in Madrid, the group was renamed the Intergovernmental Negotiating Committee (INC) for a Convention on Biological Diversity, pursuant to UNEP Governing Council Decision 16/42 of May 1991.

Formal negotiations The INC held four additional working sessions in 1991 and 1992. Its last meeting, at UNEP Headquarters, culminated in the Nairobi Final Act of the Conference for the Adoption of the Agreed Text of the Convention on Biological Diversity on 22 May 1992. The Biodiversity Convention was opened for signature two weeks later (5 June) at the Earth Summit in Rio de Janeiro. Going into the final meeting, delegates had agreed on less than half of the draft convention: 27 out of 42 articles contained square brackets. Of course, these outstanding areas reflected the most complex and controversial issues of the negotiation, such as technology transfer and financial provisions.

The matter was made more difficult by the fact that the Preparatory Committee (PrepCom) for UNCED, which met at UN Headquarters in March 1992 with a view to finalizing most issue areas, had not proceeded as far as expected. As a result, biodiversity negotiators – who had expected the PrepCom to agree on wording regarding technology transfer, which could then be transposed to Article 16(2) – would have to resolve the matter themselves.[19]

Moreover, several delegations from the Organization for Economic Co-operation and Development (OECD) had expected that the results of the recently concluded United Nations Framework Convention on Climate Change (UNFCCC), in particular its financial provisions, could be transposed to the CBD.[20] However, quite the contrary was true. Having felt "deeply colonized" by the climate change negotiations, many developing countries were determined to secure their interests through the Biodiversity Convention (McConnell, 1996). Indeed, many developing countries, including the dominating ones, felt that the climate change solution had been imposed on them by the North, and "they were therefore determined, more than ever, to obtain what they really desired" from the CBD (Koester, 1995, p. 9).

It was also contended that because the "A-Team was sent to negotiate the Framework Convention on Climate Change" (Rosendal, 1994, p. 92), the delegates sent to the biodiversity meetings would lack the political and diplomatic skill to resolve the outstanding issues. This contention reflected practical as well as political realities. Since most of the climate change meetings took place in New York under the auspices of the UN General Assembly, government delegations included staff from their respective UN missions, widely considered a plum foreign service posting. However, because most biodiversity meetings were conducted in Nairobi under the auspices of UNEP, government delegations included staff from their respective embassies and high commissions.

Another important obstacle at this final meeting was the fact that the US delegation arrived in Nairobi with a list of some 16 non-negotiable points[21] and would have preferred postponing final negotiations until after UNCED (interview with Savage, 1996). Although the US argued that extending the negotiations would facilitate a better legal agreement (Chandler), others countered that any post-Rio discussions would produce a weaker political document. Some viewed the US proposal as a strategy for undermining the Convention's prospects of survival altogether.

Despite the numerous obstacles outlined above, the INC completed its work in the late hours of 22 May, and the CBD was adopted at the Final Act Conference. What accounts for this successful outcome?

Key factors in the negotiation process   The evolution of a major international legal instrument does not take place in isolation. Within the environmental field in particular, there are important linkages to parallel events – whether they be in science or policy. In some instances, such factors facilitate the process; in others they complicate matters (Susskind, 1994, p. 82). In the case of the CBD, the range of events that impacted on the negotiations was especially wide due to the broad and complex nature of its subject matter. Conversely, the diversity of issues within the purview of the Convention had implications for other issue areas.

The concurrence of preparatory meetings for UNCED and the negotiations leading to the UNFCCC was both a burden and a blessing for the biodiversity negotiations. On the one hand, the proliferation of meetings meant that the international environmental policy community was overextended. On the other hand, the momentum created by a multiplicity of meetings, the completion of the climate change negotiations, and the pending and highly public Rio Earth Summit served as incentives for concluding a biodiversity convention. Indeed, UNCED provided an unprecedented forum for focusing worldwide attention and action on sustainable development. The fact that biodiversity was pushed forward at all as part of the Rio process was not unconnected with the slight, felt by UNEP and its Executive Secretary, when the climate change negotiations were taken over by the UN General Assembly (interview with Tolba, 2000; see also Brenton, 1994, p.200). Koester contends that without this momentum, "it is doubtful that a convention on biodiversity would have existed by now" (1995, p. 10).

Although UNCED did not serve as the original incentive for a biodiversity convention,[22] there is strong evidence to suggest that its very preparation influenced both the scope and nature of the CBD – making it more comprehensive, more complex, and ultimately more controversial through the incorporation of key UNCED themes, such as sustainable development as well as financial and technology co-operation. Indeed, following the UN General Assembly resolution, not only did the pace of negotiations pick up (going from once a year to once every few months) but the scope of deliberations was expanded in order to:

- highlight that biodiversity is essential for sustainable development;

- underscore that biodiversity be considered within a broad socio-economic context;
- take into account the implications of "new and emerging" biotechnologies; and
- address the problem of financial and technology transfers to the owners of biological resources from those who benefit from the exploitation of biodiversity, including from biotechnology (UNEP/BioDiv.2/2).

Given the issues outlined above, it was clear that there would be no turning back to a traditional conservation treaty.

Moreover, certain issues that were addressed at "higher" diplomatic levels during the preparatory meetings for UNCED had a spill-over effect for the biodiversity negotiations. These issues included biodiversity and biotechnology as well as cross-cutting issues such as financial resources and technology transfer. Thus, several of the most contentious issues within the biodiversity negotiations were also under consideration in other parallel fora. Another interpretation is that the existence of higher-level bodies outside the environmental arena may have led some OECD countries, the US in particular, to "simply stop worrying about the result of the biodiversity negotiations, confident that their interests would be secured by the TRIPS [trade-related aspects of intellectual property] regulations under the WTO [World Trade Organization]" (Rosendal, 1999).

Other important contextual factors included the CBD's adoption conference being held in Nairobi (the "Nairobi Final Act") and its opening for signature being held in Rio de Janeiro (as one of the two "Rio conventions"). These venues forced two of the key developing countries, Kenya and Brazil, into the role of mediators, brokering a united front.

Another factor that might have influenced the proceedings and outcome was the CBD's institutional host. At UNEP's 15th Governing Council in May 1989, governments debated procedural matters such as how and under whose auspices the convention should be negotiated. Several countries maintained that UNESCO, which had developed the concept of biosphere reserves, was the appropriate body. However, this proposal was defeated because of concerns (by developing countries) that the biosphere reserve concept would overemphasize conservation and (by all countries) that UNESCO might ignore a UNEP Governing Council recommendation. A suggestion made by several Nordic countries that the IUCN would be the appropriate body to oversee the process was dismissed by most diplomats on the grounds that a non-governmental organization, no matter how eminent or well-supported, could not be permitted to usurp the functions of governments or a UN programme such as UNEP.[23] Not surprisingly, the Governing Council supported UNEP's bid to oversee the biodiversity negotiations and provide a firm scientific basis for ensuing negotiations. Having "lost" the climate change negotiations to the UN General Assembly, UNEP was anxious to justify its institutional existence, highlighted by UNCED as uncertain. A convention on biodiversity, an increasingly important focal point in both scientific and policy communities, presented such an opportunity.

UNEP also provided an alternative to what many OECD countries perceived as an overly politicized Food and Agriculture Organization (FAO) arena.[24] Indeed, when the institutional issue was put on the UNEP agenda, some contend that the United States and the IUCN hoped to de-link biodiversity's conservation aspects from the more controversial aspects of utilization and economic value of – as well as property rights to – biological resources. The move to UNEP hence represented an effort to start afresh with new rules in an arena over which the US believed itself to have greater control (Rosendal, 1999).

The role of several personalities in promoting the Convention should not be underestimated.[25] In this connection, the most influential participant was Mostafa Tolba of Egypt, who served as Executive Director of UNEP throughout the duration of the biodiversity process. Emboldened by the earlier ozone negotiations, which he had overseen, Tolba was insistent that the biodiversity negotiations would not fail under his leadership. One official observed that Tolba treated delegates "more like children than representatives of sovereign states" (interview with Savage, 1996). Yet another dubbed him a "bully for the planet" (McConnell, 1996, p. 90). His tactics clearly paid off because, according to one head of delegation, "He would keep a few of us – the key delegations – up all night in his office until we just gave in... and we would have to call our capitals in the morning" (interview with Ting, 1995).

Yet another factor was the limited number of NGOs (see Table of Participants in Annex 2) as well as limited interest by the media, politicians, industry, and domestic publics (their focus being diverted to the UNFCCC negotiations and UNCED). This lack of interest may also be attributed to the complex nature of biodiversity, which does not lend itself to facile explanations. (The matter of "issue saliency" is explored later in this chapter.) Ironically, the general public indifference[26] "may have helped participants utilize the limited time available to focus their attention on achieving a result" (Koester, 1995, p. 10). Most of the final negotiations were conducted in small informal groups outside ordinary sessions. Although not very democratic or transparent, the approach was, according to some, both necessary and effective.

The location of the CBD's formal negotiations in Nairobi (a deliberate strategy, interview with Tolba, 2000) also added to the issue's low public profile. Delegates' relative isolation may have contributed to another important factor in concluding the CBD: their sense of personal and professional loyalty. Most of the chief biodiversity negotiators had been involved in the process since its inception in 1988. Many delegates also knew each other from previous or parallel environmental negotiation sets, such as those pertaining to ozone depletion and climate change. Notwithstanding important substantive disagreements, four years of meetings fostered a kind of team spirit because, as one delegate put it, "when you spend so much time and effort trying to achieve a result... nobody likes the idea of having to give up" (Koester, 1995, p. 10). Of course, delegates tend to be given a greater degree of flexibility in the final phases of negotiations in order to avoid a situation in which they or their countries are blamed for failure.[27] This enhanced "on-site" flexibility diminished the role of more rigid negotiating positions and strategies;[28] indeed, as unscripted compromises continued to emerge, delegates were contacting capitals through the final hours of negotiations.

Although the climate change negotiators tended to involve New York and Washington-based career diplomats, the CBD delegations were often led by permanent representatives accredited to UNEP who often served as their countries' ambassadors (or high commissioners in the case of fellow Commonwealth states) to Kenya. In the course of their work, most became environmentally literate; some were even posted to Nairobi because of qualifications in ecology, natural sciences, or environmental law. Despite the highly political nature and ever-evolving scope of the CBD negotiations, this substantive knowledge (in contrast to the more superficial or generalist knowledge of most diplomats) may have facilitated a more positive outcome.

The multidisciplinary character of the CBD allowed for an expanded zone of agreement (via trade-offs within the Convention itself, as elaborated below) among Parties. First, had the CBD been based solely on the natural sciences, it would likely have been a strictly conservation treaty, as originally proposed by the US. Herein lies a key insight: many developing countries argued that they are at a disadvantage in purely scientific bodies, which are often dominated by Northern-educated experts. Moreover, it is argued, science – or at least the process by which scientific studies are selected as a basis for action – is not value-free. Second, had the CBD been based on a strictly legalistic approach, it would have served as an umbrella convention to rationalize and absorb existing instruments in the field of biodiversity, as originally envisioned both by the US and the IUCN. Both the strictly scientific and strictly legalistic bases for a biodiversity convention were rejected in favour of an approach that also recognized the social, economic, and political dimensions and values of biodiversity.

1992-2002: Operation of the Biodiversity Convention

As elaborated above, many of the most contentious issues were left unresolved at the time of the CBD's adoption, thus the need for post-agreement negotiations. Therefore, in addition to the pre-negotiations and formal negotiations, a third phase of negotiations occurred following the CBD's actual adoption. In line with Lawrence Susskind's (1994) model for a "Three-Stage Global Environmental Treaty-Making Process," this third stage can be characterized as: the adoption/operation phase.[29]

By August 1993, a record number of 165 countries had signed the treaty, and by October 1993, the requisite 30 countries had ratified the Convention, thereby allowing it to enter into force in near record time on 29 December 1993. An Intergovernmental Committee on the Convention on Biological Diversity (ICCBD) was convened to oversee the Convention in the period between its adoption and entry into force. The ICCBD first met in October 1993 (Geneva) and then again in June 1994 (Nairobi). One year later, the Contracting Parties to the Convention met for the first time to discuss plans for implementation. The First Conference of Parties (COP-1) was held 28 November through 9 December 1994

Box 1.2 Intergovernmental Meetings related to the CBD

Meeting of the Ad Hoc Group of Experts to the Executive Director of UNEP on Governing Council Decision 14/26: Nairobi, 29 August-1 September 1988.

Meeting of UNEP Ad Hoc Senior Advisory Panel of Experts on Biological Diversity: Nairobi, 19-20 September 1988.

I. Ad Hoc Group of Experts on Biological Diversity
- First session: Geneva, 16-18 November 1988.
- Second session: Geneva, 19-23 February 1990.
- Third session: Geneva, 9-13 July 1990.

II. Ad Hoc Group of Legal and Technical Experts on Biological Diversity
- *Sub-Working Group on Biotechnology (SWGB): Nairobi, 14-16 November 1990*
- First session: Nairobi, 19-23 November 1990 (N.1)
- Second session: Nairobi, 23 February-6 March 1991 (N.2)
- Third session: Madrid, 24 June-3 July 1991 (N.3-INC.1)

III. Intergovernmental Negotiating Committee (INC) for a Convention on Biological Diversity
- Fourth session: Nairobi, 23 September-2 October 1991 (N.4-INC.2)
- Fifth negotiating session: Geneva, 25 November-4 December 1991 (N.5-INC.3)
- Sixth negotiating session: Nairobi, 6-15 February 1992 (N.6-INC.4)
- Seventh negotiating session: Nairobi, 11-23 May 1992 (N.7-INC.5)

IV.Conference for the Adoption of the Agreed Text of the Convention on Biological Diversity: Nairobi, 22 May 1992

V. United Nations Conference on Environment and Development (UNCED): Rio de Janeiro, 3-14 June 1992

VI.Intergovernmental Committee for the Convention on Biological Diversity (pre-entry into force)
- First meeting: Geneva, 11-15 October 1993 (ICCBD-1)
- Second meeting: Nairobi, 20 June-1 July 1994 (ICCBD-2)

Box 1.2 Concluded

VII. Conference of Parties to the Convention on Biological Diversity	
(post-entry into force)	
• First meeting: Nassau, 28 November-4 December 1994	(COP-1)
• Second meeting: Jakarta, 6-17 November 1995	(COP-2)
• Third meeting: Buenos Aires, 3-15 November 1996	(COP-3)
• Fourth meeting: Bratislava, 4-15 May 1998	(COP-4)
• First extraordinary meeting: Cartagena, 22-23 February 1999	(EXCOP-1)
• Resumed extraordinary meeting: Montreal, 24-28 January 2000	
• Fifth meeting: Nairobi, 15-26 May 2000	(COP-5)
• Sixth meeting: The Hague, 7-19 April 2002	(COP-6)
VIII. Subsidiary Body on Scientific, Technical and Technological Advice	
• First meeting: Paris, 4-8 September 1995	(SBSTTA-1)
• Second meeting: Montreal, 2-6 September 1996	(SBSTTA-2)
• Third meeting: Montreal, 1-5 September 1997	(SBSTTA-3)
• Fourth meeting: Montreal, 21-25 June 1999	(SBSTTA-4)
• Fifth meeting: Montreal, 31 January-4 February 2000	(SBSTTA-5)
• Sixth meeting: Montreal, 12-16 March 2001	(SBSTTA-6)
• Seventh meeting: Montreal, 12-16 November 2001	(SBSTTA-7)

(Nassau, the Bahamas). During the three years following the CBD's entry into force, the COP met annually. Subsequently – with the exception of an extraordinary session held in February 1999 to conclude a sub-agreement on biosafety, which was resumed less than a year later in January 2000 – Parties have convened on a biennial basis. (See Box 1.2 for a list of intergovernmental meetings related to the CBD from pre-negotiation through to the present.)

The following section examines key features of the CBD and aspects of its current operation.

The CBD's Core Characteristics and Implications for Implementation

The CBD is a framework agreement based on three central principles: national implementation, co-ordination with other agreements, and post-agreement negotiation of annexes and legally binding protocols as well as non-binding work programmes. This section reviews the Convention's structure, then assesses three key features that characterize the CBD both as a legal and as a political document: comprehensiveness, complexity, and compromise. In so doing, the chapter considers the implications of each of these "three Cs" for the Convention's current implementation and, ultimately, for its overall effectiveness as a regime.

Framework Agreement

Unlike its climate change counterpart, the CBD does not contain the term "framework" in its formal title. Despite this oversight,[30] it is widely regarded as a framework convention.[31] According to Winfried Lang, "a framework convention sets the tone, establishes certain principles and even enunciates certain commitments... As a rule, it does not contain specific obligations... nor does it contain detailed prescriptions of certain activities" (Lang, 1993, p. 19). Various authors seem to equate a framework treaty with a lowest-common-denominator outcome – one that represents "the beginning of increasingly serious and concerted attention to the problem" and seeks to "define a general direction" and "inform a process" rather than "seek to foresee the detail in circumstances in which the words will be brought to bear" (Chayes and Chayes).

As early as 1976, Alexandre Kiss described a framework convention as a document establishing not substantive rules but the institutional framework for producing such rules. Kiss writes that a framework convention:

> lays down the basic principles regarding the form of co-operation and the objectives for which the institutional framework is created. The hallmark of a framework agreement, therefore, is that it is followed by additional protocols or even complementary instruments, which are related to the main instrument but are partially or completely independent. (Kiss, 1976, p. 95)

It is important to distinguish a framework convention from an umbrella convention.[32] Although the terms are often used interchangeably, they are different in two important respects. While both umbrella and framework agreements set out basic principles and general objectives to be further specified through subsequent instruments, these are generally regional in scope in the case of the former and issue-specific sub-agreements (or protocols) in the case of the latter. Moreover, an umbrella convention (such as the UN Convention on the Law of the Sea, or UNCLOS) has legal ramifications for pre-existing agreements under its remit, while a framework convention does not. It is this "retroactivity" which essentially distinguishes an umbrella convention from a framework convention. Whereas an umbrella convention absorbs (or supersedes) related treaties, a framework convention builds upon (or supplements) existing agreements. While both umbrella and framework conventions lay the ground for future agreements (proactive), only the former has a legal impact on previous agreements (retroactive).

In conceptualizing a global biodiversity convention, several key state and non-state actors originally envisioned the creation of an umbrella convention that would harmonize existing biodiversity agreements. However, this proposal was rejected in the first round of CBD negotiations because of the "numerous practical, political and legal obstacles" it posed.[33] In this context, it is clear that the CBD is a framework agreement in at least three important ways (Glowka et al., 1994, pp.1-2).

First, the CBD creates a global structure to promote continued international co-operation and to support national implementation. Indeed, the CBD emphasizes national action relating to biodiversity within state jurisdiction, establishing a framework of general, flexible obligations that Parties may apply through national laws and policies. Elements included in the basic operational structure (for instance, those specified in the Convention text itself), as well as a sampling of subsequent bodies produced through post-agreement negotiations, are outlined in Box 1.3.

Second, the CBD allows for its own further development through the negotiation of annexes and protocols. The contemporary "framework-protocol" approach to multilateral environmental treaty-making has proven effective in transforming the often ambiguous and "soft" legal content of environment and/or sustainable development conventions into more precise and binding provisions.[34] For example, the Vienna Convention led to the Montreal Protocol on Ozone Depleting Substances, and the UN Framework Convention on Climate Change prompted the Kyoto Protocol. The Cartagena Protocol on Biosafety represents the first effort to operationalize a key and contentious part of the CBD. However, the decision to address biosafety as the first protocol under the CBD[35] has been cited as powerful proof of the treaty's lack of science-based prioritizing. Indeed, the Convention's detractors dismiss it as being a prisoner of its own politics rather than based on sound science.[36]

Box 1.3 The CBD's Operational Structure

The CBD explicitly provides for the establishment of the following bodies:

- pursuant to Article 40, a **Secretariat** to administer the CBD and co-ordinate with other relevant bodies. Following the CBD's entry into force, a Secretariat was set up by UNEP on an interim basis in Geneva. Following a vote at COP-2, the Secretariat officially established its "permanent"[37] headquarters in Montreal in May 1996.

- pursuant to Article 17, a **Clearing-house Mechanism** to exchange and share information in support of scientific and technical co-operation.[38]

- pursuant to Articles 21 and 39, a **multilateral fund** to help finance implementation in developing countries, supported mainly by OECD countries[39] and currently operated by the Global Environment Facility.[40]

- pursuant to Article 23, a **Conference of Parties (COP)** to oversee the process of implementing and further elaborating the CBD. The COP is the main policy and priority-setting body (trying to manage an ambitious agenda).

- pursuant to Article 25, a **subsidiary body to provide the COP with scientific, technical, and technological advice** (SBSTTA).[41]

Box 1.3 Concluded

These permanent bodies in turn have produced a plethora of subsidiary processes, including:

- A **Meeting of Parties (MOP)** to the Cartagena Protocol on Biosafety is scheduled to begin its work as soon as the protocol has entered into force. In the interim, an Intergovernmental Committee for the Cartagena Protocol (ICCP) has been established.

- An ad hoc open-ended inter-sessional working group on **Article 8(j)** has met twice, first in March 2000 and again in February 2002, both meetings building on the work of a formal workshop on traditional knowledge (held in November 1997).

- An ad hoc open-ended working group on **access and benefit-sharing (ABS)** was convened in October 2001, building on the work of a Panel of Experts on ABS, which met twice (October 1999 and March 2001).

- Ongoing **rosters of experts** have been established **on thematic work programmes** such as marine and coastal biodiversity, forest biodiversity, agricultural biodiversity, inland waters, dry and sub-humid lands, as well as on **cross-cutting issues** such as biodiversity indicators, incentive measures, sustainable tourism, ecosystem approach, and education and public awareness.

For many developed nations [particularly the United States], the linkage between biodiversity and the safety of biotechnology is contrived. Indeed, a UNEP study[42] commissioned in the period preceding the formal treaty negotiations found almost no linkages between the two, with those that were found tending to benefit biodiversity. However, the treaty text clearly presumes otherwise. (Raustiala and Victor, 1996, p. 7)

Third, the CBD builds upon, or supplements, existing agreements – unlike an umbrella convention, which as noted above absorbs related treaties. In contrast to previous biodiversity instruments that target specific species, sites, and/or activities, the CBD adopts a broad ecosystem approach to conservation, thereby establishing a wider context for the protection of biological diversity.[43]

Biodiversity-related agreements remain poorly integrated and could benefit from a significant organizational overhaul. However, the political processes underlying the various biodiversity MEAs are more important than the technical co-operation and memoranda of understanding agreed upon by their respective secretariats. Indeed, the group's diversity (constituent MEAs are administered by different bodies) and entrenched institutional history (biodiversity MEAs are championed by well-established constituencies and therefore subject to significant "turf battles") make substantive co-ordination difficult. Moreover, the group is dominated by two treaties with very different approaches to biodiversity: while

CITES is aimed at protecting specific species, the CBD takes a comprehensive and cutting-edge approach to biodiversity conservation, including sustainable use of its components and benefit-sharing. Many developing countries that saw their bargaining position enhanced in the CBD negotiations would likely object to harmonization with other more traditional biodiversity-related conventions. Indeed, as will be explained below, attempts to identify critical conservation areas common to all or most of the biodiversity-related agreements have proven problematic and politically divisive under the CBD.

Current intergovernmental discussions aimed at improving environmental governance have focused on co-ordinating MEAs according to various criteria, ranging from substance (e.g. grouping MEAs with common issue areas, objectives, or problem-structures) and function (e.g. pooling activities common to many MEAs, such as reporting and monitoring, scientific and environmental assessment, financial and technical co-operation, etc.) to location (either co-locating the secretariats of new MEAs or relocating existing ones) and legal status (e.g. renegotiating, with a view to merging, existing MEAs into umbrella conventions).[44] One way forward has been to place the CBD into two groupings (or "clusters"): one with the other biodiversity-related agreements (focusing on their common conservation element), and another that includes the UNFCCC and the United Nations Convention to Combat Desertification (UNCCD) (focusing on their common sustainable development objectives). Together, the three "Rio treaties" enjoy a special status within the UN system, since they are among 25 treaties identified in the Secretary-General's *Millennium Report* as central to the UN's mission.

Unlike its sister agreements on climate change and desertification, however, the CBD entered a legal field crowded with global agreements. Legal instruments are particularly prolific in relation to the CBD's first objective (conservation). In line with this goal, the CBD builds on pre-existing biodiversity conservation agreements, such as the CMS, the Paris and Ramsar conventions, and, to some extent, CITES. In relation to its second objective (sustainable use), the CBD echoes contemporaneous sustainable development regimes such as the UNFCCC (1992) and the UNCCD (1994), as well as subsequent agreements (1995), such as the International Coral Reef Initiative (ICRI) and the agreement on the Conservation and Management of Straddling Fish Stocks and Highly Migratory Species negotiated under the United Nations Convention on the Law of the Sea (UNCLOS). As it seeks to address its third objective (benefit-sharing), the Convention establishes a new regime for the international exchange of genetic resources. In so doing, it overlaps with regimes concerned with extractive and other natural resources, such as the recently revised FAO International Undertaking on Plant Genetic Resources for Food and Agriculture (IU) (see discussion regarding the international treaty below) and the recently revised International Plant Protection Convention (IPPC) under the International Union for the Protection of New Varieties of Plants (UPOV).[45] The CBD also has implications for other regimes in the areas of trade and intellectual property, such as WTO and the World Intellectual Property Organization (WIPO).[46] With the adoption of the Cartagena Protocol on Biosafety, it remains to be seen whether the

CBD facilitates the creation of a new biosafety regime or simply extends or challenges existing regimes, particularly in the area of trade.[47] Table 1.1 categorizes international agreements that impact on at least one aspect of the CBD (and vice versa) according to both scope and time period.

Comprehensiveness

The CBD's comprehensive rather than sectoral approach to conservation makes it a landmark treaty in the environmental field. The Convention goes beyond the conservation of biodiversity *per se* to encompass such issues as the sustainable use of biological resources,[48] access to genetic resources, sharing of benefits from the use of genetic material, and access to technology, including biotechnology.[49] It has been argued that the convention's central focus is on the conservation of biological resources, and that "all the rest is the methodology of how to conserve" (interview with Tolba). By bringing these "non-traditional" issues into the bargain, the CBD becomes a courageous political document but a rather clumsy and cumbersome legal text. Of course, some maintain that the CBD's near-universal membership is a reflection of its weakness – that countries sign on precisely because there is no effective way of monitoring or enforcing compliance provisions that have been described as "vague and voluntaristic" (at best) and "confusing and contradictory" (at worst).[50] Moreover, because different groups see their interests mirrored in the treaty, it has been dubbed the "omnibus convention" or the "convention for all life on Earth" (interview with A. Campeau, 1997).

The sheer proliferation of programmes and processes established under the CBD to date reflects both its breadth and its depth. However, the very comprehensiveness that makes the CBD unique among global biodiversity agreements also makes it vulnerable to overextension. The COP's overcrowded agenda (particularly in the first four years) and the proliferation of subsidiary bodies and processes have resulted in a diffusion of limited energy, attention, and resources among state and non-state actors alike. If the issues and interests it encompasses are not carefully managed, the CBD could collapse under its own weight. Fortunately, the Parties have taken steps to address these pitfalls. Not only have they organized a series of special meetings to examine the Convention's operations, but a strategic plan is being developed for adoption at the sixth meeting of the Conference of the Parties (COP-6) to be held at The Hague in April 2002.[51]

Complexity

A second feature of the CBD is the complexity (and, some would say, ambiguity) not only of the Convention text but also of the biodiversity issue area itself. Two aspects of this complexity are issue salience and the veil of uncertainty.

Table 1.1   Global Agreements and Regimes related to the CBD according to Scope and Objective

Scope:	Environment →		Economy/Trade →	
Objectives / Time period	Conservation	Sustainable use/ development	Benefit-sharing	Other
1970s-1980s	• CITES • CMS • Wetlands • World Heritage • UNCLOS	• CITES • ITTA	• IU • UNCLOS Deep Seabed Mining	• Vienna Convention and Montreal Protocol • Basel Convention • Long-Range Transboundary Air Pollution Convention
1990s	• CBD • UNCLOS (Fish stocks) • ICRI	• CBD • UNFCCC • UNCCD • UNCLOS (Fish stocks) • ICRI	• CBD • Revised IPPC	• WTO TRIPS • Basel Protocol • Kyoto Protocol
2000+	• Potential protocols under CBD	• Potential protocols under CBD	• Potential protocols under CBD • IT	• Cartagena Protocol on Biosafety • Rotterdam Convention • Stockholm Convention

Issue salience The CBD reached its peak in popularity when the US announced it would not sign in Rio. Since that time, the Convention has received negligible coverage in the mainstream media – especially when compared to its ozone and climate change counterparts. If the CBD is indeed viewed as both less popular and less prestigious than these other agreements, it is in part due to the nature of the issue area itself. Both the breadth and depth of biodiversity make it difficult to define a clear *problématique*. In essence, biodiversity lacks "issue salience".[52]

Concretely, biodiversity does not offer an uncomplicated formula that advocates can explain to policy-makers in straightforward terms and that journalists can encapsulate in headlines for public consumption. Whereas the impacts of atmospheric change, such as ozone depletion and global warming, are beginning to be understood by the average person, the "web of life"– from microscopic organisms to entire ecosystems – is an extremely elusive matter and indeed forms a topic of continuing research and discussion among ecologists. Even within the scientific community, the reality and potential repercussions of biodiversity loss have really only been recognized by ecologists, taxonomists, and biologists. Moreover, even though a number of environmental groups are working to preserve "nature", the biodiversity cause *per se* has yet to be championed by a popular group (environmental lawyers and taxonomists can hardly be said to capture the public's imagination). Again, this is in contrast to global atmospheric issues taken up by well-known professionals such as astronauts and medical doctors.

The species-specific and site-specific treaties, which pre-dated the CBD, made it easier for the public to embrace "charismatic animals", such as pandas and seal pups, and to explore "exotic sites" such as the rainforests of Borneo and Brazil. When countries such as Brazil and Malaysia effectively neutralized the forests issue within the UNCED process and they (and others) opposed any lists of globally important species and spaces within the CBD (the term "global" does not even appear in the agreed text),[53] many of the familiar connections that people had with biodiversity were lost.

Although the comprehensive manner in which the CBD addresses the biodiversity issue area may be laudable from a substantive or scientific point of view, it also serves to magnify the issue's complexity and, consequently, to diminish both the Convention's general appeal and the political will necessary for its implementation. The remedy, however, is not necessarily to return to the traditional ways of conveying the importance of biodiversity. Indeed, conservation campaigns focusing on specific sites and species are best left to well-established conservation organizations.[54] Instead, the CBD should focus on its unique nature or, in management terms, its "core competency". This entails the integration of the CBD's three key objectives of conservation, sustainable use, and benefit-sharing (as set out in Article 1 of the Convention).

The current lead-up to the World Summit on Sustainable Development presents an opportunity to showcase the CBD as a true sustainable development treaty. As one of two legally binding agreements to emerge from the 1992 UNCED, the CBD is well-positioned to serve as a global focal point for measuring progress since the Rio Earth Summit. The standing of the CBD (and its Cartagena Protocol on Biosafety) as a sister agreement to the UNFCCC (and its subsequent Kyoto Protocol) should be emphasized. By clearly identifying and creating linkages with climate change and other issues that rank high on domestic agendas (such as health and homeland safety) as well as international agendas (such as trade and security), the political and public profile of the CBD and biodiversity in general would be enhanced.

Fortunately, the COP recognized the importance of these issues and at its fifth meeting called for the creation of a Consultative Working Group of Experts on Biodiversity Education and Public Awareness. Although this joint CBD/UNESCO initiative is to be applauded, it clearly illustrates the same conceptual ambiguities that continue to plague the CBD in general. This confusion arises primarily from the fact that the working group's mandate is too broad. Rather than develop initiatives that focus on the CBD, the group attempts to address all of biodiversity. This approach rests on the misguided view of the CBD as an umbrella convention (one that consolidates pre-existing biodiversity agreements) rather than as a framework sustainable development convention (which overlaps with agreements beyond the environmental realm). A cross-cutting education and communications strategy based on the CBD itself (as a first focal point of biodiversity) would allow for involvement by a range of relevant institutions and instruments beyond biodiversity conservation *per se*. In addition, the composition of the working group itself does not encompass the expertise required to fulfil its own mandate effectively. As with many processes established under the CBD, the expert group itself reflects a narrow range of expertise, mostly comprising scientists, career diplomats, and programme officers with little experience in developing education or communications programmes. Those in the group who do possess this expertise have developed it almost exclusively in relation to biodiversity conservation. Such a focus is likely to lead to educational and public awareness programmes that emphasize the CBD's first objective over the other two rather than its key innovation – the interrelationship between conservation, sustainable use, and benefit-sharing.

Veil of uncertainty   While the uneven scientific knowledge among diplomats involved in the CBD negotiations proved problematic, the lack of information (or "veil of uncertainty")[55] regarding the various values of biodiversity may have facilitated the negotiation process. Indeed, the bargaining position of the South was significantly strengthened by the negotiators' lack of data regarding the commercial value of biodiversity within their borders (*in situ*). While developing countries are the primary holders of biodiversity, many of the relevant products (in particular, plant genetic resources for food and agriculture, or PGRFA) can be derived from the gene banks of the North (*ex situ*).[56] This fact has led some observers to conclude that any claim to victory by the South *vis-à-vis* the CBD is, in essence, a moral one.

Certainly, in the ten years since the Convention's adoption, the implications of its provisions have come into sharper focus. Among other factors, current studies of the commercial value of biodiversity have in effect weakened biodiversity-rich countries' leverage in post-agreement negotiations. This author views the recently concluded negotiations aimed at harmonizing the 1983 FAO International

Undertaking on Plant Genetic Resources with the CBD as a case in point.[57] On 3 November 2001, after seven years of protracted negotiations, the 31st Session of the Conference of the FAO voted to adopt the International Treaty on Plant Genetic Resources for Food and Agriculture.[58] However, many of the guiding principles found in the original G-77 proposal, such as farmers' rights,[59] were diluted in order to secure an agreement. According to an NGO statement issued on the treaty's adoption, the result is "a weak [t]reaty that poses few challenges to the dominant trade policy environment, technological developments and intellectual property rights regimes which tend to serve the interests of OECD countries".[60] Furthermore, in contrast to the CBD with which the new treaty was initially intended to be harmonized, the agreement has been criticized for its lack of fairness, equity, and comprehensiveness.[61] Notwithstanding these apparent "weaknesses," the treaty was adopted with 116 votes in favour, none against, and only two abstentions (from the US and Japan).

As knowledge about issue areas addressed under the CBD evolves (and as those issues themselves evolve and are operationalized through various mechanisms, including protocols), so too do the negotiating groups. Rather than following traditional UN regional groupings, unconventional alliances now form around specific interests and issue areas.

Events leading up to the conclusion of the Cartagena Protocol on Biosafety provide a compelling illustration of this phenomenon. The biosafety negotiations avoided polarization along a strictly North-South axis. As negotiations clarified the outlines of a protocol, the essential unity of developing countries (which had characterized the negotiation of the CBD itself) began to erode. Countries with nascent biotech industries, or with interests in large-scale agricultural exporting, reconsidered their interests and alignments. The most striking example was the split within the group of Latin American and Caribbean countries (GRULAC): Argentina, Chile, and Uruguay joined Australia, Canada, and the United States to form the Miami Group, while Brazil chose to retain its leadership role within Latin America and the rest of the developing world (the so-called Like-Minded Group). Industrialized countries also took up divergent positions (mainly according to their exporter/importer status), resulting in an important split within the OECD. The EU (notwithstanding major differences among its member-states) tended to move toward a more sceptical attitude regarding the benefits and safety of biotechnology and, in any event, defended its own precautionary procedures for living modified organisms (LMOs). The Miami Group maintained the view that anything more than a limited co-ordination of existing national regulations would amount to a restriction of trade based on the unspecified dangers of LMOs.

As the veil of uncertainty (which favoured developing-country interests during the initial CBD negotiations) lifted around biotech and other key issue areas under the Convention, old alliances were replaced with newer, arguably more innovative ones.[62] Indeed, it is doubtful that the CBD could have been concluded according to its existing terms in current conditions of greater issue clarity.

Compromise

From the beginning of the biodiversity negotiations, it was clear that in order to ensure a successful outcome, the divisive issue of global economic disparities, which had historically characterized negotiations between North and South, would have to be addressed. The task was to convince developing countries that the industrialized world's apparent resolve to save the globe's fast-disappearing biological resources reflected good faith rather than maintenance of the status quo. Equally essential was the task of getting industrialized countries to bind themselves to providing the necessary funds, technology, and capacity on which the practical implementation of the CBD would depend. To a great extent, the CBD succeeded in both tasks. Through a complex bargaining process, the CBD reflects a network of compromises. The Convention's adoption can be attributed not so much to the fact that both industrialized and developing countries found many areas of common ground. Rather, it demonstrates that each negotiating group had a substantial portion of their respective vital demands met within the framework of the agreed text. As Table 1.2 on negotiation trade-offs demonstrates, the CBD was the result of a distributive rather than an integrative bargaining process.[63]

The focal issues of the biodiversity negotiations can be divided into two categories according to the divergent interests that underlie them. The first category of issues consists of concessions or commitments by industrialized countries (with developing countries pressing for the strongest commitments possible). The second group of issues includes those issues that reflect concessions or commitments by developing countries (with industrialized countries pressing for the strongest commitments possible). A survey of key trade-offs within the biodiversity negotiations (with corresponding CBD Articles) is presented in Table 1.2 below.

The ultimate compromises that were achieved are reflected in the text of the CBD itself. Trade-offs took place within individual Articles, between Articles, between contemporaneous conventions (such as the UNFCCC), and even between pre-existing ones (such as CITES or UNCLOS). While developing countries' concessions and commitments (such as access to genetic resources, conservation and sustainable use, impact assessment, and national reporting) were largely negotiated in the first Working Group (WG I), those of industrialized countries (such as benefit-sharing, financial resources, and scientific, technical, and technology co-operation) were addressed in the second Working Group (WG II). On several occasions, progress in WG I was blocked or slowed when developing countries perceived lack of progress in WG II (see Svensson, pp.164-91). However, the fact that the converse was rarely true may demonstrate that although the development of a biodiversity convention was originally a Northern government/NGO initiative, the South was better able to exercise its bargaining power throughout the negotiations.

Table 1.2 Trade-Offs between Industrialized and Developing Countries

Types of trade-offs	Concessions by developing countries	Concessions by industrialized countries
Between the objectives of the CBD	Objectives (Art. 1): Conservation and sustainable use Access to genetic resources	Objectives (Art. 1): Benefit-sharing Technology transfer funding
Between the principal sets of obligations under the CBD: States have sovereign rights over their own biological resources but also a responsibility to conserve and sustainably use these resources	General measures for conservation and sustainable use (Art. 6) Identification and monitoring (Art. 7) *In situ* conservation (Art. 8) *Ex situ* conservation (Art. 9) Sustainable use of components of biodiversity (Art. 10)	Recognition of national sovereignty over natural resources (Art. 15[1]) Information exchange (Art. 17) Technical and scientific co-operation (Art. 18)
Between access to genetic resources (largely in the South) in exchange for access to the results and benefits of biotechnologies (developed largely in the North)	Access to Genetic Resources (Art. 15[2])	Benefit-sharing/biotechnology (Arts. 15[6], 19[1-2])
Between intellectual property rights (IPR) and patents (largely held by the multinational corporations and research agencies of the North)[64] and technology transfer and the rights of indigenous peoples' and local communities' rights	Protection of IPR (Art. 16[2-3])	Technology transfer (Art. 16[3-5]) Indigenous peoples and local communities (Art. 8[j])

Table 1.2 Concluded

Between the withdrawal of lists of globally important biodiversity ("global lists") advocated by several industrialized countries) and the acceptance (by developing countries) of a scientific body to advise the Conference of Parties (Art. 25) along with their acceptance of national reporting (Art. 26) and impact assessments (Art. 14)	Subsidiary body on scientific, technical and technological advice (Art. 25) Reporting (Art. 26) Impact assessments (Art. 14)	No "global lists"
Regarding the financial resources of the CBD. Developing countries accepted both eligibility criteria and "agreed incremental costs" in exchange for the North's provision of "new and additional financial resources" (Article 20[2]).	Eligibility criteria (Art. 20[2]) Agreed incremental costs (Art. 20[2])	Provision of new and additional financial resources (Art. 20[2])
Regarding the financial mechanism of the CBD. The decision to designate the GEF as the institutional structure to operate the financial mechanism on an interim basis was a compromise between North and South: the former had hoped that the GEF would be designated on a permanent basis, while the latter originally proposed the creation of a new and separate fund.	No multilateral fund explicitly mentioned GEF explicitly mentioned (Art. 39)	Mechanism for the provision of financial resources to developing-country Parties under the authority and guidance of the COP (Art. 21) GEF designated as interim institutional structure for the financial mechanism (Art. 39)

Source: Adapted from Koester (1997)

Conclusion

Assessing the major trade-offs made by both developing and industrialized countries in the course of the CBD's negotiations highlights the ways in which often divergent positions were resolved (or not) within the CBD. Despite the apparent common interest in and "perception of an integrated, interdependent ecosystem" that frame global environmental issues, the negotiation of the CBD accentuated many of the issues that divide these countries (see Miller, 1995, p. 109). Indeed, the CBD represents a network of North-South compromises achieved through a complex bargaining process.

In balancing divergent interests and positions, the final text of the CBD was more acceptable to the vast majority of states involved in the negotiation. Viewing the CBD as the best possible outcome, Veit Koester, chair of the Intergovernmental Negotiating Committee working group that negotiated the most contentious aspects of the CBD, concluded that "the Convention represents a North-South compromise, therefore the art of the possible" (interview with Veit Koester, 1995). Yet opinion concerning both the process and outcome of the biodiversity negotiations is divided. According to the chief legal advisor to the US delegation:

> It is regrettable that a legal instrument as ambitious as the Biodiversity Convention should suffer from basic conceptual and drafting deficiencies. The structure of the negotiations, the haphazard way in which crucial issues were considered, and the pressures of time contributed to a legal instrument which should cause distress for international lawyers and policy-makers. (Chandler, p. 174)

In contrast, two environmental lawyers who helped to author the original IUCN draft convention hailed the CBD as a "landmark" (Burhenne-Guilmin and Glowka, p. 17). According to Swanson, "the CBD came into existence because there exists a common interest in the co-ordinated management of domestic resources, not on account of a joint interest in a common resource. The recognition of this more complicated form of commonality is an achievement in itself" (Swanson, 1999, pp.281-282).

The CBD reflects the interaction of a variety of forces in the politics of its formation and now its operation, ranging from the nature and diplomatic context of the issue area to the activities of professional networks and lobby groups, leadership, bureaucratic co-ordination, and regional and economic bloc positions.[65] Since many of the most contentious issues were left unresolved at the time of the CBD's adoption, the post-agreement negotiations have proven particularly challenging. The level of implementation and enforcement will be the ultimate test of whether the compromise achieved during the Convention negotiations was a true success or merely an illusory one.

Author's Interviews

Interview with Burhenne-Guilmin, Françoise (IUCN Environmental Law Centre) at IUCN World Congress (Montreal: 23 October 1996)
Interview with Campeau, Arthur (Canada) at Secretariat of the Convention on Biological Diversity (Montreal: 30 October 1997)
Interview with Glowka, Lyle (IUCN Environmental Law Centre) at IUCN World Congress (Montreal: 23 October 1996)
Interview with Hirsch, Leonard P. (Smithsonian Institution, US) at Symposium of the International Studies Association (Los Angeles: 18 March 2000)
Interview with Koester, Veit (Denmark) at COP-5 (Jakarta: 15 November 1995)
Interview with McConnell, Fiona (UK) (London: 6 July 1996)
Interview with Savage, Eleanor (US) (Montreal: November 1996)
Interview with Ting, Wen Lian at COP-5 (Jakarta: November 1995)
Interview with Tolba, Mostafa K. at CSD-8 (New York: 25-6 April 2000)
Interview with Zedan, Hamdallah at UNEP (Nairobi: August 1996)

Notes

[1] Article 36 of the CBD specifies that 30 countries must depose an "instrument of ratification, acceptance, approval or accession" in order for the Convention to enter into force. As of December 2001, 181 countries and the European Union were Parties to the CBD; 12 governments – including, most notably, the United States of America – have signed the treaty but have yet to ratify it. For an analysis of the "continuing significance of the US "No" in Rio," see: Bramble and Porter (1992, pp. 313-53); Bell (1993, pp. 479-537); and Rosendal (1994, pp. 87-103).
[2] Article 2 of the Convention defines biological diversity as "the variability among living organisms from all sources, including, *inter alia*, terrestrial, marine and other aquatic ecosystems and the ecological complexes of which they are part; this includes diversity within species, between species and of ecosystems".
[3] Article 1 of the Convention outlines its three main objectives: conservation of biodiversity, sustainable use of its components, and benefit-sharing.
[4] For an extensive survey of the commercial uses of biodiversity, see ten Kate and Laird (1999).
[5] In addition to the "intrinsic value of biological diversity," the CBD preamble underscores the "ecological, genetic, social, economic, scientific, educational, cultural, recreational and aesthetic values of biological diversity and its components" as well as its importance for "evolution and for maintaining life sustaining systems of the biosphere".
[6] For an analytical overview of options for improving co-ordination and coherence among MEAs, see McGraw (2001). *Options for Improving Co-ordination and Coherence among Multilateral Environmental Agreements,* International Policy and Cooperation Branch, Environment Canada.
[7] In the lead-up to WSSD, UNEP has convened a series of conferences and consultations involving governance experts, civil society representatives, and governments (the latter culminating in a special meeting of the Global Ministerial Environment Forum held in Cartagena, Colombia, in February 2002). These meetings have in turn produced a plethora

of proposals for strengthening or reforming the existing international environmental architecture.

[8] For a thorough exposition, see de Klemm and Shine (1993).

[9] Indeed, a much greater number of regulatory arrangements – for the environment in general and biodiversity in particular – have been made under regional treaties. In the category of regional biodiversity treaties, there are more than two dozen with a general environmental focus. Some three dozen seek to conserve specific species such as fish and other marine resources (over 20), land animals (six), plants (three), and birds (one). See Sanchez and Juma (1994, p.297).

[10] Although these last two instruments were concluded in the 1980s, negotiations began in the 1970s.

[11] On 25 October 1988, President Reagan signed a joint Resolution of Congress calling for "continued US leadership in order to achieve the earliest possible negotiation of an international convention to *conserve* the Earth's biological diversity, including the protection of a *representative* system of ecosystems adequate to *conserve* biological diversity" (emphasis added) (US House Judiciary Resolution 648, 100th Congress, 2nd Session, 1988). See also Chandler (1993, pp. 141-2). At the 1991 G-7 London Summit, the U.S. position was reiterated: "We support the negotiation, under the auspices of UNEP, of an acceptable framework convention on biodiversity, if possible to be concluded next year. It should concentrate on protection of ecosystems, particularly in species-rich areas, without impeding positive developments in biotechnology" (McConnell, 1996, p.54).

[12] UNEP Governing Council Decision 14/26. Because the phrase "conservation of biological diversity" was both unfamiliar and cumbersome, a proposal was made to revert to the shorter, traditional concept of "nature conservation". However, delegates with scientific expertise argued at the time that "biological diversity" was the correct term. The shortened form, "biodiversity," was eventually adopted (interview with Burhenne-Guilmin, 1996, and with McConnell, 1996).

[13] It is important to note that the relationship with other conventions, the central issue of UNEP Governing Council Decision 14/26 for the Rationalization of International Conventions on Biodiversity, was largely ignored in the later meetings. However, the matter was taken up at very end of the negotiations (Burhenne-Guilmin, 1993, p.46) and, ultimately, was addressed in Article 22 (Relationship with Other Conventions) of the CBD.

[14] This meeting would constitute the formal beginning of the intergovernmental process that would ultimately lead to the adoption of the first legally binding instrument under the CBD – the Cartagena Protocol on Biosafety – concluded in January 2000. Biotechnology was the focus of the only dedicated sub-working group created during the pre-negotiation phase of the CBD process. Indeed, as early as the issue-framing phase, developing countries successfully argued that biotechnology be part of the package of key issues addressed in the CBD.

[15] For an exposition of the South's objections to the "common heritage of mankind" principle in global environmental issues, see Ramakrishna (1992, pp. 145-168).

[16] *Report of the Ad Hoc Group of Experts on Biological Diversity on the Work of its Third Session in Preparation for a Legal Instrument on Biological Diversity of the Planet,* Geneva, 9-13 July 1990 (UNEP/BioDiv.3/12).

[17] Letter of 19 September 1990 by the Executive Director of UNEP to governments concerning convening a meeting in Nairobi, 19-23 September 1990 (archives).

[18] Despite the expanded title, the list of participants for each "expert group" meeting reveals no significant change in the size or composition of delegations.

[19] The CBD language on technology transfer was ultimately replicated in chapter 34.14(b) of UNCED's *Agenda 21*.

[20] "Comments on Climate Change Documents as They Pertain to Biological Diversity Negotiations," UNEP internal memorandum from A. Timoshenko and S. Bragdon to M. Tolba, 23 April 1992.

[21] For an exposition of these points, see Spielmann (1992) "White House Has Serious Problems with UN Species-Saving Accord," Associated Press, 8 May 1992.

[22] The US-sponsored UNEP Governing Council Resolution (June 1987), the UNEP Senior Advisory Panel of Experts on Biological Diversity (September 1988), and the first meeting of the Ad Hoc Group of Experts on Biological Diversity (November 1988) all pre-dated the UNGA resolution to hold UNCED (December 1989).

[23] The IUCN representative proposed that the draft text could be offered to UNEP whenever the governing council decided to proceed with a convention. The UNEP Secretariat in turn indicated that proposals from IUCN and any other competent NGO or IGO would be included in background documentation for future meetings.

[24] Despite the competition among the IUCN, UNESCO, and the FAO during the CBD's pre-negotiation phase, lawyers from all three organizations were invited to take part in a special drafting group led by UNEP.

[25] McConnell (1996) provides an amusing but accurate description of 20 such individuals in her book *Dramatis Personae*.

[26] The US refusal to sign the CBD in Rio is largely credited for the treaty's sudden transition to a high-profile issue in international public and political arenas. Analyses of the US position regarding the CBD in Rio are provided by several authors, including: Bell (1993); Glowka (1993); Rosendal (1994); and Susskind (1994).

[27] A notable exception, of course, was the US whose delegation arrived at the final meeting with a set of 16 non-negotiable points. The result was its being targeted, with ensuing isolation, for not signing the CBD in Rio.

[28] For an exposition of the complex procedure of developing negotiation instructions, see Trumbore (1997).

[29] Susskind's model breaks downs as follows: Stage I (a period of six months) consists of "scoping the threat and defining the key principles"; Stage II (a period ranging from one to two years) consists of agreeing on general and specific commitments, financial and institutional arrangements, reporting and monitoring requirements; and Stage III (three years after the signing) consists of reviewing the results of the previous stage and tightening all elements of the treaty and any protocols (1994, pp. 141-147). See also chapter 4 by Le Prestre on the operation of the Convention in this volume.

[30] In 1990, the Ad Hoc Group of Experts on Biological Diversity instructed the Executive Director of UNEP to convene an Ad Hoc Group of Legal and Technical Experts on Biological Diversity with a mandate to negotiate an international legal instrument, "possibly in the form of a framework convention," for the conservation of biological diversity. Despite these explicit instructions, the term "framework" was not carried forward to the treaty's formal title. Interviews with several delegates suggest that this aspect was simply overlooked in the final rushed hours of the CBD negotiations.

[31] The CBD has been alternately referred to as: the "Biodiversity Framework Convention" (Sand, 1991, pp. 236-79); a "framework convention" (Burhenne-Guilmin and Glowka, 1994, pp. 15-8); "largely a framework agreement" (Sanchez and Juma, 1993, p.322); or "more than a framework convention" (interview with Tolba). The author has only come across one important dissenting view in the literature – perhaps not surprisingly, from an American negotiator (see Chandler, 1993).

[32] For an analysis of the relative merits of umbrella and framework conventions, see McGraw (2001).

[33] See *Proceedings of the Ad Hoc Working Group on the Work of its First Session*, Geneva, 16-18 November 1988 (UNEP/BioDiv.1/Inf.2).

[34] The development of sub-agreements (or protocols) has at times served to reinforce rather than resolve many of the political tensions inherent in the original UNCED agreements. See: D. McGraw (2000), "Multilateral Environmental Treaty-Making" in G. Boutin et al. (eds.), *Innovations in Global Governance: ACUNS Policy Brief,* Academic Council of the United Nations System and American Society of International Law, at 7 (available online at http://www.yale.edu/acuns/publications/Policy_Brief/index.html).

[35] A number of protocols under the CBD have been proposed with varying degrees of support. One proposal called for a protocol based on CBD Article 8(j), another on alien invasive species. In November 1996, the COP indicated that it would consider, among other possibilities, a revised FAO International Undertaking on Plant Genetic Resources as a protocol to the CBD (see: COP Decision III/11, par. 18, and discussion below). The eventual success of these proposals is likely to depend on political considerations, such as which groups and countries are championing a particular cause.

[36] For a presentation of political and scientific arguments against singling out biosafety as the first protocol under the CBD, see Vogler and McGraw (2000, pp. 123-141).

[37] Canada's status as host country came under pressure at COP-5 both by developing countries (calling on Canada to renew its additional $1million USD contribution to the operation of the Secretariat) and by some European countries (mainly for having taken such a hard line in the biosafety negotiations) – in particular Germany (seeking to co-locate the CBD alongside the UNFCCC and UNCCD secretariats already established in Bonn). In addition, it has been suggested that the CBD be headquartered alongside the secretariats of other global biodiversity-related treaties (in Geneva, Bonn, or Nairobi) in order to strengthen synergies and rationalize resources. The outcome of these proposals will depend largely on broader debates regarding international environmental governance (see n. 7 above).

[38] According to the CBD web site, the Clearing-house Mechanism's mission is threefold: "[to] promote and facilitate technical and scientific cooperation, within and between countries; [to] develop a global mechanism for exchanging and integrating information on biodiversity; [and to] develop the necessary human and technological network". See http://www.biodiv.org and chapter 5 in this volume.

[39] It is noteworthy that the financial mechanism is to function "under the authority and guidance of, and be accountable to, the Conference of the Parties..." This language is stronger than the relevant wording in the UNFCCC, under which the financial mechanism is to function under the "guidance of the Conference of Parties" (UNFCCC, Article 11).

[40] The GEF was initially designated as the institutional structure to operate the financial mechanism on an interim basis, subject to the condition that it be fully restructured in accordance with the requirements of Article 21 of the CBD, for the period between the CBD's entry into force and the first meeting of the COP "or until the COP decides which institutional structure will be designated in accordance with Article 21". Although the GEF appeared to be the only realistic candidate and despite having met several requirements (most notably a more democratic and transparent system of governance), COP-5 called for a second review of the financial mechanism's effectiveness during the period from November 1996 to June 2001.

[41] In its earlier days, the SBSTTA was dubbed a "mini-COP". Some actors (mainly in the industrialized world) contend that the effectiveness of the CBD will depend on the extent to which the SBSTTA can provide sound scientific advice as a basis for the COP's policy decisions. Others (mainly representing developing countries who feel at a disadvantage in strictly scientific bodies, which tend to be dominated by western-educated experts) have argued the need for a subsidiary body on implementation.

[42] Ad Hoc Group of Experts on Biological Diversity, *Biotechnology and Biodiversity,* 14 November 1990 (UNEP/Bio.Div./SWGB.1/3).

[43] Of course, the CBD articulates new norms that could also apply to pre-existing agreements. In this sense, the CBD may have the normative character of an umbrella convention without possessing its legal status. See: de Klemm and Shine (1993), and Lyster (1985).

[44] Given that each co-ordinating option has important institutional and organizational implications, additional research is needed to evaluate both their desirability (need) and feasibility (costs and benefits). For a critical analysis of these different co-ordinating mechanisms, see McGraw (2001).

[45] Prior to their recent revision, these regimes had operated largely according to the "common heritage of mankind" (CHM) – a principle that views certain resources as public goods and thus not subject to access restrictions or usage fees. However, the proposition that biodiversity should be viewed as the common heritage of humankind was rejected at an early stage of the text's negotiation on the grounds that biodiversity does not truly constitute a "global commons" (as with the oceans and atmosphere). Indeed, most of its components are situated in areas under national jurisdiction or are privately-owned property. Instead, a firm emphasis was placed on sovereign rights over biological *resources*, while recognizing that biological *diversity* itself is a common concern of humankind. "Common concern" implies a common but differentiated responsibility among developing and industrialized countries; it recognizes the international community's concern for biodiversity without making biological resources its common heritage or indeed property. Thus, broadly speaking, biodiversity-rich countries and communities may restrict access to their biological resources to those who have agreed to share the benefits arising from the use of these resources. Operationalizing this principle (and its qualifiers) into concrete arrangements has been the focus of protracted discussions and arrangements at both the bilateral and multilateral levels.

[46] For an analysis of the relationship between the CBD and the GATT, see Downes (1995, pp. 197-25).

[47] For a regime analysis of the biosafety negotiations, see Vogler and McGraw (2000).

[48] According to Article 2 of the CBD, "biological resources" include "genetic resources, organisms or parts thereof, populations, or any other biotic component of ecosystems with actual or potential use or value for humanity".

[49] "Biotechnology", as defined in Article 2 of the CBD, means any "technological application that uses biological systems, living organisms, or derivatives thereof, to make or modify products or processes for specific use".

[50] In this connection, it is worth noting that one of the reasons cited by the US for not signing the CBD in Rio was that the government took its international commitments seriously enough *not* to sign this particular treaty (Chandler).

[51] For actions taken in this regard, see, for instance, *Note by the Executive Secretary on the Strategic Plan for the Convention on Biological Diversity to the Open-Ended Inter-Sessional Meeting on the Strategic Plan, National Reports and Implementation of the CBD*, Montreal, 19-21 November 2001, pp. 1-8 (UNEP/CBD/MSP/2).

[52] An issue's saliency is derived from its simplicity, clarity, and/or familiarity. According to Oran Young and Gail Osherenko, "[s]uccess is often linked to the ability of those formulating proposals to draft simple formulas that are intuitively appealing or to borrow formulas or approaches from prior cases with which negotiators may already be familiar. The influence of salience lies in its capacity to facilitate the convergence of expectations in international bargaining" (Young and Osherenko, 1993, pp. 14-15).

[53] Although such opposition may be understood on purely political grounds, it has exacerbated the debate on issue saliency.

[54] The IUCN report *Effective Communication of Nature and Biological Diversity to an Uninterested Public* represents a case in point. It interprets biodiversity education solely in

terms of nature conservation and management. Such an approach is understandable given the IUCN's mission but remains inadequate from a CBD communications perspective.

[55] According to Oran Young, Parties involved in institutional bargaining regularly act under a "veil of uncertainty" regarding the future distribution of benefits from a regime. However, since institutions are never easily changed once they are established, this "veil" creates incentives for the Parties to opt for institutional arrangements that are more equitable so that they are acceptable to countries with different positions, interests, and resources (see also A. Hasenclever et al. (1997), p. 73).

[56] Some countries, in particular the US, claim that they recognized that the commercial value of *in situ* biodiversity was overplayed during the CBD negotiations. This contention might help explain why American negotiators were less willing to give in to what they considered unreasonable demands by developing countries, with the Nordic Group often acting as mediators.

[57] The complex and critical issue of *ex situ* collections of genetic resources acquired prior to the CBD's entry into force and the question of "farmers' rights" were left unresolved by the Convention negotiators. Resolution 3 of the Nairobi Final Act recognized the need to address these matters effectively and also recognized the FAO as the appropriate forum to do so. Both issues remained major stumbling blocks in protracted negotiations (1994-2001) under the auspices of the FAO's Commission on Plant Genetic Resources for Food and Agriculture.

[58] To view the text of the treaty, see the FAO Commission on Genetic Resources Secretariat web site http://www.fao.org/ag/cgrfa/default.htm.

[59] Developing countries sought to establish an international benefit-sharing mechanism for ensuring farmers' rights, but the new treaty effectively subordinates these to national laws.

[60] See *Statement by Public Interest, Non-profit Civil Society Organisations to the 31st FAO Conference*, 3 November 2001 (http://www.iisd.ca/biodiv/iu.html).

[61] For an analysis of the treaty negotiations, see T. Barnes and S. Burgiel (2001), *Earth Negotiations Bulletin*, vol. 9, no. 213, pp. 1-14 (http://www.iisd.ca/biodiv/iu.html).

[62] The creation of the Compromise Group, itself accommodating various positions, was particularly instructive in this regard. One delegate described the group as an "international lab" in which various proposals could be tested for broader agreement. Another innovation was the return to a diplomatic tradition called the "Vienna setting" – one that involves representation from all stakeholder groups at the negotiating table. The openness and transparency of the process made it difficult for any government or interest group to stall the process or disown the end result. Again, this outcome stands in stark contrast to the original CBD negotiations as reflected by reservations formally expressed by several governments upon the Convention's adoption.

[63] Whereas distributive or positional bargaining involves staking out definite positions that may be mutually exclusive (often resulting in "zero-sum" outcomes), integrative or productive bargaining involves searching for mutually beneficial (or "win/win") solutions See Young (1989a, pp. 349-361).

[64] The protection of IPR (Article 16(2-3)) is qualified both within the latter paragraphs and by the two ensuing paragraphs (4-5) as well as by the rights of indigenous peoples and local communities (Article 8(j)).

[65] For an in-depth analysis of these factors, see McGraw (2002).

Chapter 2

The Cartagena Protocol on Biosafety[1]

François Pythoud and Urs P. Thomas

The Cartagena Protocol on Biosafety to the Convention on Biological Diversity (or Biosafety Protocol – BP) is a multilateral agreement administered by the Convention on Biological Diversity (CBD) that represents a tightly formulated set of binding rules governing international shipments of living modified organisms (LMOs),[2] including trade in LMOs that are agricultural commodities directly used for food and feed or subsequently integrated into processed products. The BP was adopted in Montreal on 29 January 2000 after nearly five years of intense negotiations. The analytical methodology chosen for the present analysis benefits from a very extensive negotiating experience in biotechnology and biosafety and relies on official documents in order to illustrate the successive steps toward the achievement of a consensus. Because it is "neither a pure environmental nor a pure trade agreement" (Falkner, 2000), the resulting agreement is particularly complex and reflects unique dynamics.

History and Nature of the Protocol

The development of modern biotechnology over the past 25 years has shown a very high level of effervescence, thanks to the development of genetic engineering. The first field trials of genetically modified plants, so-called transgenic plants, took place in the mid-1980s. A few years later, in the mid-1990s, they started to reach the market and consumers. On the one hand, these technologies were widely seen as offering an unlimited potential for the exploitation and development of the world's genetic resources, be it in the domain of pharmaceuticals or in the breeding of new varieties and species of plants and animals. On the other hand, they raised fears in terms of their impact on environmental and food safety. This relationship between the benefits and the risks of biotechnology remains a permanent feature of the debate on the use of genetically modified organisms. This section shows how these rapid developments and this context led to the first initiatives aimed at devising international safety regulations governing the use of these technologies.

Toward the Negotiation of a Biosafety Protocol

From the beginning, the use and release into the environment of genetically modified organisms, especially transgenic plants, provoked intense debates between scientists and regulators regarding their potentially negative impact on the environment and human health. These debates led the Organization for Economic Cooperation and Development (OECD) to publish, in 1986, a "Blue Book" entitled *Recombinant DNA Safety Considerations,*[3] which represents the first document focusing specifically on biosafety to originate from a major intergovernmental body. Pertaining to the industrial, agricultural, and environmental applications of genetically modified organisms, these guidelines were intended to present scientific principles that could be used in risk assessment and risk management.

The authors realized that it was too early to formulate standards for regulating the use of genetically modified organisms. Nevertheless, by emphasizing the need to proceed on a "case by case" and "step by step" basis, the guidelines identified for the first time the basic principles that should govern the assessment and management of the risks associated with the development and adoption of genetically modified organisms. They also represented the first attempts toward international harmonization on these issues. They have subsequently been used as a reference by most industrialized countries to formulate their domestic legal frameworks on biosafety.[4]

In 1991 the publication by the UN Industrial Development Organization (UNIDO) of a "Voluntary Code of Conduct for the Release of Organisms into the Environment" represented the first contribution of the UN to the debate on biosafety.[5] UNIDO established a framework, in consultation with the UN Environment Programme (UNEP), the World Health Organization[6] (WHO), and the Food and Agriculture Organization (FAO), with the purpose of helping member countries work toward the creation of an international biosafety network. Emphasis was placed mainly on the worldwide provision and dissemination of information regarding research on and regulation, usage, and trade of genetically modified micro-organisms, plants, and animals.

At about the same time, scientific evidence of unprecedented rates of species extinction and loss of biological diversity became a serious concern for the international community. In the late 1980s, there was a call for the development of a global convention for the conservation and sustainable use of biological diversity. Very comprehensive negotiations began in earnest in 1991, and the final text of the Convention on Biological Diversity was adopted in 1992 and opened for signature at the Rio Earth Summit.[7]

During these negotiations, the seemingly unlimited prospects of biotechnology provoked increasing expectations and great hopes, particularly among developing countries. They saw benefits in the application of biotechnology to their local genetic resources, including a new potential source of revenue for development. These expectations are very well illustrated in the Agenda 21 Action Plan adopted at the 1992 Rio Earth Summit. The importance then given to emerging modern biotechnology is reflected in chapter 16, "Environmentally Sound Management of Biotechnology". It is the only chapter of Agenda 21 dedicated to a specific technology and presented as a source of opportunities for a global partnership. On the one hand, biologically rich countries, mainly in the South, lack the experience and the investments necessary to exploit these resources for economic development. On the other hand, industrialized countries (with a few Southern exceptions) possess this technological know-how. Agenda 21 places the emphasis on conditions to guarantee the "successful and environmentally safe application of biotechnology in agriculture, in the environment, and in human health care" (Paragraph 16.2), in particular through the development of international co-operative mechanisms.

The importance of biotechnology in the fulfilment of the objectives of the CBD is highlighted in Articles 16 and 19.[8] Article 16 states that access to and transfer of biotechnology are "essential elements for the attainment of the objectives of this Convention". Article 19 on "Handling of Biotechnology and Distribution of its Benefits" specifies that Contracting Parties, especially developing countries, that provide the genetic resources for biotechnological research should be given the opportunity to participate in the research. They also should have access "on a fair and equitable basis" to the results and benefits of research based on the genetic resources provided. The text adds, however, that the sharing should be on mutually agreed terms.[9]

The need to establish mechanisms for biosafety to manage potential risks associated with the use of biotechnology is also clearly recognized in the CBD. Article 8(g) urges Parties to regulate, manage, or control the risks to *in situ* conservation of biological diversity that might result from the use and release of living modified organisms. These measures would be enacted primarily on a national basis. Article 19.4 requires exchange of any available information on the potential adverse impact of LMOs to be moved across borders. Finally, Article 19.3 reflects the outcome of the negotiations of the CBD regarding the need for an international instrument on biosafety. It spells out the political will of certain countries to develop a protocol as early as diplomatically possible (a change of policy, then, would still have been possible):

> The Parties shall consider the need for and the modalities of a protocol setting out appropriate procedures, including, in particular, advance informed agreement, in the field of the safe transfer, handling and use of any living modified organism resulting from biotechnology that may have adverse effect on the conservation and sustainable use of biological diversity.

Not surprisingly, it was not possible during the early implementation of the CBD to reach a speedy consensus on crafting biosafety regulations. This is why a "two track" approach was suggested during discussions at the Intergovernmental Committee on the Convention on Biological Diversity, which prepared the first Conference of the Parties (COP-1). In order to arrive as quickly as possible at some sort of a regulatory instrument regarding biosafety, some countries suggested that the development of non-binding biosafety guidelines should begin immediately, while efforts to devise a binding agreement would continue under the umbrella of the Convention. The Netherlands and the United Kingdom were particularly active in supporting, in 1994 and 1995, the elaboration of the International Technical Guidelines for Safety in Biotechnology[10] by UNEP, which were adopted in December 1995 in Cairo.

At the political level, some countries perceived the UNEP guidelines as an attempt to avoid the development of a binding protocol. At the technical and practical level, however, these guidelines were very useful because within a relatively short time and in a less politicized atmosphere they provided the foundations of the future BP. They also played an important capacity-building role, particularly by introducing many developing-country delegates to the *problématique* of negotiating multilateral biosafety regulations. These countries were able to play a more active role when the time came to decide on the start of the negotiations in October 1995 and later during the negotiations. The position of these countries was especially difficult because they have to deal with LMOs both as importers and as exporters (Zarrilli, 2000).

The UNEP guidelines were elaborated independently from the work of the CBD. In 1994 COP-1 decided to hold a meeting of an open-ended ad hoc group of experts to prepare a decision on the protocol for the following COP.[11] This meeting took place in Madrid 24-28 July 1995.[12] It recognized the need for an international framework on biosafety and debated four options regarding its *legal standing*:

- co-ordination and strengthening of existing instruments;
- a voluntary instrument under the CBD, with specific reference to the UNEP guidelines, which at that time were still in development;
- a binding agreement under the CBD, i.e. a protocol; and
- a combination of the three options.

The majority of the delegations opted for a protocol. The 1995 Madrid meeting, therefore, represents the historic starting point of multilateral negotiations with the explicit purpose of creating a binding Biosafety Protocol. As far as the list of subjects to be covered by the future protocol was concerned, the meeting reached a consensus on most points, such as transboundary movements, mechanisms for risk assessment and risk management, information exchange, capacity-building, and the advance informed agreement procedure (Pythoud, 1996). Three sticky sets of issues, however, were left open at this stage, namely socio-economic considerations, liability and redress, and the financial mechanism and resources.

A year later, COP-2 confirmed the recommendations of the Madrid meeting and triggered the process of formal negotiations for the establishment of a BP. Decision II/5 rambles on for two pages of preliminaries and concludes with the decision to develop a BP through the establishment of an Open-ended Ad Hoc Working Group on Biosafety (BSWG) under the guidance of the COP, based on elements taken from the report of the Madrid meeting. An annex to this decision provides the terms of reference for the working group. The BSWG was to try to complete its work before the end of 1998. The COP was not successful in reaching a consensus on the question of whether socio-economic considerations as well as liability and redress should be included in the future Protocol. In fact, those issues were only temporarily concluded, at the end of the Protocol's negotiation, through the wording of Articles 26 and 27. Unsurprisingly, the two articles are rather vague and leave these important matters to be decided through future negotiations.

From Jakarta via Cartagena to Montreal: The Fundamental Issues

The BSWG, set up in Jakarta in 1995, met six times from 1996 to 1999. Its last meeting, in Cartagena in February 1999 was to be followed immediately by an extraordinary meeting of the COP (EXCOP) which would adopt the Protocol according to the rules of procedures of the CBD. The work of the BSWG, which started off as typical pre-negotiation preliminaries, became increasingly difficult. At the last meeting, unfortunately, differences turned out to be unbridgeable between the countries exporting or intending to export agricultural commodities containing or consisting of LMOs (later known as the Miami Group) and the other countries. Eventually, the EXCOP had to be suspended.[13]

During most of the negotiations within the BSWG, agricultural commodities, specifically the trade in LMOs designated for use in food, feed, or processing (LMO-FFPs), were hardly addressed as a major issue, although the US and Canada had never hidden their opposition to the inclusion in the Protocol of references to their genetically modified staple export crops. Until Cartagena, negotiations were largely dominated by reference to LMOs "for intentional introduction into the environment" and by the threats to biodiversity that might result. Seeds and fish are often given as examples of such releases into nature.

This ambiguity played a key role in the deadlock at Cartagena because it reflected – or perhaps one might say it covered up – one of the fundamental issues that shaped the whole negotiation process, namely the two-pronged question of *scope*. First, what kinds of products should the Protocol cover? Should it cover LMOs alone or "products thereof" derived from LMOs as well, such as processed foods or pharmaceuticals? Second, what products should fall within the Protocol, under the so-called advance informed agreement procedure (AIA)? The AIA was seen as a detailed and demanding information and consent procedure that could be very cumbersome for exporters of LMOs.[14]

Box 2.1 Chronology of the Biosafety Negotiations

1991
The United Nations Industrial Development Organization (UNIDO) releases the Voluntary Code of Conduct for the Release of Organisms into the Environment.
1994
November 28-December 9, Nassau: COP-1 establishes the Ad hoc Open Ended Group of Experts on Biosafety.
1995
July 24-28, Madrid: meeting of the Open Ended Ad hoc Group of Experts on Biosafety.
November, Jakarta: COP-2 establishes the Open Ended Ad Hoc Working Group on Biosafety to negotiate a biosafety protocol.
December 11-14, Cairo: UNEP adopts the International Technical Guidelines for Safety in Biotechnology.
1996
July 22-26, Aarhus: first meeting of the Open Ended Ad Hoc Working Group on Biosafety (BSWG).
1997
May 12-16, Montreal: second meeting of the BSWG.
October 13-17, Montreal: third meeting of the BSWG.
1998
February 5-13, Montreal: fourth meeting of the BSWG.
August 17-28, Montreal: fifth meeting of the BSWG.
1999
February 14-22, Cartagena: sixth meeting of the BSWG.
February 22-23, Cartagena: first Extraordinary Meeting of the Conference of the Parties (EXCOP).
July 1, Montreal: first set of informal consultations.
September 15-19, Vienna: second set of informal consultations.
2000
January 20-23, Montreal: third set of informal consultations.
January 24-28, Montreal: continuation of the EXCOP.
January 29, Montreal: adoption of the Cartagena Protocol on Biosafety.
December 11-15, Montpellier: first meeting of the Intergovernmental Committee for the Cartagena Protocol (ICCP).
2001
October 1-5, Nairobi: second meeting of the ICCP.
2002
April 22-26, The Hague: third meeting of the ICCP.

The basic difference between LMO-exporting countries and most of the developing countries lay in the latter's insistence, from the beginning of the negotiations, that all LMOs and transboundary movements should be covered by the AIA, independently of their intended use. This position was primarily based on the fact that in developing countries, even grains imported as foodstuff are often used as seeds by farmers, especially in a crisis situation (Pythoud, forthcoming); they could, therefore, directly affect biodiversity. Exporting countries, on the other hand, defended the view that the application of the AIA procedure was not appropriate for LMO-FFPs because of the specificities of agricultural products. The Uruguay Round brought trade in these products under the umbrella of the World Trade Organization; they are fundamentally treated like other goods in the trade regime (although a multitude of issues remain to be negotiated, especially the very complex provisions dealing with allowed subsidies and other supporting measures).

Another fundamental issue was the management of *scientific uncertainty* and the application of the precautionary approach in decision-making procedures. Two different views regarding the basis for risk assessment and risk management came into conflict. On the one hand, reference was made to the application of "sound science"[15] principles and practices, which consist of standardizeable, objective procedures. On the other hand, without questioning the importance of scientific knowledge and methodologies in risk assessment and risk management, emphasis was placed on the potential dangers posed by LMOs, which at this stage remain insufficiently understood and might be irreversible. Under this assumption, the Protocol would have to provide the grounds for an operationalization of the precautionary approach (Gupta, 2000a).

This assumption raised the importance of the relationship between the BP and the WTO, a question clearly related to the precautionary approach. Two options were at play. On the one hand, WTO provisions could be considered adequate safeguards for an importing country, and therefore the BP should be subordinated to the WTO. On the other hand, the BP should contain clauses to operationalize the precautionary approach, allowing an importing country to invoke this approach to withhold permission for the importation of LMO-FFPs. In the first case, the Protocol would require a so-called "WTO saving clause" giving LMO-FFP-exporting countries the right to overcome an importing country's negative decision. Hence, it could use those rights that WTO member countries have acquired under the clauses of non-discriminatory market access that are part of the multilateral trade regime. The BP's provisions would then have been hierarchically subordinated to the trade regime. It should be noted that market access rights, under GATT's Article XX, are not absolute but subject to exceptions in cases where it is necessary to protect human, animal, or plant life or health and where the conservation of exhaustible natural resources is threatened. Furthermore, WTO member countries are entitled to restrict market access through the adoption of (provisional) sanitary or phytosanitary measures "in cases where relevant scientific evidence is insufficient".[16] This provision represents, to some extent, the right of an importing country to base its decision about LMO-FFPs importing regulations on the precautionary approach. In reality, however, the WTO agreements make it quite difficult for an importing country to use such arguments effectively to prevent the importation of agricultural commodities.

The central issue here is the establishment of rules that will be authoritative in the settlement of potential disputes in cases of *scientific uncertainty*. The WTO dispute settlement system is well established. It is not just one among several options; rather, it is automatically applicable and enforceable in trade disputes. In this context, what should the rights and obligations of an importing country be in deciding whether a shipment of LMO-FFPs should be authorized? More specifically, should it have the right to use criteria based on operationalized precautionary measures that go beyond the rights already contained in WTO agreements, and if so, how should they be worded? Not surprisingly, these interrelated questions, difficult both from a political and a technical viewpoint, were negotiated as a cluster (Lin, 2000).

Procedural Issues and Successful Conclusion

The negotiations in Cartagena did not get bogged down – as they very well might have – over the still new and very complex technicalities involved in the safety of transboundary movements of LMOs, but over the protocol's scope and relations between regimes. The study of the BP negotiations illustrates how deadlocks over conflicting issues may be overcome through procedural innovations, such as the formation of country alliances across traditional geographical regions and the famous "Vienna setting".

Country Alliances, the Vienna Setting, and Timing

Even though the Cartagena meeting did not result in a consensus, it did generate an interesting outcome in terms of the negotiation process. The more than 100 delegations split into five cohesive coalitions that were not simply geographically-based, as is traditionally the case in UN negotiations, but included – where appropriate – geographically mixed groupings held together by similar objectives. They were:

- The Miami Group: Argentina, Australia, Canada, Chile, the US, Uruguay, i.e. the major agricultural crop exporters;
- The European Union;
- The Like-Minded Group: the other developing countries;
- The Compromise Group: Japan, Mexico, Norway, South Korea, Switzerland (initiator of the Compromise Group); New Zealand and Singapore joined the group before the last Montreal meeting; and
- The Central and East European countries.

The Cartagena deadlock required three additional meetings (two in Montreal and one in Vienna) to be resolved, and as is common in difficult moments during lengthy negotiations, these meetings had to be "informal," that is, not bound by the

CBD's usual rules and procedures. Indeed, they permitted the energetic chair of the EXCOP, Columbia's Environment Minister Juan Mayr Maldonado, to devise an imaginative and unusual negotiating procedure that came to be known as the Vienna setting.

The term "Vienna setting" refers to an informal procedural structure for conducting multilateral negotiations that differs from the established UN traditions with respect to patterns of participation and representation as well as the seating arrangement. Mayr managed to reconfigure the discussion in all groups, even the contact groups dealing with the most difficult issues, in such a way that each of the five coalitions was represented by one chief and one alternate spokesperson (except for the Like-Minded Group which, because of its size, was allowed to elect two alternates to make sure that Africa, Asia and Latin America/Caribbean were all represented). Instead of sitting in alphabetical order, the delegates were grouped according to their coalitions, which facilitated frank and transparent exchanges. Finally, Mayr introduced a helpful element of humour by letting the speaking order be determined through the random picking of colored balls and, later on, teddy bears. He also took an active role by asking questions and eliciting views to clarify positions and avoid nebulous position statements as much as possible. Last but not least, to ensure full transparency, all the meetings were open to all delegates, including representatives of NGOs.

The Vienna setting made a difference because under normal UN practices, Northern delegations tend to overpower the underrepresented developing countries with a large number of advisors who are highly specialized technical experts, and critical negotiations are often conducted in small closed groups with limited participation. In this case, however, having more evenly represented coalitions facing each other facilitated a more equitable and transparent dynamic. Other factors also contributed to confidence-building and ultimately to the establishment of a consensus. Each group met on its own for two days at first, which was particularly important for the developing countries, whose delegates have fewer opportunities to travel and interact than their Northern colleagues. Mayr also made sure that adequate time was available between sessions for the delegates to discuss developments among themselves (Ling, 2000).

These innovative arrangements, which allowed an equitable distribution of debating time among uneven coalitions, have been credited with making a substantial contribution to the final success of the negotiations. Obviously, the success of Mayr's approach also depended on the goodwill and co-operation of the delegations. On the whole, one may conclude that the organization of the three informal meetings after the Cartagena breakdown was an example of the working of multilateral diplomacy at its best; it was successful in bridging deep-rooted differences of perspectives and in rebuilding mutual confidence to the satisfaction of all delegations.

The resumption of the EXCOP discussions in Montreal after the Cartagena failure represented the tenth biosafety meeting (including the 1995 Madrid meeting) on the long road to the BP. It benefited not only from progress within informal negotiations but also from a changed political context. Public concern over LMOs was now being voiced not only in Western Europe and Southeast Asia but more and more in North America as well. Even more important perhaps, the meeting took place just weeks after the WTO's highly mediatized Seattle ministerial meeting. The Seattle events arguably increased the pressure on member countries to avoid another diplomatic failure on an issue that was also in the media spotlight (Gupta, 2000b).

Scope and Scientific Uncertainty

The issue of the scope of the AIA procedure was resolved thanks to the acceptance by the Like-Minded Group of the principle that the AIA's strict information and consent obligations on the part of the LMO exporter – including obtaining the agreement of the importing country within specified time limits – would apply only to the first shipment of an LMO and only to LMOs to be intentionally introduced into the environment (BP, Article 7). The Like-Minded Group changed their mind after the proposal for an alternative procedure for LMO-FFPs began receiving strong support from all other groups, including the EU.

The issue that emerged as the deal-maker after the painful Cartagena experience was the crafting of a set of decision-making criteria for LMO-FFPs that were much less demanding than the AIA procedure. The key provision in this regard was Article 11 of the BP. The heart of the procedures described in this article consists of an innovative advance notification: when a country allows the production and marketing of a transgenic crop that might be used and exported as a LMO-FFP, it has to notify all Parties through the information-sharing mechanism of the BP, the Biosafety Clearing-House (BCH). The decision-making criteria incorporated in Article 11 have the advantage of being relatively speedy while allowing an importing country to exercise some degree of sovereignty and control over the regulation of imports of LMO-FFP commodities, including reference to the precautionary approach.

The successful negotiation of Article 11 is generally credited with being one of the key turning points of the BP negotiations. It represents a well-balanced compromise between the expectations of the Miami Group that international trade of agricultural products containing LMOs should be exempt from AIA obligations and those of the Like-Minded Group that the transboundary movement of such LMOs should be covered by some sort of advance information procedure. More important, countries lacking a domestic regulatory framework to deal with these products could refer to the BP to make decisions about import regulations.

The final scope of the BP also reflects a delicate balance between the positions of the different groups. The Like-Minded Group obtained a significant concession, since transboundary movements of LMOs intended for contained use[17] are covered by the Protocol even though the AIA procedure does not apply to this group of LMOs. At the beginning of the negotiations, most OECD countries insisted on excluding contained use from the scope of the Protocol. In the final version, however, the BP contains identification requirements for LMOs intended for contained use and leaves open the possibility that future liability clauses could also apply to contained use (Gupta, 2000b).

On the other hand, regarding products derived from LMOs, OECD countries argued successfully that such products do not constitute a threat to biodiversity and consequently should be excluded from the Protocol. This means that processed food products derived from LMOs are completely exempt from the protocol's obligations. Their transboundary movements are essentially regulated by international trade agreements and national legislation. Another demand of industrialized countries, in particular the European Union, regarding the exclusion of LMOs that are pharmaceuticals for humans, was also adopted; these LMOs are excluded as long as they are "addressed by other relevant international agreements or organizations" (Article 5).

In conclusion, one may interpret the successful negotiation of the protocol, including the scope of the AIA procedure, as well as Article 11 on LMO-FFPs, as the establishment of a *four-track* approach towards LMOs and derived products and ingredients:

- A strict regulation of LMOs intended for release into the environment that is similar to the prior informed consent model applied to trade in hazardous and restricted substances (Article 7);
- A much lighter regulation largely limited to an information exchange procedure about developments in the national LMO-FFP regulatory process for the bulk of genetically modified commodities exports (Article 11);
- A transparent approach that requires some sort of identification for all transboundary shipments of LMOs, including those intended for contained use; and
- The exemption of genetically modified processed food products and most pharmaceuticals from Protocol obligations.

Let us now turn to the other fundamental issue, the management of scientific uncertainty in the decision-making procedure concerning import regulations, that is, the operationalization of the precautionary approach and the related issue of the relationship between the BP and the WTO.

First, the issue of the relationship between the WTO and the BP was resolved in a way that may seem surprising but at least has the advantage of being easy to understand. The Parties decided to conclude that the Protocol's preamble, which contains two seemingly contradictory statements, represents a simple statement of the impossibility of achieving consensus:

...Emphasizing that this Protocol shall not be interpreted as implying a change in the rights and obligations of a Party under any existing international agreements,

Understanding that the above recital is not intended to subordinate this Protocol to other international agreements...

On the one hand the Protocol should not infringe on the rights of market access because these WTO-related rights will be maintained; on the other hand, the existence of these very rights do not mean that the BP is subordinated to the WTO. This is essentially the same as saying that the Parties agree to disagree with regard to the relation between the two agreements. The Parties did, however, include the following qualifying statement before the above-cited ones:

> ...*Recognizing* that trade and environment agreements should be mutually supportive with a view to achieving sustainable development...

This seemingly innocuous if not self-evident statement in fact contains an innovative element that may help overcome the interorganizational stalemate. Indeed, since the adoption of the BP, the concept of mutual supportiveness has gained increasing recognition in international negotiations, with a view to achieving sustainable development. Consequently, it is to be hoped that should a BP-related dispute be submitted to the WTO's Dispute Settlement Body, its panel – or Appellate Body – will arrive at a ruling supportive of the goals of the BP. The opposite is also true, of course, but the CBD's dispute settlement system (CBD Article 27) – which provides the option of submitting a dispute to the International Court of Justice – is not comparable to the WTO's in terms of clout and efficiency.

Second, the intense debates over the inclusion of the precautionary approach pitted the Miami Group against the European Union, supported by the Like-Minded Group. The problem was not only different perspectives regarding the nature of the risks that might be associated with LMOs but also differences of opinion regarding the management of risk. The much-cited Article 5.7 of WTO's Agreement on the Application of Sanitary and Phytosanitary Measures (SPS) does mention risk assessment but is silent about risk management. In the end, thanks to the diplomatic and ambiguous compromise solution found in the preamble regarding the relationship between the BP and the WTO, the EU managed to overcome the Miami Group's resistance: Not only does the BP include a risk management procedure (BP Article 16) built on data gathered under the preceding risk assessment phase (Cosbey and Burgiel, 2000) but it gave the precautionary approach a considerably greater importance than it has in the SPS agreement. It is mentioned as such in the preamble and the objectives of the BP but more important, it is operationalized in the decision procedures contained in two key paragraphs (10.6 and 11.8), as follows:

> Lack of scientific certainty due to insufficient relevant scientific information and knowledge regarding the extent of the potential adverse effects of a living modified organism on the conservation and sustainable use of biological diversity in the Party of import, taking also into account risks to human health, shall not prevent that Party from taking a decision, as appropriate,...in order to avoid or minimize such potential adverse effects.

Remaining Issues

The BP is a very complex document. Even the issues on which a clear agreement was achieved are not always easy for the uninitiated to understand. Many articles refer to other articles or annexes, which creates interlocked concepts or procedures that further complicate understanding (as in the case of risk assessment). Ironically, the articles or paragraphs dealing with the lack of consensus on some unresolved issues, such as the Protocol's relationship with the WTO, are easy to understand, but some other issues are rather imprecise, such as the question as to how exactly the BP takes into consideration potential human health problems caused by LMOs. These instances of lack of clarity, purposeful ambiguity, or unnecessary complications in the legal texts are of course frequent outcomes of long and intense negotiations.

The Biosafety Protocol will enter into force 90 days after the 50th ratification. The EXCOP has established the Intergovernmental Committee for the Cartagena Protocol (ICCP) to facilitate ratification and prepare the first session of the BP's future governing body, the so-called Meeting of the Parties (MOP).[18] The task of the ICCP is to tackle issues that have not yet been settled and prepare the mechanisms of the BP that need to be ready when it enters into force.[19] As a priority, the ICCP will orchestrate the implementation of the Biosafety Clearing-House through a pilot phase and establish mechanisms to promote capacity-building in developing countries (Pythoud, 2000). Further negotiations by the MOP on two important issues are already programmed in the text of the BP itself: the identification of LMO-FFP products on their packaging and the question of liability and redress.

As far as identification is concerned, a solution was found for LMOs destined for contained use or for intentional introduction into the environment: they must be clearly identified as such in their shipping documentation. The identification of LMO-FFPs, however, was an entirely different matter because it involves the issue of requiring separate distribution channels for the bulk of genetically modified export crops. This was one of the toughest hurdles on the long road to the adoption of the BP. In fact, it happened to be the very last item to be resolved, and the success of the whole negotiation process turned on the acceptance of the following compromise by all Parties: the BP will contain a temporary requirement for LMO-FFPs to be labelled as "may contain" living modified organisms. A more permanent solution is to be found "no later than two years after the date of entry into force of this Protocol" (Article 18).[20]

The issue of product identification on packaging goes well beyond safety considerations. Identification of LMOs is also a central element of other legitimate consumer concerns, such as consumers' right to know and right to choose, which might require full traceability of the products as well as labelling requirements for genetically modified food. Europeans especially insist on being informed about the products they buy, in particular about edible products. The matter is complicated by the existence of another UN body, the Codex Alimentarius Commission,[21] jointly administered by the WHO and FAO, which also addresses labelling rules for genetically modified food. Its mandate is wider than that of the BP because it is not limited to living organisms. It not only constitutes the UN's global food code but also represents the preferred set of international standards, guidelines, and recommendations for regulating international trade in food, especially with regard to the WTO's SPS.[22] The issue of labelling is more specifically covered by the Codex Committee on Food Labelling. Moreover, in 1999 the Codex Alimentarius Commission established the Ad Hoc Task Force on Foods Derived from Biotechnology to address principles for risk analysis of food derived from modern biotechnology.

The issue of liability and compensation for potential damages resulting from transboundary LMO movements[23] has also been left to the MOP to deal with. It will presumably require lengthy negotiations. Work on this issue will certainly gain from other activities related to liability within the CBD[24] itself or other international treaties like the 1989 Basel Convention on the Control of Transboundary Movements of Hazardous Wastes and their Disposal and its related Basel Protocol on Liability and Compensation.[25]

Conclusions and Outlook: Quo Vadis Biosafety Protocol?

The adoption of the Biosafety Protocol was possible because countries realized that the compromise was better than not having any agreement at all – and because there was no loser or winner. Even environmental NGOs and the biotechnology industry expressed satisfaction with the final outcome. After the Seattle failure, the Montreal success demonstrated that with the goodwill of all partners, it was still possible to find balanced solutions between trade and environmental interests even on a difficult issue. Mayr's invention, the Vienna setting, was the joker that helped win the game. Creative diplomacy still has a place in multilateral negotiations. Moreover, the negotiation process emphasized again the importance of ensuring full transparency and participation of all partners, including civil society, at each stage of the process.

In international environmental negotiations, industry views and interests are traditionally represented within governmental delegations, whereas NGOs play a more visible role as representatives of civil society. During the BP negotiation, the biotechnology industry was able to coalesce into a single group, the Global Industry Coalition (GIC), which insisted on a status equal to that of other recognized NGOs. By the end of the process, the GIC was acting in a way similar to the five government coalitions. It was developing common industry positions and proposals. Indeed, the task of the GIC was even more difficult because it represented industrial organizations from all over the world with sometimes significant differences in sensitivities and interests. Industry's position also changed radically from a very defensive and reactive standpoint at the first meeting of the BSWG to a more pragmatic and proactive attitude by the end. As a result of its increasing involvement in the BP negotiation, industry is beginning to play a more significant role in the full CBD process.

If we take a broad look at the substance of the BP, at the regulation of modern biotechnology, and at LMOs in general, it is clear that the dynamics of the negotiations were characterized by an increasing widening of the issues discussed. As negotiations progressed, they were less and less shaped by environmental and health aspects of the evaluation and management of risks related to the transboundary shipment of LMOs and more and more by the larger socio-economic stakes involved in the development and control of modern biotechnology within the context of globalization in trade and agriculture. This observation has to be placed in the context of the public debate on those issues in industrialized countries, especially in Europe. In the beginning, opposition to modern biotechnology and the release of genetically modified organisms in the environment was essentially based on safety considerations. Now the perception has changed. Biotechnology is often seen as a symbol or a key tool of globalization in the hands of transnational corporations. Furthermore, it is widely considered to be responsible for misdeeds, particularly in the agrifood industrial sector, a charge most vocally articulated by José Bové and the French *Confédération paysanne*. This trend will continue in the near future since issues like the labelling (identification) of LMOs, liability, and compensation, as well as socio-economic considerations, will be on the agenda of the first meeting of the Parties to the Protocol.

To achieve the required 50 ratifications in a timely manner, the main priority will be to establish an effective national biosafety framework in developing countries that lack any domestic measures to address the use and release of LMOs. The Biosafety Project managed by UNEP's Geneva office and financed by the Global Environment Facility will play a critical role in this regard. This programme is intended to provide support in terms of both technical and institutional capacity-building to more than 70 Parties to the CBD. Moreover, the implementation of BP procedures like AIA and information exchange requirements is closely tied to exporting countries' obligations. The full participation of all countries with a strong biotechnology sector, including non-Parties, is therefore needed. This is particularly true in the case of the United States, the leading country in agricultural biotechnology and the main exporter of LMO-FFPs which so far, has not even ratified the CBD, a necessary pre-condition for becoming a Party to the BP. On many occasions, as at CBD-COP-5 (Nairobi, May 2000), US government officials have clearly indicated the commitment of the US to fulfil its responsibilities and to contribute to the implementation of the BP, in particular with respect to the biosafety clearing-house mechanism.[26] Finally, the BP will need further practical clarification in the operationalization of the precautionary approach in decision-making. It will eventually show full maturity through its capacity to deal with potential trade disputes on LMOs and the successful use of the preamble's notion of *mutual supportiveness* as a way of building coherence between the BP's objectives and WTO agreements.

Now that the question of biosafety has been somewhat settled, at least at the multilateral political level, the debate could further broaden and address other important issues linked to the development of modern biotechnology, such as access to genetic resources, the transfer of biotechnology, and the sharing of financial benefits arising from its application to genetic resources. Negotiations on access to genetic resources and benefit-sharing are channeled mainly through the International Treaty on Plant Genetic Resources for Food and Agriculture (IT) under FAO's leadership and more recently through separate negotiations within the CBD to implement Article 15 with regard to genetic resources not covered under the IT.[27]

Unsurprisingly, the thorniest issue is the notion that financial benefits gained from genetic resources originating in developing countries should be shared with the country or the geographical region where they originated. This concept of benefit-sharing is made much more complex and complicated by the fact that healing, nutrition and other properties of these plant genetic resources are often tied to so-called traditional knowledge (Cottier, 1998), whose holders may be difficult to determine. Applying existing intellectual property rights becomes impossible.[28] Although the issues raised in the IT and Access and Benefit-Sharing (ABS) negotiations have not even begun to come to the attention of the public, it is quite likely that they will play a part in discussions on international relations in the near future. The reason is twofold. First, research and industry need access to these genetic resources to ensure the continued development of biotechnology. Second, developing countries – including indigenous and local communities – are becoming better informed and better organized.[29] The BP will also help with the implementation of Article 16 of the CBD dealing with access to and transfer of biotechnology in order to achieve the objectives of the Convention. This issue has not been discussed since COP-2, but it is scheduled to be addressed at COP-7 in 2004.[30]

We can conclude by noting that those ten major multilateral negotiation sessions spread over nearly five years have opened the road to the establishment of an international framework aimed at addressing environmental safety as well as socio-economic issues associated with the development of genetic engineering, one of the key technologies of the 21st century. It is therefore certainly not an exaggeration to state that thanks to the adoption of the Biosafety Protocol, the international community has taken a first step in support of the sustainable development of modern biotechnology in agriculture, the environment, and human health in accordance with the objectives contained in Agenda 21.

Notes

[1] This research was made possible by a grant from the Swiss National Science Foundation. The views presented here are solely those of the authors and do not necessarily represent the views of the Swiss Agency for Environment, Forest, and Landscape.
[2] The Cartagena Protocol refers to living modified organisms (LMOs) – In national regulations, the term "genetically modified organisms" (GMOs) or in some cases "genetically engineered organisms" is more frequently used. All these terms are equivalent.
[3] http://www.oecd.org/dsti/sti/s_t/biotech/prod/safety.htm.
[4] For instance, European Union Directives 90/219 and especially 90/220.

[5] It was prepared by UNIDO with the assistance of the International Centre for Genetic Engineering and Biotechnology (ICGEB) in Trieste, Italy, for the informal UNIDO/UNEP/WHO/FAO working group on biosafety (http://www.icgeb.trieste.it).

[6] The UN tends to use American spelling in its agreements, and they will be cited accordingly, but the names of UN organizations are not consistent, e.g. American: Organization, but British: Programme.

[7] See chapter 1 by McGraw in this volume.

[8] See the text of the Convention in Annex 3.

[9] For a discussion of these issues, see chapter 7 by Blais in this volume.

[10] http://www.unep.org/unep/program/natres.

[11] Decision I/9, http://www.biodiv.org/decisions.

[12] http://www.biodiv.org/doc/meetings/COP/COP-02/official/COP-02-07-en.pdf.

[13] For daily reports, see C. Bai, S. Burgiel, L. Burney, J. Suplie, and E. Tsioumani (31 January 2000), *Earth Negotiations Bulletin*, International Institute of Sustainable Development, Winnipeg, Canada, vol. 9, no. 137, (http://www.iisd.ca).

[14] On the AIA procedure, see chapter 6 by Wolf in this volume.

[15] It should be noted that the term "sound science" does not exist in the WTO legal texts.

[16] Article 5.7 of the WTO's Agreement on the Application of Sanitary and Phytosanitary (SPS) Measures.

[17] "Contained use" refers to: "any operation, undertaken within a facility, installation or other physical structure, which involves living modified organisms that are controlled by specific measures that effectively limit their contact with, and their impact on, the external environment".

[18] Article 29: The BP's governing body is officially called the "Conference of the Parties Serving as the Meeting of the Parties to this Protocol," usually abbreviated the MOP. It will meet in conjunction with a COP or EXCOP because the Parties decided to use the same structures instead of creating new ones.

[19] For detailed daily reports and a final report, see T. Barnes, S. Burgiel, A. Gupta, and E. Tsioumani (11-15 and 18 December 2000), "ICCP-1," *Earth Negotiations Bulletin*, International Institute of Sustainable Development, Winnipeg, Canada, vol. 9, no. 173 (http://www.iisd.ca).

[20] It should be noted that the BP does not use the term "label" except in Annexes I and II; we therefore use the term "identification" here for the sake of precision.

[21] For general information on the Codex Alimentarius Commission, see http://www.fao.org/docrep

[22] See WTO/SPS Agreement, Annex A "Definitions," point 3, "International standards, guidelines and recommendations".

[23] Article 27: Liability and Redress.

[24] In 2000 the fifth Conference of the Parties decided to consider at its sixth meeting (2002) a process for reviewing paragraph 2 of Article 14 of the CBD, which deals with liability (Decision V/18). This might include the establishment of an ad hoc technical expert group, taking into account consideration of these issues within the framework of the Cartagena Protocol on Biosafety and the outcome of the workshop organized on this issue in June 2001 in Paris (http://www.biodiv.org/socio-eco/impact/ws-lr-01.asp).

[25] For additional information, see http://www.basel.int/pub/Protocol.html.

[26] The US contributes financially to the pilot phase of the Biosafety Clearing-House (http://www.iisd.ca/linkages/download/pdf/enb09173e.pdf).

[27] For documents on the CBD/ABS negotiations, see http://www.biodiv.org. For coverage and analysis of both sets of negotiations, see http://www.iisd.ca. See also chapter 7 by Blais in this volume.

[28] WIPO has recently established the Intergovernmental Committee on Intellectual Property and Genetic Resources, Traditional Knowledge and Folklore to address those issues (http://www.wipo.int/eng/meetings/2001/igc/document.htm).

[29] See also chapter 9 by Thomas in this volume for a further discussion of plant genetic resources and FAO's new treaty, intellectual property rights, and the WTO's role in this context.

[30] See COP Decision IV/16.

Chapter 3

Studying the Effectiveness of the CBD

Philippe G. Le Prestre

Is There a CBD Regime?

The growing concern of the international community over effective modes of international governance after the Cold War has been accompanied by a lively academic interest in regime theories. In contrast to the 1980s and early 1990s, scholars are now less interested in explaining the generation and maintenance of regimes than in their impact on international co-operation and their contribution to solving urgent problems. Environmental issues in particular, whether global or regional, have proven fertile ground for institutionalist theories, particularly for developing concepts and testing propositions regarding the determinants of implementation, compliance, and effectiveness of international regimes. Yet although the notion of regime has acquired great pre-eminence in international environmental politics and the study of regimes has become a prolific industry, uncertainties abound about the concept itself.

Defining and Operationalizing Regimes

States co-operate in order to reduce various uncertainties and maximize welfare. Regimes, as special forms of interstate co-operation, are answers to co-ordination or co-operation problems (Snidal, 1985). Co-ordination problems imply designing institutions that will ensure that everyone benefits from common rules, no one having an incentive to defect or cheat once the arrangement is in place because both the benefits of co-operation and the costs of defection are visible and tangible and no one can expect to improve their position by defecting. Examples are international broadcasting arrangements and arrangements governing shipping or civil aviation. Co-operation problems, in contrast, are characterized by deep conflicts of interests that give participants incentives to cheat in order to maximize their immediate net benefits at the expense of an outcome optimal for all. One example is the use of shared resources such as fisheries. Implementation and compliance issues are much more complex in a co-operation situation than in a co-ordination one. These difficulties are compounded by two elements in the CBD case: (i) since the CBD deals mostly with domestic behaviour and affairs (species and habitats), its normative and political goals tangle with sovereignty issues;

(ii) the extra-territorial consequences of behaviour that is destructive of biodiversity are minimal (in the short term), which minimizes the traditional foundation of claims for limiting the exercise of sovereignty.

A *regime* is generally understood as a set of interrelated norms, rules, and procedures that structure the behaviour and relations of international actors so as to reduce the uncertainties that they face and facilitate the pursuit of a common interest in a given issue area.[1] Norms are behavioural guidelines, which rules operationalize and procedures implement (Krasner, 1983).

This definition of *regime* has several components:

- the existence of a range or set of agreed-upon norms, rules (which include rights and obligations), and procedures (NRPs); this does not mean that all Parties will give the same importance to all norms but norms are central to a definition of a regime;[2]
- interrelations among NRPs;
- an intended (but not necessarily realized) impact on the behaviour of international actors along with a desire to reduce uncertainties by entering into an agreement on NRPs;
- a focus on a specific issue area;
- the pursuit of a common interest or a set of interests defined in common.

Is there a biodiversity regime and how would we know it? To start with, the text of the Convention defines the NRPs that Parties have agreed to support. Yet regimes may or may not stem from formal legal agreements backed by international organizations. The G-7, which lacks both, is often approached as a regime.[3] Conversely, organizations such as the Organization for Economic Cooperation and Development (OECD) are not usually thought of as regimes. Clear NRPs are essential, whether or not formally codified. Is that the case with the CBD? On the one hand, the Convention identifies clear norms, but procedures and rules are more vague. How norms and rules should be prioritized, interpreted, and operationalized remains in dispute. Indeed, one of the concerns of this study is to assess precisely the gradual diffusion of such NRPs, for regimes are also intended to socialize states into specific normative behaviour.

If we take a pragmatic approach and agree that a particular *range* of NRPs have indeed been defined through the initial legal text (although which *specific* NRPs will be realized and promoted remains contentious), can we ignore implementation? A regime, by some definitions, embodies practices and dynamics and evolves through a reflexive process. That is, rules and procedures are derived from norms and, along with experience and evolving expectations, strengthen them as well. Indeed, regimes are "living organisms", as Winfried Lang once put it, and relevant NRPs can be found in the initial covenant as well as in subsequent decisions.

Thus, some analysts have been unable to divorce the existence of a regime from its implementation and from compliance, that is, the degree to which Parties and other actors have adopted measures that facilitate behaviour in accordance with these norms, rules, and procedures. By this definition, a regime exists to the extent that the behaviour of Parties and other actors is influenced by these NRPs and expectations associated with them. For example, Puchala and Hopkins (1983) define regimes as "patterned behaviour". This approach poses epistemological difficulties, however, for it then becomes impossible to distinguish the existence of a regime from its functions and impacts. That is, one cannot define regimes as a set of norms that guide the behaviour of actors and then use the existence of the regime to explain behaviour (Hasenclever et al., 1997; Haggard and Simmons, 1987). This circularity problem has not escaped students and critics of regime theory. This problem has led some critics to deny any usefulness to the concept of regimes itself since regimes, being themselves the embodiment of co-operation, cannot explain it and, therefore, are useless independent variables.

In order to avoid this problem, one must understand "structure" as divorced from impacts: that is, defining a regime on the basis of what is acceptable behaviour according to the regime's main supporters rather than on the basis of the realization of that behaviour (whether behaviour that has actually taken place accords with the NRPs). If we did not, regimes would by definition be successful, and the task of research would be restricted to explaining their emergence.

Second, does the existence of a regime presuppose an agreement on a common interest or common goals? Apparent differences among scholars revolve around the meaning ascribed to co-operation. For example, liberal institutionalists do not assume pre-existing collective interests. Indeed, Keohane, Haas et al. (1993) seek to explain how regimes contribute to the enhancement of co-operation among states by making it more rational. For others (e.g. Oran Young), regimes are precisely instituted to solve a given problem and thus reflect a common definition of the problem (although solutions may be conflictual) and a prior willingness to co-operate.

One way of reconciling these perspectives is to better specify the independent variable and disaggregate "co-operation," which can refer to:

- the agreement on the initial set of NRPs;
- compliance, i.e. adherence to rules or rule-based behaviour – what Hasenclever et al. (1997) call "1st order co-operation";
- the result of this co-operative process, i.e. the strengthening of the regime, which includes the tightening and broadening of existing rules;
- sharing the cost of rule-making and rule-enforcement, or increasing adherence to norms – this norm-based behaviour is what Hasenclever et al. (1997) call "2nd order co-operation".

Thus, although there may be initial agreement on a range of NRPs, we should not assume that other forms of co-operation will follow. Compliance theorists and lawyers typically focus on first order co-operation, liberal institutionalists on the three others,[4] and constructivists on the last.

Although the CBD does reflect a collective will, it may or may not reflect a common desire on the part of specific states to curb biodiversity loss, promote sustainable development, or ensure an equitable sharing of benefits. This does not mean that there is no regime. Nor does it mean that the goal of creating a common understanding, concern, and project is absent and that other stakeholders do not share it. Indeed, there are numerous reasons why a state will adhere to a set of norms, rules, and procedures, such as the conclusion that internal policies depend on imposing similar rules on other countries (and potential competitors), the desire to influence a regime from the inside and prevent onerous constraints, attempts to gain advantages in other areas (such as technical and financial assistance) through linkage politics, a genuine search for common solutions to common problems, or a combination of all of these.

Yet this does not mean that regimes should be understood independently from their objectives. The apparent tautology disappears if states can be shown to have anticipated – or wished for – the effects (the resolution of the problem) of their behaviour (respect for the NRPs). There are driving forces behind each regime, and the structure of the regime reflects a certain vision of the collective interest, wherever it originated. If one wants to study the independent effects of regimes, then surely one of them is the impact they have on the evolving definition that states place on their interests. That is, to what extent does a given structure make a given behaviour more rational (the neo-liberal approach)? Further, is there a movement from a rational choice to pursue given interests defined independently from the regime to a redefinition of these national interests toward collective interests (the social institutionalist approach)? Does the CBD embody or encourage the emergence of new and common interests? Sociologists, for example, have insisted on the socializing effect of institutions, that is, on their impact on behaviour and on their contribution to the emergence of agreements regarding the nature of the problem and its solutions. Others would go further and insist on the importance of norms diffusion in this process (see Finnemore, 1996).

Also related to the problem of identifying regimes is the question of boundaries. What are the boundaries of the CBD regime? First, as the above definition emphasized, regimes pertain to specific issue areas, not to the behaviour of actors across all issue areas. Thus, we can speak of a biodiversity regime, less of an environmental regime, and even less of a unique regime governing interactions across different issue areas (e.g. economic, security, environmental). But issue areas are defined by actors according to their own perceptions, political dynamics, and the state of knowledge. Thus, this notion is fluid, and regimes transform themselves or embed themselves in others. For example, the CBD has given rise to a sub-regime related to biosafety. Second, who belongs to the regime? Should we merely include states or the institutions they have created and other non-state actors as well? If so, should we include all stakeholders and institutions whose activities are directly relevant to the purpose for which the regime was created or its implementation?

There is, therefore, a narrow and broad definition of the scope of the biodiversity regime. The broad definition is inclusive of all the actors engaged in the political dynamics of defining state obligations, implementing the Conference of the Parties (COP) decisions, and assessing how various actors impede or promote the goals of the regime. The narrow definition would restrict the analysis to the NRPs instituted by the CDB itself. The actors that are part of the regime would be the components of the convention governance system (see chapter 4), the states, and those groups and organizations that base their behaviour directly on the provision of the regime (e.g. indigenous peoples organizations). But the CBD was also more ambitious in the eyes of some of its proponents who sought to harmonize various international agreements and actions related to the protection of biodiversity.[5] Thus the secretariats of CITES and the Ramsar and Bonn conventions constitute a second circle. A third, is composed of actors whose activities impact or should reflect the NRPs of the CBD (e.g. UNDP, ITTO, WTO, WHC). Although this study restricts itself to the first circle, the ultimate effectiveness of the regime will also have to be measured in the second and third ones.

Finally, a few words about the properties of a regime are in order. Surprisingly little has been written on this topic, perhaps because of the prevalent confusion over the definition of the concept itself. Generally, the following properties have been identified. They are useful to keep in mind as a an indicator of the potential effectiveness of the regime.

- *Scope* This property refers to the range of issues, groups, NRPs, and outcomes the regime encompasses.
- *Strength* The strength of the regime is its ability to resist entropic pressures. For example, is the regime capable of withstanding internal challenges? How do stakeholders resolve conflicts?
- *Stability* refers to the persistence of the goals of the regime and to co-operation over the (re)definition of NRPs designed to sustain it over time. Support given to NRPs by stakeholders might be an indicator of stability. Scholars differ as to the determinants of regime stability. Realists and neo-liberals argue that regime stability and expansion are functions of a given distribution of power and interests; neo-liberal institutionalists maintain that the high interstate transaction costs of regime creation or renegotiation explain regime stability, even if patterns of functional benefits would recommend renegotiation; and unit-level liberals (who emphasize the importance of domestic interests in the definition of national interests) view international regimes as stable when individuals and groups adjust so as to make domestic policy reversal (or even stagnation) costly.
- *Robustness* refers to the maintenance of the regime even when the initial conditions that motivated its creation have disappeared. Neo-realists and institutionalists are in clear opposition regarding even the possibility of such an outcome.

- *Effectiveness* Central to this study, effectiveness is treated more extensively below.

Conceptualizing Effectiveness

Recent appraisals have been pessimistic about the impact and future of the CBD. Some, for example, bemoan the accelerating destruction of habitats and the assumed concurrent biodiversity loss.[6] Others are critical of the operation of the CBD or blame its Parties for the lack of progress they perceive. Problems often mentioned include lack of political support and public visibility, inability to play a meaningful role in the resolution of biodiversity crises (e.g. forest fires, coral bleaching), lack of financial resources, a scope that is deemed too large (a charge often wielded by conservationists), the appropriation of specific pet issues by some states (such as taxonomy, coral reefs, ecotourism, and marine parks) which leaves progress at their mercy and the advancement of other goals chancy, the failure of the SBSTTA to provide meaningful scientific guidance, the lack of implementation yardsticks (such as national targets), poorly developed links with other conventions directly relevant to biodiversity (e.g. CITES, Ramsar, Bonn), and neglect of trade and economic issues and other links with relevant intergovernmental organizations (WIPO, WTO).[7] All these factors are said to put the CBD's ultimate effectiveness into question. But do they really describe and explain a perceived lack of "effectiveness"? Or do these "problems" rather reflect diverse conceptions of effectiveness (not to mention of the CBD itself)?

How is effectiveness to be understood? Confusion prevails. There is often a tendency to equate effectiveness with sheer impacts, but this would only muddle the issue. Effectiveness has to be conceived in terms of the explicit objectives of the regime. Yet this approach does not take us very far, for the objectives can be variously understood as solving a problem, forcing or encouraging states (and other actors) to behave in a certain way, diffusing norms, etc. Indeed, one can identify at least seven meanings of effectiveness, depending on whether one emphasizes objectives, behaviour, or values (Young, 1996). These alternate meanings could also be approached as elements of an "absolute" or "inclusive" concept of effectiveness.

Effectiveness as Problem-Solving

This is the most common and intuitively attractive notion of effectiveness, found in a large segment of the literature. Yet it may also be the most problematic. A regime is effective when it contributes importantly to the solution of the problems that it was ostensibly created to address.[8] In this conception, effectiveness is generally thought to proceed from implementation and compliance.[9] Thus the CBD will be effective if after a minimum lag time, one notices a fair improvement in the state of biodiversity around the world. In this regard, Underdal (1992) distinguishes between two dimensions: (i) the degree to which the regime contributes to the improvement of the initial situation, and (ii) the distance between that improvement and the social (collective) optimum.

There are, however, several problems with this conception. First, effectiveness of this type often is hard to measure since precise and measurable environmental objectives may not be precisely laid out in the environmental agreement (particularly in framework treaties such as the CBD).[10] National reports may contain no specific environmental data, and these data are often inexistent. Second, it assumes that the adopted NRPs are adequate for solving the problems even though they may only reflect the relative state of knowledge and interests that prevail at a given time. Multilateral environmental agreements are not quick solutions but political frameworks for long-term co-operation and learning. Third, difficulties may arise when the problem the regime is intended to address changes or becomes contentious. Such was the case with the whaling regime when Parties did not agree on the collective goals to be pursued. Fourth, it supposes the existence of baseline data and other scientific evidence, which may not yet be available. Fifth, it sets very high hurdles and assumes a direct relationship between the output of the regime and its outcome. However, an ecosystem may have been degraded even though Parties to the regime scrupulously implemented its provisions. If success is measured in terms of minimizing threats to endangered wildlife, for example, CITES has largely failed. Conversely, if success is observed, how do we know that the regime is responsible rather than concomitant actions taken by states? This methodological issue is not insurmountable but does complicate attribution. And sixth, the conception overlooks the side-effects of regimes. These side-effects may be most important. For example, the United Kingdom's Global Environmental Change Programme (GECP 1999) concludes that "Environmental policies succeed only if they also promise social benefits such as poverty reduction and work in ways that bolster business competitiveness".

Effectiveness as Goal Attainment

This acception differs from the preceding one in that the explicit yardstick is whether "a regime's goals (stated or unstated) are attained over time" (Young, 1992). This is one of the main dimensions of effectiveness (with implementation) used by UNCED in its 1992 review (Sand, 1992). It is equivalent to problem-solving only if one assumes that the NRPs adopted are adequate for solving the problem. Thus, CITES understood as instituting procedures for regulating trade in wildlife may be effective in terms of goal attainment and a failure in terms of resource protection.[11] In the case of the CBD, one may ask whether the regime led to increases in lending for natural conservation.[12]

One difficulty in applying this approach is that the objectives of most environmental conventions are couched in highly general and abstract terms. By definition – since they are framework conventions – this is the case with the global conventions, but it characterizes many other agreements that have no measurable objectives, such as quantitative targets or technical criteria for compliance (Sand, 1992). More precise objectives, however, can be formulated by later COPs or negotiated as protocols (such as the Cartagena and Kyoto protocols). Another difficulty concerns the question of stated versus unstated goals. Conclusions regarding the effectiveness of the regime will naturally differ according to the goals and hopes of each stakeholder.

When assessing claims of effectiveness or non-effectiveness, some authors (e.g. Young, 1996) have suggested taking into account "unstated" goals for analytical purposes, assuming that one is able to surmise them. In such cases, one would, at a minimum, have to specify in relation to what goals the conclusion is reached. But what is of interest is effectiveness as a property of the regime. It is not because a particular regime falls short of the unstated goals of one or several Parties that it is not effective, unless they were explicit goals of the regime.[13] Effectiveness as goal-attainment has to be approached as an attribute of the regime itself and not in reference to the particular goals (explicit or not) that some Parties or other stakeholders may expect of it.

A second set of acceptions views regimes as effective when they have observable political effects (Haas, Keohane et al., 1993) as in the situations described in the following sections.

Implementation

Favoured as an indicator of effectiveness by policy-oriented scholars, implementation usually refers to the extent to which Parties have translated agreed-upon provisions into their legal and political systems. Emphasizing procedures, the main criteria for effectiveness identified by UNCED in its 1992 review fall in to this category.[14]

Implementation has long been recognized as crucial to the success of public policy and to the determination of the actual actions that will be taken on its behalf. In environmental matters, negotiations do not stop with the conclusion of an agreement. The signing of the CBD in June 1992 was a way of taking stock of the relative strengths of various movements and provided a basis for future negotiations. Not only do Parties have to interpret, in post-agreement negotiations, provisions that may have been left ambiguous on purpose, not only do they continue negotiating the terms of implementation (such as making implementation conditional on financial and technical support), but the very complexity of the issues ensures that Parties will not have solved all problems. It is precisely the purpose of framework treaties to give such latitude, allowing Parties to hope that the evolution of the scientific, normative, and political context will strengthen their own positions down the line. This does not apply only to framework treaties, however. The Cartagena Protocol on Biosafety is a noteworthy example of this phenomenon (see chapter 2).

Implementation can weaken, strengthen, or completely modify the purpose and effectiveness of policy. Implementation failures, that is, failure to adopt measures needed to carry out national obligations, may be wilful, stem from ignorance of the legal and policy provisions of the covenant, be rooted in a lack of resources, or be the consequence of the agreement and the measures planned having become moot (for example when the agreement has been superseded by another, or when technical progress has changed the nature of the problem). Conversely, Parties can also go beyond the minimum expected of them, as when a regime strengthens domestic political coalitions that work in favour of stronger measures by legitimizing certain actions. Implementation changes the domestic and international context of a policy, strengthening some groups at the expense of others. This can have positive or negative consequences for the regime.

Clearly, implementation has to occur for the regime to be effective, however effectiveness is defined. Thus it is a useful starting point. As Young (1996, pp. 11-12) points out, it is relatively easy to measure. But one cannot subsume effectiveness under implementation, for implementation in itself does not *guarantee* effectiveness. For one thing, Parties may be asked to undertake certain measures, but lack of conceptual clarity and vague operationalization procedures may require further collective work. For example, the CBD asked Parties to take a certain number of measures (facilitate access to genetic resources on fair terms, use an ecosystem approach, integrate biodiversity into impact assessments, etc.) that nobody really knew how to conceive, operationalize, and implement.[15] Implementation also refers to behaviour taken *in reference to* expectations explicitly contained in an agreement; it does not include solving the initial problem *per se* (although one assumes it will contribute to the solution). A focus on implementation alone leaves out important aspects of regimes. For example, it refers to explicit agreements, thus excluding implicit NRPs. Finally, one may be interested not only in knowing whether Parties have adopted the means of complying with their commitments but in actual compliance itself.

With regard to the CBD, two types of measures are to be taken, one set by the Parties to the regime acting collectively (Box 3.1) and one set by each Contracting Party (Box 3.2). One must keep in mind that these commitments are not binding but rather conditional commitments (conditional on certain undertakings by other Parties, to Parties' individual capacities, on an appropriate domestic and international context, etc.), or better yet, they are targets to strive toward rather than obligations to fulfil.

Given the nature of the resources involved, implementation under the CBD is largely a domestic matter, which considerably complicates the situation. Often, political dynamics at the international level are far different from those at domestic levels. Some groups, such as industry, may be much more active domestically than internationally. Other actors, such as states or provinces in federal systems, may hold the key to successful implementation. In the case of the CBD, the main mechanisms for implementation are national strategies and action plans, the Clearing-house Mechanism (see chapter 5), the various focal points created to liaise with the regime, and scientific, technological, and financial transfers.

Box 3.1 Regime Level Implementation Commitments

- Co-operate in providing financial and other support for *in situ* and *ex situ* conservation (Art.8, 9).
- Promote the use of scientific advances in biological diversity research (Art.12).
- Co-operate in developing educational and public awareness programmes, with respect to conservation and sustainable use of biological diversity (Art.13).
- Encourage the conclusion of bilateral, regional, or multilateral arrangements (Art.14).
- Encourage international co-operation to supplement national efforts designed to respond to emergencies (Art.14).
- Examine the issue of liability and redress for damage to biological diversity, except where such liability is a purely internal matter (Art.14).
- Recognizing that patents and other intellectual property rights may have an influence on the implementation of this Convention, co-operate in order to ensure that such rights are supportive of and do not run counter to the objectives of the CBD (Art.16).
- Promote international technical and scientific co-operation (Art.18).
- Encourage and develop methods of co-operation for the development and use of technologies and promote co-operation in the training of personnel and exchange of experts (Art.18).
- Establish a clearing-house mechanism (Art.18).
- Promote the establishment of joint research programmes and joint ventures for the development of technologies relevant to the objectives of this convention (Art.18).
- Consider the need for and modalities of a protocol on the safe transfer, handling, and use of any living modified organism resulting from biotechnology that may have adverse effect on the conservation and sustainable use of biological diversity (Art.19).
- Establish a funding mechanism for developing-country Parties. (the COP shall define the guidelines and review the effectiveness of the mechanism) (Art.21).
- Review the implementation of the Convention (Art.23).
- Establish appropriate forms of co-operation with the secretariats of relevant conventions (Art.23).

Box 3.2 National Level Implementation Commitments

General measures
- Develop national strategies, plans, or programmes for the conservation and sustainable use of biological diversity (Art.6).
- Integrate the conservation and sustainable use of biological diversity into relevant sectoral or cross-sectoral plans, programmes and policies (Art.6).

Identification and monitoring
- Identify and monitor components of biological diversity important for its conservation and sustainable use (Art.7).

Box 3.2 Continued

- Identify and monitor processes and categories of activities that have or are likely to have significant adverse impacts on the conservation and sustainable use of biodiversity (Art.7).
- Maintain and organize data derived from identification and monitoring activities (Art.7).

Measures for in situ conservation

- Establish a system of protected areas and develop guidelines for their selection, establishment, and management (Art.8).
- Regulate or manage biological resources important for the conservation of biological diversity, whether within or outside protected areas (Art.8).
- Promote the protection of ecosystems and natural habitats and the maintenance of viable populations of species in natural surroundings (Art.8).
- Promote environmentally sound and sustainable development in areas adjacent to protected areas (Art.8).
- Rehabilitate and restore degraded ecosystems and promote the recovery of threatened species, *inter alia*, through the development and implementation of plans or other management strategies (Art.8).
- Establish or maintain means to regulate, manage, or control the risks associated with the use and release of living modified organisms resulting from biotechnology (Art.8).
- Prevent the introduction of, control, or eradicate alien species that threaten ecosystems, habitats, or species (Art.8).
- Respect, preserve, and maintain knowledge, innovations, and practices of indigenous and local communities relevant for the conservation and sustainable use of biological diversity (Art.8).
- Encourage the equitable sharing of the benefits arising from the utilization of such knowledge, innovations, and practices (Art.8).
- Develop or maintain necessary legislation and/or other regulatory provisions for the protection of threatened species and populations (Art.8).

Measures for ex situ conservation

- Establish and maintain facilities for *ex situ* conservation of and research on plants, animals, and micro-organisms (Art.9).
- Adopt measures for the recovery and rehabilitation of threatened species and for their reintroduction into their natural habitats (Art.9).
- Regulate and manage collection of biological resources from natural habitats for *ex situ* conservation purposes and *in situ* populations of species (Art.9).

Sustainable use of components of biological diversity

- Integrate consideration of the conservation and sustainable use of biological resources into national decision-making (Art.10).
- Protect and encourage customary use of biological resources (Art.10).
- Support local populations in developing and implementing remedial action in degraded areas (Art.10).

Box 3.2 Continued

- Encourage co-operation between governmental authorities and the private sector in developing methods for sustainable use of biological resources (Art.10).

Incentive measures

- Each Contracting Party shall, as far as possible and as appropriate, adopt economically and socially sound measures that act as incentives for the conservation and sustainable use of components of biological diversity (Art.11).

Research and training

- Establish and maintain programmes for scientific and technical education and training (Art.12).
- Promote and encourage education, training, and research, particularly in developing countries (Art.12).

Public education and awareness

- Promote and encourage understanding of the importance of and the measures required for the conservation of biological diversity, including propagation through media and the inclusion of these topics in educational programmes (Art.13).

Impact assessment

- Introduce appropriate procedures requiring environmental impact assessment of proposed projects that are likely to have significant adverse effects on biological diversity (Art.14).
- Introduce appropriate arrangements to ensure that the environmental consequences of programmes and policies likely to have significant adverse impacts on biological diversity are duly taken into account (Art.14).
- Notify potentially affected states of such grave and imminent danger or damage to biodiversity, as well as initiate action to prevent or minimize such danger or damage (Art.14).
- Promote national arrangements for emergency responses to activities or events that threaten biodiversity (Art.14).

Access to genetic resources

- Facilitate access to genetic resources (Art.15).
- Develop and carry out scientific research based on genetic resources provided by other Contracting Parties with the full participation of providing Parties (Art.15).
- Take measures with the aim of sharing in a fair and equitable way the results of research and development and the benefits arising from the commercial and other utilization of genetic resources with the Contracting Party providing such resources (Art.15).

Access to and transfer of technology

- Provide and/or facilitate access to and transfer of technologies (Art.16).
- Take measures with the aim that the private sector facilitates access to and joint development and transfer of technology (Art.16).

Box 3.2 Concluded

Exchange of information and scientific and technical co-operation
- Facilitate the exchange of information relevant to the conservation and sustainable use of biological diversity (Art.17).
- Promote scientific and technical co-operation (Art.18).

Handling of biotechnology and distribution of its benefits
- Take measures to provide for the effective participation in biotechnological research activities by Contracting Parties that provide the genetic resources for such research (Art.19).
- Take measures to promote and advance priority access by Contracting Parties on a fair and equitable basis to the results and benefits arising from biotechnologies based on genetic resources provided by those Contracting Parties (Art.19).

Financial resources
- Provide financial support and incentives in respect of national activities that are intended to achieve the objectives of this Convention (Art.20).
- Developed-country Parties shall provide new and additional financial resources to enable developing-country Parties to meet the agreed full incremental costs to them of implementing measures that fulfil the obligations of this Convention (Art.20).

Compliance

One acception of effectiveness popular among supporters of an international order based on international law equates effectiveness with compliance (e.g. Alter, 2000). Accordingly, a regime is effective to the extent that Parties comply with the commitments they have undertaken, such as meeting emission targets or protecting certain ecosystems. The problem, then, becomes designing the right mechanism for inducing compliance (through carrots and capacity-building) or forcing it (through coercion). Often, a direct causal relationship is drawn between compliance and problem-solving (Jacobson and Weiss, 1998).

Compliance is often confused with implementation. The two may overlap when Parties have made explicit commitments to adopt given administrative or legislative measures, but they are analytically distinct. "Compliance goes beyond implementation. It refers to whether countries in fact adhere to the provisions of the accord and to the implementing measures they have instituted" (Jacobson and Weiss, 1998, p. 4) (see Box 3.3). States may have adopted laws that remain unobserved or created "paper parks" that protect no ecosystem or species. Further, many agreements do not commit states to take specific measures to achieve an objective. For example, Parties to the Kyoto Protocol may select a number of means to meet their emissions targets.

Compliance can be procedural, substantive, or normative. Procedural compliance refers to adhering to the procedural requirements contained in the treaty, such as the obligation to report, while substantive compliance refers to substantive requirements, such as controlling an activity. Compliance can also include adhering to the "spirit of the treaty", that is, the broad normative principles contained in the preamble or initial articles (Jacobson and Weiss, 1998, p. 4). Compliance is a target, never perfect and a matter of degree. To be meaningful, an assessment of compliance with a treaty must be relative to the weight of the Parties. What is important is not how many Parties are in compliance but whether the most important in a given issue area are (for example, countries with the highest biodiversity) (Jacobson and Weiss, 1998, p. 522).

Effectiveness tends to be defined in terms of compliance when environmental problems are essentially problems of co-operation and when one of the purposes of the regime is to minimize defections that may endanger the regime (such as in the cases of ozone depletion and climate change). Not all biodiversity issues, however, are collective action (or common-pool) problems.[16] In this situation, when the free rider problem is not as much of a concern, the extent to which a regime ensures compliance (rather than inducing convergence and co-ordination) becomes less central.

Box 3.3 Some Indicators of State Compliance with the CBD

Procedural compliance
- Submit national reports on measures taken for the implementation of the provisions of this Convention and their effectiveness in meeting the objectives of this Convention (Art.26).

Substantive compliance
- National biodiversity assessment;
- National biodiversity strategy and action plan;
- Support for research and training (Art.12);
- Access to genetic resources;
- Access to and transfer of technology;
- Technical and scientific co-operation; and
- Resources devoted to biodiversity protection (Art.20, 21).

Normative compliance
- Equitable sharing of benefits,
- Participation, and
- Transparency.

Although lawyers tend to assume that observed positive outcomes result from successful implementation and enforcement measures, it may very well be that compliance is, in fact, a very poor indicator of the difference that the regime has made. First, except for procedural compliance, precise measurement is elusive. Second, states can be in compliance even though they have done nothing to that end. Compliance (or "conformity") refers to the degree to which national behaviour agrees with the obligations imposed by the regime. Conformity may or may not be related to the existence of the regime. Correlation is not cause; clearly, there may be compliance without implementation (Victor, 1998; Downs, Rocke et al., 1996; Mitchell, 1994). For example, international commitments may be less stringent than existing behaviour (the International Whaling Commission, for example, used to set catch limits above annual takes) or domestic regulations (as in the case of sulfur emissions by Sweden versus the provisions of the long-range transboundary air pollution treaty). Second, Parties may have been moving in that direction regardless of the existence of an international regime.[17] Third, there could be inadvertent compliance, as in the case of Russian emissions of carbon dioxide when the economic crisis reduced industrial activity – and thus emissions – to within the range foreseen by the UNFCCC regime (Victor, Raustiala et al., 1998). Fourth, regimes may have perverse effects, that is, generate "incentives for states to defect informally thereby undermining the goals of the regime without violating the formal rules" (Saksena, 2000, p. 4). Finally, to use compliance as a measure of effectiveness assumes that the rules embodied in the original accord are clear and that expectations are well understood. Now, framework treaties such as the CBD are vague as to the precise obligations of the Parties, obligations that, most of the time, are contingent on certain behaviour by other Parties or on certain developments. Students of compliance have underscored the obvious point that the more precise the obligations, the easier it is to assess and promote compliance (Chayes and Chayes, 1995), although the reverse is not true, that is, compliance might not be weaker when obligations are vague (Jacobson and Weiss, 1998, p. 525). The CBD contains no timetables or targets.[18] Enforcement procedures are non-existent, and so are sanctions in cases of non-compliance. Thus, compliance is an "artefact of the standard embodied in the accord" and "must be understood and evaluated in context" (Victor, Raustiala et al., 1998, p. 7). At best, compliance is a continuous variable and the determination of non-compliance a political process (as in the ozone case).

Finally, a couple of trade-offs deserve to be mentioned. The first one concerns the nature of the compliance mechanism (or the insistence on a strong mechanism) and the probability of co-operation. That is, states negotiate a package deal, not individual clauses. Their decision to sign, or to ratify, depends on their evaluation of the burden that such a mechanism poses. Thus, insistence on designing strong non-compliance measures may weaken the probability that an agreement will be negotiated or ratified and thus preclude other potential benefits of the regime.[19] The second trade-off, related to the first, is between the probability of compliance and the amount of behavioural change required by regime rules (Underdal 1998).

Naturally, if behavioural change is central to ultimate problem-solving, compliance may be a poor predictor of it.

Behavioural Change

In light of the difficulties of assessing outcomes, and eager to encompass the range of situations and problems that environmental agreements tackle, many political scientists have opted for a conception of effectiveness centred on behavioural change. According to this perspective, a regime is effective "when its implementation leads to patterned behaviour that furthers the goals of the accord" (Young, 1992, p. 161), behaviour that would not have taken place in the absence of the regime. This conception stems both from theoretical concerns regarding the actual influence that institutions have on the behaviour of political actors and from methodological difficulties of attribution that pervade problem-based definitions of effectiveness (Young and Levy, 1999; Haas, Keohane et al., 1993, p. 418;[20] Young, 1992). It is also logical. Although we may ultimately be concerned with problem-solving, we must first study the behaviour of key actors that cause the problem or can solve it.

These behavioural changes can cover a wide array of situations: reinforcing pre-existing behaviour, enabling new behaviour, or changing behaviour. Examples include compliance with stated goals (reports, parks, plans, enforcement, etc.), public and private investments, personnel increases, diffusion of the norms of the regimes, broadening of the type of stakeholders involved, and changes in the distribution of power among domestic groups and institutions in favour of those supporting the goals of the regime.

Now, "effectiveness" carries a normative meaning in that we assume that it is related to the purposes of the regime. Thus, although the "impact" of the regime on behaviour may be positive or negative, we should reserve the term "effectiveness" for the former. But the latter should still be part of the analysis because a regime can have perverse effects when it redirects behaviour in ways that undermine the goals of the regime. This can happen, for example, when endangered species legislation leads to an attitude of "shoot, shovel, and shut up," when a ban on CFCs leads to the development of HCFC at least as harmful, when a ban on the exportation of threatened species actually increases rather than decreases the viability of the population, or when redirected behaviour increases the difficulty of promoting sustainable development concerns. Thus, although it makes sense to focus on this proximate impact, one cannot assume a direct connection between change in behaviour and goal attainment or problem-solving. But if biodiversity is to be preserved, behaviour has to change, and regimes are intended to promote that change.

Finally, behavioural effectiveness is not limited to states that are Parties to the regime. It makes more sense to include other Parties, targets, and stakeholders (Victor, Raustiala et al., 1998). Social groups and bureaucracies would then be included in the analysis. This is especially important in the case of biodiversity in which scientists, politicians, and civil servants have long pointed out that conservation cannot be achieved in a social vacuum.

In addition to the claims of supporters of problem-solving effectiveness who argue that behavioural change may or may not contribute to solving the problem, there are two conceptual and methodological difficulties with this conception. First, it is not always clear what behavioural change covers: the "general direction where Parties wish to go" (Bernauer, 1995) may be vague or assume consensus. For example, Parties have complained that the last goal of the CBD (benefit-sharing) has been neglected to the detriment of the first two (conservation and sustainable development). Whereas the determination – or measurement – of effectiveness as compliance or implementation can easily be made, this is not the case with effectiveness conceived as behavioural change. The causal demonstration must rely either on process-tracing or counterfactuals. Process-tracing, as Sprinz pointed out, runs the risk of magnifying initial errors, while counterfactuals rely on assumptions about trends or risks. And how should one weigh all the changes in behaviour that may be related to the regime? As Young (2001) points out, given the multiplicity of direct (states) and indirect (civil society actors) targets and the differential impacts of the regime on them, "it is extremely difficult to arrive at any overall judgment regarding the effectiveness of [a] regime measured in terms of behavioural change". But this quest is probably misguided.

Co-Operation

One can broaden the concern with impacts even further and ask whether the regime has had a positive impact on co-operation and on stakeholders' commitments in favour of its objectives and whether, ultimately, it has led actors to redefine their interests in terms of collective goals. For Hasenclever et al. (1997, p. 86), for example, international regimes "are effective in the sense that states follow co-operative policies which, in the absence of a regime, they would most likely not pursue". For example, one of UNCED's criteria for evaluating the effectiveness of MEAs was "codification programming," that is, the degree to which the original agreement led to the development of new agreements (Sand, 1992).

This conception focuses on process (as opposed to outcomes or outputs). Success, then, depends on the extent to which the regime has facilitated "processes of learning, capacity building and support building in order to address policy problems in a decentralized way consistent with the interests of the actors involved" (Knill and Lenschow, 2000, p. 6).[21]

Again, a new degree of co-operation in approaching and addressing (but not necessarily solving) common problems may or may not be related to earlier conceptions of effectiveness, although it has a clear link with behavioural change. It corresponds to what Hasenclever et al. (1997) call "second order" co-operation and reflects a successful socialization process whereby Parties and stakeholders have internalized the goals of the regime and the need to co-operate in its evolution. Note that this is considered an impact of the regime, not part of its definition. In the case of co-operation then, one could speak of a regime being "effective" (if it has directly led to that redefinition), "strong" (if the content of the redefinition is extensive), "stable" (if the NRPs evolve only slowly and if the nature of the Parties also remains constant), or "robust".

Both behavioural and co-operation effectiveness move us away from an exclusive focus on compliance. As Young and Levy (1999, p. 6) underscore:

> Activities that move the system in the right direction, even if they fall short of full compliance, are signs of effectiveness. Likewise, institutions that goad members to undertake measures that go beyond what is required for compliance are considered more effective than those that only elicit the minimum behavioural change required.

Normative Gains (Justice)

Finally, effectiveness can have a heavy normative meaning and refer to particular desirable outcomes that may not be directly related to the proximate goals of the regime (such as biodiversity conservation) but are socially desirable or to a process that promotes desirable social goals (such as empowerment and participation). For example, some authors would see regimes as institutions that should promote social change, such as greater equity within and among nations, wealth redistribution, decentralization of power, and secure human rights. In general, this conception seeks to temper an insistence on process (implementation), outputs (behavioural change), and outcomes (compliance, problem-solving) by asking at what price these desirable effects were gained.

Indeed "fairness" has been shown to play a significant role in international negotiations. Negotiations over the mechanics of compliance and implementation systems, for example, are subject to such considerations.[22] This notion is at the core of the CBD, constitutes one of its three goals, and permeates the pursuit of other objectives within the convention, such as species conservation.

Each profession is likely to favour a particular notion of effectiveness. Lawyers emphasize implementation and compliance, scientists and environmentalists problem-solving and goal-attainment, philosophers normative aspects, and political scientists behavioural change and co-operation (Young, 1999). Figure 3.1 is an attempt to summarize the relationship among these acceptions of effectiveness. It shows how they can be conceptually and empirically related but also that all do not necessarily co-vary. It also implies that "success" may be defined or assessed in a variety of ways according to the definition used.

One could easily make a strong case for each of these notions of effectiveness. They may also be conceived as elements of an overall effectiveness,[23] or as sequential intermediary factors, each deserving detailed study, that may help promote ultimate problem-solving. Because some are antecedent to others, because some may not be related to the regime (e.g. compliance), and because some are more difficult than others to assess and measure, we can still focus fruitfully on behavioural change (which must precede problem-solving) and on implementation, its necessary antecedent.[24]

Effectiveness is a continuous not a dichotomous variable. The difficulty is to assess how much NRPs and the operation of the regime account for the observed variance. In this regard, Underdal (1992, pp. 228-29) asks researchers to be specific about what they are attempting to do when assessing effectiveness: what is to be evaluated (the *object*)? what are the *standards* of comparison, i.e. the lower (e.g. absence of regime) and upper bounds (e.g. collective optimum) of implementation and behaviour? what *method* will be used to compare the object to the standard? The *object* in this book is effectiveness defined as implementation and behavioural change; the *standard* is the NRPs identified in the text of the treaty and in the decisions of the COP; and the potential *methods* are varied, ranging from statistics, game theory, and cost-benefit analysis to counterfactuals (Lebow, 2000; Fearon, 1991), process-tracing (e.g. Homer-Dixon, 1996), and text and discourse analysis.

The Prerequisites of Effectiveness

Demonstrating a direct causal relationship between regime and behaviour has proven difficult. Whereas some authors are convinced that environmental regimes matter or have appreciable effects, others are more doubtful, seeing them more as facilitators than as driving forces (Victor, Raustiala et al., 1998). Clearly, the difficulty is related to the notion of effectiveness and regime that is used. Assessing implementation, for example, is easier than assessing co-operation and justice. The problem is compounded as well by the nature of the regime itself. While some regimes have clear targets by which performance can be judged, others have failed to develop specific indicators and implementation targets. This is particularly true in the case of the biodiversity regime. Lack of specific yardsticks, however, does not mean that the regime is not effective, for it may yet move the various actors to adopt convergent policies, improve their capacities to implement them, and agree to targets, or it may change their incentive structure in a way that promotes the goals of the regime.

Given the difficulties of measuring effectiveness when the convention is relatively young, as well as the prevailing methodological and theoretical uncertainties that affect both the dependent and the independent variables (Bernauer, 1995), it would seem more fruitful at this stage to assess how the regime is putting in place various *prerequisites* of effectiveness. Thus the question becomes: to what extent does the regime reinforce factors that have been associated with the effectiveness of regimes, understood largely as behavioural effectiveness?

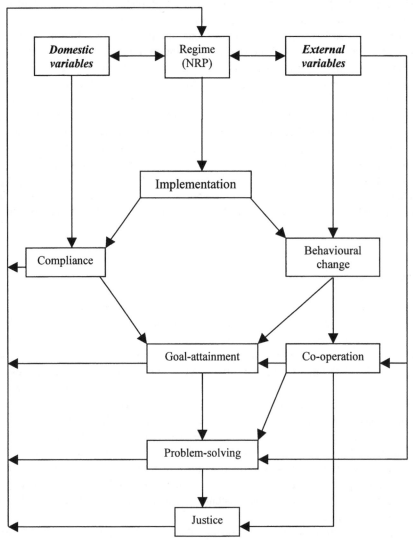

Figure 3.1 Relationships among various Types of Effectiveness

The nature of the potential independent variables is quite extensive, and relatively little work has been done in that area. One strategy of inquiry would be to try and assess how each factor might constitute a necessary or sufficient variable. Another, perhaps more realistic strategy would be to ask what is the minimum number of factors that have to be present for a regime to be effective. For example, factors f^1 to f^n may not have to be present for a regime to be effective, but the regime must at least strengthen x number among n factors.

Following Young (1996, p. 17), we may distinguish between structural and decision variables. Structural variables are aspects of the physical, biological, or social context that decision-makers cannot manipulate in the short term. They are the conditions in which decisions take place. Decision (or choice) variables, on the other hand, are those that can be manipulated by those responsible for designing and implementing regimes. They pertain to the strategies and instruments that actors can use.

Decision and structural variables correspond to what are also called endogenous and exogenous variables (Young, 1996, p. 17). Endogenous variables focus on the institutional arrangements created by the regimes (the convention governance system, for example), while exogenous variables focus on the context in which the regime operates (the distribution of power and technology, level of expertise, existing regimes and organizations, etc.).[25] Although both endogenous and exogenous factors have been considered, scholars have tended to concentrate on the latter (Victor, Raustiala and Skolnikoff, 1998; Young, 1992).

This study emphasizes endogenous variables for three reasons: (i) the number of potential exogenous variables is extremely large; (ii) the relative importance of endogenous and exogenous variables may well depend on the adopted definition of effectiveness (that is, exogenous variables may be more important for problem-solving and less so for behavioural change); and (iii) the examination of the relative weight of exogenous variables actually skirts the issue of what factors "trigger" them (that is, gives them weight in a particular issue area). For example, the notion of "political will" is so vague as to be meaningless and leads one to wonder what accounts for any lack of will.

The importance that authors ascribe to these variables may not be independent of the specific definition of effectiveness used. For example, Davenport and Bertrand (2000) use as criteria for assessing regime effectiveness (or lack thereof): the nature of commitments, the nature of the compliance and enforcement system, and participation (i.e. does it contain the most important Parties?). Clearly, these three criteria are not necessary conditions of all types of effectiveness and may be understood to revolve largely around compliance. On the basis of these criteria, the authors judge the CBD to be a "failure". Yet even if one were to accept the criteria as relevant, lack of formal participation does not prevent states from behaving according to the NRPs of the agreement, and lack of enforcement mechanisms may not doom the treaty (and may encourage countries to join or adopt a more far-reaching agreement). The nature and clarity of commitments, however, seem to be a necessary prerequisite of effectiveness insofar as they enable us to assess implementation (a necessary antecedent of effectiveness).

If one favours the political (behavioural) conception of effectiveness, different explanations may account for behavioural change (Young and Levy, 1999). Rational explanations emphasize the impact of the regime on actors' calculations of the cost and benefits attached to well-defined options that support their given and pre-defined interests or that promote the attractiveness of joint actions by mitigating barriers to collective action (Keohane, Haas and Levy, 1993). Non-rational explanations give more weight to regimes (i) as defining, legitimizing, and giving authority to specific norms that become progressively internalized and routinized (in bureaucratic structures, for example), (ii) as facilitating learning (changes in knowledge, discourses, and values), (iii) as definers of roles (and thus interests), or (iv) as agents of internal realignments through their impact on the distribution of power among the competing domestic interests that affect states.

The growing empirical record has identified a number of conditions closely related to effectiveness (Wettestad, 1999; Young and Demko, 1996). Young and Demko (1996, pp. 231-236), for example, have identified the following factors that may explain why certain regimes are more effective ("successful") than others: (i) the nature of the problem; (ii) the involvement of key actors in the negotiating process; (iii) the provisions (financial, etc.) and institutional arrangements of the regime itself; (iv) the prevalent state of knowledge as well as the degree of consensus regarding the definition of the problem, its causes, and available solutions; (v) political dynamics (especially political commitments of key players and the capacity of domestic interest groups to promote key features of the regime); and (vi) the broader institutional setting (its relationship with other regimes, notably the WTO).

The nature of the problem has obvious consequences since it shapes in part the political dynamics. It determines whether we face a co-ordination or co-operation problem, the second being much more difficult to solve and requiring sophisticated implementation and enforcement measures as well as transparent processes of decision-making and network-building (Ibid, pp. 231-232). The involvement of key actors can increase the feeling of ownership, hence the legitimacy of the regime, which may help alleviate future implementation difficulties (Ibid, p. 232).

Assessed according to these factors, one would expect the CBD to fare poorly. The biodiversity problem is multi-faceted and ill-understood. The juxtaposition of three broad and interrelated objectives complicates matters and multiplies the number and type of actors who can claim a legitimate role in the regime. Its political and public visibility is less than that of climate change even though biodiversity losses stimulate public support for the environment. The consequences of the regime on the distribution of rights and responsibilities, of resources, and of values are enormous and extremely conflictual at the domestic level. Knowledge is uncertain and policy tools controversial. The degree of consensus around the definition of the problem itself may be tenuous. The regime lacks implementation and enforcement mechanisms, and its institutions have poorly defined roles (when they do not compete with each other) or, as with the Secretariat, are embedded in a controversial institutional setting that may hamper their development. And collaboration between the CBD and other biodiversity agreements remains modest, while conflicts (actual or potential) abound with respect to the trade aspects that biodiversity protection implies. One then might have every reason to be pessimistic about the effectiveness of the regime.

Levy, Keohane and Haas (1993, p. 406) have argued that regimes matter because they make it more advantageous for states to co-operate by boosting governmental concern about a specific issue (i.e. boosting governments' and stakeholders' interest in preserving biodiversity), enhancing the contractual environment (resolving distributional, informational, and enforcement issues), and building national capacity to devise and implement solutions (technical, scientific, political, financial), often a critical cause of ineffectiveness. These "three Cs", as "causal pathways" toward effectiveness (defined either as problem-solving or behavioural change), include "clusters of factors that must change for international environmental institutions to become effective" (Keohane, 1996, p. 9). They are detailed in Table 3.1:

Table 3.1 Paths to Effectiveness according to Levy, Keohane and Haas (1993)

Role of institutions	Representative institutional activities
Increase governmental concern	Facilitate direct and indirect linkage issues Create, collect, and disseminate scientific knowledge Create opportunities to magnify domestic public pressure
Enhance the contractual environment	Provide bargaining forums that • reduce transaction costs • create an iterated decision-making process Conduct monitoring of • environmental quality • national environmental performance • national environmental policies Increase national and international Accountability
Build national capacity	Create interorganizational networks with operational organizations to transfer technical and management expertise Transfer financial assistance Transfer policy-relevant information and Expertise Boost bureaucratic power of domestic allies

Source: Levy, Keohane and Haas, 1993, p. 406

The UK Global Environmental Change Programme also identified three common elements that tend to improve the operation of environmental regimes: equitable distribution of costs and benefits, "strong but acceptable non-compliance mechanisms" and "a robust institutional structure". The first relates to general legitimacy issues and building capacity. The second also relates to capacity-building when it comes in the form of "carrots", whereas in the form of "sticks" it assumes the existence of a different regime altogether, which is not really relevant for our purpose.[26] The third refers to the operation of the regime. According to the GECP report: "Two key lessons arise from GECP research into the effectiveness of environmental regimes: Structures and rules of international environmental regimes should not only advance the formal aims of the regime, but also seek added gain in terms of trust, capacity building and social learning. Tell-tale qualities of effective regimes are flexibility and a capacity to adapt institutions, rules and procedures, but without losing sight of the overall objective".

The list could grow. Regime effectiveness, because of the multifaceted meanings of the concept, is not associated with a consistent and coherent set of prerequisites. Table 3.2 gives a sample of factors most commonly associated with one form of effectiveness or another. Many of these determinants operate at different levels and at different times and impact on each other. Minimally, to be effective a regime has to develop the authority to set new norms and rules, develop the capacity to induce action, and enjoy political support (legitimacy).

Legitimacy poses a specific problem. As the Commission on Global Governance (1995, p. 66) has underscored, "Institutions that lack legitimacy are seldom effective over the long run". Scholars of the constructivist school of international relations have insisted on a relationship between the legitimacy of NRPs and the effectiveness of a norm or institution. They ask how the regime fosters convergent intersubjective understandings of institutional legitimacy by agents in the issue network.

Regime institutions must be perceived by other actors as "fair", that is, formed and operating according to the principles on which they claim a role. In that sense, legitimacy has many sides. It refers to outcomes as well as to process. In particular, it depends on the ability of the convention governance system (CGS) to perform good governance, that is, to act in accordance with the principles of transparency, accountability, and participation. Clearly, there has been great willingness in the CBD case to adopt these principles: participation is enhanced through near-universal membership, a governing structure that reflects states' pre-eminence through the COPs and subsidiary organs, committees that give access to other stakeholders, and workshops and dialogues with interested Parties; transparency is achieved by means of specific procedures, documentation, electronic communication, and staff access; and accountability is strengthened through the COP, the SBSTTA, and their bureaux.

Legitimacy is difficult to measure independently of the other determinants of effectiveness. In fact, it is largely an implied intermediary variable between the first four prerequisites (operation, transparency, capacity-building, and networks), which originate in a rational choice approach, and the last two (consensus and learning), which relate more closely to a constructivist approach to environmental regimes that insists on intersubjective understandings and norms. We assume that legitimacy is present if the other prerequisites are, but it can best be measured through them.

Based on the nature of the CBD regime and on the theoretical and empirical literature, it would seem particularly fruitful and pertinent to place particular emphasis on the following determinants of effectiveness, which encompass much of the above: (i) operation of the CGS; (ii) transparency; (iii) capacity-building; (iv) development of issue networks; (v) consensual knowledge; and (vi) learning. These determinants are largely endogenous and reflect the notion of effectiveness in terms of behavioural change (with implementation as an antecedent) that is favoured here, although they may also contribute to other forms (or elements) of effectiveness, such as compliance and problem-solving.

Although observers differ as to the real importance of organizations for the success of regimes, the importance of the convention governance system, that is, the set of institutions created by the regime, their interplay, operation, and resources, cannot be overlooked. This element is treated in chapter 4. Young (1996, p. 18) highlights decision-making procedures,[27] financial resources, and compliance mechanisms. Others (e.g. Victor, Raustiala and Skolnikoff, 1998) expand on the nature of implementation review mechanisms, a topic that has been raised within the CBD and remains controversial. The GECP (1999) identifies as an important factor associated with effectiveness "a robust institutional structure, including a well-managed secretariat, routine meetings of member governments, mechanisms for monitoring compliance and harmonized data collection".

Chayes and Chayes (1995, p. 284) argue that successful organizations are able to combine expert management and staff with extensive Party involvement at a high level. States lie at the core of a CGS-based regime. For example, the CBD has relied and will continue relying on states assuming leadership in areas in which they hold a specific interest, ranging from knowledge construction, to building political coalitions behind certain agenda items, to the facilitation of implementation. The danger is not that a regime will move with the slowest state but that it will only move in areas where key states are willing to invest resources. This trend is exacerbated by the tendency to set up special funds for pet policies. It may be the secretariat's role in part to guard against the dissonance of such a menu-based approach; playing this role effectively, however, requires strengthening its legitimacy and overcoming some of the constraints outlined above.

The Operation of the Convention

As the GECP (1999) report stresses: "The effectiveness and legitimacy of international environmental regimes depend on how different levels of policy-making interact with one another. Yet understanding of this process is still at an early stage. Interaction varies from case to case. No general model of multi-level governance exists. The flow of responsibility and authority is specific to the regime in question, evoking a new politics and a new set of mechanisms every time.

Relations between richer and poorer countries have to be negotiated anew at every turn".

Table 3.2 Determinants of Regime Effectiveness

Nature of determinant	Sources
Capacity-building[28]	Haas, Keohane and Levy, 1993; Young and Demko, 1996; Jacobson and Weiss, 1998; GECP, 1999
CGS structure and operation[29]	Sand, 1992; Haas, Keohane and Levy, 1993; Young and Demko, 1996; GECP, 1999
Network-building[30]	Haas, Keohane and Levy, 1993; Chayes and Chayes, 1995; Jacobson and Weiss, 1998; Young and Levy, 1999
Generation, collection, and dissemination of scientific knowledge; nature of scientific consensus	Sand, 1992; Haas, Keohane and Levy, 1993; Young and Levy, 1999; Young and Demko, 1996; Jacobson and Weiss, 1998b
Monitoring	Haas, Keohane and Levy, 1993; Chayes and Chayes, 1995; Jacobson and Weiss, 1998
Learning[31]	Sand, 1992; Deutz, 1997; Haas, 1998; GECP, 1999; Young, 1999
Compliance mechanisms[32]	Mitchell, 1994a, 1994b; Cameron, Werksman and Roderick, 1996; Kokotsis and Kirton, 1997; Victor et al., 1998; GECP, 1999; Davenport and Bertrand, 2000
Transparency	Chayes and Chayes, 1995; Kokotsis and Kirton, 1997; Chayes, Chayes and Mitchell (1998); GECP, 1999
Conflict mediation processes	GECP, 1999; Davenport and Bertrand, 2000
Relationships with existing agreements[33]	Young and Demko, 1996; GECP, 1999
Convergence of global and local levels	Young, 1999; GECP, 1999
Participation (i.e. the type and number of Parties)[34]	Sand, 1992; Kokotsis and Kirton, 1997; Davenport and Bertrand, 2000
Nature of the problem	Young and Demko, 1996
Involvement of key actors in the negotiating process	Young and Demko, 1996
Scientific consensus	
Political will and domestic factors[35]	Keohane, 1984; Haas, Keohane and Levy, 1993; Young and Demko, 1996; Kokotsis and Kirton, 1997; Young, 1999b
Redefinition of clear roles and authority	Young, 1999

Transparency

Transparency is explored in chapters 5 and 6. Understood both as an open process of rule formulation (Young, 1996, p. 19) and as information-sharing, it is closely associated with compliance by many observers (Chayes, Chayes and Mitchell, 1998; Mitchell, 1998; Cameron, Werksman et al., 1996). Designed to facilitate the evaluation of implementation and compliance, as well as the dissemination of knowledge relevant to the goals of the convention, transparency is at the core of the implementation efforts of the CBD, notably through the Clearing-house Mechanism. Several careful studies have pointed out its importance, particularly when detailed regulations governing behaviour are at stake – such as combating marine pollution from ships (DeSombre, 2000; Mitchell, 1994). Transparency facilitates the co-ordination of activities, reassures Parties that all of them are meeting their obligations, and helps to deter potential violators (Chayes, Chayes and Mitchell, 1998).

A regime cannot be effective in the absence of any influence or role on the part of civil society, and that can only be achieved through transparency and multiple channels of communication. Traditional IGOs and NGOs may suffer from a lack of procedural legitimacy (or democratic deficit) and are seen as much less democratic than certain states. In this regard, the CGS may have an advantage if it opens up not only to organized interests (NGOs) but also to expertise (individual networks of researchers). Participation need not be defined in the same way or take a similar form in every case. It is in their ability to marshal the relevant expertise and clarify issues that the Secretariat of the CBD (SCBD) and SBSTTA matter.

Capacity-Building

In much of the developing world, there is no implementation of environmental agreements without capacity-building. This situation is especially acute in the case of the CBD, given lack of knowledge of the basic dimensions of the problem (i.e. the rate of extinction and the functions that species play in ecosystem stability and productivity) and given that some of the most biologically diverse countries are also among the poorest. Capacity gaps include: ignorance of the state of biodiversity or of specific provisions of the Convention; institutional impediments to change; lack of expertise (scientific and administrative), financial and human resources, and technology; and poorly developed civil society. In this context, we must answer two questions: Has the regime facilitated the transfer of knowledge, funds, and technology, and the building of a basic capacity to determine national priorities and undertake the necessary actions in light of the Convention? Has it made a difference in funding for biodiversity and in building social prerequisites for change?

Development of Issue Networks

Regimes help empower groups, form alliances, identify new interests, and link stakeholders – in short, to create a transnational community dedicated to furthering its NRP. The community includes natural and social scientists, civil servants, farmers, diplomats, indigenous peoples, activists, lawyers, and other groups.

Wolfgang Reinicke (1998, p. 40), among others, believes in the importance of global policy networks as instruments of governance and the development of an international community. An answer to globalization would be to "take public policy out of its territorial context", that is, separate governance from a structure of government. Other authors, such as Rosenau and Czempiel (1992) raise similar ideas. Reinicke sees this movement taking place in relation to specific issue areas and favouring both IGOs and civil society (including business). The underlying reasoning is based on greater adaptive capacities of both, given their dynamism and ability to respond to changes in the knowledge base.

In the context of multiple stakeholders and levels of action, effective regimes must be able to facilitate solution-oriented and implementation-driven alliances. This matrix function (facilitating the emergence of stakeholder alliances at various levels) is probably one of the most important functions of regimes. The GECP (1999, p. 12) has recognized the importance of a regime's ability to seek out organizations (including business) not formally part of the regime: "Viewed in this way, regimes provide a basis for alliances" that can help shape particular solutions to common problems (solutions attuned to local circumstances, for example).

Ideological concerns, together with pressures from NGOs and the desire to overcome local bottlenecks and reduce political surprises, have combined to put greater importance on networks in policy implementation. In this (narrow) sense, "network" refers to attempts to promote local participation in policy formulation and implementation. Faced with the substantial implementation problems of community environmental policy, the 1993 fifth Environment Action Programme of the EU emphasized "network-style and bottom-up forms of policy formulation and implementation" (Knill and Lenschow, 2000, p. 3). This approach acts in the context of policy-making and implementation. It is intended to be more flexible (to take account of local circumstances), promote increasing concern more effectively (through the provision of incentives for industrial self-regulation and social mobilization), and facilitate support and a sense of ownership on the part of implementing actors. In this sense, the horizontal, bottom-up path to effectiveness is the opposite of traditional top-down, enforcement-compliance-based models. The 1998 Aarhus Convention[36] also reflects a belief in the value of transparency and participation as a pathway toward more effective policy through the development of networks.[37]

More generally, in a system of multiple actors, overlapping goals, and general uncertainty, the CBD-CGS has the potential to serve as the hub of an extensive network linking Parties, NGOs, and the private sector. Effective co-ordination does not require a centre or an enforcer. Complex systems, for example, have positive feedbacks that reinforce behaviour of mutual benefit. As a central and focused player, the CBD-CGS (in collaboration with other actors in the network) can do more than try to reconcile divergent interests. It can play a key role in structuring advocacy coalitions, identifying and empowering actors. It can help share knowledge, promote norms, ideas, and interpretations, and ultimately shape the international understanding of an issue that will lead to policy change. The ozone regime may be a good illustration of these dynamics (Le Prestre, Reid and Morehouse, 1998).

For example, giving segments of civil society a leading role in some aspects of global policy would promote accountability (provided that the "democratic deficit" of many NGOs can be overcome), increase the legitimacy of such networks, and ensure that all interests are represented. Rather than adversaries (e.g. NGOs versus the World Bank), IGOs and NGOs become partners. These policy networks (to which state agencies would also belong) would encourage mutual learning and openness to change. The structure of the IUCN provides an example of this idea.

Consensual Knowledge

Regimes may foster co-operation through the development of common definitions of problems and agreed sets of possible solutions. This is one of the most important functions of regimes identified by Haas, Keohane and Levy (1993), especially in controversial areas where the precautionary principle is often invoked. As argued in chapter 4, an important function of SBSTTA is thought to be the socialization of delegates of developing countries and industrialized countries alike into the science and norms of the regime. For example, some countries that defined the biodiversity problem only in terms of conservation may, in the end, realize the importance of other issues, such as sustainable development or the role of indigenous populations. What matters – more than the quality of knowledge – is the existence of a political consensus on the definition of the problem, its causes, and the likely impact of various options available to remedy the problem. This is well illustrated by the climate change regime in which the IPCC is designed to promote a consensus among scientists and the Subsidiary Body for Technical Advice (SBSTA) seeks to translate that consensus into action. There is, however, no such division of labour in the CBD regime.

Learning

Regime effectiveness implies the ability to adapt regime institutions, rules, and procedures to new balances of power, new knowledge, and new needs. The difficulties that traditional IGOs have had with change have been variously attributed to the structure of interests that dominate their operations (a coalition of states and other stakeholders), to their size and operation, to the ideology it and its staff embody, and to staff training and expertise. Effective regimes are learning devices, open to the development of new consensual knowledge that leads to the adoption of new values and new problem definitions.[38]

Deutz (1997) has reviewed this question through a study of the adequacy of commitments, that is, whether or not policy prescriptions are sufficient to respond to the environmental problem for which the treaty was created, with a particular focus on the Montreal Protocol, LRTAP, climate change, and the Basel Convention. Specific review mechanisms create a dynamic regime through a continuous revision of Parties' commitments in light of evolving knowledge (Gehring, 1994). Now the engine of change is usually presented as scientific and technical knowledge, but one should also add changes in the distribution of values and political and economic power.

This learning capacity is dependent on several elements, such as the existence of scientific subsidiary bodies, regular meetings of the Parties, clear objectives, and simple amendment procedures that do not require subsequent ratification. It also depends on the constitutional rules of the regime (the procedures for adopting new amendments and commitments),[39] those governing membership,[40] the capacity to modify the structure of the regime in response to new needs, as well as on its operation. Thus one may ask: What kind of mechanisms have been created in the CBD regime for reviewing the adequacy of commitments? Has the CBD been capable of error correction, that is, of improving its performance in light of the purpose of the convention? How have its structure and routines evolved (through the creation of committees, subsidiary bodies, and new rules) in order to integrate new knowledge into its operations and respond more quickly to new demands and new information?

As Young and Demko (1996, p. 236) have remarked, rather than looking for elusive determinants that are both sufficient and necessary, it might be more fruitful to identify and explore the role that these determinants play and how they reinforce or counteract one another. Some may be preconditions of others; some may work at cross purposes. Figure 3.2 describes possible relationships among them. Consensus and learning will be facilitated by the contribution of the regime to capacity-building, network-building, and transparency, a relationship mediated by the implied variable of legitimacy. Norms are diffused through networks, reinforced though capacities, and made known through transparency. This in turn depends on a smooth functioning of the CGS. These factors may not be sufficient to ensure effectiveness (and other chapters indeed identify other factors), but they play a central and necessary role. Conversely, if the regime does not foster these prerequisites, its future effectiveness will be doubtful.

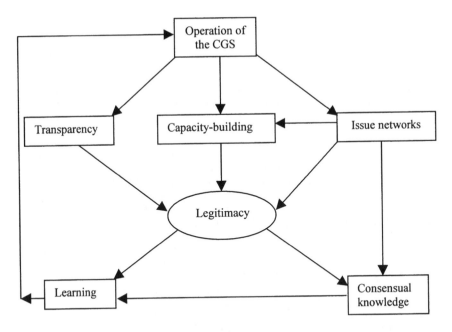

Figure 3.2 Relationships among selected Prerequisites of Regime Effectiveness

Conclusion

International politics around multiple centres of power has become the defining characteristic of contemporary international relations, characterized by interdependence, multiple actors, competing legitimacies, transnational relations, and rising uncertainties regarding the nature of the problems, the solutions, and the consequences of one's actions. In this context, protecting biodiversity effectively while ensuring fairness and sustainable developments poses profound challenges. As the GECP report points out, "There are great opportunities for more open, legitimate and flexible governance, but there are also dangers that expectations are not met". This is the challenge of assessing effectiveness, which ultimately must answer two fundamental questions: Is the regime contributing to a new form of governance of the natural world? Is it providing the tools and helping to build the conditions that will enable stakeholders to address these challenges?

Notes

[1] This definition is based on classic definitions of regimes and captures the central elements of the concept. Other definitions include: "sets of implicit or explicit principles, norms, rules and decision-making procedures around which actor's expectations converge in a given area of international relations" (Krasner, 1983, p. 2); "institutions with specific rules, agreed upon by governments, that pertain to particular sets of issues in international politics" (Keohane, 1989, p. 4), with institutions being defined as "persistent and connected sets of rules and practices that prescribe behavioral roles, constrain activity, and shape expectations" (Keohane, Haas and Levy, 1993, p. 5); "social institutions consisting of agreed upon principles, norms, rules, procedures, and programmes that govern the interaction of actors in specific issue areas" (Levy, Young et al., 1995, p. 274); "regimes are social institutions, and as such are practices that define roles, rights and the degree of organization surrounding issues of enforcement or compliance. Forming a regime not only creates new norms, but it is also a process of institutionalization, the creation of practices of decision-making, rule change and enforcement" (Bohman, 1999, p. 500).

[2] Indeed, for Kratochwil and Ruggie (1986, p. 767), norms are what sets regimes apart from other international phenomena. But some regime theorists differ as to the place of norms, arguing that norm construction and acceptance can follow the adoption of particular behaviours that are congruent with the norm (see Vogler, 1995, p. 44).

[3] See Putnam and Bayne (1987) and the work of the Toronto G-7 Research Group, notably Kokotsis and Kirton (1997). But one would have to restrict the argument to a specific issue addressed within the G-7 framework, which covers issues ranging from finance to employment, from terrorism to sustainable development.

[4] By increasing concern, strengthening capacities, and improving the contractual environment of the parties, although these factors may be more important for co-operation (2) and (3) than for (1). See Keohane, Haas et al. (1993).

[5] See chapter 1 by McGraw in this volume.

[6] But on the connection between habitat and species loss, see MacPhee and Flemming (1999).

[7] See informal workshop on strengthening the effectiveness of the Biodiversity Convention, COP-5, Nairobi, 22 May 2000 (www.iisd.ca/biodiv/cop5/).

[8] "Success or failure in solving the problems that motivate actors to create [international governance systems]" (Young and Demko, 1996, p. 230). See also: Kütting (2000); Jacobson and Weiss (1998); Sprinz (1998); Victor, Raustiala et al. (1998); Deutz (1997); Keohane (1996); Keohane, Haas et al. (1993, p. 7).

[9] "Learning about implementation and compliance is an essential first step to learning about effectiveness" (Jacobson and Weiss, 1998, p. 6). The authors conceive effectiveness as both problem-solving and goal attainment.

[10] Inded, countries resisted such precise objectives during the CBD negotiations, as shown by the conflicts over global lists.

[11] Economists like to point out the perverse consequences of well-intentioned policies. A classic example mentioned by Pearce and Warford is that of South American parrots whose mortality increased after the decision was made to ban their capture. This indeed led to a reduction in the number of illegaly exported parrots because of the risks of detection. However, smugglers captured more parrots in the wild and hid them in smaller spaces, which increased the overall mortality rate during transit. The level of smuggling decreased but the capture of a greater number of individuals to make up for seizures and mortality worked against the long-term viability of the population. See Pearce and Warford (1993).

[12] In fact, Nelson et al. (1997) have determined that more money went for brown projects to address urban pollution problems than to natural resources conservation.

[13] Young (1996, p. 10), for example, mentions that many coastal fishery regimes are

ostensibly promoted as conservation measures but that they are also intended to protect coastal fishermen from competition from foreign vessels. But one cannot start speculating about the motives of parties and deduce from it something about the property of the regime. All that one could say would be that some parties do not consider the regime effective *in relation* to the range of concerns they held. On the other hand, the IWC and ITTO, for example, were clearly created to institute a sustainable exploitation of the resource.

[14] See, for example: Knill and Lenschow (2000); Sand (1992). The criteria listed by UNCED Working Group III for evaluating the effectiveness of legal agreements (Sand, 1992) covered 1) objectives and achievement, 2) participation, 3) implementation, 4) information, 5) operation, review, and adjustment, and 6) codification programming. These criteria mix the conceptualizations of effectiveness reviewed in this section with the determinants of effectiveness discussed in the next.

[15] Indeed, one could interpret such calls as incentives to develop these management tools.

[16] In the case of biodiversity, collective action problems include resources outside state boundaries (ocean mammals and highly migratory species, both of which, however, are often regulated by separate agreements), trade in endangered species (CITES), and, potentially, intellectual property rights.

[17] Their study of the Vienna Convention, Montreal Protocol on the ozone layer, Convention on Long Range Transboundary Air Pollution (LRTAP), and the EU Large Combustion Plants Directive led Robin Churchill and Lynda Warren to conclude that agreements "represent what States have already achieved or expect to achieve, [and] so require few new actions" (GECP-UK, 1999).

[18] Indeed, India, Brazil, and other developing countries fought successfully against the wish of certain parties (most notably France) to require listings that could eventually have served such a purpose. See Tolba and Rummel-Bulska (1998), and France's comment at the time of signature.

[19] In this context, Chayes and Chayes (1995) and Chayes, Chayes, and Mitchell (1998, p. 41) insist on viewing non-compliance not as deviant behaviour to be corrected through coercive measures but as expected behaviour rooted in lack of capacity, inadvertence, ignorance, and only rarely wilful behaviour. The right model, then, is managerial rather than based on sanctions, whereby compliance is elicited through a "co-operative process of consultation, analysis, and persuasion rather than coercive punishment," which they deem ineffective and unsuitable.

[20] This working definition contrasts with their problem-based definition in their introductory chapter.

[21] See also Keohane, Haas and Levy's (1993) major functions of regimes: enhancing concern, capacity, and the contractual environment of parties.

[22] See the discussions within the UNFCCC on how to structure a compliance system for the Kyoto Protocol and within the UNCCD on how to structure a system of implementation review.

[23] For example, Wettestad, and Andresen (1991) adopt three cumulative criteria for assessing effectiveness: goal attainment, process (the correlation between expert advice and actual decisions), and problem-solving.

[24] This also follows Keohane (1996, p. 14).

[25] Oran Young adds a third type of variable, which he calls "linkage variables", that pertain to "the fit between the institutional character of a governance system and the environment in which it is expected to function" (Young, 1996, p. 17). Political support would be an example of such a variable.

[26] That is, arguing that a strong non-compliance mechanism based on sanctions (such as loss of voting rights, trade sanctions) is needed boils down to arguing that the CBD could be effective were it only different. First, we might not have had a regime had it contained such provisions (i.e. only states that are sure to comply will accept them); second, this will not

help us understand how the existing regime is boosting (or not) the conditions for its effectiveness; and third, such arguments tend to assume that strong compliance mechanisms are necessary conditions for regime effectiveness, thus ignoring other possible causes of ineffectiveness (such as poor implementation).

[27] An issue that remains pending since COP-1.

[28] Includes providing financial aid, transferring policy-relevant information and expertise, boosting the bureaucratic power of domestic allies (Haas, Keohane and Levy, 1993), sharing scientific and policy advice.

[29] Includes the factors mentioned in Table 3.1 under "enhance the contractual environment".

[30] Impacts on technology transfers and magnifies domestic public pressure (Haas, Keohane and Levy, 1993); includes involvement of key non-state actors in the policy process (including implementation).

[31] Includes procedures for revising regime procedures and commitments (GECP, 1999).

[32] Includes general regime design, rule formation, compliance and dispute settlements mechanisms.

[33] Includes synergies with related agreements (e.g. CITES) as well as with other regimes (e.g. WTO).

[34] Positive relationship, see Davenport and Bertrand (2000); Sand (1992). In this case, it is influenced by a series of factors such as the availability of financial resources, technical and scientific assistance, pressure by NGOs and other countries, the existence of flexible treaty provisions, etc. (Sand, 1992). Concert theorists, on the other hand, would emphasize that *deliberate* non-compliance is less likely when fewer states interact and when issue-relative power is concentrated.

[35] Depending on authors, may include direct political control by leaders, social pressures, and reputation.

[36] "Convention on Access to Information, Public Participation in Decision-Making and Access to Justice in Environmental Matters".

[37] But this remains a mere belief since no study has been conducted to assess the effectiveness of such an approach. Knill and Lenschow (2000) have raised some doubts about its added effectiveness in the European context.

[38] This reflects Ernst Haas's (1990) general perspective on organizational learning.

[39] For example, species listing under CITES without formal ratification.

[40] For example, ability to add new members favouring a particular evolution of the regime, as in the IWC.

Chapter 4

The Operation of the CBD Convention Governance System

Philippe G. Le Prestre

Introduction: The Search for New Modes of Governance

With the advent of global issues and the signing of important global environmental conventions, the past few decades have seen the emergence of new international environmental actors whose role and potential are neither well understood nor well defined. Each major multilateral environmental agreement (MEA) now provides for the establishment of a secretariat and other bodies entrusted with directing its implementation and evolution. Although providing significant advantages and reflecting current political realities, this proliferation has also created some concerns regarding the potential overlap among secretariats and their fragmentation, which makes co-ordination difficult, diminishes their collective weight relative to other regimes, and reduces the financial resources available to existing organizations such as the United Nations Environment Programme (UNEP). Consequently, in the context of the World Summit on Sustainable Development of 2002, UNEP and several governments have called for a general reflection on this development with the aim of finding some way back to a more centralized model of environmental governance. Yet it is not that clear that the very existence of convention-specific secretariats threatens the overall coherence and effectiveness of the global environmental regime. Rather, in a context of network-based globalization of international relations, one could also ask to what extent these arrangements might constitute the nucleus of a new model of governance uniquely able to adapt to the nature of the new international system in the making.

As existing convention secretariats reconsider or continue to define their mandate, their impact on regime effectiveness remains ambiguous and largely neglected by researchers. For some observers, secretariats are too inefficient or too weak to promote the goals of new environmental regimes effectively; for others, they have significant potential for improving international co-operation and are central to the success of multilateral environmental agreements. But secretariats are just one of the many institutions created by the new regimes. Not only is the secretariat proper of interest but also the system of institutions created by an international regime (called a convention governance system, or CGS), the factors that shape their operation and role, and their potential contribution to international environmental co-operation and states' capacity to pursue their own interests in collective harmony. Selecting the CGS as the unit of analysis may thus be more fruitful than focusing exclusively on a secretariat.[1] To assess the CGS's potential to create a new kind of environmental governance, we have to identify the hurdles it must overcome. These hurdles are numerous, including basic hostility from various actors or stakeholders; lack of capacity (intellectual, human, and financial), authority, or legitimacy; lack of agreement on the very nature or the precise obligations of the regime; its political implications; and the complexity of the subject matter.

The operation of the Convention on Biological Diversity (CBD) offers a good example of the potential and constraints of CGSs. This regime still faces considerable challenges, two of which pertain to the operation of the Secretariat (SCBD) and of the Subsidiary Body for Scientific, Technical and Technological Advice (SBSTTA). These two units are central to the implementation of the convention. The difficulties they have encountered are emblematic of the hurdles facing some CGSs in becoming truly new forms of international governance. This examination of the hurdles will be complemented by a brief discussion of other issues related to the development of a system for reviewing the implementation of the CBD.

As Young (1989) and Bohman (1999) emphasize, a regime is also a process of institutionalization, the creation of practices and rules that identify relevant knowledge and norms and govern decision-making, behaviour, learning, and enforcement. Traditionally, there have been two ways of promoting this objective: through the development of autonomous intergovernmental organizations (IGOs; in this case secretariats) or through the strong leadership role of one or a handful of states. These two approaches imply unbalanced relationships between the secretariat and the Conference of the Parties (COP). Convention governance systems, on the other hand, while recognizing the realities of international power, seek to create issue-based communities and networks that may transcend this institutional conflict.

From Secretariats to Convention Governance Systems

The first secretariats associated with environmental conventions appeared in the early 1970s. They have since multiplied. Recent treaties explicitly detail their responsibilities and assign to them functions that can, under some conditions, undergird an activist role. Their recent proliferation and the symbol they represent of the collective search for solutions to pressing global problems have led some observers to believe that they have "the potential to develop powers over states that may far exceed those of more formally established international institutions" (Werksman, 1996, p. 55). For Young and von Moltke (1995, p. 2), "the effectiveness of the secretariat is a necessary condition for the effectiveness of the regime".

Despite their growing visibility, secretariats remain largely ignored by academics. The scant literature addresses two questions: (i) regime formation, that is, how administrative secretariats influence treaty-making and how that function can be strengthened (Susskind, 1994; Sandford, 1994), and (ii) their impact on regime implementation and effectiveness (Young and von Moltke, 1995). More recent discussions have taken place in the context of efforts to promote a centralized model of environmental governance (UN University (UNU), 1999). These few studies underscore the potential importance of international secretariats in furthering co-operation among nations, but they also assume a trade-off between the effectiveness of secretariats and states' autonomy.

An approach that sees secretariats as new institutions potentially capable of carrying forward old functionalist dreams is profoundly short-sighted. First, these structures remain small and have played a relatively passive role (Susskind, 1994).[2] Second and more important, although several factors may have influenced their growing importance, such as the nature of environmental issues or the development of new diplomatic instruments (the framework treaty-protocol model of negotiation and the incorporation of financial mechanisms into treaties (Sandford, 1994)) they above all embody the desire of states to regain some control over the agenda and the evolution and implementation of collective action in highly contested areas, such as the environment. Secretariats cannot be studied in isolation. The important role given to the Conference of the Parties (COPs) in global environmental agreements and in overseeing the activities of secretariats testifies to states' concern with controlling the pace of policy change.

In contrast, the main assumption of this chapter is that regime effectiveness is enhanced not by undermining but *by strengthening* states' ability to determine, in concert, their common environmental destinies. In this context, rather than limiting oneself to administrative secretariats, one should focus on the unit of governance that they serve and represent, that is, not simply on the personnel appointed to administer a convention but also, more broadly, on the general mode of governance of a convention in which states' representatives and members of international civil society participate in the management and evolution of the regime. Ultimately, it is this system, the CGS, that is worth investigating.

CGSs are flexible, dynamic, and mission-oriented; their administrative unit – the secretariat – typically small. Through the extensive networks that they represent and build, they may develop the required conditions for effective co-operation and implementation of environmental regimes. In particular, they can play a key role in enhancing the transparency of implementation and compliance efforts, building policy capacity, developing issue networks, establishing a set of coherent knowledge, reducing competitive pressures among UN organizations, fostering convergence between international expectations and local practices, facilitating reconciliation of government priorities, and fostering learning and regime change. Of course, many of these functions could be performed by powerful organizations, provided they are adaptive. The reality, however, is that there is little political support for creating such an organization for each regime, nor would the resources exist to support it. Indeed, environmental governance is increasingly linked more to the capacity to co-ordinate individual initiatives (by various alliances of states, IGOs, and NGOs) than to developing the capacity to carry them all out in one setting.

Given the uncertainties and the changing context that surround global environmental problems and their solutions, this latter aspect is important. More than secretariats are, CGSs can be construed as learning devices, better able to encourage the development of new consensual knowledge from which new norms and new problem definitions may emerge. Given the multiplicity of conventions and the complexity of their implementation, new international institutional arrangements must be able to mobilize all relevant actors, build on their experience, address compliance issues, and steer the adaptation of the regime.

In that sense, CGSs represent evolving answers to the dilemma of governance and to a sense of a loss of control by states over the policy process[3] while at the same time acknowledging the contribution of IGOs and NGOs to the definition of and solution to common problems. Global CGSs potentially hold three attributes that states value: focus, accountability, and flexibility. *Focus*, because CGSs are only concerned with the evolution and implementation of a specific set of principles and obligations; *accountability* through the COPs and its subsidiary bodies; and *flexibility* because secretariats and COPs can quickly change their mission, tasks, and priorities in light of evolving knowledge about the state of implementation or existing constraints and opportunities.

Yet all these virtues remain incipient. Among the factors that may explain the capacity of CGSs to enhance regime effectiveness, one can identify (i) the nature of the environmental issue and relevant knowledge, (ii) the status, mandate, and resources of the secretariat, (iii) the operation and linkages that exist among CGS institutions, (iv) the relation between the latter and relevant issue networks, (v) the nature of the leadership of these institutions, notably the secretariat's, and (vi) the legitimacy of the CGS in the eyes of Parties and other stakeholders. The remainder of this paper will focus specifically on the second and third factors through an examination of the CBD Secretariat and the SBSTTA. Much of what will be said, however, may also bear on the other factors.

The Structure and Operation of the CBD Governance System

The CBD remains a weak regime. In assessing the potential of the CBD-CGS to become a key system of biodiversity governance capable of engineering a new international order, many issues relating to the operation of the convention could be examined, including:

- the ability of the SCBD to carry out its duties;
- the frequency of the meetings of the COP and the range of issues it should consider;
- the effectiveness of the COP in delivering guidance to the CBD financial mechanism (the Global Environment Facility (GEF) on an interim basis) that

can be made operational as a basis for programme planning and project selection;

- the future work programme of the COP;
- the effectiveness of the SBSTTA in delivering appropriate scientific advice for decision-making by the COP;
- the relationship among the various organs of the convention;
- the need for an additional body within the convention to oversee implementation between COP meetings;
- how to ensure that national reports become a dynamic instrument for CBD implementation;
- implementation of the Clearing-house Mechanism;
- how to devise links with civil society that promote learning;
- how to use the financial mechanism to encourage governments and IGOs to act in conformity with CBD objectives and how to do that when the financial mechanism (GEF) is a separate independent body;
- links between the CBD and other international agreements and organizations;
- the effectiveness of preparations by state delegations for COP and other meetings; and
- how to balance, even integrate, the three goals of the convention.

These are all important aspects of the operation of the convention in which any convention secretariat plays a role, sometimes minor, sometimes significant. This is due, in part, to the secretariat's permanence, its activism (which varies among conventions), and its importance as a source of information about the regime for Parties. But the secretariat is only one element of the CGS, which in the case of the CBD also includes the COP and the SBSTTA, as well as newly created open-ended bodies such as the units associated with the Cartagena Protocol on Biosafety, the Ad Hoc Working Group on Article 8(j) (AWGTK),[4] and the Panel of Experts on Access and Benefit-Sharing (See Figure 4.1).

All framework treaties institute a COP that provides a forum where the principles, norms, decision procedures, and implementation of the convention are continuously negotiated and worked out (Kiss, 1993). The COP is the supreme governing body of the CBD. It oversees the operation of the Secretariat, adopts the procedures governing the exchange of information mandated by the Convention, assesses the scientific information it receives from the SBSTTA and other bodies, ensures the coherence of the policies it adopts, and adopts protocols, amendments, or appendices to the convention. It may create subsidiary bodies and adopt procedures to resolve conflicts among Parties regarding the implementation of the convention and any measure deemed necessary for the implementation of the convention.[5] Decisions are generally adopted by consensus (Gehring, 1990, p. 37).

Now, CBD COP meetings remain frequent, annual for the first three and biennial since 1998. Some secretariats may enjoy significant autonomy when COPs are seldom convened.[6] Ramsar may be an illustration of that model. In other cases, COPs play a very active and important role in directing the secretariat and in the evolution and implementation of the convention (e.g. CITES).

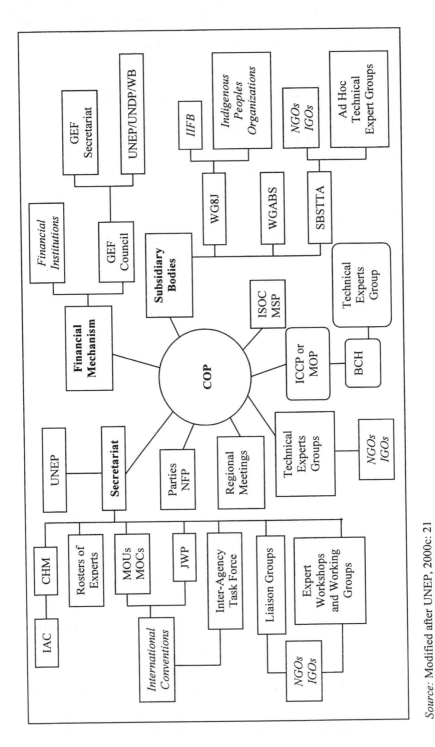

Source: Modified after UNEP, 2000c: 21

Figure 4.1 The CBD Governance System

Constraints on the Secretariat's Role

E. Brown Weiss (1998) identifies three sources of influence of convention secretariats: (i) the comprehensive knowledge of the staff regarding the state of compliance of the convention, (ii) their knowledge of the nature of the problems that have arisen at the national level, and (iii) their dealings not only with government officials but with civil society members (private-sector officials, NGOs, and interested individuals) that have or claim a role in the process of implementing the convention. The roles that secretariats will be able to claim for themselves, however, depend on an array of factors, of which the quality of the staff is but one.

The executive secretary   The relationship between the CBD Secretariat and the Parties has fluctuated according to the skills of the executive secretary and the perception that Parties have of the secretary's sensitivity to their concerns, administrative capacities, and moderation in pursuing an independent tack or in presenting them with *faits accomplis*. Parties are aware of the conflicting pressures that a secretary faces, made all the more significant by the task-oriented nature of the job, but they all emphasize the secretary's primary role as the head of a service organization. In the case of the CBD, administrative capacity and political sensitivity are the two crucial ingredients for states' support.

States that believe the executive secretary will speak for them favour a strong secretariat that will "speak for the regime"; those that do not yet pay the bills stress the secretary's administrative capacities. If the executive secretary is to serve the regime effectively, he or she must prevent capture of the secretariat by a coalition of states or stakeholders. The secretary's effectiveness also rests on his or her ability to build bridges among stakeholders, develop issue networks, and steer the regime forward while remaining sensitive to the diversity of views of the Parties regarding the nature, scope, and evolution of the regime (Peterson, 1998). "This is a delicate task requiring the development of strong informal relations of trust with some members without jeopardising the overall impartiality of the secretariat and attention to issues that are likely to become defining in the relationship between executive head and members" (Young and von Moltke, 1995).

Size   Environmental secretariats are typically small. The CBD has about 30 professionals, roughly a quarter of whom are on secondment from and funded by national administrations or other international organizations.[7] This helps to maintain good relations with countries that have a particular interest and play key roles in some issues and with IGOs with which the secretariat must co-operate. In order to increase its access to expertise and its capacity to draft needed background papers, the secretariat also makes considerable use of temporary staff and external consultants. Some governments have criticized the lack of transparency in the selection and use of such consultants, fearing that some Parties and viewpoints may be overrepresented.

Financial resources Although the budgets of secretariats increased markedly after Rio, doubling or sometimes tripling, they remain tiny compared with the means available to operational organizations. Compared with its two sister conventions (climate and desertification), the CBD budget is small, about USD 18.5 million for the biennium 2001-2002.[8]

Chronic underfunding is often mentioned as a limiting factor in the effectiveness of secretariats, but the importance of that point is unclear since underfunding also reflects disagreements about the role of the organization. The resources of the CBD come from contributions by Parties and are distinct from UN resources. On the one hand, this protects the CBD from restrictions that may be imposed by the Secretary General as a result of the financial situation of the UN. On the other hand, some would prefer secretariats' budgets to come in part from the UN general budget so that they will not be "perceived as narrowly beholden to the Parties to the treaties who are paying the bill" (Susskind, 1994, p. 59). This, however, assumes that only financially independent organizations may be able to pursue the collective good. First, being beholden to the UN budget in many cases means being beholden to a specific UN agency, which is no guarantee of farsightedness. Second, secretariats cannot hope to go further than their more advanced members. Third, being financially beholden to states does not mean that secretariats are dependent on them for all the resources they need. Multiple dependencies can create manoeuvering room.

Status Secretariats vary considerably in terms of their administrative relationship with a host organization. This relationship has been a significant source of tension in the case of the CBD. The climate change and desertification secretariats are directly attached to the UN Secretariat in New York and thus enjoy significant autonomy under the direct authority of the Secretary General.[9] On the basis of Art. 24 of the CBD, however, COP-1 designated UNEP as the administrator of the SCBD, which was subsequently located in Montreal. After difficult negotiations, the two organizations concluded a memorandum of understanding in 1998 designed to clarify their relationship and respective responsibilities.[10] UNEP's Executive Director appoints the SCBD's Executive Secretary *upon recommendation* of the COP's bureau. Although the Convention has its own budget approved by COP and made up of contributions by the Parties, "[T]he financial and common support services of the CBD Secretariat will be provided by UNEP, UNON or any other United Nations entity, as appropriate, and as agreed by the Executive Director of UNEP, in full co-operation with the Executive Secretary of the Convention"[11] and the CBD Executive Secretary must have UNEP's approval before proceeding with proposed expenses and personnel appointments. Regarding personnel, this agreement reaffirms the involvement of the COP bureau in the selection, level, terms of appointment, and appraisal of the Executive Secretary and the need for UNEP to fully consult the Secretary on all appointments, and it specifies the procedures governing staff appointment. Further, it seeks to limit UNEP's potential policy influence through the control of expenses by exempting the Secretariat from the requirement to submit cost plans and annual substantive and programme performance reports to UNEP.

The relationships of several environmental convention secretariats with UNEP acting as their "host" have often been quite conflictual, and this experience later informed subsequent models.[12] In practice, tensions were high between the SCBD and UNEP until the agreement reached in 1998 and a new executive secretary, who came from Nairobi's biodiversity office, took over in 1999.[13] These tensions cannot be ascribed solely to personalities, however; they are also structural and institutional.

The SCBD could argue that the two organizations represent different entities. States that can be Parties to the Convention but are not members of the UN or are critical of UNEP may resent UNEP's attempts to shape SCBD activities and, indirectly, the COP's. UNEP and the SCBD have different mandates: while UNEP promotes environmental awareness throughout the UN system, the SCBD supports the COP's work (and that of its subsidiary bodies) and implements the COP's decisions, which may or may not correspond to the political priorities of UNEP. Moreover, the COP with its 181 Parties (as of December 2001) could argue that it is more representative than UNEP with its Governing Council limited to 58 members (although its formal membership includes all UN members). Further, the CBD's three goals – conservation, sustainable use, and benefit-sharing – make it a true sustainable development convention, not just an environmental one. Indeed, it is the first agreement to link the two explicitly through benefit-sharing. Its mandate is therefore much broader than UNEP's. Although in its relationship with the SCBD, UNEP's responsibility is administrative, this role should not spill over into policy guidance. And too often the line is unclear or has been crossed (as with appointments). Finally, this lack of autonomy may put the SCBD at a disadvantage vis-à-vis other global sustainable development conventions since UNEP is eager to make sure that nothing the SCBD does should undermine UNEP's already embattled status or its planned activities.

So the SCBD argued for a larger mandate and autonomy as well as a co-ordinating role in order to fulfil an earlier vision of becoming the executive arm of an "umbrella regime". The immediate impact was paralysis (for example, regarding appointments and policy initiatives), working at cross purposes with governments, poor communications between the SCBD and governments, and difficulties in reaching agreements with other IGOs.

In the tug of war between the two organizations, the challenge is how to pool administrative capacities so as to promote procedural coherence and avoid wasting resources, while at the same time preventing the host organization from trying to influence policy. In this regard, Parties did not necessarily lean toward one or the other. Ostensibly, their preoccupation lay with effective management. They did not want to build up either UNEP or the Secretariat at their own expense. Indeed, in the last stages of the negotiation of the CBD, discussions over the relative role of COP versus UNEP were prominent. The emphasis given to COP reflects the Parties' misgivings toward UNEP's Executive Director and toward giving UNEP a large controlling role; it was also an attempt to assert control over the direction of the CBD. Thus, although UNEP managed to have one of its career officers appointed Executive Secretary of the Convention, this occurred after the Parties, through the COP's bureau, had asserted their role in the appointment of the executive secretary.

Location Location also greatly affects the relationship of a secretariat to its host organization. Obviously, it is easier for the host organization to prevent the secretariat from acquiring much autonomy if the latter is located in the same building and administratively dependent on it (as is ozone in UNEP and the World Heritage Convention in UNESCO). Other secretariats, on the other hand, are located away from UNEP headquarters: the Ozone Multilateral Fund and the SCBD in Montreal, CITES in Geneva, and the Convention on Migratory Species in Bonn. Locating secretariats away from their host organization is becoming more common. One material reason stems from the bidding competition among cities and governments to host them. Another factor is the desire on the part of some governments to prevent the secretariat from being captured by its host, even though the host organization usually provides the administrative resources the secretariat needs. For example, the COP of the United Nations Convention to Combat Desertification (UNCCD) decided that in order to ensure its administrative and financial autonomy, the secretariat should not be linked to a particular UN structure or programme.[14]

What Role for the Secretariat?

Environmental conventions (be they limited or global in scope) specify the mandate of the secretariat they establish. This mandate is subject to change by the COP. Some secretariats are restricted to servicing the COP; others have a broader responsibility for overseeing and promoting the implementation of the convention. Their domain of activities can also be limited (e.g. protecting the ozone layer or certain habitats) or touch on many different and sensitive areas (desertification, biodiversity).

Secretariats are small, which limits their reach and ambitions. Yet they can fulfil a variety of functions depending on the nature of the issue, the provisions contained in the treaty, and the practices that have evolved. These functions are very much an object of current debate among Parties for they are directly related to the balance of power between the secretariat and the COP. Whereas the desertification secretariat has claimed extensive responsibilities, the biodiversity secretariat is still attempting to define a role commensurate with the scope of the convention.

Secretariats do not have direct regulatory or decision-making powers. All share general core tasks, such as arranging and servicing the COP and meetings of subsidiary bodies, preparing reports on the implementation of the convention, co-ordinating with relevant IGOs and NGOs, and compiling and analysing relevant information on the request of Parties (Sandford, 1994). Additional tasks vary considerably depending on specific treaty provisions, the mandates given by the COP, or the existence of specific regulatory protocols (see Box 4.1).

Box 4.1 The Formal Mandates and Functions of the SCBD

Basis: Article 24

- To arrange for and service meetings of the COP.
- To perform the functions assigned to it by any protocol.
- To prepare reports on the execution of its functions under the convention and present them to the COP.
- To co-ordinate with other relevant international bodies; in particular to enter into such administrative and contractual arrangements as may be required for the effective discharge of its functions.
- To perform such other functions as may be determined by the COP.

Some observers have maintained that secretariats should be strong and independent, since effective implementation oversight implies the capacity for independent verification and data gathering, implementation assessment, capacity-building, financial transfers, and regime adaptation and development (Young and von Moltke, 1995). However, these tasks remain highly controversial. Others would logically entrust secretariats with the collection and appraisal of scientific and technical information. This implies a diversification of sources of information and can lead to the legitimization of particular ideas and practices (Obser, 1999).

The expansion of the role of the secretariat depends in large part on Parties' confidence in its administration, competence, and fairness. States also want to avoid being presented with advice that reflect biased perspectives and *faits accomplis*, and they want to maintain control of the process. This implies a strong and active SBSTTA and COP. Only then could the secretariat be given a mandate that would expand to the co-ordination or direct provision of training and assessment, monitoring implementation of the convention (such as by preparing country studies), or draft syntheses of current knowledge and issues for the information of the SBSTTA.

Unlike the Secretariat of the UNCCD (SCCD) which has proposed a set of tasks that would make it central to a co-ordinated system of governance on desertification matters and that may transform it into a quasi-operational organization, the SCBD's overt ambitions remain modest. No doubt this is due to its particular relationship with UNEP. But given the range of the CBD (the "domain" of which covers much more ground than that of any other environmental convention), states would also be likely to oppose such claims (as they have the SCCD's). OECD countries in particular are concerned about limiting a drift toward an operational role that would duplicate the activities and missions of existing bodies. They also fear a gradual transfer of power from the COP to the Secretariat which, in their eyes, must remain a service organization, facilitate the exchange of information, and promote concerted action and awareness. They feel that it should not be an independent source of expertise entrusted with synthesizing available knowledge or promoting a specific methodology. States have even attempted to limit the Secretariat's modest attempts to use informal expert and liaison groups to advise it and help in drafting background documents (see below).

The scientific subsidiary body, on the other hand, provides a way to deliver on this function, and states have been eager to have the SBSTTA perform this role. Again, this evolution will depend on the nature of the issue and of the existing issue-governance structure. It may be much easier to develop this role for a new issue as long as no national or international institution holds a competing claim on the role. It will prove much more difficult if governments already rely on well-established institutions as sources of expertise and operational programmes. Further, some issue areas lend themselves easily to the emergence of indicators and the construction of "objective" knowledge, others far less so, which then makes this knowledge more politically sensitive.

"Scientific information," Young and von Moltke (1995) remind us, "is rarely available in a form that lends itself directly to policy application. The questions asked by policy makers and scientists are rarely identical. Thus, the interpretation of often incomplete, contradictory or indeterminate scientific information is a critical task, but it is necessarily coloured by the culture of both science and policy. No internationally agreed rules exist for the conduct of science assessment". Therefore, since countries are reluctant to entrust the assessment function to independent scientific bodies,[15] Young and von Moltke would see secretariats as playing "a critical function in organizing the science assessment by framing questions, by selecting participants and by providing secretariat services to a process that is fundamentally indeterminate".

Yet in so doing a secretariat may raise suspicions that it is promoting the preferences of one particular group or its own. The alternative to building in-house expertise is to develop more proactive subsidiary scientific bodies serviced by the secretariat, that is, build the convention governance system, not the convention secretariat. Of course, this assumes that these bodies are staffed by experts, whereas most participants are often *de facto* dependent on a few delegations that possess the expertise. But if conventions develop successful clearing-house mechanisms and technical task forces, the problem of dependence could be circumvented. Moreover, contracting out expert knowledge, provided the sources are diversified, may help avoid the intellectual sclerosis that accompanies the build-up of in-house expertise. Pursuant to Article 25 of the UNCCD, the subsidiary scientific bodies could themselves help set up expert networks and commissions with the aim of asserting the credibility of the information provided by the secretariat. We can now turn to the SBSTTA and examine its prospects in that regard.

The Role of the SBSTTA

Article 25 of the Convention establishes the Subsidiary Body on Scientific, Technical and Technological Advice as an open-ended intergovernmental scientific advisory body for the Conference of the Parties. Its functions are summarized in Box 4.2.

Box 4.2 The mandate of the CBD-SBSTTA

Basis: Article 25

- Advise the COP and its other subsidiary bodies on the implementation of the Convention.
- Open to participation by all Parties and multidisciplinary.
- Composed of government representatives "competent in the relevant field of expertise".

Mandate

- Provide scientific and technical assessments of the status of biological diversity.
- Prepare scientific and technical assessments of the effects of types of measures taken in accordance with the provisions of this Convention.
- Identify innovative, efficient, and state-of-the-art technologies and know-how relating to the conservation and sustainable use of biological diversity and advise on the ways and means of promoting development and/or transferring such technologies.
- Provide advice on scientific programmes and international co-operation in research and development related to conservation and sustainable use of biological diversity.
- Respond to scientific, technical, technological, and methodological questions that the Conference of the Parties and its subsidiary bodies may put to the body.

The SBSTTA is asked to perform three functions that elsewhere (as in the case of climate change) are performed by different organizations: advice (the responsibility of the Subsidiary Body for Scientific and Technical Advice (SBSTA) in the United Nations Framework Convention on Climate Change (UNFCCC), assessment (the Intergovernmental Panel on Climate Change (IPCC) in the UNFCCC), and the development of methodologies (more the responsibility of countries in the UNFCCC)). Carrying out this very broad mandate is made more complex by the nature of the issue area and the diverse objectives of the Convention.

No wonder SBSTTA faces great challenges in the discharge of its duties, some of which the Parties have identified and are attempting to overcome. Indeed, it would hardly be an exaggeration to assert that the SBSTTA faces an identity crisis. In 1998 the COP asserted that it was "aware of the difficulties experienced in the operations of the Convention and in achieving its full and effective implementation".[16] And, although the COP also underscored "the need for the Subsidiary Body on Scientific, Technical and Technological Advice to focus on scientific, technical, and technological aspects of the Convention in accordance with its Article 25,"[17] the most important challenge remains defining the proper role of science in the Convention.

According to the Secretariat, "SBSTTA has an important role to play in bridging the gap between the scientific community and policy makers,"[18] in particular through the co-operative links it should set up with the scientific community within or outside IGOs. Although some countries thought that the text of the Convention undervalued the essential role of a scientific approach to biodiversity conservation, "It is generally recognized that the Subsidiary Body on Scientific, Technical and Technological Advice (SBSTTA) has an advisory role as opposed to being a purely scientific body. Accordingly, there was a need to ensure structured scientific input into SBSTTA either through arrangements similar to those of the Intergovernmental Panel on Climate Change (IPCC) or through a number of small issue-based panels, which should include members of the academic and business communities".[19]

This tension over the proper role of SBSTTA, present since its inception, reflects different conceptions of the priorities of the CBD. Some states favouring the conservation aspect of the CBD (e.g. France) would like a strong scientific SBSTTA to support all regime activities; others would like it to evolve into a kind of IPCC for biodiversity. Indeed, for the Secretariat and several Parties, "Experience with other international environmental issues shows that international action has not been forthcoming until a certain level of consensus has been achieved regarding the underlying scientific knowledge".[20] Thus, there would be a need to strengthen the SBSTTA's assessment function and build consensus before defining guidelines.

Most delegates, however, recognize that at best, the SBSTTA can only hope to help translate scientific knowledge into acceptable political options. A former president of the SBSTTA, Cristiàn Samper, saw it as "a bridge between the scientific community and the decision-maker".[21] Its function should not be to create a scientific consensus. The "need" for a scientific consensus is even questioned by some, such as Susskind (1994, p. 13) who believes that the role of the subsidiary bodies should be to present the whole gamut of available research around a particular topic rather than attempting to solve expert disagreements. However, one could also define that role as one of building a political consensus on the definition of the problem and on the range of available solutions.

Naturally, this definition would not close the debate. Should the SBSTTA debate policy or simply present policy options? Cristiàn Samper, in the opening speech of SBSTTA-5, said it would be better to "avoid entering in policy debate; instead we should give options which will allow policy decisions".[22] Should the SBSTTA also encourage and synthesize available knowledge in order to define options for the COP? According to Decision I/7[23] of the COP, the SBSTTA must only consider questions put to it by the COP, which would seem to deny it the role of initiating scientific assessments.

The COP also specified that although the SBSTTA should consider the financial implications of its recommendations, it should not make financial recommendations to the COP unless so requested.[24] Still, many delegations regularly overlook that condition, which testifies to the ambient confusion. Likewise, other delegations, generally from the North, eager to limit the range of topics under consideration, have from time to time pointed out that more competent fora exist for discussion of particular topics or courses of actions.

This ambiguity reflects and is accentuated by the composition of the body. Although Article 25 of the CBD states that the SBSTTA "shall comprise government representatives competent in the relevant field of expertise," in practice many delegates from developing countries are not specialists but the representatives who attend COP meetings; other delegations possess little scientific expertise. Scientists within and outside the delegations are fond of deploring the resulting lack of in-depth discussion of scientific issues.[25] The absence of scientists from developing countries in what are largely political delegations may make it more difficult to communicate the scientific concerns of other delegations and may impede productive discussions. On the other hand, when lack of resources limit their delegations to one or two members, governments prefer sending political representatives rather than experts. Moreover, such expertise may be limited and mostly university-based rather than government-based. These criticisms also conveniently overlook that discussions often tend to take the form of solutions in search of problems when it is precisely the definition of the problem that needs to be discussed. Many issues and concepts under discussion have no clear scientific basis but much clearer political overtones. For example, although the Convention calls for an ecosystem approach, its operationalization has been difficult because it also includes human beings and presupposes a level of scientific knowledge that is in fact absent. Likewise, the development of biodiversity indicators, although potentially extremely useful, faces considerable political obstacles that scientists alone cannot hope to solve, such as the origin of these indicators (western or local knowledge?) or the use of such indicators (which countries will become winners and losers and thus gain a different access to external funds?). Thus, the choice of indicators should be the product of a dialogue between decision-makers and scientists. Finally, since many delegates will be those responsible for following up on the scientific and technical decisions, whether or not they have any scientific basis, excluding them from such fora would seem shortsighted. Be that as it may, charges that the SBSTTA is too much like a mini-COP have prompted the COP to re-examine the SBSTTA's operations so as to improve its efficiency.

The SBSTTA has experienced difficulties in three other important respects. One has to do with poor communication between the COP and the SBSTTA and especially between their bureaux. The SBSTTA has often complained about lack of clarity in the type of advice the COP is expected, and the COP has returned the compliment.[26] One of the most important decisions of COP-4 was to adopt thematic work programmes (Decision IV/1), including cross-cutting issues (such as the Global Taxonomic Initiative, alien species, indicators, and the ecosystem approach). This has facilitated the work of the SBSTTA, which needs some guidelines in order to organize its scientific advisory bodies. Furthermore, beginning in 1999, the SBSTTA organized joint bureau meetings with the COP and adopted staggered bureau member terms to secure some continuity.

A second difficulty, related to the debate over the political versus the scientific function of the SBSTTA, has been the sheer size of the workload. This workload stemmed both from the large scope of the Convention (and constituencies competing for a place on the agenda) and the architecture of the regime, that is, the lack of a subsidiary body for implementation (see below). This situation led to an extensive agenda and precluded in-depth analysis of each item; it threatened to turn the SBSTTA into a "mini-COP" and prevented the development of communication among participants (state and non-state) which is a core function of a scientific body (see below). Some of these problems were dealt with through the creation of other subsidiary bodies, such as the AWGTK and the Expert Panel on Access and Benefit-Sharing. Further, starting with SBSTTA-6 (March 2001), the agenda of the meeting was considerably reduced in the hope that it would be better able to fulfil its role of identifying the scientific basis of policy options. For example, SBSTTA-6 was devoted mainly to the issue of alien invasive species, while SBSTTA-7 (November 2001) focused on forests.[27]

A third handicap stems from a lack of collaboration among the scientific bodies of the global sustainable development conventions. This factor is crucial because there is no external independent body of experts on the issues covered by the CBD, unlike the IPCC in the case of the UNFCCC's SBSTA. In the absence of such collaboration, states and large NGOs become the source of scientific expertise. Given the proliferation of national initiatives and programmes of works by IGOs, it is crucial for the SBSTTA not only to avoid duplicating what is being done elsewhere but above all to make sense of these initiatives in light of the goals of the regime. This means performing a "watch" as well as co-operating directly with these bodies.

But the SBSTTA has been reluctant to use or endorse the outputs of biodiversity-relevant work developed outside the auspices of the CBD.[28] No mechanism exists to channel such information and encourage its use. For example, the Global Biodiversity Assessment has not been used by SBSTTA in any systematic manner; conversely the SBSTTA needs to be able to ensure that this and future assessments generate useful knowledge for the implementation of the CBD.

The process of developing closer co-operation with other scientific bodies (the Scientific and Technical Advisory Panel, SBSTA, Science and Technological Committee, DIVERSITAS, the World Conservation Union) has been slow. Such co-operation has rested largely on the activism of the chairman and bureau of the SBSTTA rather than on formal institutional ties, and it remains limited despite the growing number of co-operation agreements signed with other IGOs.

As states have pointed out, "The Subsidiary Body has experienced difficulties in developing into a truly scientific and technical advisory body for the Conference of the Parties and in fully realizing its role".[29] Beyond the role of science and scientists, many difficulties are rooted in issues never resolved since the negotiation of the Convention. For example, should the CBD aspire to become a true "umbrella" regime (an interpretation favoured by Norway and developing countries), only one among a set of actors sharing the biodiversity domain (which influences the nature of co-operation with other bodies), or one that is relegated to residual matters (an option sometimes voiced by France and Canada)?

Difficulties also stem from the reluctance of the COP to allow the SBSTTA some autonomy, that is, its eagerness not to let a scientific body make binding decisions or present the COP with *faits accomplis* in terms of agenda-setting. Thus the challenge to the political role of the SBSTTA comes from two directions: from scientists who would like to see greater scientific expertise and more autonomy, and from those eager to limit the role of science to giving options – not recommendations – and who defend the primacy of the COP in making decisions for the regime (Group of 77). At the same time, a potential challenge to the SBSTTA's scientific role comes from the SCBD.

This competition among the various organs of the regime is illustrated by the organization of scientific advice. Several types of advisory groups have been established. Although they are designed to increase the knowledge base for decisions (i.e. scientific and social considerations), they may also perpetuate divisions and competition among units of the governance system. Currently, the Convention allows for (i) liaison groups established by the secretariat to assist it in preparing background documentation and facilitating co-operation with other bodies, (ii) ad hoc technical groups established by the SBSTTA (composed of people named by Parties and relevant groups and chosen by the SBSTTA bureau), and (iii) ad hoc working groups (such as the open-ended one on 8j) and panels of experts established to assist the COP.

To overcome the lack of in-house expertise, help prepare documentation for SBSTTA meetings, and liaise with international initiatives (such as Diversitas), the SCBD has set up informal liaison groups (composed of experts chosen by the SCBD) to advise, review, and prepare background papers.[30] For example, liaison groups have been established on indicators, on the ecosystem approach, on agrobiodiversity, and on drylands. These groups have also *de facto* been the main avenue for co-operation with relevant organizations,[31] which means that this process has been outside the control and authority of the SBSTTA or the COP.

States have expressed strong concerns about the role of these liaison groups whose composition is unknown, whose outlook may not reflect the Parties', and who may have considerable influence in shaping the agenda and subsequent debates. For example, the recommendations of the liaison group on indicators of biological diversity, which served as the basis for Recommendation III/5 of the SBSTTA (which in turn led to Decision IV/1 of the COP) "drew largely from the results of the eighth meeting of the Global Biodiversity Forum," a vehicle through which NGOs (especially the IUCN) seek to channel their concerns and shape the agenda.

Parties, therefore, have called for greater transparency regarding the composition and mandate of these groups, for the groups to be explicitly approved by the SBSTTA, and for their formation to follow a uniform methodology.[32] As a result, the COP decided in 1998 that such groups should be established in consultation with the chairman of the SBSTTA and the SBSTTA bureau.[33] It also decided to create ad hoc technical expert panels to fulfil much of the scientific functions that the SBSTTA cannot fulfil, notably the identification of knowledge gaps and the development of consensual knowledge. And third, it changed the *modus operandi* of the SBSTTA by promoting the use of rosters of experts to be named by Parties, notably on marine and coastal, forest, agricultural, and inland water biodiversity. These rosters will be "the basis through which other bodies and processes can apply their expertise and knowledge to the Convention processes and the work of SBSTTA".[34]

Instead of liaison groups, COP-5 (2000) created four ad hoc technical expert groups to advise the SBSTTA in the fields of marine and coastal protected areas, forest biological diversity, mariculture and biodiversity of dry and sub-humid lands. These groups were to use the resources and expertise of national, regional, and international organizations, of NGOs, and of the scientific community. Their membership would be regionally and gender balanced,[35] although the best available technical expertise would be the most important criterion.[36] In practice, the operation of these groups is dependent on special offers of financial support from Parties and organizations, which meant that a year after the decision to create them, only the first two were in operation.

If the SBSTTA's scientific and advisory role is uncertain and its network function embryonic and ill-defined, what is it good for? One remarkable evolution, which can be seen in other settings as well, is its contribution to facilitating links between NGOs/civil society and national delegates, to planning and publicizing international projects, to disseminating research and information outside official channels, to exploring future areas of co-operation and concerns, and to raising the awareness of delegates: in short to network-building.

Indeed, the SBSTTA's true value may lie in socializing participants in the aims, principles, and dimensions of the regime. It enables delegates to become more familiar with the process and operation of the regime and to participate in its governance. It helps to disseminate new norms and new knowledge through parallel sessions. And it legitimizes scientific parameters of decision-making and allows for a better identification of the political dimensions of the scientific discourse. In the end, the SBSTTA's functions become that of raising awareness, especially among delegates, and providing an institutional and international context for the pursuit of countries' specific scientific initiatives (e.g. on corals reefs or taxonomy).

The Nature of the System of Implementation Review (SIR)

As discussed in chapter 3, there is no effectiveness without implementation and no implementation without institutions to promote it. This is especially important with regimes that cannot rely on coercive sanctions to promote behavioural change. Implementation must foster transparency about the evolution of the issue and the behaviour of Parties, help Parties translate obligations into policies and institutions, facilitate assessment of individual and collective performance, promote individual and organizational learning, and help mobilize the resources needed for behavioural change. Thus, monitoring the extent to which the institution is furthering these objectives and how regime or national performance could be improved becomes a significant aspect of the operation of the regime. Hence the interest in what Victor, Raustiala and Skolnikoff (1998, p. 16) have dubbed "Systems of Implementation Review" (SIR) that is, the "rules and procedures by which the Parties to international agreements (as well as interest groups, administrative bodies, and the like) exchange data, share information on implementation, monitor activities, assess the adequacy of existing commitments, and handle problems of poor implementation".

The SIR of the CBD has three basic elements: national reports, the Clearing-house Mechanism (CHM), and the development of a strategic plan, to which we should add a putative fourth, the creation of a subsidiary body. The issue of the CHM is discussed at length in chapter 5 in this volume. National reports, which are traditional devices to gauge the extent to which Parties' behaviour accords with the objectives of the convention, initially suffered the ills common in many conventions: incomplete national data, late filings, and inconsistent formats, which made both comparisons and lesson-drawing difficult. In 2001 the SBSTTA adopted a common format that may help alleviate some of these problems. Indeed, national reports should be dynamic instruments of the implementation of the CBD, which starts with the development of a common format and with review procedures that will enable learning on the part of Parties and stakeholders.

The idea of a strategic plan was recommended by SBSTTA-4 and adopted in 2000 at COP-5 (Decision V/20). It would respond to several concerns: (i) the need to mobilize efforts behind the Convention's three objectives, notably access and benefit-sharing (ABS); (ii) given the complexity of the Convention and the risk of internal fragmentation and external encroachments of the CBD on other existing accords, the need to streamline and co-ordinate the organization of the work of the COP and its subsidiary bodies; (iii) ensuring that the implementation of COP and SBSTTA decisions will be reviewed within the CGS and at regional and national levels; and (iv) the need to develop a coherent set of instruments that will support the implementation of national strategies and action plans.

In its early conception, the strategic plan read much like the organization of the work of the CGS with the aim of supporting and implementing its ongoing activities (thematic and multisectoral activities), mobilizing existing and additional resources, furthering participation in the regime, co-operating with other actors (IGOs, scientific bodies), increasing regime visibility, and implementing its commitments under all articles of the Convention as well as the Cartagena Protocol on Biosafety. Elaborated by the Secretariat in collaboration with Parties during 2001, the strategic plan for the implementation of the CBD was formally adopted at COP-6 in April 2002 (UNEP/CBD/WS-StratPlan/4).

It remains unclear whether the scope of the strategic plan will be largely limited to the operationalization and implementation of the work programme of the COP and SBSTTA or whether it will broaden to include activities at the national level and the development of a broader SIR. Indeed, beyond the idea of operationalizing ongoing initiatives, Parties have emphasized that the primary objective of the strategy should be to support and facilitate national implementation through the national action plans and strategies and on the basis of the needs identified in those documents. Others have insisted on the non-coercive and flexible character of such a strategy, the aim being not to evaluate national accomplishments but to promote a collective undertaking.

What the plan does not contemplate is the creation of a new subsidiary body for implementation. In other fora (e.g. UNCCD), the G-77/China were particularly keen on the creation of a subsidiary body for implementation, whereas developed countries were reluctant to support the creation of new bodies. Proponents of a subsidiary body for implementation point to it as a remedy for several problems: (i) the workload of the SBSTTA, which would then find itself better able to focus on its core scientific mandate; (ii) the need to assess the extent to which Parties are adopting measures and policies in accordance with the objectives of the agreement; (iii) the need to mobilize the transfer of resources from industrialized to industrializing countries, particularly biodiversity-rich ones; (iv) the need to retain political control of the assessment process. Critics, however, fear (i) the costs associated with the creation of a new body; (ii) that it would be the first step toward the creation of a compliance mechanism: developing countries fearing sovereignty encroachments and developed countries fearing mandatory transfers of financial, technological, or intellectual resources. The critics also argue that the CBD is much more complex than other global environmental treaties (notably UNFCCC and UNCCD) and need not replicate their arrangements.

The idea of structural changes (implementation body or open-ended working group) was raised but did not garner significant support at the 1999 first Intersessional Meeting on the Operation of the Convention, either from developed countries, developing countries, or even NGOs. But it may surface again. Brazil and Colombia, among other developing countries, supported it at COP-5. The establishment of such a mechanism might be feasible provided it is seen not as a compliance body (with the power to sanction laggard countries) but as a body that promotes transparency, identifies obstacles to implementation, and mobilizes non-coercive means to overcome them. It might evolve on the model of the UNCCD where initial reluctance gradually gave way to cautious endorsement through, as a first step, the creation of an ad hoc inter-sessions expert committee reporting to the COP and charged with reviewing and discussing national reports and national plans (Talafré, 2001). A link with disbursements by the financial mechanism would promote both the need for such a body (given that neither the COP nor the SBSTTA have the time for such review unless it is perfunctory) and the willingness of Parties to submit their own national reports and plans for review.

Conclusion

This chapter has sought to identify some hurdles that need be overcome if the CBD-CGS is to become an effective institutional structure for the regime. The CBD regime is young, dynamic, and complex. What must happen for the CBD-CGS to fulfil its potential as an efficient alternative to centralized modes of governance? Four strands have been identified regarding where the CBD regime should be headed:[37]

- Institutionalists favour establishing more subsidiary organs, such as an implementation committee and one focusing on traditional knowledge and benefit-sharing issues. As mentioned above, the creation of a separate implementation body was rejected in 1999, but the COP in 1998 opted for an ad hoc working group on Article 8 (j) which gained the status of a subsidiary body, rather than starting negotiations on a new protocol.
- Scientists have advocated increasing the role of scientific advice and strengthening the SBSTTA. In its Decision IV/16 (1998), the COP adopted

several measures designed to address some of the problems outlined above that are in line with this perspective.

- Some countries, more interested in specific issues, favour a greater focus on programmes and operations and on the development of co-ordinated and focused actions. This approach has been evident in the development of several "initiatives" such as on coral reefs and taxonomy.
- Finally, functionalists would like to see a strong secretariat able to promote the regime, assess its implementation, and co-ordinate UN activities in this area.

Strengthening the entire CGS, however, tends to be overlooked. Yet the greater legitimacy of CGSs makes them an attractive form of international environmental governance, illustrating how states can adapt to the complexity and turbulence of the international system. As the Commission on Global Governance (1995, p. 66) reminds us "institutions that lack legitimacy are seldom effective over the long run". Moreover, CGSs present potentially significant advantages over traditional international organizations. First, CGSs are mission oriented. Second, as information webmasters, they can contribute to developing networks that link a variety of actors. Third, they are able to mediate between the global and the local level. Finally, they are displaying (or have the potential to display) more adaptability and learning capacities than larger traditional IGOs.

These observations are in line with the characteristics of successful organizations that Chayes and Chayes (1995, p. 284) have identified. They stress combining expert management and staff with extensive Party involvement at a high level. This is what they advocate for new organizations, but the size of such secretariats (a staff of hundreds if not thousands) greatly exceeds what would be politically conceivable. Developing the CGS rather than the secretariat as such ensures that expertise is not coopted in favour of specific public or private interests and promotes extensive involvement not only by the Parties but also by civil society.

The CBD regime relies on states assuming leadership in areas in which they are particularly interested, ranging from knowledge construction to building political coalitions behind specific agenda items and facilitating implementation. The danger is not that a regime will move with the slowest state but that it will move only in the areas where key states are willing to invest resources. This danger is exacerbated by the tendency to set up special funds for pet policies. The role of the Secretariat may in part lie in guarding against the dissonance of such a menu-based approach. Playing this role effectively, however, requires strengthening its legitimacy and overcoming some of the constraints outlined above.

Another difficulty that the CBD-CGS faces is intra-CGS competition, between the COP and the SBSTTA or between the Secretariat and the other bodies. A weak secretariat may not make for a strong CGS, but a strong one relative to the CGS may weaken the effectiveness of the regime. For example, a strong secretariat such as the SCCD (desertification) which wants to drive the scientific agenda, implies a significant loss of influence for the UNCCD's Committee on Science and Technology.

The North-South split also affects the evolution of the CGS. Northern countries are reasonably united in their desire to limit the Secretariat to its service role and the SBSTTA to its scientific functions, but developing countries are more divided. On the one hand, they favour strong secretariats that will help them pursue their agenda if they are headed by influential citizens from the South viewed as more responsive to their concerns. On the other hand, they also insist on the supremacy of the COP over other bodies. CGSs may represent better vehicles for democratizing international governance by providing more equal access or greater availability of political influence within the process of deliberation and decision-making (Bohman, 1999). In that context, Southern countries are better able to communicate their interests and needs. Given the inherent constraints that the Secretariat faces, the CGS option may be more promising.

Finally, other factors affecting goal attainment include the degree of international consensus on CBD priorities, the willingness of certain countries to assume leadership roles, the existence of other institutional structures where Parties can go "forum shopping," uneven understanding of the Convention and implementation bottle-necks at the national level, lack of local knowledge of biodiversity, and the clearly political character of biodiversity issues. These hurdles affect the regime and by extension the convention governance system. Building up that system, including but not limited to the Secretariat, may prove a fruitful way to overcome the hurdles and establish the prerequisites for an effective biodiversity regime.

Notes

[1] Naturally, this does not preclude examining the operation, role, and impact of secretariats as units of such systems.

[2] The question, however, remains open as to the evolution of the three global secretariats on climate change, desertification, and biodiversity.

[3] Chayes and Chayes (1995, p. 283) and others have pointed out the suspicion if not outright hostility of many OECD countries toward multi-purpose organizations, fearing inefficiencies and a loss of control over the agenda and the nature of the commitments undertaken. These observers tend to deplore the weaknesses of secretariats, in terms of resources, that would prevent them from doing much in terms of policy initiative; of course, this is precisely what states want.

[4] This article deals with the special role of indigenous and local communities in furthering the conservation and sustainable use of biological diversity and with the equitable sharing of the benefits arising from the utilization of their knowledge, innovations, and practices.

[5] On dispute resolution by the COP, see Lang (1992).

[6] This could be due to several reasons, one of which is the non-controversial aspect of the convention implementation, or to the lack of prospect that the reach of the convention will be expanded.

[7] See Annexes for detailed numbers.

[8] See Annexes. This is well short of the $25 million USD the Secretariat was requesting for the same period (UNEP/CBD/COP/5/18).

[9] Special arrangement gives those secretariats quasi-independent status, although administratively, they may use UNEP resources.

[10] Administrative Arrangement between the United Nations Environment Programme (UNEP) and the Secretariat of the Convention on Biological Diversity (CBD), signed 3 April 1998 (UNEP/CBD/COP/4/24).

[11] UNON is the UN office in Nairobi (headed by UNEP's Executive Director), *Ibidem*, note 41, par. 22.

[12] According to some accounts, the experience of the SCBD induced Parties to link the SCCD directly to the UN Secretariat in New York rather than to UNEP or FAO (interviews, April 1999).

[13] In Decision III/23, the COP invited the Executive Director of UNEP and the Executive Secretary of the Convention to clarify their respective roles and responsibilities. The agreement governing the administrative arrangements between UNEP and the Secretariat was subsequently endorsed at COP-4 (Decision IV/17).

[14] Report of the Conference of the Parties on its First Session, held in Rome from 29 September to 10 October 1997, ICCD/COP/1/11/Add.1, Decision I/3, par. 4-5.

[15] As evidenced by the hesitation to use the International Council of Scientific Unions and its related bodies for this purpose, the creation of the Intergovernmental Panel on Climate Change and the Scientific and Technical Advisory Panel (STAP) of the Global Environment Facility (see Young and von Moltke, *International Secretariats*).

[16] Preamble of Decision IV/16 (UNEP/CBD/COP/4/27:132).

[17] *Ibidem.*

[18] CBD (1999), *Report on Co-operation with Other Bodies. Report of the Executive Secretary* (18 March), p. 1 (UNEP/CBD/SBSTTA/4/2).

[19] *Review of the Operations of the Convention on Biological Diversity*, London Workshop, 5-7 January 1998, "Chairman's Conclusions".

[20] UNEP/CBD/COP/4/14, par. 37, p. 14.

[21] Opening remarks to SBSTTA-5, 31 January 2000.

[22] Opening speech by Cristián Samper, president of SBSTTA, fifth meeting of SBSTTA, 31 January 2000, Montreal, p. 2.

[23] See also UNEP/CBD/COP/1/17, p. 63.

[24] Decision IV/16(13): "Decides that, while the Subsidiary Body on Scientific, Technical and Technological Advice should consider the financial implications of its proposals, its recommendations will only include advice to the Conference of the Parties regarding financial matters, including guidance to the financial mechanism, when the Conference of the Parties has so requested".

[25] In this regard, it is useful to keep in mind that SBSTTA was originally conceived as a multidisciplinary body composed of experts from the social as well as the natural and physical sciences. (Thanks to D. M. McGraw for this point.)

[26] See UNEP/CBD/COP/4/14; UNEP/CBD/ISOC/2; and Decision IV/16(14).

[27] This decision, which identified key issues to be considered at SBSTTA-5, 6, and 7, was made at the 1998 Bratislava COP (Decision IV/16, Annex II). In fact it was reduced even further than initially planned. Decision IV/16, for example, had identified three key agenda items for SBSTTA-9 held in March 2001 (forest ecosystems, alien species, and benefit-sharing); in fact, alien invasive species was the main agenda item, and forest ecosystems were moved to SBSTTA-7 (November 2001).

[28] This may be due to suspicion about the source of that knowledge. For example, about half of the lead authors of IPCC came from the US and UK and fewer than 10 per cent from developing countries (UNEP/CBD/SBSTTA/4/2, p. 17).

[29] UNEP/CBD/COP/4/14, p. 13.

[30] See the *modus operandi* of SBSTTA and UNEP/CBD/COP/4/27, pp. 135-6.

[31] UNEP/CBD/SBSTTA/5/2, p. 5.

[32] UNEP/CBD/SBSTTA/5/L.1/Add.1, p. 3.

[33] COP Decision IV/16.

[34] CBD. (1999), *Report on Co-operation with other bodies* (18 March), p. 14 (UNEP/CBD/SBSTTA/4/2).

[35] UNEP/CBD/SBSTTA/5/L.1/Add.1, p. 4.

[36] UNEP/CBD/COP/4/14, p. 16.

[37] This typology was first suggested by Calestous Juma.

Chapter 5

The Clearing-House Mechanism: An Effective Tool for Implementing the Convention on Biological Diversity?

Geneviève Reed

Introduction

In the current international context, the political decision-making process involves a growing number of actors: governments, industries, nongovernmental organizations (NGOs), intergovernmental organizations (IGOs), and local and aboriginal communities. Because of this multiplicity of actors and the complexity of problems and issues related to the sustainable use of biological diversity, there is an increasing need for political, organizational, operational, scientific, and technical information (Busby, 1997). The development of new information and communications technology (NICT) has led to the creation of several specialized networks to distribute this information.[1] Thus, a growing number of emerging international regimes are developing information exchange mechanisms to improve the effectiveness and implementation of the commitments of the signatory nations.

In this context, the Conference of the Parties of the Convention on Biological Diversity (COP) decided at its first meeting, held in 1994, to implement the provisions of Article 18, paragraph 3, of the Convention, calling for the establishment of a Clearing-house Mechanism (CHM) to promote and facilitate technical and scientific co-operation (Decision I/3). Central to achieving the three objectives of the Convention, the CHM was set up at the second meeting of the Conference of the Parties and initially developed through a pilot phase for 1996-1997 (Decision II/3). At the third COP meeting, the delegates decided to extend this pilot phase by one year – until December 1998. In May 2000, at the fifth meeting of the Conference of the Parties, governments completed the evaluation of the CHM pilot phase by endorsing the implementation of a strategic plan and a long-term work plan and establishing priorities for developing the Clearing-house Mechanism.

The evaluation of the Clearing-house Mechanism and the desire to create a new clearing-house mechanism within the framework of the Cartagena Protocol on Biosafety raise numerous questions with regard to its role in implementing the objectives of the Convention and its impact on the behaviour of actors in the regime. How was the Clearing-house Mechanism developed? How does it contribute to the implementation of the Convention on Biological Diversity, and what is its potential impact on the effectiveness of the Convention?

According to Keohane (1984), institutions can change the behaviour of countries by getting them to adopt a broader and more long-term view of their interests, by providing them with new scientific information that clarifies policies in order to attain existing objectives, and by inducing governments to learn new objectives. Familiarity with the objectives of a convention or agreement is essential not only to implementation but also to the review of the adequacy of commitments. It is one of the institutional features needed for effective evaluation of regime implementation and adaptation, in addition to the introduction of a scientific body capable of evaluating the state of knowledge, to the presence of a permanent negotiation forum, and to the existence of procedures for rapid ratification of commitment amendments (Deutz, 1997). What is more, cognitivists argue that the control of knowledge and information is an important part of power and that the dissemination of new ideas and information can give rise to new behavioural models and play an important role in the co-ordination of international policy (Haas, 1992).

Despite the recognized importance of information in international co-operation and multilateral agreement implementation, a majority of the initiatives undertaken within the framework of regime theory have focused on the formation of regimes, their maintenance and their transformation. Although many scholars consider transparency, or information availability, to be essential and one of the factors that determines effectiveness, very little research has been conducted into transparency mechanisms in general or into those of environmental agreements in particular. Theoretical and practical comprehension of the role of transparency remains rudimentary. Most of the research that has been done has concentrated on how transparency can improve the effectiveness of agreements and compliance with obligations under these agreements. The factors that improve a given regime's transparency still need to be clearly defined.

In fact, transparency can act as a learning mechanism, not only for modifying the behaviour of actors but also for modifying it in the way the regime wants it to.[2] The impact of the Clearing-house Mechanism on the behaviour of Convention actors depends on an unequivocal conception of its role and functions, on a shared perception of the role of information in developed and developing countries, and on the level of development of institutional, technical, technological, and scientific capabilities.

This chapter describes and analyses how the CHM operates and explores factors that could compromise its transparency function. The first part deals with the theoretical concepts of effectiveness and transparency. Transparency facilitates compliance with obligations and the regime's effectiveness, as well as improving actors' ability to evaluate these two factors. The next part gives a general overview of the development of the Clearing-house Mechanism. The CHM was created to promote technical and scientific co-operation but was initially developed as a mechanism for information access and exchange on the biological diversity regime. The fact that there are so many different conceptions of the functions of the Clearing-house Mechanism probably represents the greatest obstacle to its implementation. The final part deals with a number of obstacles that must be overcome if the CHM is to contribute effectively to the implementation of the Convention on Biological Diversity and reinforce the preconditions for the effectiveness of the Convention.

Analytical Framework

Regime Effectiveness

As pointed out in chapter 3, more and more studies in international relations place special emphasis on the effectiveness of regimes, especially institutions that attempt to solve global environmental problems. However, the existence of various definitions of the concept of effectiveness still stands in the way of the construction of a sound theory on regimes and their impacts. The following analysis is based on a political definition of effectiveness according to which an effective regime leads to changes in actors' behaviour and interaction models for the purpose of contributing to the management of the targeted problem (Levy, Young and Zürn, 1995; Young, 1992). It is also based on the view that when international regimes operate effectively, they use endogenous factors, rules, procedures, and programmes to change exogenous factors, configuration of interests, distribution of power, and actors' behaviour (Levy, Young and Zürn, 1995).

Although a number of scholars have researched the role of epistemic communities (defined as networks of experts in a specific field who can claim a certain amount of authority over pertinent knowledge for public policy) in regime formation (Haas, 1992), the part played by the dissemination of technical and scientific information in implementing these regimes has largely been neglected. According to Young (1992), however, the effectiveness of international institutions varies directly in accordance with their ability to monitor compliance. This supervision or monitoring capability is closely linked to the development of the institutions' transparency mechanisms. Without any clear performance indicators or concrete, detailed obligations, the Convention on Biological Diversity has to develop transparency mechanisms that allow signatory countries to supervise the regime's implementation and progress so as to modify relevant policies if need be.

Transparency: A Source of Conformity, Learning, and Effectiveness

The many definitions of transparency found in the literature clearly reflect the conviction that the dissemination of information makes it possible to evaluate a country's policy or performance in relation to a given question. Following Mitchell (1998) we define transparency as the availability of information about a regime, its operation, implementation, and progress. The promotion of transparency fostering the collection, analysis, and dissemination of pertinent information that is regular, rapid, and specific is often one of the most important functions of a regime. In order to change the behaviour of countries, regimes must possess or create information about the activities they intend to regulate and the impact of these activities on the regime's ultimate objectives. Transparency is linked to the regime's information system, i.e. the actors, rules, and processes used for collecting, analysing and disseminating information (Mitchell, 1994). It is dependent on the reasons why the regime seeks information (the information demand), on the motivations and ability of the actors involved to provide information (the information supply), and on the strategies that the regime adopts for increasing transparency (Mitchell, 1998).

Transparency has been studied in the fields of international security, trade, human rights, and the environment. With regard to defence, for instance, transparency and information exchange were found to be useful ways of improving trust and security among nations. Indeed, most of the research done so far links transparency to compliance. In fact, by reducing the asymmetry of information through a process that improves the general level of available information, international regimes reduce the uncertainty that countries face regarding the behaviour of their partners (Keohane, 1984). According to Chayes and Chayes (1995), transparency can promote compliance with obligations in three ways: (i) it facilitates co-ordination between independent actors and the convergence of their actions on the regime's standards; (ii) it assures actors, whose compliance with obligations is conditional on similar initiatives being undertaken by the other participants, that none of them is going to obtain any unilateral advantage; and (iii) it dissuades countries from considering not meeting their obligations.

According to Mitchell (2000), there are three different ways of approaching transparency: (i) improving supervision; (ii) increasing mobilization; and (iii) facilitating rational decision-making. There have been many studies on the first type of transparency. However, in the case of the CBD, which does not contain any legally binding obligations, the third function would appear to be more useful for appreciating its impact on the regime's effectiveness. Also, since science plays an important role in the redefinition of the commitments of the Parties to the Convention, access to scientific research through the CHM should make it easier to pinpoint the links between the behaviours chosen and their consequences, and broaden the range of options.

The Development of the Clearing-House Mechanism of the CBD

From the Convention Negotiations to the First Meeting of the COP (1991-1995)

Under the Convention on Biological Diversity, nations maintain and even increase their sovereign rights over their biological resources. In return, they commit themselves, to the extent that they are able, to working towards the conservation and sustainable use of these biological resources. This entails a certain number of initiatives. For example, each Party, in keeping with its abilities, must: identify the components making up its biological diversity as well as activities that have or risk having harmful effects on it; develop national strategies, plans, and programmes; develop and/or maintain legislative and regulatory measures for protecting endangered species and populations; promote education and heighten public awareness; adopt procedures for assessing the environmental impact of projects that represent a significant threat to biological diversity; and facilitate the exchange of information on technical, scientific, and socio-economic research findings as well as on education and training programmes and aboriginal and traditional knowledge.[3]

In addition, several decisions and guidelines adopted by the Conference of the Parties require governments to present their viewpoint to the Secretariat. For this purpose, each Party must develop its own position on the basis of the best information available. The implementation of work programmes, such as the Jakarta Mandate on Marine and Coastal Biological Diversity, also involves the exchange and dissemination of pertinent information and the creation of database and expert systems. An information exchange mechanism is therefore needed to facilitate shared comprehension and co-operation in order to promote a collective approach to Convention objectives.

During the negotiations, a number of countries expressed the desire to see the clearing-house mechanism manage technology transfer supply and demand. The negotiators ended up opting for a decentralized structure fostering information exchange and facilitating scientific and technical co-operation.

In April 1994, the Open-ended Intergovernmental Meeting of Scientific Experts on Biological Diversity suggested that information exchange through a computerized network be considered as a way of collecting data and providing information for identifying scientific programmes and research and development co-operation. Subsequently, the second session of the Intergovernmental Committee on the Convention on Biological Diversity expressed the desire to see this function take the form of a global clearing-house mechanism bringing together other clearing-house mechanisms, or a "switching centre" operating a decentralized network of national, regional, and international mechanisms, using existing structures as much as possible. The committee also pointed out what was needed for the CHM to operate smoothly. For example, it stressed the importance of the usefulness and reliability of the information collected and disseminated and of clearly defined fields of study. It also pointed out that the mechanism must be based on the Parties' needs and that it should be a small-scale undertaking initially but could expand in keeping with demand and available resources. The committee felt that information sources in various fields could be inventoried in order to promote and facilitate technical and scientific co-operation. It also suggested that the CHM should align itself with the objectives of the Convention while acting as a forerunner by identifying sources of information on cutting-edge technologies and techniques in, for example the fields of biotechnology or ecosystem and species management. In addition, the committee emphasized the importance of strengthening national capabilities and the need to provide education and training support as well as financial and technical assistance. Lastly, it asked the Secretariat to take on evaluation and information collection responsibilities.

Box 5.1 Chronology of the Development of the CBD-CHM

1992

Adoption of the CBD

Article 18, paragraph 3 (technical and scientific co-operation).

1994

COP-1

Note by the interim Secretariat for the establishment of the CHM.

Decision I/3: The CHM must be established in accordance with the provisions of Art. 18, par. 3 and requests the Secretariat to prepare a comprehensive study on the subject.

1995

COP-2

Report of the Secretariat on the establishment of the Clearing-house Mechanism containing, *inter alia*, objective, scope, and functions of the CHM.

Decision II/3: The CHM shall be developed starting with a pilot phase for 1996-1997 and that the Secretariat should act as a focal point.

1996

SBSTTA-2 (Subsidiary Body for Scientific, Technical and Technological Advice)

Recommendation II/6: Recommends to the COP that the Secretariat facilitate regional workshops and establish an informal advisory committee.

COP-3

Report of the Secretariat on the operation of the CHM.

Decision III/4: States that the pilot phase shall be extended until December 1998, requests the Global Environment Facility to support capacity-building activities, recommends that the Clearing-house Mechanism should disseminate information on policy and management issues relevant to the implementation of the Convention and that the Executive Secretary constitute and co-ordinate an IAC.

Box 5.1 Concluded

1997

First International Experts Workshop (Germany)

SBSTTA-3

Report of the Secretariat on the implementation of the pilot phase of the Clearing-house Mechanism.

Recommendation III/6: Recommends that the COP request the GEF to play a substantial role as a major catalyst in the full development of the CHM and that in the launching of the independent review of the CHM pilot phase, some elements for evaluation be used.

1997-1998

Regional workshops in Latin America, Central and Eastern Europe, Asia, and Africa

1998

COP-4

Report of the Secretariat on the implementation of the pilot phase of the Clearing-house Mechanism.

Decision IV/2: Recommends that each Party organize a national clearing-house mechanism steering committee, that in building up the content of information in the CHM at all levels, major elements be used, and that the Secretariat undertake an independent review of the pilot phase.

Second International Experts Workshop (Italy)

1999

Final report of the independent review of the pilot phase of the Clearing-house Mechanism, strategic plan, and long-term work programme.

2000

SBSTTA-5

Recommendation V/2: Recommends that the COP endorse the strategic plan for the CHM and the longer-term programme of work and set up priorities of action, subject to availability of resources and relevance.

COP-5

Decision V/14: Decides that the strategic plan for the CHM shall become a component of the strategic plan of the Convention and requests that the Parties and the Executive Secretary undertake activities identified in annexes.

Development of the Pilot Phase (1995-1998)

The Clearing-house Mechanism was developed on the basis of decisions by the Conference of the Parties, working documents prepared by the Secretariat, and the opinions of the informal advisory committee (see Box 5.1). As requested by the first COP, the Secretariat prepared a comprehensive study that described ways and means of achieving the principal objective of the CHM by: (a) developing and strengthening national capabilities through human resource development and institution building; (b) facilitating the transfer of technologies in accordance with

Article 16; and (c) promoting the establishment of joint research programmes and joint ventures for the development of technologies relevant to the objectives of the Convention (Convention on Biological Diversity, 1995). This study was presented at the second COP (Doc. UNEP/CBD/COP/2/6). COP-2 decided that the Clearing-house Mechanism would begin with a pilot phase for 1996-1997 and that it should develop in a neutral, transparent, cost-effective, efficient, and accessible manner (Decision II/3). In accordance with this decision, the Secretariat was chosen as the co-ordinator for the CHM and charged with the task of encouraging the development of a network of active partners who would apply themselves to facilitating access to research and technology transfer and to strengthening national capabilities by disseminating information on the experience acquired during the implementation of the Convention.

The partners most active in implementing the pilot phase of the CHM were the World Conservation Monitoring Centre (WCMC), the European Union, Germany, Australia, Brazil, and Canada. The CHM operates in a decentralized manner, with national focal points that identify and contact regional, sub-regional, national, and local information sources, sort relevant information, and ensure that it is available in an appropriate format.

The pilot phase was developed in keeping with three principles: (i) organize and link information relative to the implementation of the Convention; (ii) facilitate the integration of information from different disciplines; and (iii) support the decision-making process by providing syntheses of global issues and priorities as stipulated by the Parties. In practice, the implementation of the pilot phase focused on enhancing the availability and use of existing data and information by improving online access. The first product of the pilot phase was the Clearing-house Mechanism's global home page. This may be why most of the Parties see the CHM mainly as an electronic information exchange mechanism. The decentralized structure can make good use of both print and electronic media, however, including but not limited to the Internet.

As for the national focal points, a number of them have developed web sites concentrating on the dissemination of national reports, national monographs, and scientific and technical contacts within their governmental and institutional system, while the CHM facilitates the exchange of information among all local stakeholders (horizontal exchanges) and between the local/national level and the global level (vertical exchanges). Concrete results of the implementation of the pilot phase of the CHM can be measured by examining national legislation, whether or not a focal point has been designated and where it is positioned in the decision-making process, the development of the network at the national level, the organization of information sessions, the amount of grants received and their use, the financial resources invested by governments, and the partnerships established at regional, sub-regional, national, and local levels.

COP-3 decided that the CHM should not only disseminate scientific and technical information but also provide information on general policy and management issues relevant to the implementation of the Convention (Decision

III/4). This decision suggested organizing regional workshops that would: i) clearly determine the scientific and technical information needs of countries and regions; ii) establish information priorities and information dissemination procedures; iii) evaluate the means that countries have at their disposal for implementing the Convention; iv) study the scientific and technical co-operation experience acquired for the purpose of supporting the Convention's objectives; and v) inventory means that would place the CHM in the best position to facilitate this co-operation. In 1997-1998 the Secretariat organized four regional workshops on the implementation of the Clearing-house Mechanism. According to the introductory document used at these workshops (UNEP/CBD/CHM/RW/1/1), although the organization of information is important, it merely represents the first stage of the CHM's development. A second stage is to be geared towards determining how interactions among partners from different fields can be used and developed. In this document, the Secretariat suggests a minimum of shared features in order to facilitate information identification for the Secretariat's Clearing-house Mechanism and for each national focal point. Some regional reports contain general recommendations on structure and co-operation in capacity building, including human resource development and institutional strengthening.

Independent Review of the Pilot Phase and Long-Term Work Plan (1999-2000)

The independent review of the pilot phase of the CHM was made public in October 1999. It confirmed that 137 Parties had designated a national focal point with the human and physical resources needed: 104 of these focal points had access to an e-mail address and 41 had developed web sites.[4]

The Clearing-house Mechanism must promote and support the following objectives: i) improve decision-making processes and make them cost-effective; ii) foster international co-operation and exchanges with regard to technology, training, education, research, information, and expertise; iii) reduce duplication or overlap; and iv) work towards better, faster implementation and greater cost-effectiveness of initiatives relating to biological diversity and of the Convention as a whole.

There is a gap, however, between the decisions of the Conference of the Parties and their implementation by the Parties. On the one hand, although the Secretariat has developed tools such as the CD-ROM and discussion list requested by the Parties, they are still not being used very much. On the other hand, the Parties, particularly developing countries, are averse to the idea of committing resources to setting up national clearing-house mechanisms, mainly because the role and functions of the CHM appear to be poorly defined and not very well understood.

By 1 November 2000, the Global Environment Facility had supported the establishment of CHMs in 55 developing nations. The beneficiary countries received an average of $12,337 USD (see Annex 2, Table A-5). The Parties that received this assistance have nevertheless asked for additional support to strengthen institutional and human capabilities. Despite their brand-new computer technology, information collection and processing appears to be a problem for several developing countries. Participants in the review also identified three common concerns: technological problems, the information gap, and communication problems, such as the limited number of languages into which CHM documents are translated.

As the independent review of the CHM pilot phase shows, there remains a strong need to describe the CHM, communicate its role and value, identify possible synergies, use clear, concise vocabulary that is easy to translate, create mechanisms of mutual support, identify infrastructure needs, monitor and evaluate activities of the CHM, and plan for the long term. Following its examination of the review, COP-5 (2000) adopted decisions that ask national focal points to describe the institutions, initiatives, and specialists active in the fields pertinent to the Convention and to set up new regional, sub-regional, and thematic focal points. According to Decision V/14, the CHM should also be directed at the population in general, the private sector, non-governmental organizations, and all levels of government. It was also felt that the information should be more useful to researchers and decision-makers.

What's in the Future for the Clearing-House Mechanism?

The Clearing-house Mechanism has reached a turning point. On the one hand, the Parties' obligations under Decision V/14 are more specifically concerned than ever with scientific and technical co-operation. On the other hand, the Secretariat has been called upon to create procedures and means that will allow the role and importance of the CHM to be better understood globally. This will require a great deal of thought about the true mandate of the Clearing-house Mechanism and its future. Up to now, its development has basically been top-down, i.e. devoted to the dissemination of the regime's objectives, work programmes, and decisions. Development of bottom-up exchanges and horizontal exchanges among Parties and among national stakeholders is still in the embryonic stage. Apart from not adhering very closely to its scientific and technical co-operation mandate, the CHM runs the risk of being reduced to a mere tool for following up on implementation or indeed for evaluating compliance with obligations, which represents a great deal less than it was initially meant to be and would increase the doubts that many developing countries have about it. These countries are indeed experiencing problems with the concept as it was developed. Some of the developing countries' CHM web sites are hosted on servers located in the North, in a standardized form. Although this assistance would appear to be a good thing at first glance, it nevertheless underscores the CHM's design limits. These limits are partly due to different attitudes with respect to information in some societies and to the absence of a strong tradition of information-sharing in certain countries, partly to a lack of human resources and the concentration on electronic media at the expense of other supports, and partly to the fact that throughout its development, the CHM has often been something of a moving target, reflecting different conceptions of its nature and functions. For example, its initial functions were gradually expanded, while in other instances certain principles of the pilot phase, such as decision-making support, were largely forgotten. This difference in conception can cause potentially paralyzing contradictions – for instance, between the desire to turn the CHM into a reference tool in the decision-making process and the desire to make it a consciousness-raising tool for civil society. The biological diversity regime also runs a real risk of becoming compartmentalized as a result of the lack of clear guidelines governing the relations between various scientific networks.

In order for transparency to be considered a deciding factor of regime effectiveness, the information system, of which the CHM is a part, must help actors: (i) evaluate progress in the management of the targeted problem and (ii) define the directions that the review and renegotiation of the regime should take (Mitchell, 1998). In addition, the CHM must disseminate the regime's standards and reinforce the political capabilities of its actors by increasing awareness of the Convention's issues, objectives, and programmes and ensuring access to recent scientific data.

Currently, the CHM widely disseminates information on Convention issues, objectives, and programmes globally. But is it really managing to reach all the signatory countries and all the people involved in the local and national decision-making process? Do the Parties have access, in their own language, to all the scientific information they need to evaluate the regime's progress and introduce corresponding national and local measures? As far as national focal points are concerned, very little has been done in the way of studies on the conditions for appropriation and national or regional development of clearing-house mechanisms. The problem is often limited to material considerations (purchasing computer equipment, developing web sites), while the cultural, political, and economic context in which the CHM has to operate is ignored. The fact that the CHM was largely designed as a means of circulating information vertically between the Convention and the Parties or between scientific powers and others also makes it difficult for local actors to adopt this tool. Development of national and local scientific expertise and its recognition via the Clearing-house Mechanism needs to be analysed more thoroughly. Ultimately, the CHM should outgrow its narrow "scientific" nature and allow dissemination of all forms of relevant expertise and knowledge, whether they correspond to western science or not.

Conclusion

The Clearing-house Mechanism of the Convention on Biological Diversity, as it has developed up until now, acts partly as a transparency tool. On the one hand, it promotes the dissemination of regime standards and, on the other, it enables the Parties to display some conformity (national reports, strategies, action plans, and monographs). However, we will have to wait for the development of thematic focal points before we can assess any real progress in managing the various areas of the

Convention. In addition, the Parties will have to "own" the Clearing-house Mechanism and improve local and regional circulation of information if they are to contribute effectively to the regime's review. Lastly, the Secretariat and supporters of the CHM must reaffirm their support of national, regional, and sub-regional initiatives, both financially and by strengthening human capacities. The transparency of the Convention on Biological Diversity and its impact on the effectiveness of the regime will depend on an unequivocal definition of the mandate of the Clearing-house Mechanism and on a shared comprehension of the objectives to be met. This task remains to be accomplished.

Notes

This chapter was translated by Linda Blythe.

[1] In fact, some of these networks are members of the Informal Advisory Committee (IAC) of the Clearing-House Mechanism: BIN21, GBIF, IABIN, IBIN, and UNEP-WCMC.
[2] See chapter 3 by Le Prestre in this volume.
[3] Ibid.
[4] In July 2001, 144 countries had designated a national focal point for the Clearing-house Mechanism; 111 of them had access to an e-mail address, and 44 had developed a web site.

Chapter 6

The Emergence and Implementation of the Advance Informed Agreement Procedure

Amanda Wolf

Introduction

The Cartagena Protocol on Biosafety (BP) is the first protocol to be negotiated under the Convention on Biodiversity (CBD). The BP promotes shared responsibility for conservation objectives in situations where they may be negatively influenced by international trade in genetically engineered organisms (called living modified organisms, or LMOs, in the BP). The "advance informed agreement" (AIA) procedure is its central mechanism. This chapter first examines the emergence of the AIA as an international norm in the trade and environment context, starting with its origins in "informed consent" around the mid-20th century. Second, the chapter examines the conceptual components of AIA/informed consent as they have been applied in biomedicine and other international treaties, highlighting the interpretive and practical challenges, and consequent strengths and weaknesses, of their application in the biodiversity context.

Until recently, informed consent was restricted to medicine, biomedical research, and social science research.[1] In all these applications, lumped together for the present purposes as "biomedical" applications, informed consent describes features in the relationship between a subject or patient (recipient) and an expert (initiator), whether doctor or researcher.[2]

Biomedical informed consent practices aim to improve therapeutic or research value, to ensure initiators engage in careful risk assessment for which they are accountable, and to show respect for the autonomy of the recipient. As Faden and Beauchamp (1986, p. 274) make clear, the term is important in two senses. First, informed consent is a "special kind of autonomous action" by a recipient. This sense is recipient-focused, rights-based, and morally grounded. Informed consent is also a set of rules governing procedures in an institutional context. Here, the emphasis is duty-based, initiator-focused, and legalistic. The two senses are clearly related, the first serving (in the ideal) to establish principles underpinning the second.

In the international context, in addition to the AIA in the BP, informed consent is the centrepiece of the Rotterdam Convention on the Prior Informed Consent Procedure for Certain Hazardous Chemicals and Pesticides in International Trade (PIC Convention). A prior consent process (Basel mechanism) is a prominent operational scheme in the 1989 Basel Convention on the Control of Transboundary Movement of Hazardous Wastes and Their Disposal (Basel Convention) even though a subsequent amendment (not yet in force) bans most exports from Organization for Economic Cooperation and Development (OECD) countries to non-OECD countries. These three international processes, like informed consent in the biomedical context, have both rights-based and duty-based senses. While the AIA may be read as a technical rule, the negotiation history of the BP reveals Parties' varied emphases on several moral and legal principles. However, AIA, PIC, and the Basel mechanism (referred to generally as "prior informed consent" in this chapter), unlike the biomedical applications, are clearly not about terms of interaction between individual recipients and initiators. Instead, these mechanisms refer to importers and exporters, as either individuals, firms, representative authorities, or states.[3] Thus, we are led to examine informed consent more closely both as an emerging norm for trade rules with significant environmental objectives and as an operating rule designed to ensure trades proceed only in accordance with certain underlying principles (Wolf, 2000). In the international setting of the BP, informed consent embodies norms of trade liberalism (the right to pursue one's own goals), respect for sovereignty, and a right to know, designed to ensure that the best possible information relevant to harm assessment is available to decision-makers. Whether or not the AIA procedure will "work" depends partly on the appropriateness of these norms and the balance among them. It also depends on a number of operational factors, which cannot be gauged or judged in the short term. Important among these factors are who bears the risks of bad decisions in the informed consent process, the breadth of risk assessments undertaken within the AIA procedure, and ultimately, the conservation effectiveness of decisions taken.

Origins of Informed Consent

Prior informed consent as a norm came together around the mid-20th century out of legal, moral, and economic origins. PIC, AIA, and the Basel mechanism are products of several converging forces: an evolving rights movement, a focus on individual liberties and social equality, the democratization of participation (Pateman, 1970), and the ongoing search for norms of co-operation among sovereign states facing common or joint problems. Prior informed consent may be the first distinct new norm since sustainable development to emerge at the interface of international environment and trade.[4] Like sustainable development, it is an aspirational norm, variously interpreted. It may prove to be largely void of true substance, as some critics have claimed when the sustainable development norm is applied in sweeping ways. Or it may serve to guide high-quality trade and environment decisions, as many participants and observers of conservation and trade treaties hope. Or it may become limited to certain procedural requirements in ways that dampen positive environmental initiative in a manner similar to what cynics charge happens in the clinical setting.

The modern idea of consent as an element in democracy has its roots in late 17th century religious beliefs about the dual roles of intellect and will in human nature (Alderson and Goodey, 1998; Herzog, 1989). While "consent of the governed" is subject to serious criticism, the core logic continues to be salient. The public clamours for more opportunities to exercise explicit choice, politically, socially, and in the marketplace. These same notions of consent prevail internationally as well, with self-determination grounding the autonomy of states. Where choice and self-determination are fundamental rights, there is often held to be an accompanying right to know. Rights to know have become important in a range of contexts in addition to those examined here, starting with workers' rights to know about the dangers they are exposed to in the workplace.

International environmental laws increasingly establish "procedural obligations" (Okowa, 1997). These obligations, including environmental impact assessment, notification, exchange of information, and consultation, require states to "observe a number of discrete procedures before permitting the conduct of activities which may cause harm" (*ibidem*, p. 275). Under the prior consultation operating principle, states owe others a duty to make known possible negative consequences of planned activities that may have spillover effects (Sands, 1995). These obligations contribute to conflict reduction by fostering, although not requiring, participation of those likely to be affected. "Consultation" in these applications does not extend as far as more recent "best-practice" norms of two-way ongoing interaction (Sterne and Zagon, 1997), but in all uses of the term, the authority of the decision-maker is assumed. Trade law emphasizes the standardization of regulations in a way that influences the information that may permissibly be used in a trade context. For example, the World Trade Organization's Agreement on Sanitary and Phytosanitary Standards allows only evidence based on "sound science" to influence a decision to impose trade constraints. In a similar vein, the Codex Alimentarius Commission develops standards to harmonize trade in food.

The term "prior informed consent" appears to have been coined by David Bull of Oxfam (UK). Bull's work influenced the Pesticides Action Network, which lobbied for curbs in what it saw as irresponsible behaviour by multinational corporations and the serious environmental and health consequences of pesticide use (Paarlberg, 1994, pp. 316-9). In 1983 the UN General Assembly adopted a resolution that provided for prior informed consent in the context of "products that have been banned from domestic consumption and/or sale because they have been judged to endanger health and the environment". Such products should only be sold abroad when a request is received or when consumption of them is officially permitted in that country (UNGA, Res. 37/137 (1983) par. 1; Paarlberg, 1994). No informed consent mechanism was proposed, however. Information disclosure was limited to the fact that a product was banned. Consent to import was assumed if the product was allowed in the country or an order for it was made.

In addition, several other strands feed into the legal evolution of the international informed consent norm. A prior consent law governs direct broadcasts picked up by other countries (Fisher, 1990). In the soft law arena, the European Union, Japan, and the United States, under the auspices of the International Conference on Harmonization of Technical Requirements for Registration of Pharmaceuticals for Human Use, completed draft guidelines in 1995 on good clinical practice, which included requirements for informed consent in pharmaceuticals research (Miller, 1997, p. 205). These guidelines are essentially about the harmonization of informed consent processes so that pharmaceuticals can be marketed in all covered countries on the basis of trials in one. The OECD has advanced a right to information on the risks created by hazardous installations, such as power plants (Smets, 1991). Each of these applications reveals a concern to balance, to one degree or another, economic imperatives with information rights.

Despite this legal history, informed consent is almost exclusively associated in the public mind with medical and research practice. The beneficence basis of medical ethics is of ancient origin. Yet, the term "informed consent" first appears in medical case law in 1957 (Faden and Beauchamp, 1986, p. 59). The period of post-war prosperity witnessed a shift from a paternalistic (and initiator-focused) medical model to an informed consumer model. At the same time, an explosion of technological developments greatly increased the complexity and cost of potential medical services, thereby adding significantly to the challenges of achieving informed consent.

Regardless of challenges, informed consent remains a mainstay of medical practice, medical and psychological experimentation, and pharmaceutical research. The potential recipient (of an experimental drug, for instance) has the right to consent or refuse. The initiator has duties, and attendant liability, to disclose the likely benefits and harms in the proposed treatment as well as alternatives and their associated benefits and harms (Faden and Beauchamp, 1986). Informed consent in an international biomedical and bioethical research context dates from the post-World War II Nuremberg Code,[5] which sought to ensure that atrocities like the Nazi experiments with concentration camp inmates would never recur (Miller, 1997; Faden and Beauchamp, 1986). Here, the impetus for informed consent stemmed from norms of basic human dignity. Gradually, informed consent spread to a range of social research areas (Kimmel, 1988). In many countries, institutional grant-givers require strict adherence to informed consent procedures as a condition of funding. Key tensions exist, as signalled above, between person-centred, autonomy-respecting ideals and necessary constraints imposed by institutional realities. A challenge arises from the particular gap between ideals of free, informed choice and practical realities in "managed care" regimes (Krause, 1999; Sage, 1999; Hall, 1997). Although managed care differs in many ways from biodiversity protection, the challenge is mirrored in the BP case in the tension between informed choice and the practical realities of trade. Importantly, economic efficiency is a driver in both managed care and trade decisions, but it is widely appreciated as at least potentially in conflict with free choice.[6]

A subtle but essential feature of biomedical informed consent is that it is not itself the means of minimizing harm. Rather, harms are minimized through prior risk assessment and ongoing management (Faden and Beauchamp, 1986, p. 223). Nevertheless, since the process requires that recipients be given information about the risks and benefits of the substance or treatment in question, initiators have strong indirect incentives to ensure that harms are in fact minimized. Liability laws can further strengthen this incentive.

We now turn to the origins of informed consent in economic theory and trade. In normative economic theory, "informed choice" is one condition for market efficiency. Consumers should have sufficient information to choose those products and services from an "opportunity set" constrained by their income that will best contribute to their overall well-being. Any policy to change the information environment for consumers should assess how information functions as a public good (and hence is undersupplied by the market) and any "market failure" caused by information asymmetry (Vining and Weimer, 1988).

This normative theory has been applied to international trade in risky products. There are several ways in which an exporter (country or firm) can contribute to the importer's free choice in the market. Pallemaerts' (1988) ladder of information provision in international trade equates informed choice with tacit consent. The bottom rung is collection and dissemination of information about a product (for instance, its toxicity) by an international agent. Next comes government-to-government information provision (for instance, about control actions taken). Next is export notification, in which importers receive information about actual exports. With each of these three bottom rungs, importers are deemed fully responsible to regulate the products within their own countries. That is, on the basis of information that they receive through general information channels, or specifically about an impending export, the government is assumed to be unconstrained, by information asymmetry or in any other way, in its response. It may make the products illegal, or it may decide to control the use of the products once in the country. However, beyond the provision of information, the exporter has no responsibility for how or whether the product is used. The balance of responsibility on the remaining two rungs shifts from the importer toward a shared responsibility between importer and exporter. The fourth rung is tacit consent or "informed choice". Exports cannot occur unless proper export notification has occurred in advance of the planned shipment and the country has not objected within a certain period of time. This level is congruent with the perfect-market norm. Prior informed consent, the fifth rung, entails explicit consent.

In summary, prior informed consent is more than the established international legal conventions of notification and consultation require, calling for an explicit decision subsequent to an exchange of information. It has evolved in a trade context, where the traded goods – including hazardous chemicals and pesticides, hazardous wastes, and genetically engineered organisms – carry (or may carry) some risk of harm to people or the environment. Informed consent is more than efficiency requires. Indeed, in economic theory, to the extent that the explicit check is not cost-free, it may actually decrease efficiency. Morally, informed consent stands as a norm of shared decision-making that establishes certain autonomy-respecting rights and duties. Table 6.1 shows the common elements of the legal, moral, and economic perspectives.

Table 6.1 Elements of Informed Consent

5. Explicit (informed) consent
4. Tacit/functional consent
3. Exchange of views/consultation/market signalling
2. Specific or implicit disclosure/notification to recipient by initiator
1. Impact assessment/risk assessment/product characterization

First, in any decision context, the relevant characteristics of the focal product or activity are assessed. This assessment results in information on the likely impacts, such as effects on disease conditions or on ecosystems from applications of that product or activity ("course of action"). This information exists initially in a common pool. At the second stage, where a specific course of action is contemplated, information from the common pool is communicated to the recipient. Third, the recipient considers the desirability of the course of action in light of the information provided. In doing so, the recipient may compare the information to the price of a good on the market or may take a more interactive role in discussing the information with the initiator. Fourth, the recipient's decision process reaches a stage in which the available information is considered in light of the recipient's interests, and a decision is made to go ahead with the transaction or not. With the last step, the decision is conveyed back to the initiator in the form of either an explicit authorization for the course of action to go ahead or a refusal of authorization.

The next section takes a comparative look at these features in international applications of prior informed consent.

Advance Informed Agreement, the PIC Procedure, and the Basel Mechanism

Prior informed consent is central to three international agreements. The Basel mechanism, PIC procedure, and AIA procedure are means for obtaining and disseminating the decisions of importing countries about proposed imports and for ensuring exporter compliance with those decisions. PIC and AIA call for product and application-specific risk assessment and the compilation and publication of decisions taken. The Basel mechanism is similar in its essential nature.

AIA applies only to the first movement of LMOs intended for intentional release – essentially uses involving exposure to the natural environment, whether they are fully "released" or under field trials. LMOs for intentional release include seeds, fish, and micro-organisms for bioremediation. An information exchange process applies to LMOs designated for use in feed, food, or processing (LMO-FFPs, or "commodities"). At present, this category includes most LMOs in trade, such as maize and soybeans that are used in food processing.

Under the AIA process, the exporter provides written notice, containing a range of specified information (set out in Annex 1) to the importer's "competent national authority". The information may come from an exporting government or from "a legal or natural person under the jurisdiction of the government who arranges for an LMO to be exported". Annex 1 information requirements include: the characteristics of recipient or parental organisms related to biosafety; centres of origin and centres of genetic diversity of the recipient or parental organism; a description of habitats where organisms may persist or proliferate; biosafety information on donor organisms; a "previous and existing" risk assessment report; and suggested methods of safe handling, storage, transport, and use. The risk assessment in turn is specified in Annex 3. The assessment should relate to the "potential adverse effects" in the "likely potential receiving environment". It should be carried out on a case-by-case basis. This assessment is intended to assist national authorities to make informed decisions.

In accordance with the BP, the importing government has 270 days to reach a decision or to elect to proceed according to a domestic regulatory framework, which must be consistent with the BP and other international obligations. The importer's decision can be: to approve the import, with or without conditions, including how subsequent imports of the same LMO will be handled; to prohibit the import; to request additional information; or to extend consideration of some specific aspect of the AIA procedure by a specified time. At the same time that the exporter is notified, the importer notifies the Internet-based Biosafety Clearing-House, which allows all countries to track every decision. The clearing-house function translates private information goods into public information goods, available for anyone's use in risk management decisions.[7]

An attenuated process for commodities requires prospective exporters to convey information that is less comprehensive than that of the AIA to the clearing-house (unless a Party has requested direct written notice). Any Party can request additional information. The clearing-house should also be provided with copies of national laws, regulations, or guidelines applicable to imports of LMO commodities. Developing countries or economies in transition that lack a domestic regulatory framework for deciding whether to import an LMO commodity may notify the clearing-house that its decision on whether to import a commodity for the first time requires a risk assessment (most likely at the expense of the exporter) as set out in Annex 3. In continuing meetings, the BP Parties are developing more detail about the operation of the clearing-house and the specific information that should accompany shipments.

AIA differs from PIC and the Basel mechanism in several ways. Most importantly, the traded goods covered by PIC and the Basel mechanism are broadly held to be inherently hazardous, whereas initiators of LMO trades believe that the products are safe (although a number of recipients and other interested Parties raise compelling concerns about these safety judgements). Both PIC and the Basel mechanism list covered products and contain processes for adding items to the lists. Listing itself is the trigger for the prior informed consent mechanism. No such list is contemplated by the AIA, although as information accumulates, it is likely to be grouped (according to type of modification, purpose, or commodity, for instance) in order to assist clearing-house users. But it is product characteristics, such as whether or not the product has been genetically engineered and its intended use, not whether a product is listed, that serves as a trigger for AIA.

Broadly speaking, both the BP and the PIC Convention aim clearly at conservation and protection of human health ends, to be achieved via trade rules. The substantive link between the composition and location of trades and the ultimate goals is unarticulated. In contrast, the Basel Convention aims first to minimize hazardous wastes. Here the trade rule is an indirect means of encouraging new waste reduction and environmentally sound treatment technologies. A second, somewhat subsidiary aim is to ensure that trades that do occur are environmentally sound. The hope is that both aims will lead to better environmental conditions.

Thus, differences in covered products and aims among the treaties point to subtle differences in the treaties' implicit norms on the relationship between trade and desired environmental goals. In the BP, trade itself is neither good nor bad for biodiversity. There is only a modest and indirect incentive for Parties to develop means for better protecting the environment. The BP hopes to avert the transfer, handling, and use of LMOs that pose risks to biodiversity, while at the same time imposing few constraints to the trade of LMOs deemed safe and essentially no oversight of their handling and use. As a general conclusion, this system provides LMO trade initiators with incentives to aim for "adequate" safety, not to develop maximally safe products. Similarly, there is little reason in trade to prefer safer products to less safe ones. The Basel Convention makes clear that trade in hazardous waste is itself bad, as the banning of entire classes of trades illustrates. In the ideal, these trades will slow and cease as countries learn to manage their own wastes effectively. The PIC Convention lies in between. It is based on the idea that trade itself is not negative, but that trades without PIC allow too much avoidable harm to occur. Because the traded products are recognized as dangerous, it is acknowledged that their use can lead to harm, which is considered unavoidable if it is more than offset by benefits. It is hoped that the PIC Convention may contribute to an overall decrease in the use of dangerous chemicals and pesticides, but this is not as central a goal as it is in the Basel Convention.

The nature and timing of prior informed consent is another point of comparison. Although subject to some modification, the AIA applies to a specific trade (product A to country B for use C at time D)[8]. Information disclosure occurs because a trade is contemplated, and it is "customized" to the intended use. The consent decision with respect to that trade is made after the importer considers the provided information in light of the importer's own circumstances. The PIC procedure (and the Basel mechanism in a less precise way) is designed to be more of a pre-approval process. Decision guidance documents are distributed to each country, which is then asked to make a decision on whether or nor it consents to the import of the products.[9] The information in the guidance document is not customized to the local intended application.

Finally, monitoring and liability systems differ. The PIC and Basel Conventions have emerging liability systems, but that is still far in the future for the BP. If the difficulty in negotiating the AIA is the indicator, it will prove exceptionally difficult (if not impossible) to achieve agreement on liability. The principal difficulties include: significant possibilities for unanticipated outcomes (such as the escape of modified DNA to a native species), which are related to the degree of uncertainty about the products; harms associated with unsafe handling or use that were not addressed in the risk assessments; and the fact that technically, informed consent in each trade is based on unique risk assessments. Related to these issues are the monitoring challenges in the BP context. In chemicals treaties, it is sufficient to track product compositions and their movements: have trades been duly authorized and is the traded substance what it purports to be? Such a system would not serve the BP objectives well because each trade (and its ensuing level of risk to biodiversity) differs from every other trade. There is no way to measure progress or success on the sole basis of trade characteristics (product and destination). A means of monitoring actual handling and use subsequent to the trade is needed.[10]

In sum, the BP is an agreement on a risk management decision process.[11] The procedures are decision-making rules that apply to trades among countries. Because the treaties have environmental objectives, the rules are instruments for attaining these ultimate goals. However, the connection between AIA and the desired environmental objectives is not a logically necessary one. In the following section, some of the implications for the AIA procedure are drawn out more explicitly, though of necessity these implications suggest the implementation challenges that lie some time in the future.

Discussion

AIA, PIC, and the Basel mechanism share a more or less common legal framework, based on a duty to inform and a right to consent. Disclosure of information to the recipient about the nature and risks of a proposed course of action and the recipient's consent are core features of all informed consent procedures. However, most writers who critically assess informed consent recognize the conditionality of both "informed" and "consent". The information disclosed should be accurately comprehended, the recipient should be competent to decide, and the decision should be made freely. In short, simply providing information and agreeing to (or refusing) a trade may meet legal criteria as set out in the AIA, for example, yet fail to extend very far toward the norms of shared responsibility for the conservation of biological diversity that are the heart of the BP. How well informed consent norms are captured in the AIA will help determine how well the BP succeeds in the long term. In the short to medium term, however, a deeper understanding of the implications of informed consent in the AIA can help Parties to be alert for unintended consequences and to improve the mechanism.

The AIA procedure's challenges, as well as they can be foreseen at this time, are examined in this section on the basis of biomedical applications of informed consent and the earlier comparison of the AIA with PIC and the Basel mechanism. In this comparative context, three features most distinguish the AIA. First, there is pronounced emphasis on the recipients' own risk assessments. Second, there is only a vague logical link between the AIA procedure and the desired ultimate outcome. Third, each application is contextual.

All informed consent procedures require risk assessments. In biomedical applications, prior risk assessments are required to ensure that only courses of action that are considered to be net beneficial to the recipient will be offered. In the view of the initiator, the recipient is asked, essentially, to confirm the judgment of benefit explicitly. The initiator expects confirmation but acknowledges that the recipient may possess special knowledge or values that will lead it to the opposite conclusion. The informed consent process allows this additional individual information to go into the decision but does not contribute to the risk assessment. In the cases of PIC and the Basel mechanism, the initiator acknowledges that the proposed activity is inherently dangerous, because risk assessments have clearly shown significant risk of harm that requires careful management. These processes leave it up to the recipient to judge whether the course of action is net beneficial based on the recipient's interpretation of its risks and the various choices that are available. Here, in essence, the initiator supplies information on risks or harms, but the recipient completes the picture by supplying the associated values. This process can be termed roughly a "joint risk assessment".

AIA requires two clearly separate risk assessments. The AIA procedure requires the initiator to prepare a customized risk assessment that takes into account the "likely potential receiving environment". As in biomedical applications, the focal activity covered by AIA is considered by the initiator to be of net benefit to the recipient, or else the trade would not have been proposed.[12] The initiator expects the trade to be consented to, but acknowledges that the recipient may have reasons not to consent. But, in contrast to the biomedical case, while using the proposed trade and initiator-supplied risk assessment, the recipient is expected to conduct its own risk assessment. As with PIC and the Basel mechanism, the recipient may supply value judgements and risk factors that differ from those of the initiator. Importantly, however, the initiator's risk assessment refers to the receiving environment as it appears to the initiator. However, not only do aspects of the physical environment differ among potential recipients, but risk scholars have also identified a number of human and social factors in risk assessment and management that may need to be taken into account. To date there is little sign that initiators will approach risk that broadly. Indeed, as Kellow notes, "risk" is frequently confused with "hazard" in international toxic risk management (1999). It is possible that "risk assessments" done according to "sound science" may be based essentially on hazard characterization and not sufficiently tuned to local conditions. The BP, however, allows recipients to take other factors into account.

As detailed above, informed consent involves both recipients and initiators in risk assessment, though in ways that differ by context. It follows that all informed consents also require that both recipients and initiators be Parties to a decision on a course of action to which the risk assessments relate. In both the biomedical and international treaty contexts, informed consent is a decision-making procedure applying to an activity that can only be undertaken by the initiator (who is responsible for ensuring that the recipient is "informed") with the express "consent" of the recipient. It is worth reflecting on the core logic or generic mechanism assumed to be operating. Why should the decision-making proceed according to the informed consent norm? What assumptions link the information disclosure and comprehension aspects with consent and ultimately, of course, with desired outcomes? The logic of the informed consent process hinges on the nature and role of risk assessment in decision-making.

In the biomedical context, the initiator is responsible for disclosing to the recipient information about the nature of treatment options and their likely results. This disclosure is based on, and necessarily follows, a risk assessment. In the ideal, the initiator translates statistical information into terms the recipient can understand. The recipient is not expected to conduct a risk assessment of his or her own.[13] The recipient may or may not engage in a decision-clarifying dialogue with the initiator. Both these factors contribute to a view that the initiator stands in some sort of fiduciary relationship with the recipient. Ultimately, by granting or refusing consent, the recipient is responsible for authorizing a course of action: the initiator cannot impose one. If, as some authors would have it, the decision is to be fully shared, the patient and doctor should jointly identify and implement the "best" treatment option, taking into account both the personal perspectives of the patient and the medical expertise of the doctor.

AIA is premised on an idea of shared responsibility among equal partners for the biosafety of LMOs. As follows from sovereignty doctrine, the exporter and importer contribute from different but equal perspectives to their respective risk assessments. The exporter, like the physician, has a duty to inform, in this case regarding "potential adverse effects" in the "likely potential receiving environment" of an LMO. The importer then makes a decision to allow the import or not and therefore assumes some responsibility for any possible harm to biodiversity, similar to a patient's decision that takes into account the physician's disclosure and the patient's self-knowledge and values. In what sense is the decision shared equally? Or, to put it differently, what does AIA achieve that another procedure would not? Again, a comparison with biomedicine can help clarify matters.

The intrinsic value of informed consent in the biomedical context is respect for autonomy. This is usually viewed theoretically as the most important reason to engage in informed consent procedures. Writers disagree on the exact mechanism through which informed consent works to identify the best option among alternatives, where "best" is measured in terms of therapeutic outcomes and/or overall patient well-being. It has been suggested, for example, that informed patients may be more "co-operative," and that informed patients make "better" decisions. However, many observers also note that the threat of legal liability for medical negligence exerts a very strong incentive for adherence to the letter of informed consent procedures if not its autonomy-respecting spirit.

How does AIA compare? As a treaty rule, AIA has, in the manner of many international norms, achieved a curious compromise. On the one hand, the negotiating position of the Miami Group, a coalition of major exporters of LMOs,[14] emphasized "positive freedoms," limiting and standardizing the informed consent procedure so that trade could be as free as possible, with decisions grounded in "sound science". On the other hand, the Like-Minded Group, comprising China and the developing countries (minus Argentina, Chile, and Uruguay), placed weight on the "negative freedoms" of a country's right to know and right to take into account a range of social, economic, and cultural values when making a trade decision. The European Union was in the middle – wanting minimal barriers to the future development of its own biotech industry but wishing to protect its current regulatory system, which includes the broader-based "precautionary" approach to LMO decision-making. Despite almost deal-destroying differences over some terms in the lead-up to the BP, the basic informed consent mechanism was widely accepted.

However, the purpose of the AIA rule as an instrument is to achieve environmental goals such as biosafety and trade goals such as lowered transaction costs. The presumed mechanism of environmental effectiveness is that only those transactions that are shown to be environmentally safe or economically sound in the course of risk assessments will be allowed to proceed. The logic in a trade setting is that information asymmetry can decrease the efficiency of trades (if a lack of information creates excess risk aversion or if a lack of caution results in environmental damage that offsets other economic gains).

With the actual logic unarticulated in negotiations, however, one could speculate about several possibilities. First, what might be labelled the "naïve" version of the logic holds that more or better information leads to better decisions. Accordingly, informed consent procedures require extensive risk assessments, and this information will be interpreted in a way that systematically favours the environment. This logic ignores phenomena such as information overload and cognitive biases. Second, more sophisticated logics may be constructed, in either positive or cynical veins. A positive logic acknowledges that the informed consent is not perfect. It is subject to cognitive biases and so on, but it is better than nothing. Operating transparently over time, informed consent will serve increasingly to allay fears about new technologies and provide people with the widest possible range of environmental safety information. When people have the information they need, they will make environmentally sound decisions. The cynical logic, in contrast, assumes that the process will always be manipulative in one form or another. If it has any value at all, it is to indemnify the purveyors of risky commodities.

Informed consent in the biomedical context is based more or less explicitly on a comparative choice. Even when the decision is limited to two options (treat or do not treat), the information disclosed (or otherwise known to the recipient) should set out the relative risks, costs, and benefits of the alternatives. The recipient may then consider this information in light of his or her own values and knowledge. However, in the AIA case, there is no explicit requirement to address any alternatives to the proposed transaction. There are weak implicit grounds, if one accepts that an importer's decision will entail a comparative risk assessment. It bears emphasizing that even though a particular course of action appears to be beneficial for the recipient, it does not follow that it should be the preferred course of action.

Biomedical writers draw attention to several critical concepts embedded in informed consent. A key condition of "informed" is the actual understanding of information. Faden and Beauchamp (1986, p. 252) define full or complete understanding as "a fully adequate apprehension of all the relevant propositions or statements (those that contribute in any way to obtaining an appreciation of the situation) that correctly describes i) the nature of the action and ii) the foreseeable consequences and possible outcomes that might follow as a result of performing and not performing the action". A person may fail to comprehend because he or she is "incompetent," perhaps because of the emotional strain of serious illness. But understanding is usually approached as a function of information communication and cognition. If we set an "expert" standard for comprehension, nearly everyone would appear ignorant (Alderson and Goodey, 1998). Moreover, numerous studies have shown that even experts have difficulty interpreting statistical information. In contrast, social theories of risk hold that desires and fears (so-called "irrational" decision influences) can be systematic and sensible

(Krimsky and Golding, 1992). Understanding may require a significant reframing of responsibility and risk (Alderson and Goodey, 1998) especially given the significant uncertainties that often accompany new technologies in trade.

Comprehension in the international arena is bound up with decision-making capacity. Calls for capacity-building assistance in risk assessment underscore the point that biosafety is best achieved co-operatively, not through piecemeal national efforts, further reinforcing the trade logic that players should be equal. Here, a lack of comprehension is attributed not to a failure to communicate clearly or to an absence of cognitive ability, but to resource constraints that limit the availability of experts and the processing of information. Capacity-building may also be supported by the Internet-based clearing-house, which creates joint value by facilitating the exchange of information. Yet the capacity debate, with its focus on equality, may miss the point that comprehension is a function of information relevant to a specific situation. Importers' consent decisions require somewhat different, and additional, information from that supplied by exporters. An importer must be able to clearly understand the nature of the proposed action and the foreseeable consequences as described in a risk assessment. But the importer also needs to understand the relevance of the information for the country's own consent decision.

Alderson and Goodey (1998) show that "consent" is variously understood. Users with a positivist definition, such as one defined legally or according to a set of "objective" measures, tend to focus on information as a thing given to recipients. Consent (or lack of consent) is then a function of how well the "thing" is communicated to the recipient. In contrast, a constructed consent allows numerous social and personal influences to shape a recipient's ability and choices. The functionalist definition recognizes that consent may be merely a ceremonial token. As a trade rule, informed consent is largely in the positivist vein. The focus in the BP negotiation, as detailed in annexes, is on the information content of the disclosure. The information required is prescriptively defined and "scientific". No mention is made of information on likely unintended outcomes that could result from errors in handling and use of a product, for instance. The Like-Minded Group failed to extend the treaty to explicitly cover social and economic consequences of LMO trade.

In the biomedical context, while a recipient initially "consents" by signing a form, there is a presumption of an ongoing obligation. A recipient is usually informed that he or she may withdraw from the course of action at any time, without having to give a reason. Similarly, in consenting to a course of action, the recipient expects to be kept up-to-date about his or her progress and about any other options that may open up over time. In the AIA context, the presumption is that consent is a once-and-for-all decision. New information about the traded item may trigger a review of the decision. But to avoid trade disputes, recipients acting on the new information must provide a specific reason to believe that the item is not as safe as earlier believed. Any such decision also needs to be trade-neutral.

Prominent in the biomedical context is the competence of a recipient to consent and, if competence is lacking, the assignment of decision-making to a competent agent. The issue of "effective competence" arises when assessing the actual locus of decision-making power. Various writers have examined the issue of the competence to consent of children, foetuses, and people with mental or emotional impairment. As with disclosure and consent, judgments about competence made in a positivist frame are likely to differ from those made in a constructivist frame. A person may be competent under one set of conditions but not another; one's religious views may lead to beliefs that make a person incompetent in the view of one judge but not another. As a generalization, the thrust of the literature is to give much benefit of the doubt to the recipient in order to minimize the use of agent consent. Consequently, a person with significant mental impairment or a child is granted as much respect as possible. A less than "optimal" therapeutic result is considered an acceptable price for this respect.

In international trade, consent is essentially by agent. The agents in an AIA are likely to be commercial exporting (perhaps multinational) entities and importing government officials ("competent national authorities"). Individuals who will be directly exposed to the item traded (such as a hazardous pesticide or a genetically modified field crop) and thus bear the greatest risks are not accorded any rights to information or consent (unless they are provided for in domestic legislation). In contrast, the elaboration of rules under the Convention on Biological Diversity for plant genetic resources states explicitly that the "consent of those directly concerned by the access activity should be sought" (UNEP, 1998f, par. 42).

As Faden and Beauchamp (1986) show, non-control is a fluid concept like comprehension, allowing for a "grey-zone" where a perfectly non-controlled decision shades into a controlled one. The key concept is "influence" (Faden and Beauchamp, 1986, p. 256). At one extreme, coercion is an intentional act performed by others, for which they are responsible and which they could avoid, that presents a credible, irresistible threat of harm. Coercion always compromises autonomy. At the other extreme, persuasion never compromises autonomy but instead improves understanding and facilitates choice through the presentation of reasoned argument. In between, various manipulations of options, rewards, or information change perceptions about the available choices in ways that are not related to understanding (Faden and Beauchamp, 1986, pp. 345-355). In the research context, for instance, institutional boards carefully scrutinize any payments to ensure that they are not manipulative. An important potential source of effective coercion is economic. If a recipient is very poor, options that would otherwise be deemed too risky but involve some economic benefits may be chosen. The issue may be further complicated when the risky activity is just one aspect of a relationship that engenders other rewards.

Conclusion

Prior informed consent is a rich norm that combines negative and positive freedoms. Thus "informed" relates to a recipient's right to not be denied information in understandable forms. "Consent" relates to the positive, enabling right to make a choice. The negative freedom dominates the expressed interests of BP Parties who emphasize environmental and health outcomes. AIA is seen as a morally grounded vehicle to ensure that the best possible information on potential harms is available to decision-makers. In this respect it is like the PIC and Basel mechanism in serving as a warning system. In contrast, the positive freedom resonates with Parties who emphasize trade. In their view, the AIA principle is primarily a pro forma ritual to smooth trade relations and minimize business-related risk. It serves as a template for, or guide to, common expectations in decision-making. Like the "initiator-centred" conception of informed consent in the biomedical context, the Miami Group emphasized the efficiency goals of the treaty in BP negotiations. Corresponding to the "recipient-centred" view, the Like-Minded Group put weight on the equity side. The Miami Group argued for narrow definitions and prescribed rules. The Like-Minded Group wanted the flexibility to take into account a wide range of risk variables.

Informed consent arose in the biomedical context in an era before "cost containment" and before the tremendous advances in health-related technology meant that the possible treatments would far outstrip their affordability. It evolved in a rights-tinged political environment and has come of age in a strongly litigious era. In contrast, prior informed consent in the international context has only recently emerged, specifically as a solution that balances some Parties' interest in an efficiency objective and others' interest in non-efficiency objectives. As a result, informed consent is heralded as a way to advance all Parties' joint objective: a trade regime that is efficient and that does not harm the environment. As a new idea, international prior informed consent has not yet experienced the full brunt of defensive risk management in the face of liability for harm. If the AIA implementation follows trends in biomedicine, we can expect to see it function more in setting broad parameters around acceptable decisions and decision-making procedures than as an actual mechanism for shared – and environmentally effective – decisions and outcomes.

However, as a policy matter, the emergence of AIA directs attention to the ongoing debate about the proper scope for direct regulation as opposed to the non-prescriptive, individual-decision-affirming information disclosure approaches. Certainly, the record of direct approaches internationally is dismal. Prior informed consent may be particularly well suited in the sense that it is the best we have to work with, in both trade and environmental contexts. Within a trade paradigm, for instance, AIA may aim for an ideal in which people (who best know their own interests) decide for themselves under perfect information conditions. In the environmental protection paradigm, AIA represents the ideal that those most affected by a decision are morally entitled to information that will assist them in arriving at their own considered conclusions in a risky situation (Wolf, 2000). If this interpretation is accurate, we must direct attention to refining the operation of the mechanism and assuring its best application.

Informed consent – in one interpretation or another – is a widely attractive norm and policy instrument. Parties can agree to conduct trades using informed consent without necessarily agreeing on why. The mechanism is substantive, not merely a symbolic veil that everyone can support. The AIA mechanism is fundamentally a way of ensuring that all decisions have the same structure, not that all decisions come out the same way.

All of these observations serve mainly to suggest why informed consent has received attention and been written into treaties such as the BP. If we are to be confident that AIA will protect the environment effectively, we need to be vigilant on a number of fronts. Those who bear risks need to be informed and to consent; countries should be free to use economic, social, and cultural variables as they see fit in risk assessments without provoking trade disputes. Ultimately, the extent to which the informed consent procedure is used genuinely to aid in environmental decision-making, and not just routinely for trade convenience, will be the key to judging its success.

Notes

[1] In addition to the international applications examined here, "informed consent" is fast emerging in a range of areas not examined in this chapter, including employment law, indigenous peoples' rights, food labelling policy, and mediation (on the latter, see Nolan-Haley, 1999; the others are from a small sample of current discourse in New Zealand and from Aroha Mead, personal communication, October 2000).

[2] At a minimum, informed consent processes include two distinct interactions: an information disclosure or pointer to information and a decision authorizing or refusing a course of action (a treatment or trade, for instance). Because the informed consent process can end with no action, it needs to be borne in mind that the recipient of information is only a potential recipient of the focal action, and similarly for the initiator.

[3] In biomedical applications, a recipient may be represented by an agent, if he or she is a child, for instance, or deemed otherwise incompetent to participate in the informed consent procedure. The "initiator" may appear to the recipient as a team or even as an institution. Nevertheless, the relationship is clearly considered in the literature of informed consent to be a one-to-one, decision-making process. Legal precedent, based in the law of battery and negligence, reinforces this view (Faden and Beauchamp, 1986).

[4] In addition to the three treaties considered in the text, two other major trade/environment treaties are built around mechanisms that can be interpreted as collective decision versions of informed consent. The Montreal Protocol and other ozone layer treaties give effect to a set of allowed and prohibited trades (denoted by ozone depleting substance, country, year, and use) to which the signatories "consent". The Convention on International Trade in Endangered Species of Wild Fauna and Flora (CITES) may be similarly interpreted. Here, regular meetings of the Parties serve to refine the collective "consent" of the Parties to species' inclusion on annex lists, to set quotas, and to other aspects of affected trades under the Convention. In both cases, sharing information relevant to the treaties' objectives is prominent. Legal trades under the conventions have the "prior informed consent," in this

broad interpretation, of the treaty Parties. This consent differs from a consent that may exist under WTO agreements, for instance, because of the specificity of the affected trade.

[5] The Nuremberg Code is part of the judgement in the *Doctor's Trial* conducted in the US Military Tribunal No.1 (*United States v. Karl Brandt, Trials of War Criminals Before the Nuremberg Military Tribunal under Control Council Law No. 10*, 1948; see Miller, 1997, pp. 207-8).

[6] For instance, fully informed free choice may be very costly. Transaction costs detract from efficiency, as do a number of other "market imperfections". More to the point, efficiency is an aggregate quality, applied to a market system or a set of exchanges. Free choice, by contrast, is a quality of individuals. In managed care, the efficiency of the institution may mean that certain options for care will not be offered to individuals, thus constraining their choice.

[7] This point was suggested by an anonymous reviewer of my recent article (Wolf, 2000) in a comment that highlighted the learning-feedback loop of informed consent.

[8] The recipient can choose to allow subsequent trades without prior informed consent at the time of first authorization.

[9] Despite these requirements, follow-through has been slow. As of 31 May 2000, a total of 1,886 decisions had been registered (of which 19 per cent were consents), while there were 2,690 of non-response (responses that did not address importation or failures to provide responses). (Data from UNEP, 2000b, p. 4.)

[10] Article 19, par. 3 of the CBD calls for AIA in the "field of the safe transfer, handling, and use…" of LMOs.

[11] Krueger (2000) refers to PIC as a "governance structure".

[12] This is not necessarily to say that the initiator believes the risks to be minimal, although that appears to be the case among today's main exporters – rather, that any projected costs are outweighed by projected benefits.

[13] The risk of making the wrong decision or the risk of not truly knowing one's own mind are everyday usages of "risk" that are not consistent with technical usage.

[14] Argentina, Australia, Canada, Chile, United States, and Uruguay.

Chapter 7

The Fair and Equitable Sharing of Benefits from the Exploitation of Genetic Resources: A Difficult Transition from Principles to Reality

François Blais

Introduction

The Convention on Biological Diversity (CBD) has three objectives: protecting biological diversity, the sustainable use of its components, and the fair and equitable sharing of the benefits generated by the exploitation of genetic resources. This chapter addresses the third objective and seeks to explain the reasons why it remains so difficult to achieve. Following a brief overview of the provisions of the CBD for fair and equitable sharing, and what has been achieved so far by those mandated to implement it, I will describe the three components common to all redistribution projects and review the difficulties associated with each.

The fair and equitable sharing of benefits raises institutional, political, and intellectual challenges of great complexity. Our purpose is to highlight some of these challenges, while stressing the need to continue experimenting with existing agreements and at the same time, as much as possible, continue reinforcing the role of international and national agencies responsible for improving these agreements and the conservation of biodiversity.

The CBD and the Fair and Equitable Sharing of Benefits

The general preoccupation that led to the clauses of the Convention with distribution implications is intuitively easy to understand. First of all, by mere chance biodiversity is distributed unequally on the planet, and developing countries are often located where biological diversity is richest.[1] Conversely, the financial, technical, and scientific means necessary for the commercial exploitation of the genetic components of biodiversity are more commonly found in developed countries.

Considering that the objective of protecting biodiversity[2] is now seen as a "common concern of humankind,"[3] and that the appropriate measures to attain this goal will necessarily generate considerable economic costs or "opportunities," the CBD clearly specifies that developed countries must provide support to developing countries to help them achieve this goal.[4] One way of conceiving the distribution question implied in the goal of maintaining biodiversity would be: ensure that the necessary efforts and costs required are shared among all countries while, one would expect, taking into consideration the paying capacity of each. The required effort is of course impossible to calculate. There are millions of animal and plant species to protect, and specific interest in protecting any individual species can vary considerably according to circumstances and period, as will the resources available for achieving it. Probably the only imaginable solution is to start by defining certain governmental priorities and ensure international support for the efforts of these countries (Swanson, 1997).

This chapter does not deal with this first conception of distributive justice but rather with another one, just as strongly asserted by the CBD: the practices and difficulties associated with achieving the goals of Article 19, which is intented to guide the sharing of various benefits flowing from biogenetic manipulations for commercial purposes. Clauses 1 and 2 of this Article state respectively that:

> Each Contracting Party shall take legislative, administrative or policy measures, as appropriate, to provide for the effective participation in biotechnological research activities by those Contracting Parties, especially developing countries, which provide the genetic resources for such research, and where feasible in such Contracting Parties.[5]

and that:

> Each Contracting Party shall take all practicable measures to promote and advance priority access on a fair and equitable basis by Contracting Parties, especially developing countries, to the results and benefits arising from biotechnologies based on genetic resources provided by those Contracting Parties. Such access shall be on mutually agreed terms.[6]

Although the sovereignty of states in legislative matters and in the use of their natural resources, particularly genetic "resources," is entirely recognized by the Convention, the signatory Parties nevertheless agreed to provide guidelines for this right by introducing new responsibilities:

> Each Contracting Party shall endeavour to create conditions to facilitate access to genetic resources for environmentally sound uses by other Contracting Parties and not to impose restrictions that run counter to the objectives of the Convention.[7]

Thus, the Convention seeks to facilitate access to genetic resources for purposes associated with maintaining biodiversity (surveys, research, protection measures). However, it also requires the targeted country's permission for this access, especially if the purpose is commercial, because it is in such situations that benefit-sharing issues truly arise. "Equity" is therefore initially understood as a property and rather extensive usage right over the resources located in the territory of all contracting states.[8]

In parallel to this recognition, Article 16 (2) clearly reaffirms the protection of the intellectual property rights of biotechnologies. It recognizes intellectual property rights, and each Party pledges to facilitate access to new technologies, and their transfer, on the basis of mutually advantageous agreements. In the case of technology subject to patents and other intellectual property rights, such access and transfer shall be provided on terms that recognize and are consistent with the adequate and effective protection of intellectual property rights.

Of course, in the absence of an institutional structure with minimal requirements and explicit criteria for the sharing of costs and benefits, many observers have been sceptical about the possibility of attaining this objective (Beurier, 1996; Miller, 1995, pp. 109-28; Pallemaerts, 1995; Hulbut, 1994, pp. 379-409). However, typical of large international agreements, the CBD, in the quest for a consensus, wanted initially to reiterate the rights and privileges of each participant to the agreement. We must now try to mold these rights and privileges, and this will be achieved through a long negotiation process among the signatory Parties, which is only now beginning.

A Response from the Conference of the Parties

Putting the objective stated at the Rio Earth Summit into concrete form is part of a long and sometimes arduous process ranging in this case from negotiations among states to compromises between suppliers and users of genetic resources. It was mainly during a succession of meetings of the Conference of the Parties (COP) that the establishment of an institutional mechanism that could help achieve the fair distribution objective was discussed.

As early as the first meeting (COP-1, 1994), a mid-term work schedule was drawn up,[9] requesting the Secretariat of the CBD, among others, to prepare a general report on access and benefit-sharing. This study was presented at COP-2 (1995)[10] which in its Decision II/12 requested a preliminary study of the impacts of intellectual property rights in regard to the conservation of biodiversity and the sharing of benefits from its use. The ensuing report was submitted at COP-3 (Buenos Aires, 1996).[11]

Following up on Decision III/5 (1998), two notes from the Executive Secretary were the subject of items 16 (1) and 16 (2) on the agenda of COP-4 (1998).[12] It was then requested, through Decision IV/8, to establish a panel of experts composed of representatives of the private sector as well as of local and indigenous communities. The objective was "to draw upon all relevant sources, including legislative, policy and administrative measures, best practices and case-studies on access to genetic resources and benefit-sharing arising from the use of those genetic resources, including the whole range of biotechnology, in the development of a common understanding of basic concepts and to explore all options for access and benefit-sharing on mutually agreed terms including guiding principles, guidelines, and codes of best practice for access and benefit-sharing arrangements".

The panel's conclusions were included in the Report of the Panel of Experts on Access and Benefit-Sharing,[13] which was submitted to COP-5 (2000). At the same meeting, an ad hoc panel with unrestricted participation was created (Decision V/26) to examine various factors related to access and benefit-sharing. In particular, these issues were raised: the prior informed consent procedure and the conditions governing any mutual agreement; the role, duties, and participation of the agreeing Parties; benefit-sharing mechanisms based, for example, on technology transfer and joint research and development activities; how to ensure the respect, conservation, and maintenance of the knowledge, innovations, and practices of local and indigenous communities; and the question of intellectual property.[14]

In spite of all these discussions and prolific report production, no specific line of conduct, norm, or policy has yet been determined by the signatory Parties of the Convention. However, this institutional vacuum has not prevented the signing and implementation of agreements between suppliers and corporations, as we shall see in the following section.

Four Examples of Benefit-Sharing Agreements

Four examples of agreements promoting a degree of benefit-sharing in the commercial use of genetic resources give us a better understanding of the issues at stake.

Without doubt, the best known and most quoted is the agreement signed in 1991 (predating the CBD) between the American pharmaceutical company Merck and the Instituto Nacional de Biodiversidad (INBio) of Costa Rica. Their agreement stipulated that in return for granting the exclusive right to conduct pharmaceutical and agricultural research on samples of indigenous wild species identified and conserved by INBio, Merck agreed to (i) give, through INBio, approximately one million dollars to this biodiversity-rich country; (ii) concede to the government of Costa Rica a fixed monetary share of the entire revenue earned by the multinational firm for commercial products developed from biological specimens obtained through the agreement; (iii) give the equivalent of $180,000 USD in equipment; (iv) train competent technical personnel on-site to accomplish the major tasks (OECD, 1999; Rolston, 1995; Hulbut, 1992).

In a very different context and with very different arrangements, Laird and Lisinge (1998) studied an agreement signed in Cameroon concerning the use of two specific plant resources: *ancistrocladus korupensis* (a plant potentially useful for treating HIV) and *prunus africana* (a tree with bark having recognized medicinal properties against hyperplasia [cancer] of the prostate) (OECD, 1999). The 1992 agreement on *ancistrocladus korupensis* brought together Korup National Park, the University of Yaoundé, and the government of Cameroon on the supplier's side and the National Cancer Institute (NCI) of the United States, the Missouri Botanical Garden, and Purdue University on the side of the users. The contractual terms stipulated, among other things, that in exchange for access to the resource, the NCI agreed to communicate the results of its tests, collaborate in matters of research, and pay dues and give other forms of compensation (equipment, support for infrastructures, technological transfer) to its Cameroon partners (OECD, 1999). As for *prunus africana*, the protagonists were the villages of Mapanja and Bokwongo, the Mont Cameroon Project, and the Ministry of Environment and Forests of Cameroon on one side and the French firm Plantecam-Medicam on the other. This agreement, signed in 1997, was designed specifically to reduce massive illegal harvests: "it guarantees, to each village, the purchase by the firm of a maximum of 10 tons per month, paid to the harvesters on the basis of the price paid to intermediaries, 7 percent of these gains being deposited to a Village Development Fund (OECD, 1999, p. 47).

Moran (1998) reports on a trial project in Nigeria in the 1990s that sought to establish a viable arrangement for benefit-sharing in bioprospecting. On the suppliers' side, the Parties were local traditional healers organizations, Bioresources Development and Conservation Programme (BDCP), an NGO based in Nigeria, and the University of Nigeria; on the users' side were the American firm Shaman Pharmaceuticals (whose expertise lies in developing plant-based therapeutic products) and its subsidiary NGO, the Healing Forest Conservancy (HFC), which is dedicated to conserving the biodiversity of tropical forests. In summary, the agreement included the long-term payment of dues by Shaman Pharmaceuticals to its collaborators through HFC. Dues are to be paid on an equal basis "among all collaborators having worked with the firm, and this whatever the origin of the sample or the traditional knowledge used" (OECD, 1999, p. 47).

Finally, another agreement model presented by Gillaud (1998) and known as Biodivalor was proposed by a French NGO, Pro-Natura International (PNI) and financed to the extent of up to seven million francs (approximately one million dollars US) by the French government. PNI acts as an intermediary between a prospector and a supplier country during the process of obtaining samples and ensures that the obligations of all Parties are respected. At the centre of this mechanism is the Special Ecodevelopment Fund, which takes in all the profits from the sale of samples and half of all revenue received when a sample leads to a commercial product. A trial agreement of this type has also been in effect in Gabon since 1996.

In summary:

> The Biodivalor contract seeks to establish a long term relationship between Pro-Natura International (PNI), a scientific supplier organization and the industrial users to which a limited exclusivity is initially granted, which could be extended at the request of the user. With the creation of the Fund, the local communities are also participating Parties to the contract although, until now, only as beneficiaries of the local development project. (OECD, 1999, p. 48)

It is important to note that the type of "benefits" received by either side in this kind of agreement generally have a monetary and a non-monetary component. Because such collaborations are still relatively recent, non-monetary advantages have prevailed the most, being independent of the materialization of commercial products from the research of pharmaceutical firms. For the supplier, these advantages usually lie in technology transfers for bioprospecting, in shared research results (sometimes even in the status of the author of the results), in support for priority medical research, and in the setting up of a fund to finance local development projects; for users, advantages come in the form of access to genetic resources and local knowledge, the use of local infrastructure, shared authorship of the results obtained, and public profile. As for monetary benefits, the most significant are: (i) dues received by suppliers for samples of biogenetic material and in some cases for commercialized products; and (ii) profits received by biotechnology firms on the sale of developed products protected by industrial patents (OECD, 1999). These arrangements will be discussed in the following section.

Defining an "Equitable" Compensation

The objective of the fair and equitable sharing of benefits arising from the exploitation of genetic resources creates not only practical but also theoretical difficulties. This objective demands that three complementary requirements of distributive justice be defined as clearly as possible: i) the *nature of the benefits* in question (the *distribuendum*); ii) the *agents that possess a right* to these resources (the *distribuendis*); and iii) the *criteria* according to which the sharing can be said to be "equitable" (the *distribuens*).

What Do We Share (the Distribuendum)?

If the CBD has included the principle of equitable compensation among its objectives, it is primarily because there is a commercial value attached to the use of certain resources. Of course, this value is neither given nor immediate. If that were the case, those closest to the resource would exploit it themselves. However, under present circumstances, they must collaborate with partners already capable of developing the economic potential of the resource.

Today, two large sectors of economic activity use genetic resources: the agrofood industry and the pharmaceutical industry. Their needs, however, may differ. The agricultural industry usually seeks genetic material that could eventually be used in other environments. Thus, we talk about the "exportation" of genetic materials from a supplier country. The pharmaceutical industry, on the other hand, is generally looking for more specific properties that it can "copy" and integrate into its products. Thus we talk about "incorporating" information of a genetic nature (see Swanson, 1995). The contribution of genetic resources in these biotechnology fields has become more crucial, although for most part genetic research remains essentially a laboratory pursuit. In fact, most biotechnology corporations prefer to invest in replacement technologies rather than in bioprospecting, which remains costly and requires a lot of time and in which truly marketable discoveries are more the exception than the rule (although this could change).

Biotechnology incorporates several elements that range from the genetic resource itself (strategic potential, availability, accessibility *in situ* or *ex situ*, etc.) to the in-house know-how of the corporation (research and development, transformation, links with consumers, etc.). If market conditions are favourable, it is possible to earn revenues that can be shared in various ways between the supplier of the resource and the partner who transforms it and exploits it commercially. The preceding section cited a number of examples of current practices aimed at equitable compensation, ranging from dues on anticipated or actual profits to payment of a continuous revenue, but the spectrum of possibilities is probably infinite.

The non-monetary advantages aimed at "enhancing the capabilities" of supplier countries are also noteworthy. In fact, if we examine practices of the last ten years, they have clearly dominated their monetary counterparts (access rights and dues). Compensation of this type can vary: hiring indigenous people, technology transfers to supplier countries, free training of skilled workers, sharing of research results, establishing a fund to finance local development projects, etc. Most of the time, the immediate goal is to integrate the local community rapidly into bioprospecting work.

The hope is that supplier countries will gain other benefits as well, such as a greater share of the profits and, more important, a better mastery of the process leading to commercialization. This would help them become more autonomous from large multinational corporations one day and eventually market their products themselves. Finally, non-monetary benefits may be considered as a means of improving the overall economic level of the supplier country by accelerating its progress in economic development or sustainable development.

The forms of compensation are therefore as important for equity as the level of equity itself. Strictly monetary benefits are probably necessary, but they may reflect an essentially short-term perspective if they are the only kind of benefit included. Non-monetary benefits are part of a longer-term logic, aimed at increasing the autonomy of supplier countries.

Who Has a Right to the Sharing (the Distribuendis)?

In principle, in any transaction of this kind there is a supplier of genetic material, generally a developing country, and a private firm that wishes to use it commercially and usually has its head office in a developed country. Following a commercial logic, one might think that benefit-sharing should be left entirely to the discretion of these two Parties: the supplier of the raw material and the private firm with the skills. However, reality is more complex. Indeed, it is far from easy to determine which Parties are involved and what their respective rights are.

Among those who should normally have a say in the sharing of benefits, consumers of the products derived from the resources rank first. Their primary interest is to obtain useful and effective products at a reasonable cost. In the end, it is consumers who consent to the funds needed for compensation, and their capacity to pay is of course limited. Next are the firms that invest the capital necessary for bioprospecting and possess the expertise and skills. They are aware that they are taking significant risks and hope that their investment will reap profits. In exchange for the recognition of the property rights of suppliers over samples taken, firms at minimum expect that patents on products developed in their laboratories will be respected.

For supplier countries, the situation is even more complex. In many cases, indigenous communities living near the resource have accumulated a traditional knowledge of its use. Their lifestyle can be negatively affected by bioprospecting or the intensive cultivation of certain rare resources. Compensation for the inconveniences they suffer, in monetary form or otherwise, is generally entirely justified. However, their "property right" to the resource is not always formally established. In that case, they must seek to obtain it, and depending on the laws and customs of local authorities, the process may not be easy or even obvious. Local communities are in a similar situation. Bioprospecting and commercial exploitation of a particular genetic resource may cause degradation of their immediate natural environment while at the same time improving their livelihood through, among other things, the influx of capital and the creation of jobs. Local universities or research centres are usually involved in bioprospecting agreements. Their local knowledge is recognized, and they are the first to be able to offer a well-trained work-force.

Experience has shown that the national governments of supplier countries are generally part of the process leading to a co-operation agreement. Their participation will often prevent, among other things, a non-sustainable exploitation of the resource. More than private organizations, governments generally tend to see their role as that of a protector of the resource for future generations, a concern reflected in legislation or national institutions dedicated to overseeing such agreements, as in Australia, Brazil, Cameroon, Costa Rica, and Indonesia. It would be helpful if the states in which the head offices of multinational firms seeking to exploit resources are located would reflect these policies and oversee the firms to ensure that they respect the same operating principles inside and outside the country. We will return to this issue in the conclusion.

Of course, the increasing number of players involved, their very different "contributions," their wide range of circumstances, and their often incompatible interests do not help in the search for a satisfactory solution to fair and equitable benefit-sharing. Some products require the intensive and continuous harvest of a resource, which is likely to impact negatively on the environment. Other products may be synthesized in the laboratory. The "contribution" of each Party to the process that will eventually lead to the commercialization of a genetic resource is not easy to determine, and the solution does not depend only on the good faith of the Parties concerned. Economics teaches that, ideally, the "efficient" solution to the sharing of revenues resides in identifying the property rights (or usage rights) of each of the Parties involved in the transformation process beforehand. In situations where the Parties to the transaction are not clearly defined or their "contribution" recognized, as is often the case, an agreement on a voluntary basis appears much more difficult to achieve.

To these difficulties must be added the fact that two types of complementary rights must be recognized in order to achieve a co-operation agreement that may lead to benefit-sharing: on the one hand, the right to the resource itself and the use of its genetic material; on the other hand, the intellectual property right required for firms to undertake the research and development necessary for the transformation of the product. That the CBD explicitly recognizes these two rights does not mean that a consensus exists on their nature – to the contrary. The assertion of these rights has, in fact, given rise to an immense literature marked by opposing viewpoints. Some authors entirely challenge the intellectual property rights that are often appropriated by firms from developed countries (Stenson and Gray, 1999; Fowler, 1995; Hobbelink, 1995; Shiva, 1995; Shiva and Holla-Bohar, 1993). Others take an opposite view, calling for a limit to exclusive rights to the resource (Svatos, 1996; Rolston, 1995; Michael, 1995; Russell, 1988). Notwithstanding the theoretical aspect of the debate and the often quite extreme viewpoints, a dose of pragmatism is required. Usage rights considered by one of the Parties as exaggerated would simply make it impossible to reach any agreement. In a world where alternative solutions are still possible, Parties have a vested interest in finding a balance between their differing expectations and in being realistic. Experience over the last few years seems to indicate that this balance is still achievable today. However, the existence of compensation agreements does not obviate the question of determining whether benefits are being fairly and equitably shared. If a good understanding of each other's interests is often enough to engender co-operation among humans, that does not automatically make all forms of co-operation "fair".

According to What Criteria Should We Share (the Distribuens)?

The choice of a guiding principle for benefit-sharing does not follow from the teachings of a positive science, such as economics for example, but from more general considerations of social justice. As a discipline, economics is absolutely silent on the issue of equitable sharing of revenues. Economics can of course specify the general conditions under which these revenues can exist and even bear interest. It can also propose hypotheses on the level of distribution that will allow its "optimization". However, optimization must not be confused with equity, which is more sensitive to the redistribution impact (Okun, 1975).

The definition of a sharing principle is therefore in the domain of public debate, but it still must acknowledge economic and political realities. The distribution of revenues according to a previously defined criterion while ignoring the real exchange conditions between Parties could lead to a suboptimal situation and even prevent the conclusion of agreements deemed "acceptable" by the majority of Parties. The circumstances leading to an eventual co-operation between firms and suppliers of genetic resources are so different from one case to the next that forcing the Parties to agree to a given benefit-sharing scheme would simply jeopardize the signing of many agreements. Economic collaboration generally requires a great deal of flexibility in defining arrangements, and when not strictly necessary, unilateral norms that do not correspond to the needs or expectations of the Parties concerned should be avoided.

For practical reasons, but also as a question of principles, if international norms are ever established on sharing the benefits of the exploitation of genetic resources, it is almost certain that these norms will be relatively vague and will not define all the details of the sharing agreement in advance. Indeed, as long as the principle of the sovereignty of states over their resources remains the accepted norm, we will have to accept, in the interest of the same principle, a wide margin for negotiation between Parties. The norm to which we could ask them to conform would not define the level or the nature of the benefits to be shared in advance but would probably establish certain constraints or procedures to "validate" the agreements. Of course, procedural constraints of this type, or others we could think of, are not sufficient to make any agreement "fair" or "equitable". There are several reasons for this, but the main one will always be disproportion in the balance of power between Parties. In some cases, the multinational firms negotiating these agreements have revenues exceeding the GNP of supplier states. The capacity of the Parties to negotiate is therefore not at all the same, and this can create several distortions prejudicial to the minimal requirements of an equitable agreement. Furthermore, firms usually have alternatives when they cannot reach an agreement with their supplier. They can, for example, obtain their resources elsewhere or try to create a synthetic substitute in the laboratory. The suppliers, generally developing countries, do not have as many options. Under these circumstances, they can hardly expect to obtain a very high revenue. Those who believed that such agreements could lead to a new El Dorado probably overestimated the real outcome.[15]

Disproportion in the balance of power is one of the reasons (although not the only one) why we can never entirely be sure that a voluntary agreement will result in an "equitable" compensation scheme. There are too many contingent factors involved in the signing of these agreements for them to be entirely satisfactory in terms of equity.

Conclusion: Seeking a Balance between the Various Objectives of the CBD

The quest for "equity" primarily concerns the principle of respect for basic human rights. In the present case, that means making it possible for all groups that consider they have a right to equitable compensation to be heard. This constraint, however, remains fairly minimal. It prevents the worst abuses of economic colonialism and biological "piracy," but it does nothing to ensure the establishment of a procedure that would guarantee an equitable result. Stating that negotiated voluntary agreements are equitable from the outset brings us back, in a way, to the "formal" concept of rights defended by radical liberals such as Friedrich Hayek or Robert Nozick. It also amounts to saying that the state should not establish any wealth redistribution mechanism and remain content to enforce the "spontaneous" revenues accruing from work or from capital. This minimalist concept of distributive justice is considered quite marginal nowadays and is certainly at odds with the very spirit of the CBD.

In an ideal international community, a "Leviathan" would probably exist to oversee better distribution of global wealth among people. This world does not exist. We can, however, hope that over the upcoming years, the Conference of the Parties or the CBD Secretariat will make a number of proposals to improve the situation and "even up" the forces involved. Developed countries can also make a major contribution to this effort. The majority of biotechnology firms have their head office in these countries. It is therefore easier for developed countries to influence these firms directly, for example, by establishing legislation and monetary or fiscal incentives that would compel them to behave in a sustainable and equitable way when dealing with developing countries. The governments of developed countries have access to better mechanisms than international organizations do to play the role of guardian of the principles of the CBD. Therefore, they have a moral responsibility to do so.

Finally, we must recall that genetic resources have both a private value and a public value. The private value comes from the resource's commercial potential as an element in the development of a pharmaceutical or agricultural biotechnology product. The public value is linked to other social objectives that are equally important: quality of life, the beauty of landscapes, and the conservation of biodiversity. These two values can sometimes be opposed: striving for equitable sharing by no means guarantees that conserving biodiversity will be any easier.

The complex nature of the environmental "value" must not be forgotten in our future reflections. The sharing of benefits derives from two different logics, which may very well prove to be at odds. We may first consider transactions between suppliers and producers as "private". In that case, each Party only seeks to maximize its own benefits, and the purpose of the bargaining is to determine each Party's share. The risk with this method, of course, is that the agreements it produces will ignore other objectives of the Convention, such as the conservation of ecosystems, the maintenance of biodiversity, and the protection of local communities, simply to maximize profits. For example, a very lucrative agreement for the supplier countries of a resource that is very rare and difficult to synthesize might well lead to unsustainable exploitation of the resource. This would be in complete contradiction to the spirit of the CBD. According to the simple logic of maximizing mutual profit, "fair and equitable sharing" would occur to the detriment of the primary objective of the Convention. Since there is no private market for the conservation of biodiversity because it is a public patrimony, competent authorities must intervene so that agreements on sharing revenues from exploiting genetic resources pay sufficient attention to the public property. We must therefore find ways of reconciling the maximization of revenue with the other objectives of the CBD. Setting up parallel funds financed through agreements for the use of genetic resources may be one of those ways.

The Conference of the Parties and the Secretariat for biodiversity now have a fundamental role that they must keep in mind: limit the possibilities for conflict between the objectives of the CBD. These institutions will be effective at playing this role if they remain well-informed about existing benefit-sharing agreements and then police them to prevent the logic of private bargaining from prevailing over respect for the public heritage.

Acknowledgements

I sincerely thank Marcel Filion, who researched the pertinent literature for this chapter and made a preliminary synthesis. This research has received funding from the Social Sciences and Humanities Research Council of Canada for a team research project led by Marie-Hélène Parizeau.

Notes

This chapter was translated by Patricia Wood.

[1] Tropical forests, which cover approximately 7 per cent of terrestrial areas, probably possess more than 50 per cent (perhaps up to 90 per cent) of living species. A relatively small country, such as Madagascar, has approximately 150,000 endemic species. Brazil, with slightly more than 6 per cent of the Earth's area, has 22 per cent of its plant species. See : Miller (1995, p. 110); Panjabi (1997, p. 221); Yamin (1995, pp. 530-1).

[2] For an overview of estimates of the decrease in biodiversity on Earth, see Panjabi (1997, pp. 225-7).

[3] "Affirming that the conservation of biological diversity is a common concern of humankind," (CBD, 1992; preamble and p. 335).

[4] For example, the CBD stipulates that: "the Contracting Parties shall promote international technical and scientific co-operation in the field of conservation and sustainable use of biological diversity, where necessary, through the appropriate international and national institutions" (Article 18.1) and "the developed country... Parties shall provide new and additional financial resources to enable developing country Parties to meet the agreed full incremental costs to them of implementing measures which fulfill the obligations of this Convention..." (Article 20.2). See Ibid, pp. 365 and 367 respectively.

[5] CBD, Article 19.1 in Ibid, p. 366.

[6] CBD, Article 19.2 in Ibid, p. 366.

[7] CBD, Article 15.2 in Ibid, pp. 363-364.

[8] "[r]ecognizing the sovereign rights of States over their natural resources, the authority to determine access to genetic resources rests with the national governments and is subject to national legislation" (CBD, Article 15.1 in Ibid, p. 363).

[9] UNEP/CBD/COP/13.

[10] "Access to Genetic Resources and Benefit-Sharing Legislation, Administrative and Policy Information" (UNEP/CBD/COP/2/13).

[11] "The Impact of Intellectual Property Rights Systems on the Conservation and Sustainable Use of Biological Diversity and on the Equitable Sharing of Benefits from its Use" (UNEP/CBD/COP/3/22).

[12] "Measures to Promote and Advance the Distribution of Benefits from Biotechnology in Accordance with Article 19" (UNEP/CBD/COP/4/21); "Addressing the Fair and Equitable Sharing of the Benefits Arising out of Genetic Resources: Options for Assistance to Developing Country Parties to the Convention on Biological Diversity" (UNEP/CBD/COP/4/22).

[13] UNEP/CBD/COP/5/8.

[14] In October 2001 the Ad Hoc Open Ended Working Group on Access and Benefit-Sharing adopted the "Draft Bonn Guidelines on Access to Genetic Resources and Fair and Equitable Sharing of the Benefits Arising out of their Utilization," which are to be submitted to COP-6 in April 2002 (UNEP/CBD/COP/6/6).

[15] See Kerry ten Kate and Carolina A. Laird (1999).

Chapter 8

The Role of Indigenous Peoples in Conservation Actions: A Case Study of Cultural Differences and Conservation Priorities

Catherine Potvin, Jean-Pierre Revéret,
Geneviève Patenaude, and Jane Hutton

Introduction

This chapter examines the role that indigenous peoples (IP) or local communities play, or could play, in conserving biodiversity. The Convention on Biological Diversity (CBD) recognizes the importance of traditional ecological knowledge for the protection of biological diversity and the role that IP and local populations can play in its conservation. It tries to ensure that these roles are taken into account by the Parties to the Convention through Articles 8(j), 10(c), 17(2), 18(4) and related articles that specifically focus on IP and local communities. Above all, it is Article 8(j) that sets out the signatories' obligations in terms of IP and traditional knowledge (TK). Accordingly, each Contracting Party must:

> ...respect, preserve and maintain knowledge, innovations and practices of indigenous and local communities embodying traditional lifestyles relevant for the conservation and sustainable use of biological diversity and promote their wider application with the approval and involvement of the holders of such knowledge, innovations and practices and encourage the equitable sharing of the benefits arising from the utilization of such knowledge, innovations and practices[.]

Recognition of the importance of this human component has led to a model of "community-based" conservation grounded in traditional ecological knowledge (Gadgil et al., 1993). Many observers advocate increased involvement of local communities in the planning and management of protected areas (e.g. Western et al., 1994). For example, under the CBD, new development projects are subjected to impact assessment to determine *a priori* the consequences for biological diversity. Article 14(a) indeed requires that each Party to the Convention:

Introduce appropriate procedures requiring environmental impact assessment of its proposed projects that are likely to have significant adverse effects on biological diversity with a view to avoiding or minimizing such effects and, where appropriate, allow for public participation in such procedures[.]

The present-day practice of environmental impact assessments has begun to give more explicit consideration to traditional knowledge in parallel with scientific knowledge. Although there is still debate on the optimal way to approach biodiversity in impact studies, this is certainly another area in which traditional knowledge must be recognized in the implementation of the Convention.[1]

In the general context of this book, we ask in this chapter whether involving indigeneous people in conservation actions would influence their effectiveness. Given the wealth of biological resources in existence, the extent of the prevailing crisis, and the financial constraints, it is impossible to protect everything. The question then becomes, *What should we protect?* (Parizeau, 1997). Research on strategies to resolve the biodiversity crisis has put much effort into prioritizing conservation issues for action. This effort is essential since Article 8(c) of the CBD states that each Party must:

Regulate or manage biological resources important for the conservation of biological diversity whether within or outside protected areas, with a view to ensuring their conservation and sustainable use[.]

We believe that the possible role of indigenous people in protecting biological diversity and its effectiveness hinges on the following two issues. First, the effectiveness of traditional knowledge in conservation action pertains to the difficulty for scientists to obtain sufficient data on the status of many species, especially in biodiverse regions of the world. Conservation biologists have examined different methods of assessing biodiversity (Kerr et al., 2000) including indicator species, hierarchical approaches, community surveys, or rapid assessment methods (e.g. Noss, 1990; Karr, 1991; Kremen, 1993; Oliver and Beattie, 1993; Rodriguez et al., 1998). Increasingly, traditional ecological knowledge is suggested as an alternative or complement to scientific methodologies (Huntington, 2000). Local perceptions of resources or resource decline could provide a useful "short cut" (Kerr et al., 2000) to assess biodiversity, thus augmenting the effectiveness of locally-based conservations strategies. We developed this theme at length in another publication (Dalle and Potvin, submitted).

Second, it is increasingly recognized that cultural perception is an important component of conservation action (Weeks et al., 2001). On both theoretical and practical grounds, respect for and inclusion of local decision-making processes is advocated (Norton, 2001). "Adoption " of conservation priority by local populations is indeed a key element of the success of conservation action (Butler and Regis, 2001). Given the increased popularity of the notion of traditional knowledge, it is therefore legitimate to ask the following question: *Do indigenous people and local groups have the same conservation priorities as the international or scientific communities?* If indigenous people, politicians, and scientists perceive conservation issues and actions in a compatible way, "community-based" conservation could be the ideal way to go. However, if these groups of stakeholders see different realities, the implementation of Article 8(j) might prove complicated.

The logical starting point for this question is representation – the place of nature and biodiversity in one's worldview. This, together with socio-economic considerations, partially underlies the definition of conservation priorities. The relevance and meaning of the biodiversity concept is not necessarily the same at the international, national, and local levels. Biodiversity is a western scientific and political construct that is influential at the international and national levels.[2] At the local level, the concept might be either not understood or considered irrelevant, since ecosystems are viewed in terms of the resources they provide for direct and in some cases indirect use. In general, it may be said that between the international level – the level of the Convention – and the national and local levels, the focus shifts from indirect use (e.g. the "existence value" of biodiversity) and non-use (e.g. the "option value") to more direct use of its components.

Weber and Revéret (1993) emphasized the importance of representation in determining the potential use of a natural resource. In the West, the elements of nature are classified as either "useful" or "harmful," this latter category being absent from the imagination of many peoples. *Representations* of nature are based on value systems, on extensive systems of classification of things and persons, and on the relationships between persons and things. Representations of nature tell us what can be eaten and what cannot; they allow us to distinguish between the beautiful and the ugly, the useful and the useless, the clean and the dirty, the "correct" and the "not correct" (Douglas, 1971). A system of representation constitutes the first level of a regime of ecosystem appropriation. It relates to what Elinor Ostrom (1990) called "constitutional choices". If local populations project their culture onto the surrounding environment, the same is true of scientists whose work is based on classification or experts who classify the elements of nature according to what interests them. Weeks, Packard and Martinez-Velarde (2001) demonstrate the importance of cultural perception in assessing conservation priorities. Citing examples of foresters, engineers, and peasants, among others, they emphasize how the values and training of each shape their reality: "Forest-dependent villagers, for example, may look at a forest and see fuel, medicine, fruit, housing materials, shade, fodder, and perhaps a sacred space. An ecotourist may see a place of adventure, an area in which to view animals, or an unspoiled place 'to commune with nature.' A lumber company and its employees may see the forest as a source of income".

We shall begin by examining the international conservation agenda, then the manner in which scientists view biodiversity and have attempted to answer the question of what to protect. Since biodiversity protection in the field takes the form of actions at the local level, we shall go on to consider representations of nature and the priority-setting process in local-scale conservation. We will conclude by discussing different options for melding traditional knowledge and modern science in the service of effective conservation.

Implementation of the CBD's Article 8(j): The International Agenda

As a first step in our analysis, we sought to find out what has been done since the CBD came into force with regard to the implementation of articles pertaining to indigenous and local peoples. In particular, we considered how the point of view and recommendations of indigenous people were taken into account in the decision process of the CBD itself. The Conference of the Parties (COP) is the major decision-making body of the CBD. As such, it represents the decision-makers and their viewpoints regarding the positions of IP and local communities. The third meeting of the COP (COP-3) took place in Buenos Aires, Argentina, in November 1996. Decision III/14 of COP-3 asked that an intersessional meeting be held to discuss issues pertaining to traditional knowledge and its role in the conservation of biological diversity. This was the purpose of the Madrid Workshop on Traditional Knowledge and Biological Diversity, a forum organized by the COP in which indigenous and local peoples were specifically invited to participate. The COP, in Decision III/14, specifically asked that the Executive Secretary of the CBD "invite representatives of indigenous and local communities embodying traditional lifestyles relevant for the conservation and sustainable use of biodiversity to provide input to the meeting" (UNEP, 1997). The workshop is thus considered of great importance in the continuing evolution of the roles of traditional communities in conservation.

Of all CBD-related meetings, the regional Global Biodiversity Fora (GBF) appeared to be the settings in which the wishes and views of indigenous and local peoples were most strongly expressed. Before the Madrid Workshop, two regional biodiversity fora (Africa and Latin America and the Caribbean) had been held by participating countries to elaborate on issues relevant and specific to a region. The meetings involved the participation of governments, NGOs, and indigenous organizations. The Latin American Biodiversity Forum took place in Santa Marta, Columbia, in May 1996 and focused on the following four themes:

- successful experiences in the region concerning conservation and sustainable development of biological diversity;
- the current state of governmental policies related to the implementation of articles of the CBD;
- access to genetic resources, intellectual property rights, and equitable distribution of benefits; and
- recognition, valuation, and protection of the TK of local communities.

The report of this forum notes that "116 participants from 19 countries representing governments, NGOs, and both local and mainly indigenous communities" were present at the meeting. It further states that the results of the forum will hopefully "be taken into account in the different international, hemispheric, regional, national and local fora related to biological diversity" (Ortiz Quinjano, 1996).

The corresponding forum for the African continent took place in Nairobi, Kenya, the same year. This was a subregional meeting with participation mainly from East African countries. It focused on the following issues pertaining to the CBD:

- national strategies, action plans, and programmes;
- identification, monitoring, and assessment;
- knowledge, innovations, and practices of indigenous peoples and local communities;
- agricultural biological diversity;
- access to and development and transfer of technology, including biotechnology;
- access to genetic resources; and
- financial resources and mechanisms.

Results were formulated into recommendations to the COP of which three specifically dealt with indigenous peoples and local communities.

We analysed the final reports and decisions from the three COP meetings (COP-1, COP-2 and COP-3) and the reports of the Latin American and African Regional Biodiversity Fora leading to the Madrid Workshop to obtain information about the congruency of their decisions and recommendations. Our objective was to discover the extent to which the desires of indigenous peoples and local communities were being considered by the various actors of the CBD. We treated the recommendations of the Latin American and African fora regarding IP as expressions of the desires of indigenous and local peoples with respect to the implementation of the CBD. In total, 24 individual recommendations of African and Latin American Biodiversity Fora were amalgamated and used as a template upon which recommendations of the Madrid Workshop and decisions of the COP were compared. For each of the 24 template recommendations, the presence or absence of a similar recommendation or decision in the reports of the Workshop or the COP was recorded. The data were subjected to an analysis of similarity, using Jacquard's coefficient (Legendre and Legendre, 1999).

We searched for indications that attention to indigenous peoples and local communities have been increasing since the Convention came into force. In this regard, comparisons of the meetings yielded interesting results. The number of COP decisions that overlapped with the 24 recommendations of the regional GBF increased from COP-1 to COP-3. For COP-1, two of the 24 recommendations were represented, for COP-2, five, and for COP-3, seven. This suggests that indigenous peoples and local communities were given increased importance. On the other hand, the recommendations of the Madrid Workshop were very similar to those of the Latin American forum but different from the African (Table 8.1). A possible explanation for this observation is that of the 75 indigenous peoples and local community organizations present at the Madrid Workshop, 34 were specifically Latin American and two were African. We also suggest that the concept of IP might not have the same meaning or reflect the same reality across the developing world. As demonstrated at the Madrid Workshop, in the context of the CBD, Latin American NGOs and other groups established to promote the needs and rights of IP were more prominent than African ones. Apparently, some Latin American IP see the CBD as a potential new legal framework in which to assert their land claims (Davis and Wali, 1994). In contrast, the main concern for local communities in African countries appeared to be the loss of traditional knowledge (ACTS, 1996). There might be an historical explanation for this observation. In Latin America, there is a clear distinction between the people who colonized the continent after the 16th century and those who inhabited the land earlier. The latter group, called IP, constitutes a minority in Latin American countries. Therefore, societal struggles involving IP (such as land ownership conflicts) might have a different significance in Latin America than in Africa, where IP are the majority.

Thus, in the context of the implementation of Article 8(j), efforts have been made to listen to and act upon recommendations made by the indigenous community. It appears that preoccupations of indigenous people are become increasingly important, thus justifying our interest in the comparison of perspectives of the indigenous and scientific communities on conservation issues. Our results, however, suggest geographical differences in attitudes toward biodiversity and call for caution toward considering indigenous people as a homogeneous group. This caution should be kept in mind when analyzing our case study.

Worldviews and Priority-Setting: The Scientific Standpoint

Until the Rio Earth Summit, biological diversity was seen by many in industrialized countries as part and parcel of humanity's shared heritage. With its transformation into "biodiversity," it has acquired a status that it does not necessarily possess in the eyes of the local communities making daily use of its components. Early approaches to priority setting, such as identifying species-rich "hotspots" (Myers, 1988) or "megadiversity areas" (Mittermeier and Werner, 1990) and endemism favoured the selection of certain areas according to species count and rarity (Muller, 2000). Johnson (1995) looked at biodiversity assessment criteria and found that in general, priorities are set on the basis of a small number of criteria: species richness of an ecosystem, rarity, threat, species representativeness, and function. For Miller, Allegretti, Johnson, and Jonnon (1995), the importance of biodiversity may be estimated on the basis of genetic information, species richness, and ecosystem or landscape characteristics.

In terms of biodiversity's genetic dimension, conservation tends to target three objectives:

- ensure representative genetic variability of a species within protected populations;

- identify populations with the largest genetic variability; and
- conserve populations representing the geographic range of each species.

Gene-level conservation is generally reserved for species with significant economic value or species represented only by small isolated populations. Thus, for the conservation of genetic resources, biologists tend to work with a small number of species, striving to conserve all their available genetic material. Regarding species with high commercial value, the 1970s debates on optimal management strategies for fish stocks, notably cod, may be relevant in this context. Arguments based on population genetics suggested that a maximum number of individuals of the same species should be maintained, whereas arguments from bioeconomics sometimes indicated strategies leading to the extinction of one or more populations as optimal solutions (Revéret, 1991).

A majority of biodiversity protection organizations base their interventions on a species-level analysis of biodiversity (but see Norton, 2001, for a critique). The central scientific importance of species is justified because species are the basic components of ecosystems and are easily classified by taxonomists. One particular advantage of species-centred approaches is that they make it possible to focus actions on the most endangered species. Two examples follow.

The province of Quebec, Canada, like many countries, has an endangered species law, the 1989 *Act respecting threatened or vulnerable species* (Huot, 1993). It gives the government powers relating to knowledge, protection, management, and designation of threatened or vulnerable species. Under the Quebec government's policy on threatened or vulnerable species, a species is threatened if the size of its population and/or its range are restricted or greatly reduced; it is vulnerable if a reduction in its numbers or range are observed. Hence, the status of a species in Quebec depends largely on its abundance.

Internationally, the best-known biodiversity prioritization system is undoubtedly that of the World Conservation Union (IUCN), which draws up "red lists" of species in need of protection around the world. The IUCN assigns a status to each species studied: critically endangered, endangered, vulnerable, near threatened. A species is classified as critically endangered if it meets any of the following criteria:

- population size reduction of 80 per cent over the last ten years or three generations;
- geographic range of less than 100 km^2 or area of occupancy less than ten km^2;
- population size numbering 250 mature individuals showing signs of decline or grouped in a single population;
- population size estimated to number fewer than 50 mature individuals; and
- quantitative analysis finds a 50 per cent probability of extinction within ten years or three generations.

Thus, the international system for identifying species conservation priorities is based on species abundance. This must, however, be viewed in an historical context. The status of a naturally rare species is less worrisome than that of a formerly common species that has suddenly become rare.

Conservation priority-setting at the ecosystem level is done on a more global basis. Generally, the process considers ecosystem richness, the presence of endemic species, the representativeness of an ecosystem or its exceptional nature, ecosystem processes, and the disturbance regime. The underlying idea is that the conservation of representative ecosystems in a region will *ipso facto* ensure the conservation of a majority of the region's species. This approach was used by the Worldwide Fund for Nature (WWF) in its Canadian campaign "Endangered Spaces". For the WWF, what is important is to identify persistent landscape elements and then establish a system of protection to ensure that a sampling of these elements is represented. The methodology developed by the WWF assumes that ecosystems and the biodiversity they contain are closely linked. Climatic, physiographic, topographic, geologic, and edaphic conditions interact to determine the associated vegetation cover and fauna (WWF, 1995).

The ecosystem-based approach differs fundamentally from the species-based approaches discussed above in that it demands protection of samples of every persistent landscape element identified, not just a choice of elements. Critics argue that ecosystem-based conservation methods appear to be satisfactory in their protection of the essential elements of biodiversity but are not effective in protecting rare species. In response to this objection, the WWF proposes to add other dimensions to the analysis of persistent landscape elements, such as the presence and concentration of rare species in an area, species-rich areas, sites of rare ecosystems (e.g. old growth forests), sites of animal concentration, and high-value watersheds.

Representation of the World and Local-Level Priorities

It is increasingly evident that the effectiveness of biodiversity strategies depends on their implementation at the local level. For example, the late 20th century saw the concept of "natural park" as a protected, inaccessible space evolve into that of a park in which human beings can coexist with nature (Potvin, 1997). This peaceable coexistence of humans and nature is similar to the concept of sustainable development put forward in the Brundtland Report. In that connection, various authors have stressed the importance of using local knowledge as a substitute for or complement to scientific knowledge in identifying conservation priorities (Joyal, 1996; Ticktin, 2000; Velasquez Runk, 1998).

This issue is at the heart of the discussion that follows, which is based on a long-term case study of the Emberá in the Republic of Panama. The members of this indigenous group are of South American origin and currently live in Colombia and Panama (Cansari, 2001). Their total population is about 50,000, of which

18,000 are in Panama. Of the five main indigenous groups of Panama, the Emberás are considered to reflect their traditional lifestyles most closely. They are a hunting and gathering people who practise rudimentary slash-and-burn agriculture. They also use and depend upon a large number of plants and animals in their daily lives.

We worked with the community of Ipeti-Emberá, a village located on the bank of the Ipeti River near the foothills of Serranía de Majé (9°00'N, 78°05'W), province of Panama. Ipeti is organized as an indigenous *tierras colectivas,* territories of semi-autonomous administration. The land of Ipeti-Emberá, comprising 3,198 ha, is bordered on the north by the Pan American highway and located approximately five hours (by bus) east of Panama City. When the Bayano hydroelectric reservoir was created in the mid-70s, some of the Emberá people living in the area were relocated to Ipeti, and the village now comprises 50 houses with a population of around 400 people. The largely forested indigenous territory is embedded in a matrix of land used by colonists for cattle ranching. The local economy appears to be rather diversified. Men and women work for day wages in various *colono* enterprises, such as farms and logging companies, or in private homes. All households also engage in subsistence agriculture, fishing, and hunting when game can be found. In the last two decades, basket-weaving for women and, to a lesser extent, wood-carving for men have become important sources of supplementary income. The handicraft products are sold mainly to tourists in urban areas.

Close contact with this people over the last five years has led us to the conclusion that the Emberá place importance on biodiversity, or rather on the renewable resources that are its most tangible expression, according to a value system fundamentally different from that of scientists. The value of biodiversity seems to be intimately linked to the utility of a species. Traditional Emberá nomenclature exists only for species having a use. Even striking-looking flowering plants will not be named if they are good for nothing. Visiting birders may, to their delight, spot a red-billed scythebill – extremely rare in Panama – on Ipeti-Emberá territory, yet the villagers have no use and hence no name for it. Another incident compellingly illustrates the different perceptions of the value of biodiversity. In July 1996, in Darién National Park, an Emberá hunter killed a giant anteater, considered to be one of the most endangered animals in Panama. The dead animal was simply left lying on the ground. One of the authors asked why the anteater had been killed, and the hunter replied that he had feared for the safety of his hunting dog. He explained that without the dog, it would be very difficult to hunt, and without hunting, he could not feed his family. Therefore, the dog was much more important to the hunter than the anteater.

We thus hypothesized that rare species are less commonly used and therefore less important than common ones (Dalle and Potvin, submitted; Patenaude, 2001). Various activities, ranging from workshops to formal questionnaires, participatory observation, and ecological inventory, were conducted in Ipeti to test this hypothesis. Over 90 per cent of the 50 households in the village participated in the project, and results from the questionnaire and informal interviews were in general agreement. Twenty-two plant species were ascribed a significant traditional value by the villagers; without exception, all of these plants have a use. We found eight tree and eight palm species used to build houses and for various domestic purposes (basket-making, food, thread, etc.). Three species provide the raw materials for Emberá craftwork – one of the largest sources of income for the community. Finally, three species are important for their symbolic or spiritual value (Table 8.2).

A list of priority animal species was drawn up in a similar way. The most important species have multiple uses and are strongly represented in all sociocultural spheres of Emberá daily life (Table 8.3). The agouti, for example, is hunted and represents an important source of protein for the Emberá (Torres de Arauz, 1972; Bennett, 1968). Its meat and various by-products are sold to people in the community and to outside merchants. It is also used in the preparation of a powder central to a ritual practice called umbiligation. A powder made from the bones, teeth, or dried claws of an animal is inserted into the newborn's navel to endow the baby with the particular traits of that species (e.g. strength, speed, etc.). But it is equally important to consider the cultural and spiritual roles of each species as well as its representations in the community. During traditional dances and ceremonies, Emberá women perform the dance of the agouti, mimicking the activities and movements of the animal. During shamanistic practices, the *jaibana* (shaman) must possess the *jaï* (spirit) of the agouti to practice certain healing rituals. In addition, the agouti, an agile, smart, bold animal, represents one of the main characters in traditional Emberá tales.

In addition to having multiple uses, animal species of highest importance are all edible. Only the armadillo, kinkajou, and howler monkey, which ranked low in importance (Table 8.3), were not unanimously identified as edible. In light of this observation, we hypothesized that certain uses and/or representations account for the perception of importance better than others. We tested this second hypothesis using an ethnographic questionnaire that focused on the sociocultural variables, representing the uses or functions of the animals (e.g. edibility, shamanism, decoration, domestic uses, traditional medicine, sale) that best explained the notion of "importance". Only the *edibility-importance* correlation was significant (0.86 p>0.001). In addition, cluster analysis showed that the *subsistence and local economy* group of variables was grouped with the *importance* variable, meaning that the majority of species considered important are also edible, domesticated, and/or commercialized. Therefore, the most important species would appear to be edible ones.

We then searched for a relationship between species abundance and importance, since this relationship is key to scientists' approach to biodiversity. For plants, abundance was determined directly by sampling 150 24-metre-diameter quadrats. The abundance of these plant species on Ipeti territory varied between zero and 2,071. We counted six species with more than 200 individuals, and five others represented in the quadrats by more than 20 individuals. For eight species, fewer than ten individuals were found. The Emberá appear to be unanimous in considering four plant species to be particularly important: chunga, guagara, jira, and kipara (Table 8.2). Chunga provides a fibre that is used to make the woven baskets sold cheaply as tourist items. Guagara and jira provide, respectively, roofing and flooring material for huts. Kipara produces a vegetable dye used in body painting. Our ecological inventory indicates that while three palm species are found abundantly on the territory, kipara is rare, with only nine individuals counted. Therefore, there does not appear to be any relationship between utilization, importance, and abundance (Dalle and Potvin, submitted). The status of the animals is similar. Eight of the 19 species named by the villagers as important are listed in Appendices I and II of the Convention on International Trade in Endangered Species of Wild Fauna and Flora (CITES), while three are considered vulnerable by the IUCN. Other species, such as the white-tailed deer, agouti, and toucan, are very common in Panama.

Our analysis shows that in the quest to increase indigenous participation in establishing conservation priorities, it would be naïve to assume that stakeholders share the same views on biodiversity or that scientific and local concerns will match. If conservation action were largely based on locally derived priorities, target species would differ from the species list derived by scientists. The challenge then becomes that of bringing together traditional knowledge and modern science, not as a substitute for one another but coexisting within the decision-making process. It also forces us to explore the relevant implications of such findings for community-based management systems that are often propounded as the answer to the biodiversity crisis.

Conclusion: From Global Thinking to Local Conservation Action

Concerns over the loss of biological diversity are very real and have been enshrined in the CBD, giving rise to increased international awareness of IP and traditional knowledge. However, despite this clear enunciation of global concern and the success of such agreements in building international consensus around conservation policies, local implementation of these policies has often been ineffective. A key reason lies in the common failure to understand and include local interests, priorities, and management systems in high-level conservation projects. It is becoming increasingly clear that the local perspective must have its place within such conservation projects if biodiversity is to be preserved. Local knowledge and local cultural systems are essential for the preservation of biodiversity. In fact, the lists of conservation priorities (flora and fauna) published by the IUCN and CITES are good examples of the unilateral scientific prioritization of biodiversity. Indigenous livelihood can conflict in many ways with these conservation concerns. Consider the example of the tapir, at 180–300 kg the largest neotropical mammal. From the standpoint of the IUCN and CITES, the tapir is valued because its survival is threatened. More than 70 per cent of its Central American habitat has been deforested in the last 40 years, its population is fragmented and regenerates slowly, and the number of mature individuals has sharply declined (Martola, pers. comm.). In addition, it is heavily hunted (Torres de Arrauz, 1972; Bennett, 1968). The tapir is valued by the Emberá primarily for subsistence nourishment and was identified by Vasco Uribe (1993) as one of their four most highly valued game species. It is also valued for livestock, for representation in traditional dances, for medical uses, and for shamanistic rituals and umbiligation. A villager told us that if a tapir (extremely rare in the region) were to pass through the village, he would kill it so that he could taste its meat once again. Thus, importance does not translate into protection. Furthermore, the criteria defining importance may be fundamentally different, even contradictory, at the local and international levels. For example, the use of species for commercial or subsistence purposes comes into direct conflict with the conservation objectives for endangered species.

Local support for conservation strategies is likely to be further undermined by the fact that rare species may be of little or no interest to local populations or may represent a choice food item. In the Emberá cultural context, rarity does not seem to be perceived as linked to overexploitation through hunting and subsistence activities. This is illustrated by the Tale of the Peccary.

The Tale of the Peccary

The tale of the peccary, collected by one of the authors (GP) from a community member of Ipeti, Bonifacio Flaco, illustrates the ecological role and significance of a *wandra* (guide of certain animal species (Lonsonczy, 1987)). The story tells how an Emberá man, unsuccessful at hunting, becomes the protector of the peccaries. While hunting one day, he follows a female peccary into the Netherworld:

> *It is said that he walked and walked, he walked and walked, until he arrived at the opening of the cave. It was the home of the peccaries. A very dark entrance. An immense hole.*
> *It is told that after resting, he walked into the cave, on the path, into the hole. He walked and walked and walked. When one day, suddenly, he reached the end of this hole. There he saw beaches and pure white sugar cane. There was a magnificent river, with three female peccaries cavorting nearby. He stood there, astonished.*

This part of the story reveals two levels of the cosmogonic space: the Human World, where the Emberá live and where animal species feed, and the Netherworld, a place of refuge and rest for the animals. The tale of the peccary then goes on to tell how the Emberá man became accepted as the protector (*wandra*):

> *The mother peccary said to her young ones: "...If you do not kill him, this man will become your chief, he will show you all the places you must go. This man will take care of you so that the Emberá do not hunt too many of you. This man will become your guide".*

This expresses the role of the *wandra* as a protector of species, one who guides them far away from hunters. For the Emberá, the rarity of animals may also be due to the actions of the *jaïbana* (shaman), whose role is that of a healer. The term *jaïbana*, composed of the morphemes *jaï* (spirit) and *bana* (possession, abundance) clearly describes the nature of this shaman. The *jaï*, according to Emberá beliefs, are the spirits responsible for human ills and illnesses. The shaman fights disease by seducing, negotiating with and capturing them. These spirits are of various types: animal, place, character, etc. One of the shaman's roles is to seduce the spirits and negotiate a person's healing process with them; the *wandras* are among these spirits. As a negotiating tactic, the shaman may, even to the detriment of his own community, encircle the prey and try to enclose them within a magic boundary in order to limit hunting activities and seduce the *wandras*. He, too, then, becomes a regulator of abundance and rarity.

If animal species are absent or become rare in the vicinity, then they must be elsewhere, encircled, protected, or taking refuge in the Netherworld. This magical cosmological discourse represents a language of interpretation serving to bridge the gap between the known and the unknown. This conception could lead to unsustainable hunting practices, overexploitation, and local extinction of fauna, which may historically have been the origin of the Emberá's migrations (Herlihy, 1986; Bennett, 1968). It has, in fact, been shown that nomadic peoples who are not tied to a defined territory do not generally tend to use the available resources sustainably (Gadgil et al., 1993).

Thus, for the Emberá, the size of animal populations is determined by factors independent of traditional hunting activities:

- protection of species by wandras;
- multidimensional cosmogonic construction: the existence of places of refuge for animals;
- encircling of animal species by the shaman; and
- hunting by colonists, large-scale deforestation, other exogenous influences.

We believe that local decision-making processes and land use dynamics (Dalle and Potvin, submitted) may be crucial to implementing management plans for biodiversity. In view of all the cultural differences, it would seem that mixed strategies taking account of both the biological and cultural importance of species would maximize effectiveness. Indeed, if conservation priorities are set on the basis of purely biological criteria (such as abundance and endemism), conflict with local populations is likely to arise. Conservation strategies focusing preferentially on rare species may exclude species that are heavily exploited or of high cultural importance. Furthermore, we view it as important to recognize explicitly the representations of the world held by the people who use the natural resources that others wish to manage. Failing to do so not only evinces a lack of respect for the group concerned but will probably result in the failure of the management strategies in question.

In the World Heritage Convention's definition of biosphere reserves, for example, the importance of taking account of both local and international priorities is mentioned. The former takes the form of vital subsistence needs and integration into the market economy, as well as the preservation of traditions, and the latter, the conservation of endangered species. Although it is complex, we do not see the possibility of convergence as unthinkable. Might it be possible, for example, to issue seasonal hunting permits that are sensitive to different species' reproductive and regenerative cycles, while regulating or even proscribing hunting activities for species considered gravely endangered by virtue of their small numbers? It would then be important to take account of the prevailing appropriation and management regimes, not to mention the capacity of the state to enforce such regulations, often in a context of scarce resources and different cultural perceptions, as illustrated by Emberá attitudes.

In some cases, it is possible to reconcile such attitudes through hunting and fishing season regulations. For example, in the Ivory Coast, the story of the *Gun Kuala* whale told by fishermen on Ébrié Lagoon near Abidjan is used to "manage" the lagoon fishery. The gist of this myth, forged over generations, is that it was impossible to fish during certain periods when the fish were thought to be hiding under the whale. A village sage was called in to rid the lagoon of the whale and free up the fish; the fishery then resumed until the return of *Gun Kuala*, which the sage would announce (Verdeaux, cited in Revéret, 1991). Under such circumstances, collaboration between modern science and traditional knowledge around fishing permits and seasons seems plausible. Rather than a unilaterally imposed fishing season, a dialogue with the sage could be conceived, serving to chase away *Gun Kuala* earlier or later, based on biological considerations. But this requires great professional humility as well as an interdisciplinary dialogue between the biologist and the anthropologist, who acts as an intermediary between the sage and the biologist. Maximizing the effectiveness of conservation action calls for a dialogue between scientific and indigenous knowledge – one that acknowledges inherent differences in value systems as well as a shared concern for all life, human and non-human.

Table 8.1 Similarity Matrix comparing the Recommendations of the Two Regional Biodiversity Fora with those of the Madrid Workshop

	Africa	Latin America	Madrid
Africa	1.00	0.50	0.50
Latin America		1.00	0.86
Madrid			1.00

Table 8.2 List of Plant Species deemed Cultural Priorities by the Ipeti-Emberá Community*

Spanish name	Scientific name	Use	Number of plants counted	Harvest frequency (1–6)
Bejuco motété		Food baskets, posts for houses, hen cages	13	4
Bijao	*Calathea latifolia*	Wrapping buns and tamales, utility baskets, wrapping food covered with salt, hats	272	1
Pita con espinos	*Aechmae pubescens*	Thread	55	2.5
Nawala	*Carludovica palmata*	Structural elements for decorative chunga baskets, chaume, utility baskets, wrapping for buns, bellows, hats	553	2
Chunga	*Astrocaryum standleyanum*	Decorative baskets, posts for houses, food, sugar presses, ornamentation for shaman's home, hoe blades, spears	466	2
Wagara	*Sabal mauritiiformis*	Chaume, posts for houses	361	5
Jira	*Socratea exorrhiza*	Flooring, fencing, *para cinta y chuso*	644	5
Uvita	*Bactris coloniata*	Pliers, food, arrows, construction materials	2071	3
Jagua	*Genipa americana*	Body and hair painting, soothing skin lotion	9	2
Maquenque	*Oenocarpus mapora*	Pilions, utility baskets, food, ornamentation for *jaïbana* houses, beverage, chaume, sugar cane press head, flooring, oil	92	5

Table 8.2 Concluded

Balsa	*Ochroma pyramidale*	Stairs, dolls, river rafts for cargo, plates, pillows	504	5
Malagueto	*Xylopia fructescens*	Construction materials	56	5
Cedro espino	*Bombacopsis quinata*	Boats, boards	32	3
Cedro amargo	*Cedrela odorata*	Boats, boards	70	3
Nispero	*Manilkara sp.*	Construction materials, axe handles, food	0	6
Chiru		Traditional Emberá woodwind instruments	1	6
Kidave	*Manettia reclinata*	Substance for the purpose of hardening and protecting teeth	0	6
Bejuco real	*Heteropsis sp.*	Food baskets, binding for the construction of materials, hats	0	6
Pita sin espinos	*Aechmea setigera*	Food	0	3
Tinta roja		Dye for chunga fibres	0	2
Cocobolo	*Dalbergia retusa*	Animal sculpting, construction materials, black dye for chunga fibres	0	2
Trupa	*Oenocarpus bataua*	Oil, beverage	0	3

*The number of plants is based on our sample of 50 quadrats as described in the text and represents the total number of individuals found. The frequency of use was obtained by a questionnaire administered to all households in the village. The answers are coded as follows: 1 - weekly harvest; 2 - monthly harvest; 3 - annual harvest; 4 - biennal harvest; 5 - infrequent harvest, about once every five years; 6 - rare or nonexistent harvest.

Table 8.3 Selected Priority Animal Species

Use and functions Selected priority animal species Importance: Frequency mentioned		Food	Ritual	Domestic	Traditional	Economic	Divinatory	Medical
White-tailed deer, *Odocoileus virginianus*	6	X	X	X	X	X		
Iguana, *Iguana iguana*	6	X	X		X	X	X	X
Tapir, *Tapirus bairdii*	5	X	X	X	X			X
Turtle, *Testudines sp.*	5	X	X	X	X	X	X	X
Collared peccary, *Tayassu tajacu*	5	X	X	X	X	X	X	X
White-lipped peccary, *Tayassu pecari*	5	X	X	X	X	X		
Squirrel, *Sciurus sp.*	5	X	X	X	X			
Agouti, *Dasyprocta punctata*	5	X	X	X	X	X		
Paca, *Agouti paca*	5	X	X	X	X	X		X
Keel-billed toucan and chestnut-mandibled toucan, *Ramaphastos sulfuratus, Ramphastos swainsonii*	4	X		X	X	X		
Geoffroy's tamarin, *Sanguinus geoffroyi*	4	X		X		X		
Grey-headed chachalaca, *Ortalis cinereiceps*	4	X	X	X		X		
Great curassow, *Crax rubra*	4	X		X	X			
Great tinamou and little tinamou, *Tinamous major, Crypturellus soui*	4	X	X	X		X	X	
Macaws, *Ara sp.*	4	X		X				
Nine-banded long-nosed armadillo, *Dasypus novemcinctus*	4	X	X	X		X		X
Blue-headed parrot, *Pionus mestruus*	3	X	X	X		X		
Kinkajou, *Potos flavus*	3	X	X		X	X	X	X
Howler monkey, *Alouatta palliata*	2	X		X	X	X		X
Jaguar, *Panthera onca*	–		X	X	X	X		X
Giant anteater, *Myrmecophaga tridactyla*	–		X	X	X			
Tiger-herons, *Tigrisoma sp.*	–							
Common potoo, *Nyctibius griseus*	–					X	X	
Ferruginous pygmy-owl, *Glaucidium brasilianum*	–			X			X	

Acknowledgements

This research was conducted with financial support from a Social Sciences and Humanities Research Council of Canada team grant in applied ethics to Marie-Hélène Parizeau (Catherine Potvin and Jean-Pierre Revéret) and from an International Development Research Centre grant to Catherine Potvin. Above all, we are indebted to the Emberá people of Ipeti, who welcomed us into their lives and allowed us to carry out this research. Special thanks to Bonarge Pacheco and Lisandro Flaco, *caciques* of the *tierras colectivas* of Ipeti.

Notes

[1] The IUCN maintains active ties with and is hosting a debate between the two communities of practitioners of environmental impact studies and biodiversity conservation.
[2] See also chapter 10 by Guay in this volume.

Chapter 9

The CBD, the WTO, and the FAO: The Emergence of Phytogenetic Governance

Urs P. Thomas

The debate on intellectual property rights and the environment is one that is generally characterized by more heat than light.

Graham Dutfield

Introduction

The term "governance" is commonly used in the discussion of global environmental issues to denote the more or less binding application and enforcement of norms, rules, and procedures in a given issue area. This chapter analyses ongoing multilateral negotiations on the development of regulations in the interlocking fields of the protection of agricultural biodiversity, biotechnology, North-South relations, and trade in food crops. The importance of the economic and ecological stakes explains the complexity and highly political character of these negotiations. They have intensified markedly in the past few years, mostly because of the introduction of the issue of property rights to plant genetic resources in the wake of scientific advances in the genetic engineering of seeds. Furthermore, these negotiations now involve not only non-binding declarations and principles, the operationalization of which would require the launching of a new negotiation process, but also binding rules of international law, which may be used in the settlement of disputes.

Doing justice to such a broad and complex topic would therefore require an in-depth study of the development of public international law and interorganizational and intergovernmental relations. Only a synthetic overview will be possible here of an issue area that so far has received too little attention. The fast pace of negotiations on various fronts, however, clearly indicates that this area will command more and more attention from the media, academia, politicians, and civil servants in the foreseeable future.

This survey will proceed in three steps:

- A discussion of the wider framework governing negotiations on the relations between multilateral environmental agreements, such as the Convention on Biological Diversity (CBD), and the World Trade Organization (WTO); the chapter then turns to a discussion of the stepwise introduction of intellectual property rights (IPRs) to plant genetic resources primarily through the creation of the WTO's Agreement on Trade-Related Aspects of Intellectual Property Rights (TRIPS) and its conflicts with the CBD, especially with regard to farmers' ancient rights.
- Based on this discussion, the next section sketches out the negotiations that led to a tenuous reconciliation – under the umbrella of the Food and Agriculture Organization (FAO) – of the TRIPS agreement and the CBD through a new binding agreement, the recently adopted International Treaty on Plant Genetic Resources for Food and Agriculture (IT); the *leitmotif* for this reconciliation consisted in the guarantee of access to germplasm for plant breeders (i.e. for the seed industry), in the protection of developing countries' national sovereignty over seeds, in related benefit-sharing mechanisms, and thus in efforts to improve global food security.
- The last section analyses from different perspectives the compatibility among the four main agreements regarding the protection and equitable use of plant genetic resources (International Union for the Protection of New Varieties of Plants (UPOV), CBD, TRIPS, and IT). This analysis is followed by a brief reference to the Biosafety Protocol in order to arrive at a conclusion concerning the emerging shape of phytogenetic and phytosanitary governance.

Emerging Efforts to Reconcile Economic Globalization with the Protection of Ecosystems

Phytogenetic and phytosanitary negotiations have intensified considerably since the creation of the CBD in 1992, and they have accelerated in recent years. To an important degree, this can be explained by the introduction of genetically modified (GM) crops and by the potential that the international community sees in these agricultural biotechnologies. At the same time, concerns have arisen regarding potential impacts on agricultural biodiversity. In spite of advanced breeding techniques, plant breeders continue to depend to a significant extent on seed varieties used by indigenous peoples, so-called land races, as well as on their wild relatives, in their search for new varieties of the world's leading staple crops, especially wheat, rice, corn, and beans (Tuxill, 2000, p.32). Therefore, how to improve incentives for protecting plant genetic resources (PGRs) is becoming an increasingly important issue in the emerging new international biological order (Swanson, 1999).

New Challenges for a New Era

Agriculture has long been a highly politicized sector in most countries because it cuts across many concerns, such as food security and food safety, the national economy, history and culture, environmental and landscape protection, job maintenance and creation, internal migration, and political alignments. Biotechnology now further complicates agricultural politics and policies in the North and in the South. Consumer resistance to genetically modified food products is currently very strong in Western Europe as well as in several developing countries. Even in North America, where acceptance of genetically modified food products was nearly unanimous for the first few years after their introduction, opposition to bioengineered food varieties and demands for labelling are increasing. This movement is led by a small number of specialized small or medium-sized NGOs, such as Genetic Resources Action International (GRAIN, Spain), ETC group (formerly RAFI, Canada), Solagral (France), and the Institute for Agriculture and Trade Policy (IATP, US), and several large international organizations, such as Greenpeace and the Worldwide Fund for Nature (WWF). They are generally well-informed about the status of ongoing international negotiations, the contents of scientific reports, and the positions of the regulatory authorities in various countries. Thanks to a skilful use of the Internet, these NGOs manage, in spite of relatively modest financial expenditures, to build global networks that allow them to take collective action with regard to biodiversity and seed patenting (Purdue, 2000, p. 97).

It is noteworthy that they and other NGOs rely heavily on electronic communication for many of their activities, which in some cases made their emergence possible in the first place (Thomas, 2000, p. 554).[1] Indeed, four phenomena that all exert a powerful influence on shaping the modern world emerged very recently and simultaneously in 1994:

- the creation of a rule-based, binding, and enforceable global trading system through the adoption of the Marrakesh Agreement Establishing the World Trade Organization with all its annexed agreements;
- the appearance of a more or less organized social movement targeted specifically against economic globalization;[2]
- the technological maturation and virtual explosion of the Internet in its present user-friendly form; and
- the introduction of genetically modified crops on world markets (Phillips and Kerr, 2000, p. 63).

These four important developments, which have gained rapid prominence, are closely intermingled and interact with each other in dynamic and unpredictable ways. They reach directly or indirectly into most spheres and aspects of today's society and exert a powerful influence on the issues discussed in this chapter. All are directly related to the wider trend of globalization: the creation of the WTO and the Internet have been crucial forces behind globalization and have pushed it to unprecedented levels. The introduction of GM crops exerts a twofold impact: on the one hand it catalyzes the expansion of corporate control over different sectors of agricultural production, such as seeds, fertilizers, pesticides, and machinery; on the other hand it has done much to signal the urgency of providing for "centralized development planning" and for the establishment of incentive mechanisms that improve the protection of agricultural biodiversity (Swanson, 1999, p. 331). The anti-globalization movement, for its part, tries hard to slow down this trend at all levels, be it in the realm of culture, the economy, food and agriculture, or politics in general.

Trade and Environment as a Field of Negotiations and Analysis

The creation of the WTO and its Committee on Trade and Environment[3] focused attention on these questions more specifically than any previous initiatives. The 1990s have seen an increase of interest in negotiations and other discussions on the relationship between Multilateral Environmental Agreements (MEAs) and the WTO (Nordström and Vaughn, 1999; Charnovitz, 2000). They provide the conceptual, organizational and diplomatic context of the present chapter. The appropriateness and usefulness of this framework for the analysis of phytogenetic and phytosanitary governance is justified on two counts: (i) the relationship with WTO agreements lies at the centre of the negotiations on FAO's International Treaty on Plant Genetic Resources and on the Biosafety Protocol, and (ii) neither of them are pure trade or pure environmental agreements. The stakes involved in these negotiations can only be truly understood in the context of the wider trade and environment debate.

If one looks at the trade side of the trade and environment equation, it becomes quickly apparent that the main interface of interest for the CBD is largely centred on the following four multilateral trade agreements, which were adopted together with about 15 others in Marrakesh in 1994:

- GATT 1994 (General Agreement on Tariffs and Trade)
- SPS (Application of Sanitary and Phytosanitary Measures)
- TBT (Technical Barriers to Trade)
- TRIPS (Trade-Related Aspects of Intellectual Property Rights)

The first comprehensive analytical study of the interface between trade law (in our case WTO law) and international environmental law – two bodies of public international law that are very different in their orientation and in their legal and political foundations and history – appeared in 1992 (Charnovitz, 1992). The investigation of this domain has emerged from the need to reconcile MEAs and trade law. The first cases that generated such discussions were the treaties governing international trade in wildlife (CITES, 1973), ozone depleting substances (Montreal Protocol, 1987), and transboundary movements of hazardous wastes (Basel Convention, 1989). The processes and organizations that may lead to a reconciliation of trade and environment concerns continue to be the subject of lively debates at roundtables and expert meetings of intergovernmental organizations such as the United Nations Environment Programme (UNEP), the UN University (UNU), and the United Nations Conference on Trade and Development (UNCTAD), as well as increasingly at the WTO, and in academic research.[4]

The Biosafety Protocol is of particular interest in the discussion of trade and environment issues in general because it pioneered in its preamble an explicit statement that is essentially applicable to all MEAs with trade implications, namely that "trade and environment agreements should be *mutually supportive* with a view to achieving sustainable development". This innocuous-sounding phrase may have some hidden teeth. In a dispute before the WTO over the accusation of setting up unjustified or discriminatory trade barriers against the importation of GM crops, the WTO's Dispute Settlement Body (DSB) will presumably have to take this concept into consideration, especially if both Parties have ratified the Protocol. This integrative vision is strengthened by the fact that the new International Treaty on Plant Genetic Resources, which we shall discuss below, also contains a nearly identical formulation in its preamble. The concept of mutual supportiveness – together with its companion concept of *deference* – indeed represents a crucial element in reconciling conflicting trade and environment stakes:

> ...because of the interdependencies between trade and environment, rules and principles on international trade will have an effect on the environment, and environmental regulation will have an effect on trade. Therefore, while each regime should focus on its primary competence, it is not prevented from adopting measures having an effect on the other regime. However, it should take into account the concerns and interests of the other regime, and it should *pay deference* [italics added] to the competence of the other regime. This deference requires that each regime does not judge the legitimacy or the necessity of measures adopted by the other regime. (Perrez, 2000, p. 524)

A new and crucial element in this debate concerns the role of developing countries in multilateral negotiations; they tend to be at best hesitant and more often strongly opposed to the integration of environmental concerns into trade negotiations (Le Prestre, 1997). This attitude is to some extent understandable because their fear that industrialized countries will try to use the environment as a trade barrier may sometimes be justified. However, the much vaunted trade discipline of the WTO agreements should easily help overcome this problem. It should be feasible to link capacity-building and technical assistance in the implementation of the WTO agreements – not to mention better consideration of their short-term and long-term trade concerns through differential treatment provisions – to generate a more forthcoming attitude on environment and trade issues among developing countries. It would be dangerous for the WTO to underestimate the needs and frustrations of developing countries. These frustrations, after all, lay in part behind the Seattle fiasco. Since developing countries are usually more dependent on agricultural exports than industrialized countries, which can relatively easily change their agricultural suppliers or use substitute products, trade-related environmental issues in the agricultural sector have a disproportionate impact on developing countries' economies and societies. Hence, it is ultimately in the interest of all countries to improve the coherence and consistency of trade and environmental agreements and to work toward their ultimate convergence.

In the medium term, consistency between WTO rights and obligations on the one hand and MEA trade measures on the other could be improved through the negotiation of one of the following options (Stilwell and Turk, 1999, p. 19):

- *amending Article XX of the GATT* to include trade measures in MEAs under its list of permitted exemptions;
- *interpreting Article XX* so that trade measures in MEAs are deemed presumptively consistent with existing exemptions; and
- *negotiating a separate WTO agreement on MEAs,* acknowledging that MEAs and WTO rules have equal status and exempting them from WTO challenge.

Integration, in order to be effective, must be made visible: there needs to be a feedback mechanism linking the environmental impact of international policies in any given sector with ongoing negotiations. The only way to achieve this goal is to integrate the cost of environmental degradation into the price of the appropriate goods and services: "Without this feedback, individuals, corporations, and governments systematically undervalue the environmental consequences of their decisions, leading to over-consumption of resource capital and degradation of the environment" (MacNeill, Winsemius, and Yakushiji, 1991, p. 32). In order to develop what has been appropriately called an *integrative responsibility* (Juma, forthcoming), appropriate standards, criteria, and indicators need to be developed and implemented.

Global Phytogenetic Governance

The negotiations over PGRs are different in nature from most other negotiations because of the large number of issues, agreements, and organizations involved and because the key issues are interlinked to an unusual degree. The dynamics of these negotiations are influenced by two forces that give the whole process a distinctive flavour. First, in many if not most cases, the fault line cuts between the financial objectives of industrialized countries and those of developing countries – this North-South tension is always present, at least in the background. Second, reconciling the objectives of PGR conservation, trade liberalization, protection of intellectual property rights, and international equity is fiendishly complicated because progress on one issue affects member countries' interests in the other issues. In fact, progress is itself often difficult to gauge, which explains why one observer likened the negotiation process to trying to swim out of a whirlpool: ultimately, one winds up swimming in circles in an effort not to get sucked down (Barnes et al., 2000). Furthermore, the length of the negotiations – almost two decades long – resulted in numerous changes in the composition of the delegations and added layer upon layer of unfinished results.

Box 9.1 Key Steps in the Development of Phytogenic Governance

1961	First UPOV agreement adopted.
1978	Revision of the UPOV agreement.
1983	Adoption of a non-binding International Undertaking on PGRs.
1991	New revision of the UPOV agreement.
1992	Signature of the CBD at the Rio Earth Summit.
1994	Revision process of the International Undertaking on PGRs launched.
1994	WTO Agreement adopted at Marrakesh.
1996	Fourth Technical Conference of the Commission on Genetic Resources for Food and Agriculture (CGRFA) at Leipzig.
1996	*Rome Declaration* of the World Food Summit.
1999	Start of the process of revising the WTO/TRIPS agreement.
2001	International Treaty on Plant Genetic Resources for Food and Agriculture.
2001	Ministerial Declaration of WTO's Fourth Ministerial Conference at Doha, Qatar (Paragraph 19 decides to "examine" the TRIPS-CBD relationship, the protection of traditional knowledge, and the development dimension).[5]

The Stepwise Introduction of Intellectual Property Rights to Plant Genetic Resources

To a large extent, international negotiations on PGRs deal with the protection of a specific kind of intellectual property rights, namely plant breeders' rights (PBRs) covering new plant varieties that are stable and uniform. A first agreement was achieved in 1961 with the signature in Paris of the International Union for the Protection of New Varieties of Plants, usually called by its French acronym UPOV.[6] This first version entered into force in 1968 but was later replaced by subsequent Acts, namely UPOV 1978 and UPOV 1991, which entered into force in 1981 and 1998 respectively.

These agreements represent PBRs for commercial breeders as alternatives (usually called *sui generis* systems) to patent regulations. At present, UPOV has approximately 40 member states, mostly industrialized countries, and most of them adhere to the much more flexible 1978 version. In many developing countries, especially in Africa, the private sector's involvement is currently quite limited in the areas of plant breeding and seed supply (Dutfield, 2000, p. 29). It should be noted that new members can only sign on to the 1991 version. The difference between the two versions reflects the trend toward a considerably stronger emphasis on exclusionary PBRs, although they are less stringent than patents since they allow for some exceptions for farmers (Cullet, 2001a, p. 213). Cullet (2001b, pp. 2, 12) therefore considers this system inappropriate for African countries where conditions are very different from the OECD countries that have adopted them. Given that PBR provisions under UPOV 1991 are exercised at the expense of age-old farmers' rights[7] to re-sow harvested seeds, many NGOs – such as the Delhi-based Gene Campaign (Sahai, 2001, p. 12) – are trying to persuade developing countries not to join. These farmers' rights represent one of the key contentious issues of the PGR negotiations: To what extent can farmers re-plant their own crops? What rules should govern re-planting for personal consumption and for the market? To what extent are PBRs transferred to new varieties originating from protected varieties? For how long should the terms of protection be valid for different plant species? How can biopiracy be prevented? In this regard, farmers face two kinds of biopiracy: patenting knowledge that is in the public domain, and making profitable use of significant discrepancies that exist between different countries (Cullet, 2001a, p. 224).

One of the most elusive issues is an adequate definition of farmers' rights, which are sometimes compared to human rights but are not yet legally codified in a binding multilateral agreement (ten Kate and Diaz, 1997, p. 289). The CBD provides only limited guidance because as a framework convention, it leaves many crucial questions open or ambiguous, for example the question of rights:

> Developed countries and transnational corporations wanted as few restrictions as possible on access to biological resources. Perhaps not surprisingly, most of the uses of the words 'right' or 'rights' in the CBD are to affirm that they belong either to states or to intellectual property owners. It is commonly supposed that these IPR owners are corporate patent-holders. In fact, in the CBD there is no *explicit* reference to who such rights holders should be. They could be governments, private individuals, community holders of traditional knowledge and technologies, or companies. (Dutfield, 2000, pp. 33-34)

There are many reasons why the operationalization of the concept of farmers' rights is so difficult. To start with, the term "farmer" is not clearly defined. The CBD's term "indigenous and local communities embodying traditional lifestyles," although vague, better encompasses activities that protect genetic diversity assets such as non-timber forest products or medicinal and herbal plants. Also, it is often unclear who the holders of these rights are and who should be the beneficiaries.[8] In contrast to the clearly designated holders of PBRs, holders of farmers' rights may be individuals, clans, communities, or other more or less clearly distinct groups (Dutfield, 2000, p. 104). Under UPOV, farmers' rights depend on national legislation. The 1978 version is favourable to farmers in this regard, whereas in the more restrictive 1991 version "...an age-old practice has become an exception to the rights of plant breeders" (Walker, 2001, p. 29, fn.79).

In 1983 FAO established an intergovernmental commission on plant genetic resources, now called the Commission on Genetic Resources for Food and Agriculture (CGRFA). Also in 1983 the FAO Conference adopted a non-binding International Undertaking on Plant Genetic Resources (IU)[9] with the objective of supporting the protection and use of PGRs and making them available for plant breeding and other scientific purposes. It started off with an idealistic emphasis on farmers' rights of access to seeds but was not adopted by consensus. It had over 100 members, but some of the major countries with important agricultural constituencies, such as Brazil, Canada, China, Japan, Malaysia, and the US, were not part of it.[10]

The unresolved problems surrounding farmer's rights are a key reason why we are witnessing a "dichotomy" (Swanson, 1999, p. 327). On the one hand, we have the success of the industrialized countries in defending the rewards accruing from education and well-financed technological infrastructures. On the other hand, we have to observe the developing countries' failure to obtain financial compensation for the supply of their raw germplasm necessary for research and development of new seed varieties, cosmetics, and pharmaceuticals. This state of affairs is not only ethically inequitable but it has for the North and the South the disastrous consequence that the biodiversity-rich and economically poor Southern regions of the planet lack the incentives they need to maintain and manage their biological resources. Worse, the poverty of the latter often forces them to engage in ecologically destructive practices.

One of the most important factors influencing the construction of a new international biological order is the application of multilaterally negotiated intellectual property rights – more specifically plant breeders' rights (sometimes called plant variety protection) – to plant genetic resources or plant germplasm. Firms specializing in the development and commercialization of new seed varieties now can improve or protect the financial returns on their investment in plant breeding by imposing ownership on these varieties through the application of IPRs based either on patents or on alternative *sui generis* systems. This introduction of IPRs to living matter represents an "enclosure of what was previously common property" (Walker, 2001, p. 28) and signals, as we shall see, a fundamental shift in agricultural practices. This development contrasts with previous agricultural practices, which were shaped by the "green revolution" and which essentially continued to allow farmers to re-plant harvested seeds for the next crop. They relied to a large extent on public seed banks that allowed farmers and plant breeders free access to seeds.

This new thinking started to manifest itself around the end of the 1980s. In 1989 FAO members agreed that plant breeders' rights were compatible with the IU (Walker, 2001), and subsequent negotiations moved away from the emphasis on farmers' rights and took a more PBR-friendly position. The adoption of the CBD in 1992 marked further important changes. The Convention has placed biological diversity under the stewardship of national sovereignty. It gives states the sovereign right to regulate access to germplasm according to their prior informed consent and on mutually agreed terms with regard to the sharing of benefits. On the other hand, states must facilitate access and cannot impose restrictions that run counter to the objectives of the Convention. These two fundamental concepts are linked and subsumed by the term of "access and benefit sharing (ABS)".[11]

The adoption of the TRIPS agreement marks the conclusion of a real paradigm shift in international law with far-reaching consequences both with regard to agricultural biodiversity and with regard to trade. As far as trade is concerned, we need to look briefly at some of the characteristics that make the WTO a uniquely powerful organization. The conclusion of the often tense negotiations of the Uruguay Round through the signature of the WTO agreement finalized, among other results, the quest of the industrialized countries for a binding multilateral IPR regime, which is subject to the WTO's Dispute Settlement Understanding (DSU)[12] as are the WTO's other agreements. To appreciate the implications of this diplomatic achievement, one needs to realize the extent to which the unique character of the WTO derives this status (and with it much of its power and influence) from the DSU.

To start with, DSU procedures are far more speedy and predetermined than those of other intergovernmental courts (such as the International Court of Justice) which in many cases lack effective enforcement powers (unlike the WTO). Its two most important features are found in Articles 23 and 22. Article 23.1 represents an "exclusive arbitration clause," which means that the application of DSU procedures is automatic and mandatory when a WTO member brings a claim against another member to the DSU.[13] And under certain circumstances detailed in DSU Article 22, members can use cross-retaliation, that is, they can for instance penalize another member through punitive measures that lie within their national sovereignty for violating the TRIPS agreement. Retaliation can take the form of a suspension of benefits that the other member is entitled to under the GATT agreement, such as economically crucial market access.

The key TRIPS provision with regard to the CBD is the much-cited Article 27.3 (b) on *patentable subject matter,* which contains exceptions related to life-forms that WTO members may exclude from patentability under specified conditions:

> Plants and animals other than micro-organisms, and essentially biological processes for the production of plants or animals other than non-biological and microbiological processes. However, Members shall provide for the protection of plant varieties either by patents or by an effective *sui generis* system or by any combination thereof. The provisions of this subparagraph shall be reviewed four years after the date of entry into force of the WTO Agreement. (WTO, 1994, p. 379)

This subparagraph of Article 27 is arguably the single most contentious element of the WTO agreements. It has huge potential implications for agribusiness and for biotechnology industries in general. The subparagraph, however, leaves many questions unanswered, and its scope is not at all clearly defined. For instance, the difference between plants that a member country may exempt from patentability and a plant variety that must be protected by patents or an effective *sui generis* system is unclear (is a transgenic grass a "plant" or a "plant variety"?). In any case, as long as there is no WTO case law on the exact scope of the TRIPS agreement, doubts remain about its boundaries, for example regarding the definition of micro-organisms. Attorneys for Novartis and the Max-Planck Institute have claimed, for instance, (and they have received some support for these claims from the European Patent Office) that plant cells and DNA sequences are to be considered micro-organisms; if the WTO Dispute Settlement Body accepts this reasoning, they would be covered by the TRIPS agreement (Dutfield, 2000, p. 22). As a matter of fact, it turned out that the question of the precise definitions of relevant genetic material was the last one that needed to be solved before the International Treaty on Plant Genetic Resources could be adopted (Barnes and Burgiel, 2001, p. 5).

A high level of uncertainty about the meaning of some key terms with far-reaching socio-economic and ecopolitical implications and institutional ramifications is not the only flaw of this paragraph, however. The fundamental concern of developing countries lies in built-in biases that accrue from the fact that patent protection must be extended to high-technology fields like biotechnology but that there are really at this time no practical answers for the protection of their traditional intellectual property rights. As developed economies rely more and more on intellectual input for the creation of value and competitive advantage, the protection and monopolization of this input through IPRs tends to increase the North-South gap. To add insult to injury, resorting to courts with the knowledge and experience to adjudicate extremely complicated disputes between different patent holders may be completely beyond developing countries' financial means; in many cases such courts may not even exist (Dutfield, 2000, p. 18). These points represent the main arguments used to justify the need for much greater concessions to developing countries in the ongoing review of the TRIPS agreement!

The CBD is particularly concerned about the fact that the TRIPS agreement is designed for the protection of formal knowledge but very unsuitable for collectively held and often intergenerational farmers' rights, which often do not fulfil the patent rights' requirement of novelty. Furthermore, the allocation of property rights on knowledge may be contrary to a community's belief system in some cultures (Walker, 2001).[14] Last but not least, the unresolved legal and scientific questions of Article 27.3 (b) are perhaps less cumbersome for the WTO than the general political and ethical question: is living matter patentable? The positions with regard to this question are widely divergent and hotly debated, especially in Europe, where public opinion is very sensitive to agricultural and food politics in the wake of the bovine spongiform encephalopathy (BSE) disaster and other food-related public health problems. The politics of this debate is of course closely intermingled with the clash over GM food.

As Article 27.3 (b) specifies, plant varieties do not need to be protected by patents, but if a government chooses an alternative approach, it has to be an "effective *sui generis* system". This provision may appear innocuous but it is not! The term "effective" is not defined, but it has to be interpreted in the context of the TRIPS agreement and is therefore very demanding. In particular, it has to cover, according to TRIPS Article 1.2, the full scope of intellectual property obligations, and it has to provide to the holder of the IPRs covering a plant variety "an additional right, i.e. a right which is not foreseen anyway by the TRIPS agreement" (Leskien and Flitner, 1998, p. 57). That means, for instance, that if a government were only to require the registration of a new plant variety as a trademark for the protection of the IPR embodied in this variety, it would be in violation of the TRIPS agreement since this *sui generis* system would not go beyond what the agreement already allows. The fact that a great deal will depend on the interpretation of the term "effective" by the WTO's Dispute Settlement Body (Maljean-Dubois, 2000, p. 965) adds to the uncertainty spread by this subparagraph. Not only that, but these doubts were hanging over the negotiators, and they were forcefully taken advantage of by some of the delegations. This represents a powerful example of the phenomenon of *regulatory chill*, which will be discussed at the end of this analysis – in fact the question of effective *sui generis* provisions represented one of the key obstacles in the negotiation of the International Treaty on Plant Genetic Resources.

The question also arises whether farmers' rights might qualify as a *sui generis* system, which seems unlikely since they tend to be regarded as opposing a property rights system, a counterbalance to IPRs. They could, however, be included in such a system in order to enable indigenous holders of IPRs to claim compensation for their efforts in developing a plant variety during past centuries. Industrialized countries are applying pressure on developing countries to adopt UPOV 1991 – which is widely considered as fulfiling the requirement of "effectiveness" in the sense of Article 27.3 (b) – as their *sui generis* system if they do not want to assume the very considerable burden of protecting patent rights on plant varieties. Walker (2001, p. 35), however, goes as far as considering the possibility that a revised TRIPS agreement could specify UPOV 1991 as the relevant effective *sui generis* form of plant variety protection as a "worst case scenario". In any case, it should be stressed that the development of an effective *sui generis* system would be "extremely demanding" (Cullet, 1999, p. 653) for a developing country.

As far as the environmental consequences of the conclusion of the TRIPS agreement are concerned, the main problem lies in a strengthening of the ongoing trend toward the concentration of land ownership and larger and larger monocultures at the expense of land races and agricultural biodiversity (Dutfield, 2000, pp. 44-46; Walker, 2001, p. 40) because traditional agricultural practices represent the principal storage sites of *in situ* biodiversity of food crops (Monagle, 2001, p. 18). Unfortunately, there is a serious lack of long-term studies of agricultural productivity in developing countries but signs of "slow yield declines, caused by increased pest pressure, depletion of soil micronutrients, and buildup of harmful chemicals from low-quality irrigation water" (World Bank, 1992, p. 138). Intellectual property rights will undoubtedly favour the further expansion of monoculture practices as a result of the patent-protected introduction of genetically modified seeds. This will of course deepen concerns over their impact on the surrounding ecosystem and over long-term productivity.

The TRIPS agreement is probably the most contested WTO agreement in a North-South perspective: "It seems that in many countries there was little awareness of intellectual property rights when the TRIPS agreement was signed. The problem was most pronounced in developing countries" (Mishra, 2001, p. 172). The agreement never really obtained the backing of most of the developing countries; they agreed to it under strong economic pressures originating from knowledge-based industries located mostly in industrialized countries in the hope of improving their market access to the industrialized world. During the negotiation process that led to the WTO's Fourth Ministerial Conference in Doha in November 2001, many representatives from developing countries stressed that these hopes had been largely dashed. Ironically, because the large preparatory effort for the 1992 Rio Earth Summit coincided with the very complicated and complex TRIPS negotiations, developing countries followed the process largely from afar (Juma, 1999).

These North-South divergences may be one reason why the agreement incorporates, after some transitional periods for developing countries and formerly centralized economies, a continuous biannual review process.[15] One should therefore expect politically tense negotiations around these reviews. These tensions may explain why implementation delays on the part of developing countries have so far been met by a relative flexible attitude on the part of industrialized countries. In view of these problems, especially after the Seattle experience, a vigorous policing of the official implementation schedules might cause a domino effect of recalcitrant reactions (Chiappetta, 2000, pp. 337, 381). The ongoing reviews will presumably bring about some modifications, but it is rather unlikely that the structure of the TRIPS agreement will be fundamentally transformed in the foreseeable future because it is a key component of the outcome of the Uruguay Round.

Rather, current trends point toward the global spread of even more stringent intellectual property rights on plant genetic resources, which in many instances will be achieved through bilateral and regional treaties.[15] The US and the European Union, in particular, have already succeeded in negotiating numerous so-called "TRIPS-plus" agreements with developing countries in the context of trade, investments, development co-operation, and scientific co-operation. These TRIPS-plus agreements interfere with the very spirit of the IT which is based on the realization that countries are interdependent and need to find multilateral solutions. Some of these treaties specify UPOV 1991 as the only acceptable alternative to patents; others refer to the 1980 Budapest Treaty on the International Recognition of the Deposit of Micro-organisms for the Purpose of Patent Procedure. This treaty, with about 50 signatories, so far mostly industrialized countries, obliges countries to accept as disclosure requirement – which is a condition for the granting of a patent – the deposit of a sample of the micro-organism in a recognized international depository authority, instead of the usual description. These and other TRIPS-plus developments point to the co-ordinated negotiation of a globalized patent regime on PGRs with fewer exceptions than TRIPS, if any, on the patentability of life-forms.

A Long-Awaited New Beginning: The International Treaty

The signing of the International Treaty on Plant Genetic Resources for Food and Agriculture in Rome on 3 November 2001 marks a new era in multilateral negotiations regarding food security and agriculture. Its purpose consists essentially in reconciling the interests of the internationally active plant breeding industry and local farmers. Under the treaty, plant breeders obtain access to PGRs as well as a far-reaching protection of the intellectual property used in their breeding efforts. On the other side, holders of traditional knowledge and nations or indigenous communities that harbour these genetic resources can now hope to obtain some sort of benefit-sharing from the proceeds of these breeding efforts, which is a vital incentive for them to safeguard their crop diversity.

There was considerable speculation initially that the agreement would become another protocol to the CBD. Instead, a very innovative solution was found "by closely linking this Treaty to the Food and Agriculture Organization of the United Nations and to the Convention on Biological Diversity" (Article 1.2). It should be noted that the new name for the treaty was applied only at the last minute before the signing; until then it continued to be known as the International Undertaking.

It should also be stressed that the IT represents a *de facto* framework agreement; it is comparable in the breadth of its ambitions and objectives to the climate change and biodiversity conventions. That of course means that a broad and general consensus has been found on many issues but that a great deal of detail work remains to be negotiated, possibly through one or more protocols. As might be expected after seven years of often acrimonious negotiations, the text is convoluted and interlocked, and it leaves great latitude to the governing body. Regrettably, the US has not only abstained from signing the IT (Japan was the only other country), it also seems to have precluded a ratification at a later date because of the absence of a "national security clause," i.e. it insists on preserving the right to use seeds as a political tool by placing an embargo on their export.

The fundamental process driving negotiations on the international regulation of PGRs, especially since the conclusion of UPOV 1991, can be called a shift from "free" to "shared" access to germplasm, with sharing strictly regulated and limited to the member countries of the IT. Under the original 1983 version of the IU, access to seed samples for the purpose of scientific research, plant breeding, or genetic resource conservation was to be "free of charge, on the basis of mutual exchange, or on mutually agreed terms".[17] Since the CBD had placed PGRs under national sovereignty, the IU had to be revised and harmonized with it (Correa, 2000, p. 169). Accordingly, the members of the Commission on Genetic Resources for Food and Agriculture decided in 1993 to initiate negotiations with the objective of arriving at a revised agreement, which would not only be compatible with the CBD but also replace the agreement's voluntary nature with binding provisions.[18]

Its official name was temporarily changed to "IU on PGRs in Harmony with the CBD" to reflect the international community's intent to establish an explicit linkage with the CBD, even though the nature of the linkage remained undefined. Compatibility would be achieved through the creation of innovative procedures making it possible for indigenous farmers to receive compensation for the access they provide to plant breeders. Furthermore, the agreement would create incentives for communities to maintain and manage these valuable biological resources. On a larger political and diplomatic level, however, the momentum exerted by advances in biotechnology and by concurrent developments in the field of IPRs were arguably much more influential in shaping the negotiations. It is important, therefore, to keep in mind that negotiations on the TRIPS agreement were nearing completion at the time that the revised IU negotiation process was launched at the commission's first extraordinary session in November 1994 (Cooper, 1993, p. 158). The challenge before IT negotiators, therefore, was to harmonize the agreement not only with the CBD but also with the TRIPS agreement. The revision process of the IU/IT and of the TRIPS Article 27.3 (b) have been proceeding at the same time and with great difficulty in both cases.

Once the WTO agreement had entered into force on 1 January 1995, and with it the TRIPS agreement, it was relatively easy to extend IPRs covering PGRs to the food and agriculture sector. This process was essentially finalized through the Fourth Technical Conference of the CGRFA in Leipzig in June 1996 (Purdue, 2000)[19] and the 1996 *Rome Declaration* of the World Food Summit, which took place in November of that year. The liberalization of trade in food crops, however, could "cause havoc to rural communities" (Mishra, 2001, p. 18). Furthermore, the introduction of IPRs through the WTO may bring "a boon to some countries, and may spell a disaster for many others," according to Mishra (Ibid) who concludes that all the advantages of genetic engineering "will be of no use if a patentee... decides to exercise monopoly abuses associated with it" (Ibid, p. 21).

There is no doubt that the outcome of the ongoing negotiations and the implementation of the two agreements on PGRs and intellectual property rights will determine the nature of phytogenetic governance for years to come. The CBD is directly concerned in these negotiations because of the need to achieve harmony between it and the IT. The treaty's fundamental objective is to improve the world's food security. This is to be achieved largely through a binding agreement covering a specific *listing* of food crops strangely called the Multilateral System (MS) which provides for facilitated access to a few dozen food and forage crops for member countries. The composition of the MS has been one of the most hotly debated issues in the IT negotiations. Given that the CBD puts PGRs under national sovereignty, it was up to the member countries to decide which crops they would include. Unfortunately, what transpired was a hotly negotiated trade-off between more or less concrete prospects for some benefit-sharing on the one hand and inclusion of more crops in the MS for access by plant breeders on the other. In view of the fact that many developing countries were disappointed over the benefit-sharing mechanisms, they kept many crops such as soybeans, groundnuts, and sugar cane excluded: "no more money, no more crops"; furthermore, there were squabbles among certain countries over the inclusion of specific seeds placed under their sovereignty: "it was not a pretty scene".[20]

The MS essentially stipulates the following privileges and obligations for member countries:

- to conserve the world's major public *ex situ* seed collections, which are held in a network of 16 autonomous research centres loosely co-ordinated by the Consultative Group on International Agricultural Research (CGIAR)[21];
- to facilitate access to seeds for research purposes by keeping them in the public domain;
- to develop a mechanism for the sharing of financial benefits accruing from the development of new varieties based on seeds from these public seed banks; and
- to protect *in situ* crop diversity by improving local communities' livelihood through initiatives at the international and national level aimed at the development of legal frameworks for the exercise of farmers' rights.

Although these four points represent only a very simplified summary of the negotiation stakes, it is clear that the negotiations cut across public rights and private IPRs. The stakes involved in the IU/IT revision process were large because they pitted the financial interests of various segments of agribusiness against the need to protect the world's food security faced with rapidly declining agricultural diversity (Halweil, 2000, p. 15). The IT can be considered an attempt to build a bridge between the TRIPS' trade perspective and the CBD's sustainable perspective. This attempt to reconcile two very different approaches lies at the root of the difficulties involved in turning the non-binding IU, which represented more or less a declaratory instrument, into the binding legal text of the IT. Article 12.3 (d) dealing with intellectual property was particularly hotly debated and in the end was left sufficiently fuzzy to leave some clarifications up to the governing body or to future negotiations.[22]

In this context, it is not surprising that the negotiations of the CGRFA have gradually become both more frequent and politically tense. There were eight regular sessions from 1985 to 1999, six extraordinary sessions from 1994 to 2001, six intersessional contact group (IUCG) meetings on the revision of the IU from 1999 to 2001, and an important experts' meeting in 1999. The IUCGs involved approximately 40 countries attempting to prepare a consensual draft for the plenary extraordinary session. This accumulation of meetings signals that the implications are important and that the objectives of the main protagonists are far apart.

In view of the importance and urgency of protecting agricultural biodiversity for future generations, there is a need to devise "new approaches based on shared interests in preserving genetic resources and enhancing social and economic development" (Cottier, 1998, p. 560). There is also a need to engage in a wide and inclusive debate over new concepts that can be useful in advancing better socio-economic equity and ecological benefits and to reflect on their political implications. The term usually employed to designate the knowledge of indigenous communities or of individuals in these communities with regard to PGRs is traditional knowledge (TK). This term, however, may not be concise enough for many applications, and that has led to the development of the concept of traditional resource rights (TRR) which can be considered as a "bundle of rights". An interesting contribution to this complex debate has been made by Cottier (1998, pp. 565, 573) who proposes the more specific term traditional intellectual property rights (TIP rights) to emphasize the intellectual and mental nature of the knowledge that may be held by communities or individuals.

There is a need to elaborate these and related concepts in a qualified multilateral forum in order to achieve a consensus on the meaning of terms that are new to international law. The recent creation by the World Intellectual Property Organization (WIPO) of an Intergovernmental Commission on Intellectual Property and Genetic Resources, Traditional Knowledge and Folklore[23] is an important and positive step in this direction. It has begun to explore new issues such as contractual agreements for accessing genetic resources and benefit-sharing, and the enforcement of rights based on TK.[24] WIPO has also commissioned, in co-operation with UNEP, a number of case studies that provide lessons on how the effective protection of intellectual property rights can support the sharing of benefits arising from the use of genetic resources.[25]

In 1999 a CGRFA-convened experts' meeting yielded a number of much-cited "chairman's elements" on which future debates could be based. Unfortunately, differing interpretations of these elements by some of the delegations led to subsequent meetings of the IU contact group that were generally very tense, except for the third one (IUCG-3, Teheran, August 2000) which went surprisingly well. At IUCG-4 (Neuchâtel, Switzerland, November 2000) however, some countries changed their position and deadlock over many issues returned (Barnes et al., 2000). The situation was so bad that it was impossible to conclude the negotiations as scheduled on the occasion of FAO's council meeting in November 2000, and an extension had to be granted by the council. The challenge for negotiators was to create a new kind of binding multilateral agreement that contained the following set of incentives, which had to be made compatible with the TRIPS agreement:

- industry must be motivated to continue to develop new seed varieties;
- access to seeds for research and experimentation by breeders and farmers must be assured;
- individual and group holders of TK, local communities, indigenous peoples, and developing countries must find it in their financial and cultural interest to preserve and protect the unique and precious wealth of their biodiversity; and
- funding and political support must be generated from industry and governments to make the whole endeavour pragmatically workable.

Clearly, these incentives will be very difficult to implement. Indeed, to some extent, they conflict with each other. For example, the interests of indigenous farmers and transnational biotech corporations clash in many areas, and governments are much more likely to support national research projects than distant seed banks for the common good. The situation is made more unpredictable by the possibility of the TRIPS agreement undergoing significant modifications with regard to PGRs in the near future. Taking these questions into consideration, we may subsume and group the main issues of the IU revision and of ongoing IT negotiations, as shown in Box 9.2.

Box 9.2 Summary of Negotiation Topics in Phytogenetic Governance

Legal issues
- the IT's relationship with the TRIPS agreement and with the CBD;
- separate ABS provisions for regulating the use of phytogenetic resources for pharmaceutical and cosmetic purposes outside the IT framework;
- the elaboration of specific and detailed lists or annexes of plant species that are covered by regulations regarding ABS – especially the scope of the Multilateral System for food and for forage;
- the requirement of novelty: definition, application, implications;
- the patentability of whole species in general;
- the patentability of varieties, or even whole species, that are used by indigenous farmers (land races);
- the patentability of varieties, or even whole species, originating from public *ex situ* collections;
- the patentability of wild species and varieties that are not yet included in *ex situ* collections;
- the legal definition and implication of the notion of "heritage of humankind" and its relationship with national sovereignty; and
- the implementation of so-called Material Transfer Agreements (Dutfield, 2000, p. 106).[26]

Science and technology issues
- the contribution of science, and of traditional breeding techniques, to global food security through germplasm remaining in the public domain for researchers and farmers for the purpose of breeding new varieties;
- conservation of the germplasm through incentives for creating and maintaining in situ and ex situ collections;
- the modalities of the inclusion of existing in situ and ex situ collections, especially the CGIAR centres;
- the relationship between public and corporate ex situ collections;
- various kinds of access conditions to germplasm: free, free but not free of charge, based on mutually agreed terms; and
- the scope and modalities of applying patents on widely used biotechnological processes and techniques, such as screening, mapping, and engineering genes, or tissue culture methodologies (Correa, 2000, p. 171).

Consumer and civil society issues
- origin, traceability, and quality of imported food;
- potential health problems due to genetically modified food products;
- fair trade considerations; and
- ethical considerations of biotechnology.

Box 9.2 Concluded

- the definition of cultural and grassroots political and social concepts, especially traditional knowledge, traditional resource rights, traditional intellectual property rights, farmers' rights;
- prior informed consent procedures concerning patented varieties in order to minimize instances of biopiracy; and
- compulsory indication of geographical origin(s) of IPR-protected germplasm.

Economic and equity issues
- the assessment of equitable benefit-sharing;
- modalities of and procedures for implementing mandatory or voluntary benefit-sharing;
- the assessment of the actual benefits to be shared; and
- the determination of the beneficiaries of entitlements to shared benefits.

Administrative issues
- details of the funding mechanism; and
- establishing procedures for ensuring the implementation and monitoring of the treaty's provisions.

The FAO has established a Global System on plant genetic resources, which in addition to the CGRFA and the IT consists of a Global Plan of Action, a fund for PGRs, a world information and early warning system, guidelines for the collection and transfer of PGRs, and international networks of *ex situ* seed banks and *in situ* crop-related conservation areas. As one can readily understand from the above list of issues, negotiations at the commission's regular, extraordinary, and contact group meetings have been going on for a long time, and they deal with a staggering number of interlinked questions. Therefore, a comprehensive and effective implementation and enforcement of the IT is unthinkable in the near future. More likely, we are going to see a continuation of the present negotiation process based on the adopted treaty framework. We therefore shall not attempt to delve into the complexities of any of the specific IT issues on this occasion. Instead, we shall conclude this section by summarizing the main questions requiring further discussions.

The IU has always been on shaky grounds politically because of the unstable balance between farmers' rights on the one hand and plant breeders' rights or industry's intellectual property rights on the other. The IT has not solved this tension: it recognizes farmers' rights in the relatively unimportant preamble, but in the more important actual text (Article 9.3) it has skirted the issue by simply leaving it up to national legislation. It is not surprising, therefore, that the above-mentioned notion of access and benefit-sharing, which is located at the core of the industry-farmers conflict of interests, represented and continues to represent probably the toughest conceptual problem of these negotiations. ABS issues, moreover, are closely intertwined with the *scope* of the agreement, i.e. the exact listing of seed species to be included in the Multilateral System. This connection arises because not all seeds have the same economic value:

> ...countries are not prepared to commit certain categories of genetic resources to international access without agreement on the terms under which these resources will be made available. Similarly, it is impossible to define the terms for access to genetic resources without considering the economic, political and scientific significance of the resources themselves. (ten Kate and Diaz, 1997, p. 286)

The scope of the IT is severely limited. It does not cover pharmaceuticals and cosmetics, *in situ* seed collections, seeds for plants that are not used for food, and seed collections that are older than the CBD. All these cases are covered by more recent ABS negotiation processes initiated by the CBD. It is also important to realize that the much increased cost of research as a result of genetic engineering techniques adds to the quandary; in fact, it may have completely changed the equation in recent years. The concentration process among agribusiness conglomerates (Halweil, 2000, p. 14) has been driven by, among other things, the high cost of developing genetically modified seed varieties and bringing them to the market across the numerous regulatory hurdles. As a result, we are now observing the development of essentially a global oligopolistic agribusiness industry with deep pockets and long-term objectives. This industry is able to exert more or less subtle pressure on governments, especially in developing countries, in order to advance its goals. Unlike government delegations, which often come from different and often badly co-ordinated ministries to the negotiation of agreements such as UPOV, CBD, TRIPS, the Biosafety Protocol, the IT, and the Codex Alimentarius Commission[27] (where industry representatives are very commonly included within in the delegations) or to attend meetings of the governing bodies of organizations such as UNEP, FAO, WIPO, or WTO, industry takes a more cohesive approach at the different fora thanks to this concentration, which generates a new kind of dynamics. It was deeply involved in the IT negotiations, especially through the International Association of Plant Breeders (ASSINSEL) which is based in Nyon, Switzerland.[28] It will undoubtedly take several years to clarify the relationship among these regimes and organizations in general and especially between the two ongoing processes of the IT and the TRIPS negotiations.

The main outstanding issues of a more general and political nature that will be implicitly or explicitly included in future IT negotiations or clarifications of vaguely worded articles include:

- Financing of phytogenetic governance: what should be the relationship between benefit-sharing or royalties paid by industry and government contributions, and should either or both be mandatory?

- Should TK about plant genetic resources be lumped together ("omnibus approach") – for strategic reasons – with folklore, or should the economically much more important PGR issues be negotiated separately?[29]
- Is the issue of North-South equity one of the key stakes of the negotiation? Is there any realistic chance that developing countries will ever obtain substantial economic benefits from the implementation of the IT, and under what conditions could a more equitable system be constructed?
- Is the "access" issue of low importance to industry, as is claimed sometimes, because it has sufficient resources in its own or in other accessible collections, or is this issue downplayed by industrialized countries below its real importance for tactical reasons? To what extent does this question depend on specific seed species? and
- Is there a gradual convergence of biosafety and plant genetic resources negotiations, or will these two streams of negotiations remain completely separate and distinct?

An important first step has now successfully been concluded, but of course the IT framework agreement leaves many questions unanswered for the time being, as the discussion of its difficult relationship with the TRIPS agreement has illustrated. Nevertheless, sooner or later countries will have to grapple with these issues more specifically than through a framework agreement. To meet the challenge of worldwide food security, which depends on sharing resources and knowledge (Cullet, 2001a, p. 216; 2001b, p. 2), the international community must endeavour to find an appropriate balance between conflicting objectives: it must encourage scientific research, which relies on the protection of IPRs, and at the same time it must provide the necessary incentives and support structures for indigenous communities, which are necessary for the conservation of PGRs.

Towards Phytogenetic and Phytosanitary Governance

The difficulties of achieving the adoption of an IT that is compatible with both the CBD and the TRIPS agreement can easily be explained by the problems related to the application of IPRs on PGRs (Walker, 2001: Box 6 The International Undertaking):

> The positions of negotiators turn on the question of ownership and control. Developing countries are generally wary that free access to germplasm will result in a flow of genetic materials to the plant breeding industry, to be adapted and made subject to IPRs with inadequate sharing of benefits. Developed countries advocate free access to genetic resources, while arguing that germplasm subject to IPRs should be outside the 'free' multilateral exchange system.

What is really meant by global governance or by international regulation in this specific context? As we have seen, this question really boils down to bridging, reconciling, making compatible, and managing the two fundamentally different perspectives of, on the one hand, the CBD (including the Biosafety Protocol)[30] and the IT and, on the other hand, the relevant agreements of the WTO, i.e. SPS, TBT, GATT, and TRIPS, as well as UPOV, which though a separate entity is widely considered to be compatible with the TRIPS agreement. It is also necessary to distinguish between two related but distinct types of plant-related governance: phytogenetic and phytosanitary governance cover roughly the same issue area but have different objectives. Phytogenetic governance seeks to set up international provisions governing access and benefit-sharing with regard to PGRs and to create an incentive framework for their continued *conservation*, whereas phytosanitary governance (embodied by the Biosafety Protocol) focuses on the *protection* of this biodiversity against potential trade-related threats from living modified organisms.

Compatibility between agreements has a very specific meaning in the interface between trade and environment regimes. In the context of PBRs, it means essentially that a *sui generis* regulatory system put in place by one government is sufficiently stringent to make it unlikely that another government could contest it successfully before the WTO's Dispute Settlement Body if it feels that the IPRs held by its seed companies are not protected adequately. It is characteristic of trade-related environmental measures that it is often difficult to judge whether they are conflicting or compatible with WTO provisions because of the way the WTO's Dispute Settlement Body is interlocked with multilateral environmental agreements: the DSB can only decide on the conformity of such measures with the WTO agreement after a dispute is raised. This fact very much applies to the IT as well once it has entered into force; in fact, it has been a major reason for the negotiations' difficulties (Barnes et al., 2000).

Is there a *legal* incompatibility between the CBD and the WTO? How would a WTO dispute settlement panel and its appellate body rule if a government should claim that the exercise of IPRs is deleterious to its local agricultural biodiversity? The fact that "the two regimes are based on different conceptual premises and were negotiated independently" (Cullet, 1999, p. 655) may indeed give rise to such a claim. The outcome of such a dispute remains highly uncertain until a case involving these different rights is brought before the DSB (Tansey, 1999, p. 29) and because the actual impacts of IPRs on biodiversity are difficult to evaluate and prove (Kothari and Anuradha, 1999). In the case of the TRIPS agreement, this legal uncertainty is fully recognized by the WTO Secretariat:

> The WTO Secretariat cannot offer authoritative interpretation of any Uruguay Round agreement, since that right is reserved to the WTO member governments, acting jointly and in accordance with the provisions of the agreement concerned. That caveat applies with particular force to a commentary on the TRIPS Agreement. The agreement is a highly complex legal system, the provisions of which have yet to be tested by the

institutions and mechanisms of the WTO, including those on dispute settlement. (WTO Secretariat, 1999, p. 209)

The relationship between the IT and the TRIPS agreement has to be placed in the context of the wider environmental impact of the trade regime. The WTO likes to take credit for contributing to trade-related environmental improvements brought about by win/win synergies[31] – and it is indeed very much entitled to claim due credit for reducing environmentally destructive subsidies in areas such as energy, fishing, or forestry. The trade regime has a strong environmental impact, sometimes favourable, sometimes not. In this context, it is important to realize the limitations of the WTO's Committee on Trade and Environment. It serves as a valuable discussion forum on trade and environment issues but by no means represents a negotiation forum for reconciling trade and environment conflicts. These negotiations take place within the various trade, environmental, and hybrid trade/environmental agreements themselves. UPOV, the CBD, the Biosafety Protocol, and the IT are all prime examples of such hybrids, which explains why they represent a particularly concentrated cluster of flash points between trade and environmental concerns. The IT has a unique feature in that regard because it explicitly recognizes and expresses this cross-sectoral nature in a paragraph of its preamble (it should have added North-South relations for the sake of completeness):

Aware that questions regarding the management of plant genetic resources for food and agriculture are at the meeting point between agriculture, the environment and commerce, and convinced that there should be synergy among these sectors...

The most serious environmental critique of the trade regime is arguably the assertion that some of the WTO's agreements exert a discouraging influence on environmental negotiations and regulatory developments, even when a wide consensus exists on the need to take international action to protect the ecosystem. This phenomenon is often called a "chilling effect" or "regulatory chilling" with regard to regulatory processes dealing with the environment and sustainable development (see for instance Martin, 2001, p. 151; Stilwell and Turk, 1999, p. 5). More or less the same idea is conveyed by the term "deterrent effect" (Cannabrava, 2001, p. 7).

This, of course, is in direct opposition to the need for *integration* of the two issue areas. These problems of inter-regime coherence are not really a surprise; they were anticipated before the conclusion of the Uruguay Round. This concern finds its expression in Principle 4 of the Rio Declaration which states that "In order to achieve sustainable development, environmental protection shall constitute an integral part of the development process and cannot be considered in isolation from it".[32]

The analysis of phytogenetic and phytosanitary governance is particularly interesting and pertinent in illustrating this chilling effect. In the case of the IT negotiations, the clash between conflicting rights and obligations was and continues to be at the heart of the disagreements. On the one hand, WTO member governments have the obligation, under the TRIPS agreement, to provide patentability for micro-organisms and microbiological processes and to apply stringent TRIPS-compatible protection for IPRs on plant varieties. On the other hand, they have, under the CBD, the right to institute legislation to protect agricultural biodiversity, to develop this resource sustainably, and to establish mechanisms for the equitable sharing of financial benefits from these genetic resources. The TRIPS obligations, however, make it difficult if not impossible for a government to exercise those rights. If, for example, a plant variety finds its origin in breeding experiments by indigenous communities over generations, and if a seed supplier subsequently claims PBRs on it on the basis of having implemented an improvement that is difficult to demonstrate, how can a government, in this situation, elaborate regulations that provide for sharing the financial benefits from this plant variety with the indigenous community, given that the recognition of collective property rights is currently exceedingly difficult?

At the same time, this government is obliged under TRIPS to protect the exclusionary rights of the plant breeder, which makes the chilling effect on the national regulatory process more evident. Furthermore, one may have to assume that the seed supplier has far greater financial resources than the local community to defend its claims by hiring expensive, highly specialized legal and scientific experts. Of course, the chilling effect takes place not only at the national level but more so at the multilateral level in the negotiation of these hybrid trade/environment regimes, because it is obvious that international law is far better equipped to implement IPR systems, such as patents, than regulations for the enforcement of traditional intellectual property rights.

As far as the CBD is concerned, the discussions and negotiations focus on three Articles: Article 8(j) on indigenous and local communities, Article 16.5 on the compatibility between intellectual property rights and the CBD objectives, and Article 22 on the relationship between obligations derived from existing international agreements and the protection of biological diversity. Contrary to the TRIPS agreement, however, those Articles do not create explicitly binding obligations. Clearly, there is a long way to go to reach a balance between trade and environmental objectives and imperatives.

In the case of the Biosafety Protocol, a comparable conflict of interests occurs between, on the one hand, the obligation of a government under GATT to provide market access to other countries' exporters and, on the other hand, the right under the Biosafety Protocol to limit this market access as a precautionary measure in the case of a justified risk to the environment. As a matter of fact, the breakdown of negotiations in February 1999 in Cartagena in the case of the Biosafety Protocol and in November 2000 in Neuchâtel in the case of the IU is largely attributable to these two clashes. In both cases, trade interests exerted heavy pressure on the negotiations over these environmental stakes. Such pressures are not applied by the

WTO itself, but trade proponents use the WTO agreements and the clout of its dispute settlement mechanism to move the results of the negotiations towards their own objectives. In view of the fundamental conceptual discrepancies between the trade and environment regimes, the WTO's chilling effect is very real, which means that its impact on global environmental governance should not be disregarded or belittled. The IT and the Biosafety Protocol negotiation processes represent two cases of MEA/WTO[33] relations that are intertwined to a particularly high degree. In this issue area, the WTO can truly be considered an organized global ecopolitical force (OGEF) (Thomas, 1997, p. 231), thanks to its unique DSU.

The WTO faces a double challenge from biodiversity and other environmental concerns and from issues related to socio-economic equity and cultural integrity. This dual challenge has led, especially over the past ten years or so, to the creation of a number of NGOs specializing in this complex *problématique*. They have developed two distinct but related "discursive frames" (Purdue, 2000, p. 62) to address these two issue areas. Through their globalized electronic networks, personal contacts, and informative presentations, they attempt to influence delegates participating in multilateral negotiations as well as the media. Between sessions, they are in touch with civil servants in the capitals and at intergovernmental organizations. They have managed to acquire a counter-expertise (Purdue, 2000, ch.4) in this complex issue area by assembling flexible and overlapping coalitions of networks whereby each coalition develops knowledge and recognition in its specialized niche, while at the same time attempts are made to achieve synergy by co-operating on the more general questions. Their effectiveness in these highly complex debates is difficult to assess, but one may certainly observe that they have been quite successful in linking connected issues, in articulating the wider implications of specific negotiation topics, and in preventing governments from acting as if trade, environment, North-South equity, and sociocultural issues were disconnected and could neatly be tackled separately. This latter mechanistic worldview is still widely represented in the trade community and represents a major obstacle in the negotiation of these hybrid trade and environmental agreements.

The distinct roles of the various organizations and regimes implicated in phytogenetic and phytosanitary governance, not to mention the sheer number of important actors, is confusing even to well-informed observers of international environmental affairs. A metaphor might help make sense of this complexity. The basic image representing this double governance process is that of a very large bus carrying six billion passengers. Its engine is the TRIPS agreement, bilateral and regional treaties boosting intellectual property rights act as a turbocharger that drives the process of expanding the application of IPRs, and it runs on seeds. The engine's starter is UPOV 1961 and its fan is WIPO, which cools the engine with fresh ideas on traditional knowledge. The IT serves as its clutch to allow fine-tuning of the linkage between the engine and the rest of the vehicle according to road conditions. The wheels that touch the earth can only be the FAO. The bus is further equipped with an emergency brake (the Biosafety Protocol) and a first-aid kit (the International Plant Protection Convention).[34]

Outside the bus, we find the CBD functioning as the government with a number of different tasks, the Codex Alimentarius Commission as the inspection agency, and of course the Bretton Woods institutions serve as the bank. Last but not least, we also have a team of drivers – governments and transnational corporations – holding the WTO steering wheel and expected to follow the road map that was given to them back in 1992, i.e. *Agenda 21*. Unfortunately, the traffic police, consisting of ministers representing a number of different portfolios, do a poor job of providing harmonized directions. Two problems have yet to be resolved: the brakes have never been tested, and the liability insurance (the Biosafety Protocol's Article 27) is still under negotiation.

There is a clear need for concerted efforts to render environmental and trade regimes more compatible. As far as plant genetic resources are concerned, Cullet (2001b, p. 25) warns that a *sui generis* system should not be developed in isolation but should be closely integrated with CBD and TRIPS requirements.[35] Unfortunately, what we lack is an appropriate term standing for the interface between the sciences of ecology and economics, which can thus facilitate the dialogue not only among academic disciplines but more importantly, among decision-makers in both sectors. I am proposing, therefore, to use the self-explanatory terms *ecolomics* or *the ecolomy* to convey the need to explore new approaches aimed at improving the equilibrium between the two spheres.[36] An ecolomic approach will be particularly useful in assessing the real importance of the phenomenon of regulatory chilling in trade and environment negotiations because it focuses the analysis on this *interface* rather than on the technicalities of one sphere or the other. We can conclude, therefore, that we are dealing here with a particularly interesting case study of ecolomic institution and regime-building that can undoubtedly yield useful lessons for the analysis and negotiation of other international environmental agreements.

Notes

Helpful comments by Philippe Le Prestre, which went well beyond the usual editorial screening, are gratefully acknowledged, and comments by Graham Dutfield have been very valuable.

[1] This observation increasingly applies also to scientific publications, such as the e-journal *IP Strategy Today* published by Cornell University with co-operation from World Bank staff (www.biodevelopments.org).

[2] The first major street demonstrations protesting against the effects of economic globalization took place in October 1994 in Madrid on the occasion of the Bretton Woods Institutions' 50th anniversary.

[3] WTO Committee on Trade and Environment: http://www.wto.org.

[4] For recent overviews and a variety of perspectives, see Sampson (2001), and Sampson and Chambers (1999).

[5] The prospect for improvements in developing countries' traditional intellectual property rights are uncertain, however, given the US and EU resistance so far to discussing these issues at the WTO; they want to relegate these rights to WIPO where they would have far less weight because it lacks the WTO's dispute settlement features ("The Doha Declaration's Meaning," by editorial team, *Bridges*, November/December 2001, vol. 5, no. 9, pp. 1-6 (6)).

[6] Union internationale pour la protection des obtentions végétales.

[7] In a larger sense, the term "farmers' rights" also includes the compensation of farming communities for their contributions to the modern agricultural system. The term was coined by Pat Moony of ETC group, formerly RAFI, as a counterpart to breeders' rights (personal communication by Graham Dutfield).

[8] For a discussion in the context of access and benefit-sharing, see chapter 7 by Blais in this volume.

[9] FAO Conference Resolution 8/83 (http://www.fao.org/ag/cgrfa/iu.htm#documents).

[10] *Earth Negotiations Bulletin* (25 June 2001), vol. 9, no. 192 (www.iisd.ca).

[11] CBD, Article 1. See also chapters by McGraw and Blais in this volume.

[12] Understanding on Rules and Procedures Governing the Settlement of Disputes; see WTO (1994: Annex 2, pp. 404-433).

[13] "When members seek the redress of a violation of obligations...they shall have recourse to, and abide by, the rules and procedures of this Understanding".

[14] See chapter 7 by Blais in this volume.

[15] Article 71.

[16] July 2001 Report by GRAIN (Spain) on bilateral and regional TRIPS-plus agreements (http://www.grain.org/publications/ or http://216.15.202.3/docs/TRIPS-plus-en.pdf).

[17] Article 5 of the 1983 IU.

[18] Resolution 7/93 of the Commission on Plant Genetic Resources.

[19] Purdue (2000) devotes all of chapter 6 to this conference, which is interesting not only for the analysis of the negotiations' actual achievements but also because of the spirited account from a participating NGO perspective, which can be considered as quite representative of the role of NGOs in MEA negotiations.

[20] ETC group (formerly RAFI, Winnipeg) (1 December 2001), *Translator,* vol. 3, no. 1, p. 7 (www.etcgroup.org).

[21] The CGIAR network is financed and governed by the World Bank, FAO, national governments, and bilateral arrangements (http://www.cgiar.org).

[22] ETC group, op. cit., p. 4.

[23] WIPO (2001), *Intellectual Property Needs and Expectations of Traditional Knowledge Holders, WIPO Report on Fact-Finding Missions,* WIPO, Geneva.

[24] WIPO/GRTKF/IC/1/3, 16 March 2001.

[25] WIPO/GRTK/BNE/01/2, 16 May 2001.

[26] These MTA agreements limit or prevent the application of intellectual property rights on germplasm that has been obtained from an *ex situ* collection situated in the public domain; they are particularly pertinent for material originating from the CGIAR network.

[27] This is a joint FAO-WHO body that acts as multilateral food safety standard, which is explicitly recognized by the WTO; it is relevant to the discussions in this chapter because it has lately become involved in the risk assessment of GM food (http://www.codexalimentarius.net).

[28] This is the French acronym for Association internationale des sélectionneurs.

[29] At WIPO these completely different kinds of TK are currently lumped together.

[30] A discussion of global environmental governance issues in the domain of agricultural biodiversity, food crops, biotechnology, and the trade regime, must include the CBD's Biosafety Protocol. The objective of the Protocol is the protection of biological diversity – and to some extent human health as well – from potentially adverse effects that could be caused by trade in living modified organisms. See chapter 2 by Pythoud and Thomas in this volume.

[31] See, for instance, the discussion of sectoral win/win outcomes at the Committee on Trade and Environment's (CTE) meeting on 13-14 February 2000 (http://www.wto.org

[32] *Agenda 21: The United Nations Programme of Action from Rio* (1992), UN Department of Public Information, New York, p. 9.

[33] We may consider here that the IT is technically an MEA because of the above-mentioned Article 1.2, although it is *de facto,* as explained, a hybrid agreement.

[34] The objective of this Convention is to maintain and increase international co-operation in controlling pests and diseases of plants and plant products and in preventing their introduction and spread across national boundaries. 1997 version: http://www.dpie.gov.au/corporate_docs/publications/cover_page/marketaccess/biosecurity/plant/icippc.html.

[35] In June 2001, the Organization for African Unity developed a Model Law for the protection of the rights of local communities and the regulation of access to biological resources, which can be adjusted by each country that wishes to explore the *sui generis* option according to its own specific needs (http://www.grain.org/publications/oau-en.cfm).

[36] Steve Charnovitz (1995, p. 60 and n. 12, 13) supports the same idea but coined the term "ecolonomy," which is linguistically more logical but somewhat cumbersome to use.

Chapter 10

The Science and Policy of Global Biodiversity Protection

Louis Guay[1]

Our atom of carbon enters the leaf, colliding with other innumerable molecules of nitrogen and oxygen. It adheres to a large and complicated molecule that activates it, and simultaneously receives the decisive message from the sky, in the flashing form of a packet of solar light: in an instant, it is separated from oxygen, combined with hydrogen and (one thinks) phosphorus, and finally inserted in a chain, whether long or short does not matter, but it is the chain of life. All this happens swiftly, in silence, at the temperature and pressure of the atmosphere, and gratis.

Primo Levi, *The Periodic Table.*

Introduction

Policies and practices of environmental protection have been founded on new knowledge, new values, new needs, and new wants. Though people have always seen their environment as a necessary component of their well-being, attitudes toward it have differed greatly. In human ecology terms, the environment is almost everything. It is where life begins and ends; it is what constitutes life's richness or poverty; it is what acts as stimulation to innovation, proposing models that may be imported into human activities. Forms of human reaction to a changing environment have in the past as well as today been diversified: benign neglect, smooth or fierce adaptation, migration, and finally, since migration and neglect are no longer possible, conscious measures to change humanity's relation to nature and improve its quality as a means of preserving people's sustainability on Earth.

The problem of biological diversity comes after a long series of environmental problems that have been on the rise for at least a century. In his comprehensive environmental history of the 20th century, J. R. McNeill (2000) has documented how the past 100 years have radically transformed the Earth's environment. Following pioneer publications (Simmons, 1993; Turner, 1990; Thomas, 1956) though covering a shorter time span, McNeill shows how population, technology, needs, and aspirations have combined to transform the planet at an unprecedented pace, creating problems that humanity can no longer ignore. Informed by an ecological approach – a major scientific breakthrough of the 20th century (Deléage,

1992; Drouin, 1991; Acot, 1988) – McNeill reviews humanity's transformations of the "spheres" (lithosphere, atmosphere, hydrosphere, and biosphere) within and upon which it has grown and, for some nations, prospered over this short but decisive time period.

This environmental history is impressive. We may rejoice at it, but our excitement is not whole-hearted: it has an undertone. People may be glad that so much has been done in so short a time, but though standards of living have improved for a significant part of humanity, we are, at the same time, worried by this recent evolution. First, not all of humanity shares the increasing wealth. Global reports on the state of the world, such as those by the World Watch Institute and the World Resources Institute (2000) as well as the recent contribution by the United Nations Environment Programme (UNEP) to world reporting and trends analysis (1999c), have consistently shown that inequalities on a global scale persist, even amplify. Second, progress has been made "on nature's back", so to speak. Humanity could not have prospered without damage to the environment. Not long ago, Georgescu-Roegen (1979) reminded us that we cannot escape the second law of thermodynamics, namely, general and inexorable entropy. The gains we have acquired are nature's losses. Though Georgescu-Roegen placed his analysis within a very broad and long-term perspective, he certainly had a point.

Now, how are we to react to this? One of the lesson of the previous century is that we have concentrated our activities on increasing flows – flows of people, goods, animals, plants, ideas, technologies, institutions, and organizations – but we have depleted stocks (Theys, 1999). And over the long haul, depleted stocks lead to decelerating, even halting, flows. Economically, socially, and culturally, we have given a great deal of energy, effort, and attention to moving information, things, and people around – but less to assuring that these movements are sustainable. When the World Commission on Environment and Development (WCED) published *Our Common Future* in 1987, the message was clear: development, in which we have invested so much, must be sustainable if it is to continue. The needs of present generations must be addressed and met, but those of future generations must not be discounted. We must strike a balance between the present and the future in using nature's resources and preserving nature's integrity.

This chapter presents an analytical framework for the biodiversity problem that places the problem in two different contexts: first, in the context of the evolution of ideas about environmental protection; and second, in the context of public decision-making on environmental problems, where science and politics meet and at times clash, and where science is a necessary guiding principle of action, but (alas! some would say) not the only one. In placing biodiversity in these contexts, I also intend to look at it in relation to other global ecological problems, in particular climate change. The bulk of the chapter focuses on the second aspect, the decision-making context; the remaining parts remind us that the biodiversity problem is complex.

The biodiversity issue is a good example of the process of designing a policy in which science is called to task. The relationship between science and politics, or policy-making, is not simple, nor of one type only. This chapter includes a typology of the relationships between science and policy-making. It also discusses a model of how an environmental issue emerges and evolves. This model is built on the idea that many environmental issues emerge as the result of the production of an "environmental message," which often originates from scientific research and from scientists. However, as the message moves through public space, including the policy-making process, it is appropriated, or used, by a variety of actors and social interests. In the process, the message may change. This change is often due to uncertainties, scientific or otherwise, in the formulation and implication of its content.

In this chapter, I adopt a broad constructivist perspective. Environmental problems such as biodiversity can be seen as societal problems emerging from a tense and difficult relation between contemporary societies and nature. At least in the minds of many social actors and institutions, these problems need to be solved, partly or completely. However, unlike various other kinds of problems confronting social institutions, environmental problems change constantly, largely because the environment is not a stable system.

Many critiques, often passionate, have arisen against a constructivist stance in analysing problem, in which science and politics, or more broadly society, interact. This approach has spawned a large literature and triggered intense debates, epistemological, methodological, as well as ontological, which this paper cannot review or discuss in detail. Suffice it to say that a constructivist perspective does not negate the reality of the world out there, nor does it mean that all forms of knowledge are equivalent, which is quite different from saying that they are all worth studying.

Biodiversity in the Context of Environmental Ideas

Though the concept of biodiversity (or biological diversity) is in scientific terms quite recent, its implicit use and a broad understanding of it are not. Scientists do not even all agree on its scientific definition, or more precisely, they are often reluctant to give it a definition. But a good Cartesian can not eschew the definition stage in his or her research.

The most agreed-upon definition appears to be that of the Convention on Biological Diversity (CBD) (Art. 2):

> Biological diversity means the variability among living organisms from all sources, including, inter alia, terrestrial, marine and other aquatic ecosystems and the ecological complexes of which they are part: this includes diversity within species, between species and of ecosystems.

A similar version is given by the US Office of Technology Assessment:

> The variety and variability among living organisms and the ecological complexes in which they occur. (cited in Dobson, 1996, p. 10)

Definitions, however, can be reifying processes and do not always capture the variety of ways of studying such a complex natural phenomenon as the diversity of life. In his history of the emergence of the idea of biodiversity, or biological diversity, Takacs (1996, pp. 47-50) shows slight but significant variations on a common theme. When asked how they define biodiversity, the scientists Takacs interviewed were not always forthcoming, and some found the question difficult to answer. Several responses are worth quoting. For David Ehrenfeld, biodiversity has different meanings to different people: "...it obviously means to some people species diversity; other people expand that to include populations. To other people it means really genetic diversity, heterozygosity, allelic diversity, often within population. To many, it means variety of ecotypes or ecosystem types, landscape types". Paul Ehrlich conceives biodiversity as: "the living resources of the planet". To others, biodiversity appears as method ("a measure of difference" – Donald Falk), the result of natural processes ("the product of organic evolution" – Terry Erwin), a universal feature ('a fundamental property of life" – G. Carleton Ray).

The inclusive definition that comes out of printed reports and textbooks tends to minimize differences. There is an effort, quite legitimate, to arrive at a consensual understanding. However, although all agree that life is very diversified, one must not ignore the deep differences. For the French biologist Christian Lévêque (1998), different views of biodiversity can be explained by disciplinary traditions. Scientists work within scientific traditions, or paradigms. These paradigms are strong organizing frames of meaning coupled with strong working practices. Paradigms also define to a normal scientist, one still in training as well as the more experienced, what the problems are, how to attack them, and with what sorts of instruments, methods, and working hypotheses. For instance, an ecologist will conceive biodiversity slightly differently from a population biologist. They share a similar understanding of interactions and complexity between organisms and their broader physical environment. On the other hand, a geneticist, who may also manifest an interest in biodiversity, will look at problems from a different perspective. Biologists like to say that they all share a global view of nature and life, constructed on evolutionary principles, but when they get to the business of research, the research programmes, instruments, and conceptual frameworks no longer march in one step. Specialization produces variety and makes integration and coherence more difficult to achieve. A good case in point is the public debate around the introduction and regulation of genetically modified organisms in which scientists, depending on their scientific traditions and expertise, were confident or less confident about the risks of transgenic plants grown in open fields and sold in markets (Limoges et al., 1993). Whereas geneticists were confident that transgenic plants possess low levels of risk, biological ecologists were much more wary, concerned about the long-term effects of transgenic plants, which have, in their view, not been thoroughly studied.

Diversity of viewpoints among scientific communities is a fertile ground for disagreements among social interests when it comes to participating in a policy-making process. Since science cannot speak in one voice, how can one make decisions that depend so much on what scientists have found? We shall return to this intriguing question when we examine the relationship between science and public policy.

Now, environmental ideas have evolved significantly, not to say radically, over the past century. Environmental policies regarding biodiversity protection have gone through several steps, not all of which are linked closely to a better scientific understanding of the diversity of life.

Biodiversity protection has followed three main lines of representation and intervention: 1) the preservation of natural landscapes, at times more concerned with geological features than with biological characteristics; 2) the conservation of natural resources for future use; and 3) more recently, the restoration of damaged and degraded ecosystems, either back to a state that approaches the pristine or at least introduces a greater richness of life and thus biodiversity.

Environmental protection arose during the long debate that opposed conservationist and preservationist views of nature, particularly in North America (Hays, 1987, 1959). Preservationists held the view that for aesthetic, religious, and symbolic reasons, part of nature should be kept aside. Conservationists believed that scientific principles could be used to manage nature and extract valuable resources. With the passing of time, however, and in a more secular society, the religious feeling that inspired the first perspective has gradually been replaced by a more utilitarian view of nature: nature is worth preserving because it provides services to humans, only one of which is recreational. But this approach raises new questions: services for whom? and what kinds of services? Here the science of ecology has contributed to our definitions of nature, and, as far as scientific conceptions are concerned, to guiding principles in environmental policy-making.

In a series of articles on international environmental policy-making over a century (1870-1990), David Frank and his co-researchers have shown that conceptions of nature in international treaties changed substantially (Frank et al., 2000; Frank, 1997). On the basis of a content analysis of these treaties, in particular of the preambles, they observed that the conception of nature was increasingly shaped by scientific progress and scientific views of nature.

Frank (1997) offers a typology of nature conceptions built around two dimensions: whether nature is conceived in spiritual or physical terms, and how nature is linked to society (that is, nature against society, nature subordinate to society, nature united to society). The combination of these dimensions produces six types. Not all are found in the treaties analysed by Frank, but two emerging patterns can be seen. First, the aesthetic and religious conception of nature, a foundation of some treaties at the beginning of the period, is being gradually replaced by a conception that emerged following the advancement and consolidation of the science of ecology. The ecosystems approach is dominant in grounding international environmental treaties today, notably the CBD. Second, and perhaps more significant, whereas early on, many treaties conceived nature almost exclusively as a source of economic goods for humans, this conception has been replaced by a less instrumental view of nature, which is now viewed as an array of utilities and functions:

> At the beginning of the period, nature was noticeable to humans mainly for instrumental (primarily economic) reasons. By the end of the period, nature was conceived as the biogeochemical undergirding of human life. Thus, the same mountain that was a wart-like excrescence in the early modern period, and a store of iron in 1870, may now be considered a vital part of the biogeochemical support system, performing critical roles in [the] hydrological cycle, for example, and hosting an irreplaceable genetic pool. (Frank, 1997, p. 412)

This double process, which Frank called physicalization and functionalization respectively, is a clear indication of the potential impact of science on the very conception of environmental policy. Science, as an important part of the secularization process, has relegated religious conceptions to the private sphere. One can still believe that preserving huge tracts of wilderness is good for the soul, but today this conception is not likely to lead to environmental policy. On the other hand, because of the way ecological science has described it, nature offers a vast array of functions and services. Not all of them are for human needs and purposes. There is a wholeness, defined in scientific terms (namely, in precise and often quantified mechanisms) that emerges in the scientific understanding of nature. This conception, however, is a far cry from holiness and holism. Is the Convention on Biological Diversity not a logical extension of this historical process, nature being seen as a whole in all its diversity and for the benefit of all its inhabiting species, as a common patrimony of all humanity? But has the Convention taken this path, or has it restricted nature's dominion?

Biodiversity Science in the Context of Public Decision-Making

Science (and scientists) interacts with politics and public policy in many ways. There are areas of public decision where nothing can be done unless there is scientific input in the form of reports by practising scientists, mostly applied scientists employed by a government or a publicly funded agency. The approval of food and drugs for human consumption and for medical prescription is a good example. When public health matters, authorizations and regulations are grounded on scientific expertise. Modern life has expanded the common area of interaction between public policy and science. This is a fact of public life. Much of the encounter between science and regulation happens inside organizations that have developed, over long periods of time, their own procedures. Their workings do not attract public attention, and appeals for change are relatively rare. However, radically new products or new domains of regulation are highly contested, and most of the development phases often take place in the public eye. Since the environmental movement of the 1960s, environmental decision-making is not completely left to organizations and public administrations. Consultation processes have developed and are required by law when there is significant impact on the environment. But critics complain that consultations and open processes are used only in the planning of a physical project. When a policy is being developed, public consultations are more rare. Transgenic seeds, for example, have been authorized in Canada for a decade, without any public consultation. Today, there are strong demands for a closer look by the public at the risks and benefits of transgenic plants. These demands concern a policy, or a set of practices, not a physical project.

This raises three important questions. First, what kind of science is used in and applied to decision-making, in particular environmental decision-making? Second, how can we represent in broad terms the social and political response to environmental problems, including biodiversity? Third, given that there are a variety of public decision-making processes – as a result of history, political culture, links between civil society and the state, political and economic ideologies, etc. – what role and place do science and scientists have in these processes?

Interactions between Social Worlds

Modern society is highly differentiated. Though sociologists like to analyse all social institutions and practices through the same lenses, they do not conclude that institutions and practices are all alike. The Parsonian project of constructing the social system of modern society, and for that matter the social systems of all societies, is a good case in point (Parsons, 1951). Parsons postulated different functions in societies but also showed how these different functions follow similar mechanisms.

Science can be approached in a similar fashion. It is a social institution with a different function but inside that function the mechanisms of social interactions are not too dissimilar to those encountered in other social institutions. In the heated debate between realists and constructivists in the analysis of science in society, the constructivists adopt the view that science must be viewed not in relation to its product (scientific truth) but like any other social institution, that is, through the interactions of people, the social mechanisms whereby production and reproduction of people, values, ideas, goods, organization, and specific outputs – be they scientific facts, technological artefacts, political ideas, or even material goods – are the result of intentional and non-intentional social action within constraints, physical as well as institutional. Science studies – and the perspective is highly relevant when one examines environmental policy-making – have been blamed for not taking the activities of science seriously. This means, for critics, that science is a special and unique activity, defined by its result, not by the mechanisms that produce them. In a "naturalistic" philosophy of science, it would be bad sociological science to treat one institution entirely differently from all the others. We would not today accept geology treating the Earth, because it is inhabited by humans or because people believe that God made the Earth hospitable to humans, differently from, say, Venus or Mars, though they both have different characteristics (different atmospheres or lack of one, for example). This does not mean, as some critics have said, that all truths are worth holding and defending. It only means that science as a social institution must be treated like any other social institution. Nor does it mean that this particular institution has not developed its own norms of social behaviour or that its outputs are the same as any other institution. On the contrary: like planets, all institutions are different, but the social processes, or mechanisms, leading to these end-results are, like natural processes, universal, common to all.

This discussion leads to a representation of the interactions of science with political institutions and social actors in making environmental policies.

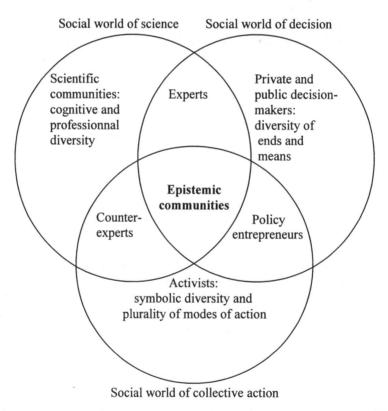

Social world of science   Social world of decision

Scientific communities: cognitive and professionnal diversity

Experts

Private and public decision-makers: diversity of ends and means

Epistemic communities

Counter-experts

Policy entrepreneurs

Activists: symbolic diversity and plurality of modes of action

Social world of collective action

Figure 10.1 Interacting Social Worlds in Environmental Policy-Making

We can conceive participants in environmental decision-making as actors belonging to different social worlds. Social worlds are, in Howard Becker's apt terms, built by "people doing things together".[2] Social worlds are more or less social institutions. Between the two concepts, there is a difference not of nature but of degree. Like institutions, social worlds are the product of social interactions. However, whereas the institutional perspective emphasizes constraints on actors, the role ascribed to them that they must play (social worlds, in the perspective of symbolic interactionists, who invented the concept and used it widely) emphasizes the continuing process of constructing social settings.

Figure 10.1, which resembles interconnecting Venn diagrams, expresses the interaction of three social worlds that take part in decision-making on environmental policy. The three worlds are:

- the social world of science, composed of scientists whose main task is to advance knowledge of the natural world. This social world is, of course, divided into subgroups and at times fragmented. Special cognitive, professional, or economic interests may lead to conflicts over the proper use of knowledge in particular situations. For example, as mentioned before, ecologists are more cautious than geneticists with respect to assessing the risks of transgenic plants.

- the social world of political and economic decision-making. The business of its members is to run the institutions that mark the modern world. With respect to the environment, government and business are the two institutions whose decisions have the greatest impact on the environment. Their members are called by the appropriate collective term of decision-makers. Governments are mainly in the business of social regulation. They regulate negative externalities ("costs" imposed on third parties) and create collective advantages that may be difficult to provide privately, such as a healthy environment or the protection of biodiversity on which it is hard to tag a price.[3] Business has gained a great deal of autonomy in modern society to pursue its purpose of providing goods and services privately in response to consumer choice. But it also is a highly diversified subgroup whose participation in the environmental policy process depends on the issue at stake and on the potential impact of a policy on its members' interests and well-being.

- the social world of collective action or activism, made up of members whose main purpose is to bring about change in the dominant social institutions. Though social institutions may change internally, many changes come from outside. Sociologists have paid great attention to social movements that have contributed significantly to changing policies, decisions, practices, even values and worldviews. The environmental movement has had an important impact over the entire 20th century, even though it was not the sole actor or factor in these changes. This social world, despite its common purpose, is also highly differentiated. While grouping actors and organizations in social worlds on the basis of what they do together or share together, we cannot avoid dividing them at the same time into subgroups and sub-social worlds. Society is a very diversified lot...

Figure 10.1 represents zones of interaction between actors in these different social worlds. Environmental policy is about interactions. At the intersection of two social worlds are actors whose role is to help social worlds communicate. For instance, the expert's job is to translate scientific data into policy. There are also counter-experts who act as communicators between the world of science and the world of activism. Some scientists have been close to the environmental movement, providing it with the understanding necessary to participate in a policy process.

Finally, the zone where the three worlds meet includes actors whose main role is communication and mediation. Peter Haas (1992, 1990) has labelled these actors *epistemic communities*. These communities share a common understanding of the problem at hand and a common understanding of what is feasible in social and policy terms and may act as mediators among the three (or more) groups of actors who may be in conflict. Perhaps no environmental solution or decision is arrived at without actors mediating and sharing a common understanding of the issues.

Now, since all graphical representations are an imperfect representation of social processes, caution is necessary. First, the social world of science is only one world of knowledge relevant to environmental policy-making – or to any other policy process for that matter. Other forms of knowledge contribute to environmental policy-making. In her personal account of the negotiating history of the CBD, Fiona McConnell (1996) clearly shows that the knowledge used in the preparation of the Convention was diversified, though legal knowledge was highly prominent. What is called technical knowledge includes scientific, legal, and administrative knowledge, without which no international convention could be properly prepared and signed. Also, traditional ecological knowledge (TEK) could be called upon much more regularly, though not much was used during the negotiations.[4] Second, graphical representation cannot account for all the dynamics of interacting actors and institutions. Actors belonging to social worlds may move from one world to another, though the probability of moving greatly depends on the structure and culture of public decision-making. In an open and pluralistic environmental policy-making process, actors may more or less easily cross boundaries, whereas in a less open and more technocratic culture it may be more difficult for them to do so. For instance, in an open process, counter-experts linked to environmental NGOs may become experts for governments. In international environmental policy-making, expertise from NGOs has been valued and integrated, though still timidly, into policy-making.[5] Richard Benedick (1991) gives a convincing account of the role of NGO experts in the making of the Montreal Protocol. However, if the "mode-2 science" thesis (see below) is true, flows of actors, norms, rules, and, in part, practices between social worlds may become more frequent.

This simple model can be applied to environmental policy. Coupled with models of the public policy process that focus on the steps through which policy develops, the social world model can be very fruitful, for the latter focuses on key actors in the process whereas the former concentrates on the process itself.

Public policy literature has traditionally divided the policy-making process into the following stages (Hempel, 1996, p. 1): i) problem identification and definition; ii) agenda-setting; iii) formulation; iv) selection of means and choice of instruments; v) implementation; vi) monitoring, evaluation, and correction of the course of action, if necessary. In this model, internal as well as external actors can contribute ideas and impose solutions on others. Also, as Hempel has shown, not all actors have a strong interest in a satisfactory conclusion to the process. There may be "political saboteurs," external or internal, who do not wish the policy process to come to a decision.

This conventional model is helpful but concentrates too much on what the administrative structure does. In the case of environmental issues, a large part of the process takes place outside the sphere of government. It is the wider society and economy that are concerned with an environmental problem. We need a proper representation of this wider process, which often leads to the initiation of a public policy process as described above.

Environmental problems can be viewed as a social construction that develops in three stages: i) problem construction, mainly by science; ii) problem diffusion in a larger social setting; iii) problem utilization, by a variety of actors since the problem and the solution it may command may affect these actors' interests. This three-stage model resembles the model suggested by Hannigan (1995, p. 42) who labels the stages differently: assembling the facts; presenting the problem; and contesting it. There is, of course, a fourth stage in which the problem finds a negotiated solution.

This view of environmental issues as problem-solving and as a social construction is certainly not new, though it tries to combine two approaches, one inspired by engineering and social engineering, the other by the interactionist perspective in science studies and in science and policy studies. Before applying this model to biodiversity, a word about science and types of science relevant to environmental decision-making is in order.

Science in the Context of Environmental Policy

That science is increasingly linked to practical needs and decisions has become commonplace. Many authors have emphasized a change in the relation between science and its social, economic, and political context. Funtowicz and Ravetz (1994) have called this type of science "post-normal," following the distinction Kuhn introduced between normal science and revolutionary science, revolutionary science being a state in which a scientific paradigm has reached its limits and cannot explain mounting anomalies. Revolutionary science and paradigm change are rare moments in the history of science. Most of the time, scientists perform normal science, that is, they work within theories, methods, and instruments that possess some sort of stability. Their task is to expand the paradigm's capacity to explain natural processes. Kuhn (1970) would say that normal science as well as revolutionary science are mainly inner-directed, though many would also say that external factors play an important role, particularly in the revolutionary phase. In the Kuhnian perspective, problems and new questions emerge internally, from scientists wanting to make their theories and explanations more and more general (for a similar interpretation of Kuhn, see Fuller, 2000).

For Funtowicz and Ravetz (1994) however, science has entered a new stage. It is driven not only by its practitioners but also by external social forces and factors. According to Boehme and his co-researchers (Schäfer, 1983) contemporary science is driven by practical problems. This is the much discussed "finalization thesis". Gibbons et al. (1994) have developed a similar idea: owing to its success, traditional science, or "mode-1 science," is being replaced by "mode-2 science," the development of which is more tightly linked to outside demands and considerations. Mode-2 science is knowledge "generated in the context of application" (Nowotny et al., 2001, p. 1). Science policy, as Ruivo (1994) has shown, has evolved along similar lines. Whereas, science policy after the Second World War concentrated on funding basic research in the hope that scientific discoveries and progress would make positive and profound effects on the economy and society, beginning in the 1960s science policy aimed at making science more responsive to social and economic needs, however defined. In the 1980s and 1990s, science policy has not retreated from this idea but has introduced a longer time frame. Strategic research is the combination of basic science and practical needs, a close collaboration between industry and research centres in order to develop future technologies. In Canada, this co-operative effort has an institutional basis, called Networks of Centres of Excellence (NCE), which first covered a dozen areas in the mid-1980s.

However, the post-normal science thesis has a particular twist to it. Post-normal science is science confronted by two new contexts. First, the more we know of something, the more things appear complex. Complexity is a challenge for science. Classical physics was simple, clear, and predictive. It reduced the complexity of the world to some overarching principles and formulas. Today's physics deals with micro as well as macro complexity. Complexity has the peculiar property of emergence ("emergent complexity" in the words of Funtowicz and Ravetz). This means that prediction, a deep belief of classical science, is more difficult to attain. There may be a set of future states that models can predict with some certainty, but there may also be other possible states that escape model predictions.

Second and consequently, uncertainty is a normal characteristic of post-normal science. This has important consequences for policy-making in areas where the public and decision-makers demand clear advice from science. Current debates on global warming and on genetically modified organisms (GMOs) represent interesting cases in which science is called upon to deliver, but cannot, the certainty required for sound public decisions in order to ensure people's health and security as well as the health and integrity of the environment.

However, whereas most authors agree about science's new uncertainties, Funtowicz and Ravetz (1994) go one step further. Because of the complexity that exists in the world, largely the product of our evolving scientific understanding (though, with globalization, social differentiation, and technological progress, modern society has created its own complexity) knowledge is full of ignorance. Since its ascent in 17th-century Europe, science has fought ignorance, to a point where ignorance is just a starting point for further investigations: if we do not know, let us investigate and know. But complexity has created zones of ignorance, and it would be ignorant of scientists not to be conscious of this ignorance. As Ravetz (1993) has said, ignorance of ignorance, or ignorance squared, would be a "sin of science". Now, if uncertainty (or ignorance) is a fact of science, how can decision-making, which relies so much on science, be justified?

Politics and science are two independent activities that interact more and more frequently. In spite of these interactions, they remain distinct. Politics is about social regulation and distribution – and, in a Hobbesian worldview, one must add, pacification – whereas science is about producing knowledge about the external world and about the one we have constructed. The French political scientist Jacques Theys has drawn interesting comparisons between modes of interactions of science and politics in different countries (Theys, 1999). For him, the French mode of interaction is built on a strong expertise centred on the national state. The *grandes écoles* produce the technical and administrative *cadres* of the French state. Expertise and thus policy-making are mainly the responsibility of the state. Scientific activities are at arm's length from the state. State experts are responsible for translating scientific information, when it has some bearing on policy-making, into workable public decisions. This is more or less the classical technocratic model, of which France is a good representative. American administrations have pursued a more open process and recognized that expertise and knowledge-generation cannot be concentrated solely in the hands of the state (Hoberg, 1997). This pluralist model is built on the idea that there is no monopoly on knowledge and that social interests may have their own experts to counter those of other social interests and those of the state. Policy-making, therefore, is a long process not only of translating scientific information into public decisions but of confrontation in a sort of market of knowledge, ideas, scientific expertise, and proposed solutions to problems. This process has been working fairly well in environmental policy-making, though some authors have shown that the underside of the pluralist model is that science is "coloured and tainted" by social and economic interests. The same data are interpreted differently, sometimes in opposite directions, a situation that is not independent of the presence of uncertainty in science (Regens and Rycroft, 1988; Zehr, 1994).

These two models are certainly not sufficient to describe all concrete policy-making practices. For instance, depending on the problem at hand, the Canadian policy-making process can be adequately described neither by the pure technocratic model nor by the pure pluralist model. The Canadian federal state model, particularly regarding climate change policy, resembles a sort of neo-corporatist model in which selected social and economic interests are called upon to help formulate policy (Guay, 1999). And there is the possibility of a fourth model concentrated on the broad participation of a large variety of people and interests, which on the whole the Dutch and Danish processes of science and technology assessment approach (Faucheux and O'Connor, 2000).

Now, since science and politics constitute two independent social processes, there are critical variables that distinguish and characterize them. For politics to be effective, it has to be built on consensus. Democratic and modern politics is about legitimacy, which is related to consensus-building. Science, on the other hand, deals with the critical variable of uncertainty. No science can be coded and introduced in textbooks for training new scientists if it has not been widely accepted within the relevant community of practitioners. Acceptance is based largely on uncertainty reduction. In the Popperian model of scientific methodology, science does not provide definitive truths but eliminates unpromising avenues, a process of uncertainty reduction (Whitley, 1984). We can express the relationships between science and politics in policy-making by the following matrix:

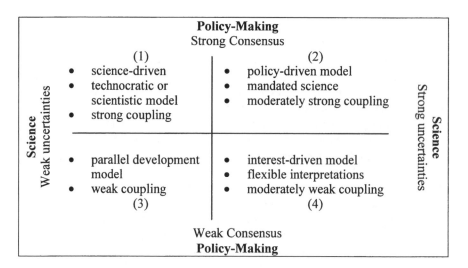

Figure 10.2 Models of Science and Environmental Policy-Making Relationships

Each quadrant shows how science and politics interact or are coupled. The first quadrant summarizes the idea that science and politics are closely linked and that science has a crucial if not decisive role in decision-making. A good example is the science and politics of nuclear technology in which a strong consensus was built among scientists, the military, regulatory authorities, and commercial interests after the war. Uncertainty, which was certainly high when nuclear science and technology expanded from the military into commercial electricity generation, has been reduced, making nuclear electricity-generating plants relatively safe. This case can be described as science at the command, though military needs and safety regulations were important factors in designing the technologies.

The second quadrant represents what Salter (1988) has called "mandatory science". This science is produced and used in making decisions about product safety and risk assessment. Politics, or regulation, imposes safety and security standards on new products and technologies, which producers must meet in order to market their products. One can say that science is being pushed by policy requirements, though these very requirements are the result of previous standard already attained by scientific expertise. The relationship is moderately coupled because, as Salter (1988) and Janasoff (1990) have shown, standard-setting is a difficult business and the science of standards is not as rigorous as decision-makers would like.

The fourth quadrant represents the science and politics of ecological problems quite well. Here scientific uncertainty is the norm rather than the exception. Scientific information and models are only tentative devices for understanding complex and evolving phenomena. Though, in time, science can reduce the level of uncertainty, success is far from certain. On the other hand, because ecological problems can seemingly have important social and economic consequences, policy-makers tend to ask a degree of precision of science, which cannot always be quickly met. In the context of the debate on climate change, Shackley and Wynne (1996, 1995) have shown what policy-makers expect of scientific data and modelling, in particular at the regional level, which science is expected to address. A dynamic of claims and demands sets in: data and models pouring out of laboratories and printed in scientific journals create expectations on the part of policy-makers for more precise data and models and for further uncertainty reduction. Future funding for research may depend on it.

Now, the science and politics of ecological problems (typically, ozone depletion, global warming, acid rain, biodiversity loss) may move from one quadrant to another over time. Not all combinations are possible, of course. With uncertainty reduction and the development of a stronger consensus, the science and politics of an ecological problem may move, say, to quadrant 2 or to quadrant 1, where policy-makers and scientists have a greater confidence in their models, data, and the capacity of science to "deliver the goods" that political decisions require. However, there may be limits to such a "natural" evolution, if complexity is a property of ecosystems. The scientific community working on the global warming hypothesis seems confident of reducing the uncertainties that characterize its understanding of climatic change (Houghton, 1995). Likewise, acid rain research has benefited considerably from public funding, which has helped to reduce critical uncertainties. Though research on ozone depletion held large uncertainties when the process of controlling ozone-destroying chemicals began, models and data were later refined and came to provide strong evidence as to the causes and actual mechanisms of stratospheric ozone depletion (Litfin, 1994). Where and how does the science of biodiversity fit in this mapping?

Biodiversity, Uncertainty, and Environmental Policy

The Convention on Biological Diversity is an important landmark in the landscape of international environmental policy. It is an encompassing convention that breaks with the conventional legislation on protecting biodiversity. Although it is important to keep in mind that the term itself is fairly recent, the practice of studying biological diversity has a longer history. American biologists whom Takacs (1996) interviewed had been in the business of conservation biology for some time, had been studying biological diversity, and worried about its decline. Harold Mooney, a pioneer in conservation biology, has published an intellectual biography (1999) in which he documents how biological diversity evolved slowly as a scientific question worth studying and as an environmental question worth tackling. Rapidly, he says, biodiversity as an ecological problem demanded that it should be dealt with internationally. He himself participated in international conferences to exchange findings about an emerging field of research and raise people's and governments' awareness of the danger of biodiversity loss.

This message has been taken up by international governmental and non-governmental organizations, such as UNESCO, UNEP, the World Conservation Union (IUCN), and the Worldwide Fund for Nature (WWF) (Juma and Henne, 1997, p. 388). IUCN's *Strategy for Conservation*, published in the early 1980s, was an important factor in creating an international agenda for biodiversity protection. This strategy invented (co-invented or popularized, it is difficult to say) the expression *sustainable development*, which became a key organizing concept in the 1987 Brundtland Report (Vaillancourt, 1995). This report contained an important chapter on biodiversity protection, and proposed the creation of biosphere reserves. It also suggested that 10-12 per cent of national territory should be designated as protected areas. Thus, if the 1992 CBD was a landmark, its ground had been prepared beforehand by environmental non-governmental organizations (ENGOs) and by some scientists who believed that biodiversity loss was a major problem.[6]

But why should we be concerned with biodiversity loss? In view of the many ecological problems that humanity faces, why was it so important that an international convention on biological diversity should be signed by a majority of the world's nations in 1992? Is it more important than water pollution and scarcity, air pollution, and related health problems? More urgent than feeding the world and providing many people with drinkable water? Should we allocate significant economic resources to something about which our knowledge is still in infancy? These are difficult questions for policy-makers.

There are strong reasons why we should be concerned about biodiversity loss (Tuxill, 1999; Hughes, Daily, and Ehrlich, 1997; Lévêque, 1997). These reasons are economic, ecological, cultural, and cognitive. Biodiversity has actual or potential economic value. From a biotechnology perspective, biodiversity means resources for genetic knowledge and experimentation with applications yet to be invented. From an economic development viewpoint, it means the potential development of new tourist activities through ecotourism or the commercial development of particular species. From a biological viewpoint, it is an insurance against natural catastrophes and the large-scale decimation of the plants that nourish us and feed the animals we eat. There are good reasons to believe that biodiversity maintains the processes of biological evolution and helps to regulate global geochemical processes and the hydrological cycle. It also contributes to soil fertility, participates in the elimination of pollutants, helps to cleanse water, and provides other services and goods (Tilman, 2000; Baskin, 1997).

From a sociocultural perspective, biodiversity provides a host of other values and usages in support of human societies. It offers a source of food, material, and fuel for many people. Culturally, biodiversity, or part of it, may be valued for aesthetic, religious, and ethical reasons (Wood, 2000; Sagoff, 1998). It is a source of creativity in the arts and a source of invention. Ethically, biodiversity may have an intrinsic value. Generations may feel that they have a moral obligation to pass on an environment as diversified as if not more diversified than the one they inherited.[7] In many religious teachings, biodiversity, or more properly nature, is the work of a transcendent being; tampering with it for no good reason is hubris and may be reproved. Also, biodiversity protection may be a means to an end, that is, the protection of human or cultural diversity. Finally, there is at least one good cognitive reason to protect biodiversity. It is the best possible laboratory for understanding living mechanisms and life's evolution.

Is biodiversity a science or a natural phenomenon? And if it is science, is it a discipline, an all-encompassing discipline, or a perspective common to all biological disciplines and domains? If it is a natural phenomenon, how can it be studied? Takacs (1996) speaks of the *idea* of biodiversity, but what kind of idea? New ideas are strong organizing principles upon which much of scientific progress depends. Seventeenth-century natural philosophers broke with the past by inventing new ideas from which modern science emerged. Is biodiversity likely to do the same? But the same to what? Or is biodiversity a new common idea giving new meaning to what biologists have been doing all along?

We should not be surprised that the word *biodiversity* cannot be found in Ernst Mayr's book, *The Growth of Biological Thought*, for the term had not been coined when his history of biology first appeared in 1982. Nor can we find the expression *biological diversity* in the index. Yet the entire book is about diversity. Chapter one, which follows a long introduction, is called "Diversity of Life" and begins with the paragraph: "Hardly any aspect of life is more characteristic than its almost unlimited diversity. No two individuals in sexually reproducing populations are the same, no two populations of the same species, no two species, no two higher taxa, nor any associations, and so *ad infinitum*. Wherever we look, we find uniqueness, and uniqueness spells diversity" (Mayr, 1982, p. 133). His entire history is about diversity, in the context of evolution and inheritance, two terms appearing in the book's subtitle.

The same impression arises from a reading of the *Global Biodiversity Assessment*, the major international scientific endeavour to respond to the need for a "comprehensive review of current knowledge in the broad field of biodiversity" (Heywood, 1995, preface). Now, this comprehensive review reads like an extensive and up-to-date course in biology, for section after section reviews what is known about many if not all aspects of the biological sciences. From genetics and molecular biology to ecology, evolution, and palaeontology, it seems that all important domains of biology are represented. Of course, not all of biology could be included in the book: plant physiology or other highly specialized and technical aspects have been left out. But biological diversity seems to be the most important question for all of biology: it is a universal property of life that has to be explained.

There is some agreement among authors and scientists that biodiversity should be viewed as a global approach to life that is integrating and dynamic: "Biodiversity is not systematics, genetics, nor ecology. Biodiversity uses these different disciplines in a global approach. Biodiversity is a dynamic notion of the living world" (Lévêque, 1998, p. 38, my translation).

Uncertainty is an important feature of biodiversity. The *Global Biodiversity Assessment* does not mask uncertainties regarding what scientists know and do not know about biodiversity. First, nobody seems to know with any relatively high degree of certainty the number of species that inhabit the world and the number that may disappear as a result of natural factors or human action. Variations are very wide, which to some critics is already problematic (Martin, 2000). Since species are integrated in larger wholes – ecosystems – science cannot tell with precision the number of species that an ecosystem may lose without irreversible damage. There is some evidence that certain species may act as key species without which an entire ecosystem may fail. Second,

practices have changed from species protection to whole habitat, or ecosystem protection. Though this practice is scientifically sound, conservation technology has yet to define more precisely how wide a protected habitat must be. No scientist can afford to ignore that ecosystems, like species, evolve (Lévêque, 1998). Consequently, how can conservation strategy take this basic feature of life into account? The size of the protected area, its relation to surrounding areas, the possibility or impossibility of invasion by other populations are all questions that need to be addressed more thoroughly. Finally, though some areas of biology have used and developed mathematics and mathematical modelling, some scientists feel these instruments are still not used widely enough to obtain precise knowledge of some objects of biology, including biodiversity (Dyson, 1999). If we compare the *Global Biodiversity Assessment* with the "scientific assessment" in the *Climate Change* issued by the Intergovernmental Panel on Climate Change (IPCC), the one crucial feature that differentiates the two international scientific initiatives is the presence of numerical modelling in the IPCC reports and its absence in the biodiversity assessment. Despite its drawbacks, numerical modelling helps to produce an overall understanding of a global process. Also, the UN Framework Convention on Climate Change had at its disposal, before the Rio Earth Summit, a strong scientific assessment, which had been prepared internationally during the 1980s, whereas the scientific assessment on biodiversity came after the Convention on Biological Diversity was signed. One explanation for this difference lies in a stronger international institutional basis for climatology (on this, see Boehmer-Christiansen, 1993, 1994) compared to conservation biology, even when taking into account that nature conservation has a long international history.

The 1992 Rio Summit produced two major international conventions: one on biological diversity and the other on climate change. There are many differences between them, some of which are worth noting. An important one is that a key international actor, the United States, has not yet ratified the former convention (though the Climate Change Convention may be in jeopardy because the American government has announced that the United States will not ratify the Kyoto Protocol). I would like to point out other aspects while reviewing the emergence of the biodiversity problem, which Aubertin and her co-authors have analysed in some detail (Aubertin, 2000; Aubertin et al., 1998; Aubertin and Vivien, 1998). Their analysis illustrates again that ecological problems are social constructions and the role that science plays in this construction.

Aubertin and her co-researchers show that though the idea of biodiversity is a product of scientific research in the sense that scientists became worried about the decline of biodiversity, it has been picked up by ENGOs such as the World Conservation Union. Discussed in the 1970s and 1980s at national and international scientific conferences (Hawksworth, 1997), biodiversity came to the forefront of national and international news in the late 1980s and early 1990s. International scientific institutions, such as the International Council of Scientific Unions, were key actors in this process. A message on the importance of biodiversity loss has been building. Most practising scientists, though perhaps personally concerned with the problem, for various reasons have not been publicly active on the issue. However, some were, and their scientific and ecological "message" mattered.

There is a pattern in the evolution of attempts to solve environmental problems. It normally starts as a message, a scientific and environmental message. Whether the message originates only from science and scientists or from other social actors as well is not always clear. Environmental problems could emerge from non-scientific knowledge, from people seeing a changing environment and worrying about the change. Local environmental problems can be identified by local actors using what anthropologist Clifford Geertz has called "local knowledge". But large-scale environmental problems cannot be properly identified using local knowledge. It is also entirely possible that such identification results from a combination of empirical knowledge and scientific knowledge.

In the case of biodiversity decline, the public has been aware for many decades that some species may decline and even disappear. Activists, concerned citizens, as well as scientists have joined efforts to document such dangers. Measures have been taken for the protection of animals and plants. There is a long history of conservation embodied in the creation of national parks and protected areas and in national legislation on endangered species (McCormick, 1989). Moreover, two important international conventions preceded the CBD: Ramsar and the Convention on International Trade in Endangered Species of Wild Fauna and Flora (CITES) (see chapter 1).

International ENGOs have been active in the preparation of such legislation and conventions. But governments also like to root their decisions in science. Scientific associations, scientists working inside government, and leading research scientists are all called upon to prepare what will become law, treaty or convention. The Royal Society of Canada and the National Academy of Sciences in the US are scientific institutions that have taken on the role of providing scientific advice to their respective governments. The Board on Biology of the American National Research Council, the "operating agency of both the National Academy of Sciences and the National Academy of Engineering," organized a major scientific forum in 1986 (followed by a second in 1997) which was highly instrumental in transforming biodiversity loss into an environmental and public issue. The message took shape and reached major national institutions. It brought biodiversity to the attention of a wide audience of scientists and other individuals with the publication of the proceedings of the conference, simply called *Biodiversity* (Wilson and Peters, 1988). Even the term "biodiversity" first appeared in 1985 in the context of conference preparations. It was coined by Walter Rosen, who found it more appealing (Heywood, 1995, p. 5).

Was the message clear? Was the science of biodiversity sure of itself before the CBD and certain about an ecological issue deemed dangerous for human societies? Clearly, no. The science of biodiversity was just beginning; important progress has since been made. So how can a major international convention be considered a major step toward the protection of biological diversity? Was the scientific message strong enough to warrant such a convention? Did scientists have a clear view of what was at stake? Clearly, some were quite eloquent about the diversity problem. Edward Wilson and fellow biologists have been very active in "transforming" scientific knowledge into an environmental and public issue. The message passed from the scientific community to a wider public and, with the CBD, to governments. However, as Aubertin (1998) has claimed, this passage is in large part the result of ENGOs having put these questions on the international agenda.

Despite uncertainty regarding many aspects of the science of biodiversity, governments felt obliged to act. They responded to some public pressure, in particular to environmental groups, which had been very active at the 1992 Rio Earth Summit and had lobbied for a convention on biodiversity at the international level. While science continued to progress on the question of biodiversity, civil society was contributing to the agenda, particularly after the Convention.

Sociologists of science thrive on scientific controversies. They study them closely. They are interested in them because they see science in action and all the means scientists use to bring about closure. Controversy is an open court of knowledge and closure, which is the court's supreme judgement. After long debates, intellectual and social, rhetorical and rational, a consensus is reached within the relevant community of practitioners as to the meaning of new ideas, facts, theories, and measurements, or the proper use of instruments and techniques. Science is then codified or, as sociologists say, "black-boxed". Scientific disciplines advance with closure: facts are deemed valid, hypotheses are widely tested and verified, theories become strong enough to explain a wide array of natural phenomena and processes.

In principle, if we were strict rationalists, no action regarding environmental problems would be taken before all the facts were assembled. However, this process is unending. Whether it be climate change or biodiversity loss, science continues to evolve. Moreover, not only does knowledge of the natural world change, but ecosystems change as well. Biodiversity loss is still in progress, under pressure from population and production and consumption needs. This poses difficult problems for science and constitutes the main reason why international conventions that rely so much on scientific data and models have built formal procedures and institutions to integrate new science into the workings of the conventions. And international conventions have also begun adopting the precautionary approach, which states that action should not be deferred when there are good reasons to intervene to prevent serious and irreversible environmental damage, even in the absence of scientific certainty (Godard, 1999).

But science is not the only factor, nor are scientists the main actors, in the response societies give to ecological problems. Various social interests are also at play. The examples of acid rain, ozone thinning, climate change, and biodiversity loss indicate clearly that from the social world of science to the social world of decision-making and politics, huge transformations of the ecological message occur. In the case of the biodiversity problem, international ENGOs transformed the message of biodiversity loss, with all its uncertainty, into a message of a great threat to life on Earth and human life in particular. Framed in these terms, it means that we are all responsible for the loss of biodiversity and for its protection and restoration. The implication of this transforming operation is to define biodiversity as the common heritage of mankind.

The consequences of such a transformation, had it been accepted, would have been significant. Since nations have sovereignty over their territory and resources, it might have meant that international organizations – or a single state – could intervene to protect humanity's common property, since it is the common heritage of mankind. According to Aubertin and her co-authors (1998), governments were quick to ensure that this would not be allowed. The CBD states clearly that nations have full sovereignty over their natural resources.

A second transformation happened. The Convention (and the discussions that preceded its signing) became more and more focused on one type of biodiversity, namely, genetic biodiversity. The Convention aims to maintain the sovereign rights of nations but also to make use of the richness of biological diversity for bioprospecting. It values property rights, contracts, and legal arrangements that nations can strike with one another or with private firms.[8]

How can we interpret this transformation, or utilization, of the ecological message on biodiversity loss? For Aubertin and her colleagues, it is proof of the effectiveness of the liberal and contractual approach to international and environmental problems, and it is also a further step in the commercialization of life. This further step results from many factors. First, economic interests were active during the preparation of the CBD. That the United States did not sign the Convention at Rio is significant. Property rights on genetic resources, as transformed by biotechnology, were not sufficiently protected. Second, biotechnology is a highly promising industry. Genes may become the next basic commodity, as cotton, steel, and cars were in past technological revolutions (Freeman and Soete, 1997). With the electronic chip and perhaps the fuel cell, genes may be driving the world economy in future decades. Genes, or "life" as opponents complain, have been adapted to property and patent rights. There is money and profit to be made in the gene business (Yoxen, 1983). No wonder that economic interests, agribusiness and pharmaceuticals, have been concerned about insufficient protection of the fruits of invention and innovation and the investments that led to them. Since inventions and technological innovations are the name of the economic game, intellectual and patent rights must be better protected.[9]

Furthermore, there may be another reason why the message was transformed. The new biotechnology is the brain-child of molecular biology and genetics. It is highly funded and occupies a strong position inside the biological sciences. It is close to chemistry and physics, and its methods are experimental. On the other hand, the rest of biodiversity science, though rich in methods, models, and field experiments, is not as well-integrated. It calls upon many disciplines and subdisciplines, and the variety of its contexts and methods casts an image of fuzziness. Molecular biology is reductionist, while the science of biological diversity is systemic. Finally, I should venture, molecular biology is highly technology-oriented, that is, it can be directly used in technology development, as mechanics is used in engineering. Biodiversity science has not yet invented its technology, "and it is not a technology that can be easily sold in the market place" (Chevassus-au-Louis, 2000).

This brief analysis of biodiversity as an ecological problem shows how a scientific message is produced, disseminated, used, and, in the process, transformed. From the concerns of a group of scientists and activists, it was appropriated by a variety of actors who used the message differently. Some wanted to use biodiversity in terms of the common heritage of mankind, whereas others, states and biotechnology corporations, were not too keen on, even opposed to, such an approach. The former wanted to reinforce their sovereign rights over their own resources ("it is not the property of all, and in signing the CBD, we want to affirm that we are responsible world citizens and determined to play our part, with some help from the North, in protecting biodiversity"). The latter wanted to have guaranteed access to genetic resources. They agreed on some form of compensation to local communities when they extract valuable genetic resources but were keen to preserve, even reinforce, property and patent rights. In this long process the scientific message seems to have retreated into the background as a sort of Big Bang background radiation. And this is due to framing mechanisms, which are a powerful social and political dynamic in many environmental issues (Miller, 2000). If there is a "new international, or global, biological order" in the making, it may be more genetic than biological, for the transformations of the CBD regime are only one indication of the crucial importance that the new biotechnology is taking on in the world economy and polity as well as in the public mind.

Conclusion

There is no doubt that global ecological problems present new threats to humanity and new challenges to the world polity. The 1992 Rio Earth Summit was an important moment in the attempt to consolidate international environmental action. The CBD is one of the building blocks of global environmental regimes. Compared with other international regimes, it may appear weak. But if my analysis is correct, its weakness is due to many factors. Weakness comes with newness. Biodiversity as a major global concern, though not entirely new, has not yet been through a long history and practice of negotiations, consensus-building over the definition of the problem, development of strong scientific advice, and, dare I say, a deep shared concern about the role every nation has to play in making Planet Earth more hospitable to today's and tomorrow's inhabitants. We still have to digest and fully integrate into policies and practices the teachings of the Brundtland Report. Biodiversity as well as climate change, forest management, sustainable urban development, and water quality and supply are truly global environmental problems.

It is not clear that the global environmental problems that we are now trying to understand are seen as urgent by all. The IPCC efforts to understand and diffuse a complex problem such as climate change are unprecedented. But in spite of these efforts, climate change – the facts as well as the policies – remains a controversial issue. The IPCC's scientific reports are, however, the best scientific assessment so far of any global ecological problem. One can hope that the global biodiversity problem will give rise to similar efforts. For that to happen, strong institutions must be designed, nationally as well as internationally: an international convention is a first building block but just the beginning of a long construction process. But it is not all that is needed. Institutions will be strong and effective as long as they have a clear idea of what they are trying to achieve and are adaptable to new situations. Now, with ecological problems, a clear idea of problems to be dealt with and goals to be pursued depends on sound scientific advice, which itself depends on science being able to reduce some uncertainties or at least to teach policy-makers how to live with uncertainty.

But our very notion of "science" or relevant knowledge may also have to change in the process. A greater integration of traditional ecological knowledge is certainly something that the Convention would benefit from, though integration may not be easy. We have come to believe that science and ethnoscience are worlds apart in thought and methods of exposing ideas, as well as in facts and general propositions. But to protect biodiversity, as well as cultural diversity, perhaps "world society" cannot do without the empirical and highly diversified knowledge of the environment possessed by local communities. And there may be nothing more fruitful for protecting cultural diversity than preserving – and making use of – people's knowledge of their environment and of themselves. There is a need for international recognition, inside the world's main institutions, of the local knowledge that cultural communities have accumulated over very long periods of time. Whether the two modes of thought can cohabit respectfully and co-operatively, and whether each can learn from the other, remains to be seen. This is a great challenge for advisory committees of experts – thus an enlarged epistemic community – upon which the Convention's success so greatly depends.

The biodiversity issue remains complex. Its science seems not yet prepared to provide sure and policy-relevant advice. Though biologists may share a global vision and broad understanding of the Earth and the biosphere in what Richard Williams has called the "modern Earth narrative," constructed on two fundamental ideas – deep or geologic time and biological evolution – it remains for them to suggest how to translate this global view (a true global perspective if there is one!) into workable policies. Otherwise, interests will continue to define what is at stake and what should be accepted as laws, conventions, and regulations. I am not pleading for the adoption of a strong technocratic decision-making model but for science (and traditional knowledge, for that matter) to be a stronger actor (though not the sole or preponderant one) and play a larger and closer role in the process of preparing a safe road to what the sociologist Edgar Morin calls a "cognitive democracy".

Notes

[1]This research was funded by the Social Sciences and Humanities Research Council of Canada. I am very grateful for its support of my research on the sociology of ecological problems over the years.
[2] Social worlds in this conception (people doing things together) suppose quasi face-to-face interactions and are analytically more appropriate at a micro level of sociological analysis. However, we can expand this conception, *mutatis mutandis,* to broader social processes and institutions, since people belong or feel attached, by geography, history, and socialization,

to large wholes, which provide them with norms, rules, codes of conduct, ideals, resources, etc., and to which they contribute. These social worlds can also be seen, with due adaptation, in light of Giddens's structuration theory (Giddens, 1984).

[3] See chapter 11 by Revéret and Webster in this volume.

[4] For the use and impact of other forms of knowledge, see, in this volume, the chapter by Potvin et al.

[5] Fiona McConnell (1996, pp. 18-19) relates that when the British delegation included, as early as 1990, a representative from an environmental NGO, some other national delegates were surprised, even shocked, arguing that international policy-making is the sole responsibility of governments. What seemed natural to some delegates was unthinkable for others. McConnell explains that the British Department of Environment (DOE) had, in the past, established strong co-operative links with environmental NGOs. Political culture does matter!

[6] See chapter 1 by McGraw in this volume.

[7] Some philosophers distinguish intrinsic value from inherent value: "Inherent value is the value that an entity possesses on account of being prized for itself rather than for its utility...Both instrumental and inherent value, it will be noted, depend upon the existence of an external valuer or beneficiary. Intrinsic value, by contrast, is understood to be the value that entities have of themselves, and therefore does not presuppose the existence of any external valuer at all" (Bowman, 1996, p. 15). Clearly, the intrinsic value idea used here comprises both types of values.

[8] See also chapter 7 by Blais in this volume.

[9] See also chapter 9 by Thomas in this volume.

Chapter 11

Economics and Biodiversity Management

Jean-Pierre Revéret and Alain Webster

Introduction

The implementation of the Convention on Biological Diversity (CBD) builds on the foundations of the Rio process and the broad acceptance of its concept of sustainable development. However, it also comes within a context of trade liberalization, globalization, and the development of a hegemonic school of thought according to which the market should play an increasing role in all sectors of society while the state seeks to diminish its own role. These two background factors change the rules of the game for conservation: here as elsewhere, less state and more market is the watchword.

Thus the field is open for economics, the pre-eminent science of the market, and almost without exception, all stakeholders are knocking at its door for both a diagnosis and a prescription. In particular, Article 11 of the Convention calls on the Contracting Parties to "adopt economically and socially sound measures that act as incentives for the conservation and sustainable use of components of biological diversity". Article 14, too, which calls on the Parties to:

Introduce appropriate procedures requiring environmental impact assessment of its proposed projects that are likely to have significant adverse effects on biological diversity with a view to avoiding or minimizing such effects and, where appropriate, allow for public participation in such procedures,

indirectly bolsters the role of economists, since economic valuation of damage is increasingly being used in the context of environmental impact assessments. This ideologically favourable context for economics conditions how the discipline will contribute to the conservation of biodiversity – a field of study that has traditionally been the preserve of biologists.

The methodology developed for environmental economics and natural resources management is being transposed with all of its strengths and weaknesses, i.e. strong internal coherence and often fragile analytical assumptions. The two central issues of environmental economics – the determination of total economic value (TEV) and the development of economic management tools – are equally central to biodiversity management. These conventional economic approaches will be adapted, but not specifically developed, for each category of biodiversity (though these categories are artificial in any case, since each of them is included within a higher level). The analytical assumptions, lines of inquiry, solutions, and in short, the paradigm of environmental economics are being transposed, *mutatis mutandis*, to biodiversity.

Valuation of Biodiversity

A variety of existing methods for monetary valuation can be applied to biodiversity. In addition, "[i]gnorance and uncertainty concerning the ecological role of biodiversity limit our ability to value its full contribution to human welfare" (OECD, 1996). Usually, monetary valuation is applied to only one component or at best a group of components of biodiversity. The most frequent approach is to measure the value associated with a species or a category of specific functions. The simplest situation is that of a marketable resource, where the market price gives a first approximation of value. As examples, annual world wood exports were worth $97 billion USD in 1990, including $11.1 billion USD for tropical wood; fish imports are worth approximately $35 billion USD, while trade in furs, reptile skins, tropical fish, shells, coral, and natural pearls is estimated at $5 billion USD. Ecotourism accounts for 4-22 per cent of the $55 billion USD generated by world tourism. In parallel with these marketable resources produced in most cases on an industrial scale, new markets are developing for more traditional products, such as non-wood forest products (NWFP).

The Convention, though, does highlight the fact that biodiversity's value derives from many sources that cannot be reduced to market value, whence the need to enlarge the concept of value to encompass these sources. Economics has developed a "rational" – indeed now the conventional – approach to this valuation. The approach depends on an expansion of the concept of value to consider the components of the natural environment as "natural assets" in any of three senses: i) they are used as production factors in economic activity; ii) they are subject to direct final use by consumers; or iii) the maintenance of natural ecosystems contributes to individual welfare.

Total Economic Value

The concept of *total economic value* (Pearce et al., 1989) comprises the sum total of these sources of value, i.e. all use values, option values and non-use values (Figure 11.1). Briefly, the concept of "Use Value" includes all benefits arising from the present-day use of a resource, whether in the context of a commercial, recreational, or subsistence activity. "Option Value" refers to the price people are willing to pay to preserve future access to an environmental good. Finally, "Non-Use Value" is defined as the economic value assigned by individuals to the knowledge that the resource exists in nature, even if it is never used at any time, present or future.

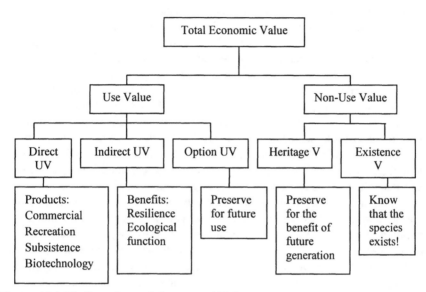

Figure 11.1 Biodiversity and Sources of Value

It is also possible to identify an "intrinsic value" – which is indeed recognized in the Convention as a component of biodiversity's value. The preamble to the Convention refers to the Contracting Parties' awareness of "the intrinsic value of biological diversity and of the ecological, genetic, social, economic, scientific, educational, cultural, recreational and aesthetic values of biological diversity and its components". As the guide to the CBD produced by the World Conservation Union (IUCN) (1996) indicates, use of the term "intrinsic" may seem surprising in a document of this nature. It should be noted that certain economists reject existence or intrinsic value as a valid type of non-use value because it derives from the biocentric rather than anthropocentric view that the environment should be preserved for the sake of nature and nature alone. Such recognition of living organisms' right to exist inexorably comes into conflict with models of economic rationality, for it allows actions to be motivated by considerations other than utility maximization by individuals (Pearce and Turner, 1990).

The concept of TEV, when applied to biodiversity, should encompass all its associated benefits at the genetic, specific, and ecosystem levels. Thus, the economic dimension of genetic variability is strongly marked by its use in pharmaceutical, agricultural, and food biotechnology. The economics of biodiversity at the species level deals mainly with species having commercial value and is in keeping with the income-based approach developed by renewable resource economists for fisheries and forestry. Methodological progress on the measurement of non-use values has made it possible to assign values, however preliminary, to non-market species and ecosystems.

Various direct or indirect valuation techniques are used for this purpose. For biodiversity in particular, two frequently used methods are the *travel cost method* and the *contingent valuation method*. The travel cost method is based on the hypothesis that individuals manifest a demand for a recreational site according to the travel costs they incur to get there and stay there. The relationship between total trip cost and number of trips taken yields a demand curve from which the consumer surplus associated with the site can be determined. Recent work has attempted to extend the method to the valuation of medicinal plants according to the time spent by traditional herbalists on collecting them; in this case, the opportunity cost was calculated by comparison with the average remuneration for a day of farm work in the region (Lescuyer, 2000). However, since the travel cost method only considers the costs borne by visitors, it measures direct (recreational) use value to the exclusion of other possible benefits associated with a given site.

The chief advantage of the contingent valuation method, in contrast, is that it takes account of both use and non-use values. This method attempts to simulate the operation of a normal market by using a survey to create a hypothetical market in which respondents reveal their preferences for certain non-market goods. Respondents to the survey are told of the potential consequences of a given event on biodiversity and are then led to disclose their maximum willingness-to-pay to avert or achieve those consequences (depending on whether the consequences are positive or negative).

The total value associated with the changed availability of an environmental good is then defined as the summation of willingness-to-pay for all concerned individuals. Contingent valuation therefore conforms to the principle of "consumer sovereignty," according to which individuals are assumed to know the utility of any given item to them (Mitchell and Carson, 1989). One critique of the method is that it tends to *create* rather than *reveal* preferences (Diamond and Hausman, 1994; Willinger, 1996). In the specific context of biodiversity valuation, there is also a type of bias known as the embedding effect: in some cases, people's willingness-to-pay to preserve a set of biological resources has been found to be the same for the whole set and for various combinations of its components. In other words, individual values calculated by contingent valuation cannot be assumed to be additive where this effect operates.

But irrespective of methodological bias issues, it should be remembered that these methods do not claim to determine the total value of biodiversity as such, only some of its components – in general, a species or an ecosystem harbouring it. In a typical illustration of this approach and its limitations, Gardner Brown Jr (1989) estimated the economic value of Kenyan elephants by both the travel cost and contingent valuation methods, based on the economic surplus derived from tourist "safaris". The safaris as a whole were valued at $200 million USD per year, of which the elephants accounted for 13 per cent, for an annual benefit of $20-30 million USD. Although a useful order-of-magnitude estimate was attributed to the value foreign tourists place on being able to see elephants in Kenya, the total value of this species clearly cannot be reduced to that dimension.

In short, assigning a value to biodiversity or its components may help decision-makers rank conservation objectives by order of priority and develop the economic incentive measures necessary to achieve these objectives (OECD, 1996), but as Muller (2000) points out, what is being measured is never biodiversity itself – an essentially non-operational concept at this level – but only some of its dimensions, the additivity of which is questionable.

Transposition to Developing Countries: Limits

A wealth of literature deals with the limitations of economic valuation methods in the context of developing countries (see the interesting summary by Hampicke, 1999). Lescuyer (2000) offers a particularly interesting set of arguments against using contingent valuation to calculate non-use values in tropical forests. His empirical study in the forests of eastern Cameroon showed that this environment is perceived as a space for human activities, one that is inseparable from the uses to which it gives rise. When he attempted to determine villagers' willingness-to-pay to save the forest, most of them refused monetary compensation, which they saw as a source of problems. They preferred collective compensation – a result at odds with the criterion of maximizing individual utility. For Lescuyer, what is lacking in essentially non-market societies is not just the existence of a market for the environmental good but the concept of a market itself. In this case, market mechanisms do not satisfactorily explain individual behaviour.

Economic Management of Biodiversity

Optimization and Sustainability

Through redefining the concept of value and developing new monetary valuation techniques, economic theorists have attempted to propound a cohesive methodology for the determination of biodiversity's economic value. Once the "benefit" of any given act of conservation is defined, a standard cost-benefit analysis can be performed for conservation and compared with the net benefits of alternative land uses. On this model, conservation is justified when it maximizes net benefit to society. This produces the following decision-making criterion (leaving aside temporal considerations):

$$[(Bc - Cc) - (Bd - Cd)] > 0$$

where Bc and Cc are the benefit and cost of conservation, and Bd and Cd the benefit and cost of any alternative land use (Pearce, 1996).

Here as before, the transposition of such a decision-making methodology from industrialized countries – where the market is already the privileged mechanism of resource allocation – to developing countries is problematic. This is a major reason why opinion is not unanimous about the advisability of applying this approach to biodiversity and to environmental issues in general. In contexts where certain resource allocation decisions are not mediated by the market, it is not at all clear that the consequences of an unquestioned transposition of this method would be positive. On the other hand, it would be naïve to suppose that people in developing countries know nothing of markets and that no aspect of their exchanges is monetized.

If the role the market should play in various societies is open to question, there is equal cause to question the sustainability of an approach based on optimization. As Faucheux and Froger (1993) put it, "The methods for valuing the depletion of non-market natural capital lead to a confusion between economic optimum and sustainable use of this capital. Yet nothing guarantees that the economic optimum will necessarily correspond to the sustainable use threshold" (translation).

Milon (1995) sheds some interesting light on this debate by stressing that the manner in which sustainability is defined can have a major impact on the calculation of TEV. Solow's weak sustainability concept, for example, extends the neo-classical theory of economic growth to natural capital by assuming that it and fabricated capital are substitutable for one another. Holling's strong sustainability concept assumes that the peculiar stability and resiliency of natural systems, and hence the maintenance of their capital, cannot be duplicated by substitution of fabricated capital. If one accepts the second definition instead of the first, an analysis based on maximization of individual benefit becomes impossible, since a decrease in natural capital cannot be offset by an increase in fabricated capital. These sustainability concepts therefore lead to different measures of TEV. The result is that TEV cannot be used as a criterion for selecting a sustainable and efficient policy, since there is no unique way to measure it (Milon, 1995).

The foregoing argument casts doubt on the concept of economic optimum as a rational decision-making criterion. Not just the accuracy but the very *possibility* of an economic valuation of biodiversity as a whole becomes doubtful, for independent of accuracy, the principle of optimization assumes that natural capital and fabricated capital are interchangeable. But this denies the special features of natural capital. When a decline in biodiversity results in an irreversible loss of irreplaceable natural capital that is essential to the maintenance of an ecosystem's resilience, this approach must be discarded.

The question of the interchangeability of natural and fabricated capital must be restored to a central position in the current debate on sustainable development and biodiversity. Given the uncertainty about substitutability and the relationship between biodiversity, resiliency, and ecosystem maintenance, the *precautionary principle* demands that any decrease in biodiversity should be contemplated with the utmost circumspection.

Precautionary Principle and Minimal Standard

Strictly interpreted, the precautionary principle suggests that "where there are threats or a likelihood of serious or irreversible biodiversity loss, lack of full scientific certainty should not be used as a reason for postponing cost-effective measures to prevent that loss" (OECD, 1996). In such cases, biodiversity maintenance must be considered an external constraint to be defined in non-economic terms. For Barbier (1996) this means that the protection of ecosystem sustainability or resilience becomes an explicit, primary objective.

Such a normative approach serves to determine an *a priori* level of environmental protection. It may be likened to the "safe minimum standard" approach developed since the early 1950s. For Perrings, Folke, and Mäler (1992) a safe minimum standard constitutes an essential part of a biodiversity conservation strategy, given the considerable uncertainty surrounding the future environmental impact of economic activity, the status that environmental assets possess as non-market public goods, and the irreversibility of species extinction and lost ecological functions.

Decisions made according to a minimum standard (or critical capital) concept may be diagrammed as in Figure 11.2, in which they are located along the vertical axis representing the degree of alteration of natural assets and the horizontal axis representing the degree of irreversibility and/or importance. Decisions at the lower right can be made on the basis of individual benefit maximization. Decisions in the centre of the figure are often made collectively by various public agencies with the aid of conventional cost/benefit analysis. Decisions at the upper left, however, have potentially catastrophic, irreversible effects. These decisions are often made by collective choice, as determined or constrained by legislation. For these decisions, it is necessary to organize the information differently, focusing on the minimum standard of preservation and the most efficient means of attaining it. The question becomes where to draw the lines between these different types of decisions and which information is most useful to decision-makers, particularly at the boundaries between zones.

Standard economic theory asserts that an answer to this question depends fundamentally on determining individual willingness-to-pay. Bingham et al. (1995) summarize the limits of this approach:

Although improved economic methods can lead to improved environmental decisions, economics cannot substitute for collective political decisions about distribution issues, including rights to resource use to future generations or within the present generation. Thus for some types of decisions, the issues of sustainability and ecosystem values ultimately will require collective choices within the political process... [In this context,] decisions makers do not need sophisticated benefit-cost analysis to justify actions to prevent irreversible environmental effects of large magnitude. Under such circumstances, analysis of the cost effectiveness of different policies or actions for preventing such consequences is appropriate. The question, however, remains how large is too large?

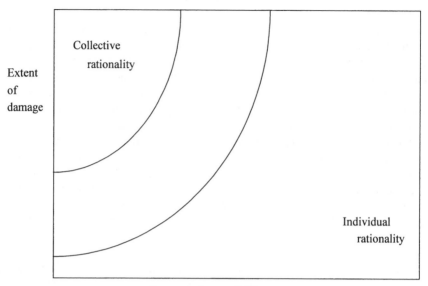

Degree of reversibility

Source: Bingham, 1995

Figure 11.2 Scope of Application of Valuation Methods

Victor (1994) likewise stresses that such questions about the quantity of natural assets that must be maintained "are not questions that economics alone can answer. The answers to these questions are largely social, political and ecological and are relevant at global and local scales".

Revéret et al. (1990) concur when they argue that ecology and environmental science must provide the data needed to determine the constraints that society wishes to impose on the maximization of economic production. The role of economics, say these authors, should be to indicate the lowest-cost option for meeting those constraints – that is, for preserving those values that society considers as transcending the economic sphere. The economic valuation then provides decision-makers with a realistic basis on which to negotiate with various stakeholders. In this context, monetary valuation of biodiversity no longer revolves around the measurement of individual willingness-to-pay but rather around the total costs that must be incurred if society is to preserve or achieve a given level of sustainable development. Thus, two competing paradigms are in play (Norton, 1995).

Faucheux and Noël (1995) rightly point out that "the version of sustainability typical of this approach may be termed conservationistic...Though it does give pride of place to intergenerational equity, it is more problematic in its treatment of intragenerational equity. Putting energy use and production on hold in the developing world could indeed interfere with the achievement of a "sustainability" which must, let us not forget, be economic, social and ecological in nature. The economic and social concerns must not, as here, be sacrificed to the environmental ones".

Considerations of intragenerational equity make it clear that the determination of minimum standards cannot be dissociated from the financing of such measures: the development prospects they allow and the payment of compensation they may necessitate. Since the benefits of biodiversity are global but the costs of its conservation are inequitably distributed among nations, international compensation mechanisms may be considered an indispensable feature of any global strategy on biodiversity (Barbier, 1996).

Economic Incentives

Regarding economic incentive measures, economic theory teaches that if a flaw in the market prevents it from playing the role of optimal resource allocator, then the flaw must be corrected. In the case at hand, the real price of goods must be re-established by including the cost that their production or consumption inflicts on the environment. This principle, when applied to genes, leads to the recognition and formulation of intellectual property rights and the introduction of royalties. It entails that states, communities, and individuals take account of the cost of their maintenance but not the cost to the environment. The concept of property rights is also applied at the species level (OECD, 1996). At the ecosystem level, various types of incentive measures have been tested (Loureiro, 1996).

The dominant trend, as we have noted, is to give more weight to market mechanisms, and in this context, the literature discusses various economic measures designed to promote the conservation and sustainable use of biodiversity. Whether or not the optimal level of conservation in a society is ultimately determined by an economics-based approach, economists have certainly proposed many incentive measures to assist in its maintenance. Noteworthy in this regard is the emergence of a consensus to the effect that an assessment of the economic impact of biodiversity loss is not a necessary prerequisite to economic incentive development. Governments are free to implement incentives without first undertaking costly valuation studies – which moreover possess the limitations discussed earlier.

Positive incentives, both monetary and otherwise, are those that provide a benefit to governments, organizations, and individuals if they preserve biological diversity; disincentives or deterrents internalize the costs of using and/or damaging biological resources and thus deter activities that deplete them. Indirect incentives are commercial mechanisms or institutional arrangements for improving or creating markets and price signals for biological resources, thus encouraging the preservation and sustainable use of biological diversity (OECD, 1996). In the development and implementation of such measures, it is important to identify and eliminate existing ones that may be termed perverse, i.e. those that run counter to the goal of preserving biodiversity. There are indeed many industrial subsidy programmes with potential perverse effects of this type.

Furthermore, the equity of any given measure must be considered. It is essential to identify clearly the likely winners and losers as a result of an incentive programme. It is also important to revise and/or establish a suitable legal and institutional framework for the implementation of effective incentive measures. Finally, the involvement of local populations at all levels is crucial to the success of incentives. A strong sense of appropriation by the affected populations is essential to ensuring a minimum of efficacy and sustainability.

Toward a General Theoretical Framework

Many authors have stressed the limits of a pure-economics approach, arguing that it cannot alone provide the theoretical framework and tools necessary for managing biodiversity and ecosystem resources used directly and/or indirectly. Given this oft-repeated observation, one can elucidate the various emerging and coexisting trends and – without claiming to provide a definitive framework – consider how they may complement one another.

Analysis of appropriation regimes   The establishment of property rights in biological resources is seen by many as essential to the success of conservation measures. In the discourse of the OECD (1996), not dissimilar from that of other international organizations, "[w]here property rights do not exist at all, then open access conditions prevail". If so, then the solution is to allot exclusive usage rights by privatizing resources. But this is only a partial, not a universal, truth.

Hardin's "tragedy of the commons" (1968) is indeed played out where access to commercial resources is unrestricted, particularly relevant examples being certain northern commercial fish and game species. In numerous other cases, however, resources have been maintained at acceptable levels of abundance (Ostrom, 1990; Berkes et al., 1989), in particular through social control of access[1] (Weber and Revéret, 1993). Communal ownership and freedom of access are not synonymous; a conflation of the two helps legitimate the pure-economics approach that seeks to re-establish or institute individual property rights in all situations. In this regard, a distinction should be drawn between ownership and appropriation regime. By analysing specific examples of appropriation regimes for biological resources, taking account of various levels of representation, use, arrangements and access control, transferability of access rights, and distribution and sharing, it becomes possible to provide a more comprehensive reading and understanding of real situations. This facilitates the adaptation of theoretically sound management strategies to suit local socio-economic contexts.

The development of socio-economics as a fully-fledged discipline (Bürgenmeier, 1994) takes a step in this direction: indeed, its basic assumption is that economic models alone afford an inadequate analysis of economic problems and that human behaviour is too complex to be reducible to the economic rationality of individuals (particularly in less market-based economies). For socio-economists, economics is a social science, one whose sphere of inquiry encompasses economic policies and the conditions of their application. It addresses the interactions between individual behaviour and the institutional framework.

A socio-economics of this kind is compatible with and complementary to the work on common pool resources (Knudsen, 1995; Ostrom, 1990; Berkes et al., 1989) being conducted by researchers in diverse disciplines (biology, anthropology, political science, etc.) which analyses the management of a wide range of resources (forestry, game, fisheries, etc.) in both Northern and Southern geo-socio-political contexts. Not only does this work demonstrate the non-universality of the tragedy of the commons, it contributes to the development of a management regime that more comfortably accommodates local social realities and institutions. A common property regime consists of a well-identified resource and group of users, plus a set of institutional arrangements governing the use of the resource, including penalties for noncompliance.

The heritage approach A heritage-oriented approach is another promising theoretical framework that more adequately accounts for the real behaviour of individuals and societies (Ollagnon, 1989; De Montgolfier and Natali, 1987). Godard (1989) argues that this approach is broader than the pure-economics and regulatory approaches to the management of nature and the environment. The following discussion on the heritage approach is based on Weber (1996) and takes as its point of departure the observation that human beings are an integral part of any ecosystem eyed for preservation: there can be no success without their co-operation. This, moreover, is consistent with the ecosystem-based approach adopted by the Convention. In short, it is asserted that from both an ethical and a pragmatic point of view, and in accordance with the World Conservation Strategy, it is appropriate to give local populations a central role in conservation programmes.

It follows that local people must be involved in the development of conservation objectives from the outset. For example, discussions may be held with stakeholders on the *long-term objectives in which the resolution of a conflict or the management of a problem should be situated.* The long-term is defined here as a time horizon on the order of 25-30 years so that present-day stakeholders are obliged to negotiate not only for themselves but also for their children. It is this placing of short and medium-term commitments within a long-term framework agreement that lends the approach its heritage character. It is founded on the hypothesis that although long-term events are not predictable, they are partially *determinable* and that *to plan is to govern* (Weber and Bailly, 1993).

The long-term collective point of view entails negotiation and hence mediation between differing representations of the past, present, and future. The result must consist of:

- long-term objectives (at least one generation);
- medium-term management scenarios combined with an ecological, economic, social, and institutional feasibility assessment; and
- development of a negotiated management structure.

Logically prior to the mediation process is the establishment of an *initial situation* (Rawls, 1987) in which the stakeholders are clearly identified and informed of their differences from one another, as well as their common dependence on a solution to the problem giving rise to the negotiation. This initialization step paves the way for a confrontation between equally legitimate and subjective *perceptions*. The process is grounded by the stakeholders' agreement that their present-day dispute is less important than the unacceptable negative consequences for their children's lives of allowing current trends to continue unchecked.

The challenge is to induce the stakeholders to elaborate a long-term charter – a kind of social contract – in which both the ideal and the material find expression. Myths, symbols, and ancestors may very well come into the discussion. Based on a shared disagreement with current inertial trends, or a desire to see some of them continue, it becomes possible to discuss the elements of a *desirable* future.

Since the long-term objectives must be of a "heritage" nature – i.e. indisputable, intangible, "constitutional" – they must be both legitimated and ritualized. *Legitimization* is the procedure whereby agreement among a group of people is accepted as binding on all stakeholders, present and absent. Most often, it involves making public the terms of the agreement, along with a written declaration *in the presence of an authority governing on a wider scale* than the problems giving rise to mediation. *Ritualization* takes the form of a public expression of the terms of the agreement in the form of a ceremony appropriate to the context and culture. Its purpose is to situate the long-term agreement within the symbolic order, thereby rendering it inalienable, non-monetizable and difficult to transgress.

Agreement on long-term objectives precedes and legitimates the definition of medium and short-term management arrangements for the natural heritage. Economic analysis may help define these objectives and arrangements, but it does not constitute the only decision-making criterion. Various heritage management experiences are underway, in Madagascar for example, where this approach is being used to design and implement a regulatory framework for renewable resources known as *gestion locale sécurisée*; it involves the signing of environmental stewardship contracts between the national government and local communities.[2]

Conclusion

Regardless of one's own conviction as to the role the market should play as a resource allocator in society – and as a corollary, the role the state should play – it should be borne in mind that the market is a social construct. It is a tool used by a society to achieve its own objectives. In this sense, it does not fall to the market to establish conservation priorities, particularly when inter- and intragenerational equity is involved, as is the case with biodiversity. Economic analysis as embodied in standard environmental economics methodology cannot by itself make sense of the complex social and ecological dynamics underlying the use of terrestrial and aquatic ecosystems and their resources. Therefore, in biodiversity management, monetary valuation should be viewed merely as one decision-making aid among others. Economics does have a predominant role to play, though, in determining the most effective way to adhere to the sustainability constraint. It can and must contribute to developing effective, efficient, and equitable approaches to achieving these conservation objectives.

It may thus be said that where biodiversity is concerned, the "development of a unified paradigm clearly comes under the domain of interdisciplinary research" (OECD, 1996) in which, beyond biology and economics, several other social sciences have their place. Economics must contribute to the development of this new paradigm without claiming to be the only science that can determine the rules of the game. As we have seen, several coexisting approaches can complement or substitute for the environmental economics approach. One can only hope that they will indeed be developed and applied to the real world in a complementary fashion.

Notes

This chapter was translated by Peter Feldstein.

[1] See also the conclusion of chapter 8 by Potvin et al. in this volume.
[2] See also chapter 13 by Hufty and Muttenzer in this volume.

Chapter 12

Development of Canadian Policy on and the Protection of Marine Diversity

Paule Halley[1]

Introduction

The 20th century has left us a sizeable and complex legacy of international conventions and treaties designed to protect the environment and its resources. These instruments were developed as a result of ecological disasters, overexploitation of natural resources, and the impact of human activities on environmental quality and natural resources. Most of these initiatives were undertaken in response to specific problems. However, since the 1992 Rio Earth Summit and the signing of framework conventions such as the Convention on Biological Diversity (CBD), there have been significant changes in the handling of pollution prevention and environmental resource management.

All of these treaties and conventions signed by states require a great deal of effort to implement so that commitments made in the international arena can be met. I will be looking at Canada's experience here. This example will illustrate the role played by the CBD in the development of environmental policy in a developed country. In this regard, it is important to note that before the 1992 Earth Summit in Rio, there were many similarities between the development of international environmental law and that of Canada's environmental and resource protection policy. Recent developments also show that, since the Rio Summit, Canada's public authorities have embarked on a renewal of their intervention strategy for biodiversity protection.

Canada was convinced of the importance of the Convention on Biological Diversity and played an active role in the talks that led to its introduction in Rio. Canada was also one of the first countries to sign the Convention and the first to ratify it. Since then, Canada has continually stressed its commitment to sustainable development and biodiversity conservation and its firm intention to abide by the terms of the Convention. Canada is the home of 70,000 known species of animals, plants, and other organisms, and new species are being discovered every year. Studies show, however, that a growing number of species are endangered. According to the Committee on the Status of Endangered Wildlife in Canada, a total of 380 species were at risk as of May 2001. This number includes over 20 marine mammal species that are extirpated (no longer existing in the wild in Canada but occurring elsewhere), endangered, threatened, or of special concern.[2]

Over the two decades leading up to the Rio Summit in 1992, important efforts were made on the international scene and by numerous countries to protect the environment and biological resources. These initiatives, however, fell short of ensuring environmental quality and resource sustainability. As it gathered in Rio, the international community drew lessons from this first wave of public intervention and proposed new intervention strategies. It was no longer a question of adding to the list of activities to regulate or environments and species to protect. The new commitments were based on new guiding principles and ultimate goals as well as on fundamental changes in decision-making processes. In this context, I plan to examine what the Rio commitments in the field of biodiversity are intended to solve and to identify the main solutions adopted and the implementation challenges they entail for Canada.

In recent years, a number of initiatives have already been taken in Canada on behalf of sustainable development and biodiversity protection. In this chapter, I will be taking a look at changes in Canadian policy in order to show how Canada is implementing the Convention on Biological Diversity and to what extent it is contributing to the effectiveness of environmental and resource protection systems. The abundance of Canadian systems geared toward biodiversity protection makes this difficult and unnecessarily complex to analyse. Therefore, I will be concentrating essentially on Canada's initiatives in the marine biodiversity sector. Specifically, this is a study of the effects of public policy renewal on the regulatory framework developed to protect marine biodiversity. Marine ecosystems represent an interesting field of study in many respects, although Canadian literature has so far shown more interest in terrestrial biodiversity. Canada has the longest coastline in the world, and marine resources are fundamental to its economy.[3] The marine environment comes under the exclusive jurisdiction of the central government, which avoids the need to address issues of Canadian constitutional law in this chapter; more important, these ecosystems offer the most innovative biodiversity protection initiatives.

With these factors in mind, I will begin by presenting the problems that the international community and Canada's public authorities considered needed to be solved by renewing their intervention strategy for biodiversity protection. To this end, I briefly review the steps taken before these problems arose. I then describe how biodiversity protection policy is currently being renewed in the international arena and in Canada since the adoption of the CBD. Finally, a number of observations on the essential requirements for this renewal will be raised and several challenges awaiting Canada's public authorities outlined.

Emergence of Policies and Legal Protection for Marine Biodiversity in Canada

Over the course of the 20th century, pressures exerted on the environment by human activities and the precarious situation of wild species prompted the international community to commit to protecting the environment and its biological resources. This commitment was borne out by the adoption of several international charters and conventions advocating this protection, as we shall first illustrate. The following subsection argues that the substance of these legal instruments reflected the fact that the development of Canadian environmental policy was not entirely unrelated to Canada's signing of numerous treaties and conventions and to its commitment to implementing them. As far as environmental protection and Canada's biological resources were concerned, however, the results proved to be disappointing: the first wave of public intervention did not solve environmental problems as the final subsection will show.

First Wave of International Conventions and Treaties

These legal instruments do not form a coherent whole: they are basically a series of measures developed in response to specific problems relating to pollution and species and habitat loss. Since they were developed for a distinct purpose, they were not all inspired by the desire to gradually construct an international environmental law. They therefore only provide limited answers to environmental problems. This international framework suggests a number of general remarks with regard to the protection of marine environments and resources (Dyoulgerov, 2000).

Most international conventions dealing with ocean pollution have to do with spills from ships. The first international convention of this type, the Convention for the Prevention of Pollution of the Sea by Oil, signed in London in 1954, concerned ship safety and marine pollution caused by crude oils. As a result of a number of major oil spill disasters, other conventions set out detailed measures for preventing pollution caused by toxic substances transported by ships and provided for casualty compensation and emergency measures.[4]

Another source of marine pollution involving ships is the dumping of waste. In this case, the international community preferred to develop a framework distinct from that applied to pollution caused by ships. The Convention on the Prevention of Marine Pollution by Dumping of Wastes, which was signed in London in 1972, defined "dumping" as: "the deliberate disposal at sea of wastes from not only vessels, but aircraft, platforms or other man made structures, as well as the deliberate disposal of these vessels or platforms themselves". Regional – as opposed to international – agreements were drawn up to deal with other sources of marine pollution, such as the pollution that can result from ocean-floor exploration and exploitation (VanderZwaag, 1995, pp. 220-64).

Although pollution from land-based sources represents the most serious cause of degradation of the marine environment, no formal international framework regulates it – unlike pollution from ships – only non-binding guidelines.[5] It is true, however, that this form of pollution is difficult to regulate: it involves a wide range of contaminants that are released by countless industries and can be airborne, delivered via rivers, or leached from the soil.

Very few marine species are subject to international regulation: a few marine mammals, certain migratory birds and fisheries. For example, a regional convention in 1916 concerned migratory marine birds such as penguins, and the first international convention designed to manage the durability of a marine resource, in 1946, dealt with whales.[6] Later, saving the whales prevailed, and the International Whaling Commission ratified a moratorium on commercial whaling. Conventions geared towards protecting wetlands and controlling international trade in endangered species were signed in 1971 and 1973. They protect certain rare marine species such as the polar bear and walrus and protect coastal habitats – for what they are rather than as natural resources to be used by an industry.[7]

Finally, there are a large number of regional agreements regulating the management of transboundary marine resources by the signatory Parties to the agreements (Myers, 1992). It should be pointed out that these agreements were not originally concluded to protect biodiversity but rather to avoid a collapse of fish stocks, which would be detrimental to the hunting and fishing industries.

On the whole, the first generation of international agreements dealing with marine environments and resources grew up around obvious, alarming problems: they were designed to solve or alleviate specific problems such as oil spills, dumping of waste at sea, overharvesting of whales, and loss of wetlands. Although a few of these agreements directly addressed protection of the environment and species, most of them were more concerned about the limited nature of marine resources and the need to share their use and prevent their depletion.

Rapid Development of Canadian Environmental Policy and Protection of Marine Biodiversity

By signing these international conventions, Canada promised to translate its commitments into concrete actions and decisions. Gradually, the federal and provincial governments developed environmental protection policies for intervention geared toward pollution sources and conservation of wild species and their habitats. For the most part, these Canadian environmental policies involved economic incentives, national programmes, and regulating detrimental human activities. Traditional legal instruments such as laws and regulations were used abundantly in this first generation of environmental policy (Juillet, 1998, p. 168).

Examination of the countless statutes and regulations adopted as of the end of the 1960s shows that Canada's public authorities were trying to conform to proposals formulated on the international stage. Although national law and conventions differed in many respects in terms of content, they shared the same purpose, assumptions, and problem-solving approach. This kinship is illustrated, in particular, by the reactive and fragmentary nature of the actions of public authorities: interventions were geared toward specific problems that were obvious and serious.

This special trait also applied to the marine environment. There were no laws adopted for the express purpose of protecting the marine environment during the first generation of public interventions. Therefore, a whole series of laws and regulations had to be consulted in order to understand how public authorities intended to control pollution and protect marine species. Also, these first-generation statutes and regulations are generally considered to have been founded on the traditional "command and control" approach. In other words, laws and regulations were used to prescribe conduct and punish offenders.

With respect to prevention of marine and ocean pollution, the chief federal interventions designed specifically for marine environments were aimed at controlling pollution from ships and pollution stemming from the dumping of waste.[8] It should also be pointed out that several laws were passed to control air and water pollution from land-based sources.[9] Although they were not adopted for the purpose of protecting marine environments, they could have this effect because they target the greatest sources of marine and ocean pollution. These legal instruments control the way polluting activities are practised, using authorization, operating permits, and standards relating to the quality and quantity of contaminants that can be released into the environment (VanderZwaag, 1995, pp. 308-38).

Over the course of this period, protection of marine species reflected the priorities adopted internationally: interventions specifically targeted migratory birds, cetaceans, walruses, narwhals, belugas, seals, and trade in rare species.[10] A number of special laws were also passed dealing with fisheries management.[11] These instruments were based on prohibitions against taking rare species without authorization and, for other species, permit and quota systems.

However, marine habitat protection remained virtually non-existent. Although general laws authorized the creation of marine parks, attention remained focused on land environments. It was not until 1990 that Canada got its first water park, a freshwater park.[12]

Failure of Public Interventions

The first generation of public intervention aimed at fighting pollution and protecting wild species was harshly criticized at the end of the 1980s: it had failed as far as the environment was concerned. Despite numerous public interventions, environmental pollution and loss of wild species and habitat had not been eliminated.

The normative framework developed during that period has also been criticized. With respect to biodiversity, it is censured for not doing enough, intervening too late, and intervening in too fragmentary a fashion to be effective.

Not doing enough   For example, it is said that parks and other protected areas (refuges, deeryards, nests, "residences," etc.) are too small and do not take the use and purpose of areas adjacent to the area being protected into consideration. It is also said that public authorities do not do enough when it comes to implementing legal protection instruments. This is the case, in particular, with the Convention on International Trade in Endangered Species of Wild Fauna and Flora (CITES), which was implemented in 1975 in two existing federal statutes, the *Export and Import Act* and the *Game Export Act*. In a recent study, Marshall notes the weaknesses of these instruments, which remained without any real effect for 20 years. She points out that the first of these laws fails to prohibit the importing into Canada, possession, purchase, or sale of protected species products, that the second does not prohibit possession of live game, that customs control is limited to passengers while commercial freight is ignored, and that the officers responsible for implementing these instruments are not very well-trained and insufficient in number (Marshall, 2000, pp. 44-7).

Intervening too late   The issue with public interventions is that they are reactive. Possibly because of misplaced optimism, Canada's strategy focused essentially on problem-solving. In other words, public authorities reacted to environmental emergencies, providing a specific solution tailored to each case: they rectified production methods, restored damaged areas, increased natural resource stocks, etc. Legal instruments for protecting threatened and vulnerable species represent a good example of this approach (Haeuber, 1996, pp. 12-13; Rohlf, 1994). Although endangered species need to be protected, "ambulance chasing" is not the best way to prevent the endangerment of wild species. The reasons are simple: there are too many species to attempt to manage them one by one; a large number of them are still unknown or not known well enough to decide whether or not they need protecting; and finally, the listing process takes so long that a species can change from being "threatened" to "extinct" or from being "vulnerable" to being "threatened" in the course of the process.

Intervening in too fragmentary a fashion   Public interventions are carried out separately, and a special solution is found for each problem. For instance, to regulate the specific problems related to water pollution and marine species management, the federal government adopted different regulations dealing with pulp and paper mills, the meat and fowl industries, potato processing, metal mines, oil refineries, mercury in effluent from chlorine plants, ichthyotoxic substances, whales, narwhals, belugas, seals, walruses, and so on (see *Fisheries Act*, R.S.C. 1985, c. F-14). These regulations introduce specific, individual protection systems that are separate from those adopted by other federal and provincial authorities qualified to intervene in these areas. This means that none of these authorities has an overall picture and they all disregard the impact of their actions and activities on the environment. This is true with a river such as the St. Lawrence, which is used as a waterway, is a venue for swimming, fishing, and recreational activities, provides water for human consumption, agricultural and industrial production, and generation of electricity, and supports numerous fish, mammal, and bird species.[13] Generally speaking, the increase in the number of legal protection instruments and the dispersed nature of the authorities involved make it difficult to co-ordinate public policy dealing with protection of marine species and environments.

Finally, in a more general way, public intervention founded on legal instruments such as statutes and regulations and the "command and control" approach was also criticized at the end of the 1980s. Businesses find that these interventions are too expensive, slow, and severe and that they prevent them from remaining competitive. Citizens do not think that the development and implementation of these instruments take their concerns sufficiently into account. They all agree that there is a need for greater participation in development and implementation of standards.

Sustainable Development, Protection of Biodiversity, and Renewal of Canadian Policy

Despite the efforts made during the first wave of government intervention in the field of environmental protection, human activities still threaten the quality of the environment and the diversity of its biological components: pollution, habitat destruction, overexploitation, overcultivation, etc. It is these negative results and the criticism of first-generation interventions that Canadian public authorities are attempting to address by renewing their strategy. This calling into question and the innovative documents signed at the Earth Summit held in 1992 in Rio de Janeiro go hand in hand.

Sustainable Development and Protection of Marine Biodiversity

At Rio, the international community adopted a number of commitments defining the framework for a new form of development called "sustainable development". They are the Rio Declaration on Environment and Development, the Convention on Biological Diversity, the United Nations Framework Convention on Climate Change, the Non-Legally Binding Authoritative Statement of Principles for a Global Consensus on the Management, Conservation and Sustainable Development of All Types of Forests, and *Agenda 21*.[14]

This new common framework has to allow for progress towards a form of development that meets the needs of present generations fairly without compromising the needs of generations to come.[15] This approach to development is based on the idea that the biosphere has a limited capacity and that human activities must be altered to take these limits into account. There is no one principle for sustainable development. The most complete reference in this respect is the 27 principles set out in the declaration and the documents signed in Rio. This section takes a look at the objectives and principles governing the protection and sustainable use of marine biodiversity and outlines their requirements.

In terms of public policy, *Agenda 21* notes that many countries still tend systematically to compartmentalize economic, social, and environmental factors when they develop policy and in connection with planning and management (*Agenda 21,* 8.2). The general aim proposed is therefore to restructure the decision-making process so that economic, social, and environmental considerations are fully integrated, thus ensuring that development is economically real, socially fair, and ecologically rational all at the same time (*Agenda 21,* 8.4). With this action plan, laws and regulations play a key role in implementing environmental and sustainable development policy because of their mandatory nature and their normative effect on economic planning and market instruments (*Agenda 21,* 8.13).

The biodiversity objectives stated in the Convention on Biological Diversity are the conservation of biological diversity, the sustainable use of its components, and the fair and equitable sharing of benefits derived from utilization of genetic resources (Article 1). Biological diversity encompasses all living organisms and aquatic ecosystems (Article 2). A series of measures are provided to help the signatory Parties meet objectives. They include development of a national strategy, action plans, and a series of obligations relating to identification, supervision, conservation, and sustainable use of biological resources. In general terms, the signatory Parties noted that: "the fundamental requirement for the conservation of biological diversity is the *in situ* conservation of ecosystems and natural habitats and the maintenance and recovery of viable populations of species in their natural surroundings" (preamble).[16] The Convention also has the mission of ensuring the integration of biodiversity and development considerations and thereby offering a solution to the problems of co-ordinating countless biodiversity protection instruments and the different users of these resources.

The protection of marine biodiversity is dealt with specifically in the *Agenda 21* chapter devoted to the protection of oceans and seas.[17] From the outset, this document stresses that the provisions of the United Nations Convention on the Law of the Sea,[18] which has been in force since 1994, constitute the standard in the field of marine habitat and resource protection. These provisions presuppose the adoption of new integrated management strategies for policies and decision-making processes that include all Parties involved in order to promote compatibility and balance between different users (*Agenda 21,* 17.1 and 17.5). These new integrated management approaches are supposed to apply precautionary and preventive principles to planning activities, take the interests of small-scale artisanal fisheries and indigenous peoples into account, and allow concerned individuals, groups, or organizations to gain access to information, to be consulted, and to participate in planning and decision-making at the appropriate levels (*Agenda 21,* 17.5 and 17.74).

The integrated management of marine areas was the first component of the Convention on Biological Diversity work programme on marine and coastal biodiversity adopted in 1995.[19] This programme uses the ecosystem approach for the analysis of matters relating to the conservation and sustainable use of marine biological diversity and for the sustainable management of marine areas. The ecosystem approach is defined as follows:

> The ecosystem approach is a strategy for the integrated management of land, water and living resources that promotes conservation and sustainable use in an equitable way... An ecosystem approach is based on the application of appropriate scientific methodologies focused on levels of biological organization which encompass the essential processes, functions and interactions among organisms and their environment. It recognizes that humans, with their cultural diversity, are an integral component of ecosystems.[20]

The ecosystem approach takes the different relationships existing between organisms and their habitats, including human activities, into consideration and is based on a natural space rather than on a jurisdictional space or on property (see Figure 12.1). Many people feel that it would help overcome the fragmentary management in practice up to now.[21] It should be pointed out that it does not replace earlier governance approaches based on controlling polluting activities and protecting specific species or habitats: it attempts to integrate them so that interactions between these different systems can be considered.

To sum up, the Rio commitments, unlike the fragmentary initiatives during the the first wave of international interventions, are based on generic, integrated, and holistic objectives, principles, and approaches for conserving and protecting marine biodiversity. The substance of the instruments has changed: there is no longer any question of naming endangered species or habitats or controlling specific activities. Instead, the idea now is to prompt or co-ordinate action plans on which states will base their own policies. Finally, to return to the original question, integrated management or ecosystem approaches for sustainable development are proposed as an essential ingredient for solving environmental and biodiversity problems, which the fragmentary approaches have been hitherto unable to solve. As we will see, the Rio commitments, and particularly those made in connection with the CBD, are very definitely gaining ground in Canadian policy.

Renewal of Canadian Policy and the Protection of Marine Biodiversity

Canada participated actively in the United Nations Conference on Environment and Development in Rio, and it supported the declarations and conventions presented, the various principles introduced, and the sustainable development objective. It is within this general context that the federal and provincial governments of Canada have undertaken to renew their environmental policies and translate their commitments into concrete actions and decisions.

This second wave of environmental policy has brought important changes. Even though it is still too early for an outcome assessment, current changes in Canadian policy are already clarifying intentions and the kinds of initiatives to be

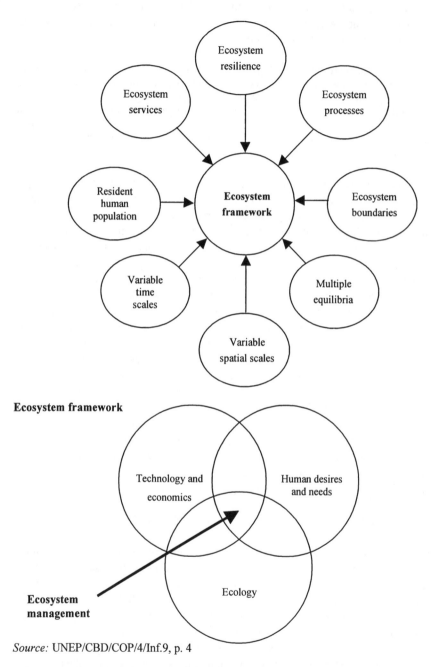

Ecosystem framework

Source: UNEP/CBD/COP/4/Inf.9, p. 4

Figure 12.1 The Ecosystem Approach

taken with respect to sustainable development and the biodiversity sector. Clearly, there is a desire to change the fragmentary approach and to pay more attention to the marine environment.

One of the important initiatives for integrating sustainable development into federal policy was the creation in 1995 of the position of Commissioner of the Environment and Sustainable Development. The commissioner is charged with the task of supervising progress in this field and must report annually to Canada's Parliament.[22] Twenty-eight federal departments and agencies are required to draft a sustainable development strategy, update it every three years, and annually report their progress to Parliament. In 1998 the commissioner examined the first batch of sustainable development strategies submitted by federal authorities and noted two significant weaknesses, the second of which is especially relevant for our purposes:

> Many strategies appear to represent less a commitment to change in order to promote sustainable development than a restatement of the status quo. Those strategies tend to focus more on past accomplishments than future directions. Less than one half identify specific policy, programme, legislative, regulatory or operational changes that would be made to implement the strategy.[23]

It should also be pointed out that this federal initiative is based on a decentralized approach to sustainable development in that each department has to account for itself without being subject to a common national framework or national priorities. In this regard, the commissioner indicated in his reports that since some of the most urgent problems concern more than one department, effective co-ordination is an essential condition for achieving sustainable development goals (Commissioner, 1999, par. 50).

Also of note is a remarkable increase in Canadian federal and provincial government references to the concept of sustainable development and its underlying principles, such as "biological diversity". Recent parliamentary and administrative activities bear eloquent witness to this trend. For example, since the Earth Summit, the expression "sustainable development" has been incorporated into 13 different federal statutes and the terms "precaution," "biological diversity," and "ecosystem" have been included in the main federal environmental laws.[24] It still remains to be seen, however, to what extent these principles, which mostly appear in the preambles and introductory provisions of laws, will bind and influence the actions and decisions of public authorities. The ecosystem approach has also appeared on the national stage. It was proposed in 1996 by the Canadian Council of Ministers of the Environment (CCME) to encourage harmonization, co-operation, and co-ordination between federal and provincial governments (CCME, 1992). This approach is conceived in terms similar to its international representation (see Figure 12.2).

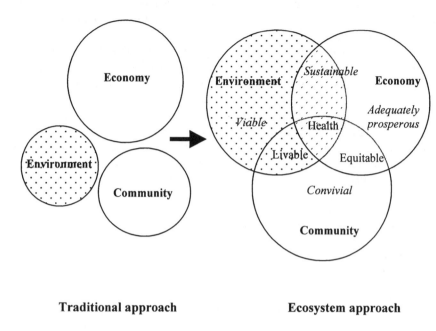

Traditional approach   **Ecosystem approach**

Source: Canadian Council of Ministers of the Environment, 1996, p. 3.

Figure 12.2 The shift from Traditional to Ecosystem-Based Decision-Making

With respect to biodiversity, Canada's public authorities clearly demonstrated their commitment to the Convention on Biological Diversity during and immediately following the negotiations. Beyond that, Canada has developed the strategies, national reports, and inventories called for by the provisions of the Convention and the decisions of the conference of signatory Parties.[25] Concerns connected with biodiversity have therefore begun to make their way into Canada's national institutions.

Canada's chief initiative in response to the Convention has been the development of the *Canadian Biodiversity Strategy*. This strategy introduced the innovative ideas from Rio into the national arena and, in particular, revised objectives geared toward the conservation of biodiversity and sustainable use of biological resources, the improvement of knowledge and of ecosystem and resource management approaches, and the introduction of incentives and legislative measures promoting the twin goals of conservation and sustainable use (Canada, 1995, pp. 3-4).[26] It also reiterated the importance of legal instruments for the implementation of Canada's new biodiversity protection policies. The national strategy pointed out, however, that past experience suggests that new legal instruments should be introduced and certain existing instruments changed. There was clearly a desire to change the fragmentary approach adopted up to that point:

Such changes require a greater harmonization of efforts among governments and non-government agencies, as well as more integrated resource management approaches that integrate biodiversity conservation and sustainable use of biological resources with economic, social and cultural objectives. (Canada, 1995, p. 11)

With regard to marine biodiversity, the federal government noted that it had not paid much attention to protecting the marine environment in the past. It stated in the *Canadian Biodiversity Strategy* that from now on it should "make every effort to...accelerate the protection of areas that are representative of marine natural regions" (Canada, 1995, p. 24). The federal government decided to centre its marine biodiversity intervention on the conservation and protection of special areas.

Since the early 1990s, Canada's public authorities have been changing the way they manage the conservation and sustainable use of biodiversity. Although these reforms are not yet completed, they have already laid the groundwork for the new federal strategy. When we look at government actions from the marine biodiversity angle, two trends appear to stand out: reinforcement of the existing normative framework in order to make pollution prevention and resource protection instruments more effective and use of a new normative framework for marine biodiversity.

Reinforcement of existing environmental legislation   After Rio, Canada's Parliament began reinforcing some of the existing legal instruments to make them more effective and adapt them to the new sustainable development objective. Many of these initiatives concerned marine biodiversity.[27]

The *Canadian Environmental Protection Act* (CEPA) is the central component of the federal strategy for promoting sustainable development and addressing its commitments under the Convention on Biological Diversity.[28] It was completely revised in 1999, and the concept of "sustainable development" and the guiding principles of "prevention," the "ecosystem approach," "biodiversity," and "precaution," as well as the wide range of new approaches to regulating polluting activities, were incorporated into the new CEPA.

Marine biodiversity was particularly affected by the revision because special attention was paid to protecting oceans. For example, CEPA now provides for the establishment of objectives, guidelines, and codes of practice for preventing marine pollution from land-based sources (s.120) as well as measures for fighting international water pollution (s.175). Provisions regulating the dumping of waste at sea were also amended to take changes made to the international instrument into account (s.122). The most innovative aspect of these provisions is the introduction of the precautionary principle as the basis for the new system. The premises governing regulation of this activity have been overturned. For instance, dumping waste at sea used to be authorized unless the waste in question was included on a list of exceptions, whereas dumping is now prohibited unless the waste is included on an exclusive list of substances that can be dumped – provided that the permit applicant can show that dumping the waste at sea is the most environmentally sound option (Schedules V and VI).

Most of the systems for controlling land-based sources of pollution contained in the new CEPA and other legal instruments that were recently amended have an effect on marine biodiversity even if they do not target ocean protection directly, because these polluting emissions can penetrate the marine environment, alter marine habitat, and damage biological components.

On the whole, this second wave of public policy development remains vaguely defined. Changes were not just limited to a list of new concerns included in the agenda of Canada's public authorities – it is a lot more complex than that. We are also seeing the introduction of new approaches to regulating polluting activities. What these approaches have in common is that they represent departures from the traditional model in which the state adopts statutes and regulations in order to prescribe conduct, supervise its enforcement, and punish offenders. The reforms introduce new ways of developing and applying standards and are notable for the variety of forms adopted: greater participation by the public and citizens; more flexible standards; individualized standards; a predilection for self-regulation; generalization of self-control; etc.[29] Three examples help illustrate these forms.

Greater participation by the public   In accordance with its international commitments (Rio, Principle 10), the federal government reinforced CEPA so as to promote greater participation by the public in environmental decision-making (Canada, 1995, ch.3). Supplementary rights relating to access to information, consultation, participation, and instituting suits were introduced in the act: public register; application for investigation of presumed offences; environmental protection actions; non-divulging of the identity of informers; national pollutant release inventory, notice of opposition contesting a draft regulation, formation of a review committee; etc. The old version of CEPA already granted many of these rights, but they were more limited in scope and they were not exercised very efficiently.[30] For instance, the Minister of the Environment received notices of opposition to draft regulations under the former act but had never exercised the power to follow up on them by forming a review committee. Parliament was sensitive to this problem, and the act was amended so that the filing of a notice of opposition by an individual would automatically lead to the formation of a review committee in the case of certain draft regulations (s.333 (3), (4), and (6)).

New ways of developing standards   The federal government also stressed its intention that voluntary approaches should play an important role in its administration of the new CEPA. These approaches come under self-regulation practices, and standards developed by citizens are considered voluntary or non-regulatory because they intervene peripherally with government control and the restrictive framework of the act. These measures come in different forms: codes of practice; agreements; draft agreements; guidelines; letters of intent; etc. The federal government has pointed out that these initiatives can represent an alternative to regulatory standards or inspire their content: "More importantly, the results of these initiatives [of current non-regulatory initiatives] can help focus the government's regulatory regime. Used effectively, non-regulatory action can be used to determine if, when and to what degree regulations are required" (Canada, 1995, p. 21).

New ways of implementing the act   Mechanisms authorizing flexible and individualized treatment of businesses were also incorporated into the new CEPA. These mechanisms authorize the government to exempt citizens from the obligation to comply with the norm set out in the act or in a regulation. For example, the system referred to as "environmental protection alternative measures" (s.295) authorizes any business that does not observe the terms of the act to negotiate an agreement with the government with respect to the steps it will take to comply with it, in exchange for which the government agrees to suspend the effect of the act for as long as the business continues to abide by the terms of their agreement. The purpose is to help and encourage businesses acting in good faith to comply rapidly with the act without recourse to lawsuits. This is not a new practice, and it tends to be a general approach in Canadian environmental law. Sensitive to concerns about preferential treatment and betrayal of the environmental objectives of the act, Canada's Parliament formalized this practice in order to reduce the discretionary leeway enjoyed by public administrators and address criticism (Halley, 1998).

There are also provisions authorizing public administrators to exempt a business from the obligation to adhere to standards set out in the act or in regulations dealing with implementation of the act. An exemption may be granted in exchange for applying an individualized standard to the specific situation of a citizen, which acts as an alternative to the standard contained in the act. Thus, CEPA provides that in the case of the control of hazardous waste movement, the Minister of the Environment may issue "permits based on equivalent environmental safety level" for activities that do not comply with the provisions of the act (s.190).

There is no lack of new instruments, but are they really effective? It is important to pause and let this new information settle before answering this question. I will come back to it in the last part of this chapter. One fears, however, that studying the profusion of new instruments and systems may be a waste of time because their newness may conceal the fact that they merely represent an improvement on the first generation of public policy.

New normative framework for marine biodiversity   Noting the lack of attention paid to marine resources and habitat up to then, federal authorities decided to set up systems designed to promote the conservation and sustainable use of marine diversity in a special way. Thus, with the renewal of federal policy, we now have a brand-new normative framework for protecting the marine environment and its resources.[31]

Most of the developments are concerned with habitat protection. The most important initiative was the coming into force of the *Oceans Act* in 1997, the first Canadian statute focusing on protection of the marine environment. With its integrated management instruments, it also introduced the most innovative aspects of the new federal strategy in the field of biodiversity protection.

Right at the beginning, in its preamble, the *Oceans Act* stresses that "conservation, based on an ecosystem approach, is of fundamental importance to maintaining biological diversity and productivity in the marine environment" and "promotes the integrated management of oceans and marine resources". Part II of the act, which is devoted to oceans management strategy, introduces two integrated management instruments: a national strategy for the management of estuarine, coastal, and marine ecosystems (s.29) and plans for the integrated management of all activities in or affecting these ecosystems (s.31). The act provides for the Minister of Fisheries and Oceans to lead and facilitate development and implementation of the national strategy in collaboration with "other ministers, boards and agencies of the Government of Canada, with provincial and territorial governments and with affected aboriginal organizations, coastal communities and other persons and bodies" (s.29). The act briefly provides for the national strategy development process, merely stating that it must be based on principles of sustainable development, integrated management of activities, and prevention (s.30).

With regard to development and implementation of the plans for integrated management of all activities affecting the ecosystems, the act repeats the same list of Parties with whom the Minister of Fisheries and Oceans has to collaborate (s.31). It also points out that these interested Parties may co-operate on the establishment of marine environmental quality guidelines, objectives, and criteria (s.32 (d)) and the creation of a national system of marine protected areas (s.35 (2)). It has now been almost five years since the *Oceans Act* came into force, but a national strategy still remains to be adopted and consultations are still underway.

In practice, it is difficult to find one's way around. Surprisingly, the expression "integrated management" was not defined. Because of the polysemous nature of this concept, it is impossible to precisely pinpoint the conditions for its exercise and the limits assigned to it. Although the preamble suggests that integrated management of activities be based on the ecosystem, it might be limited to activities of the same nature without reference to any specific ecosystem. By the same token, the cursory provision for the consultation of third parties during development of the national strategy and integrated management plans undermines the new act's effectiveness: the act fails to specify how Parties are to be consulted, does not provide a consultation time frame, does not say how these consultations are to be reported, and fails to provide for how the strategy or management plans can be changed or revised once they have been developed. One might reasonably ask how these new instruments can be expected to improve protection of the marine environment and its resources.

A priori, the purview of the act leads us to believe that the national strategy should guide all ocean management initiatives and consequently that its development should precede the development of management plans, marine environment quality guidelines, and marine protected areas. In practice, this is not the case. The Department of Fisheries and Oceans appears to be doing things backwards – opting to develop specific programmes before it develops the general orientation programme. Here are a few examples.

The department's web site lists a number of current integrated management initiatives as well as quality standards developed for certain marine environments.[32] Undertaken peripherally to the development of a national strategy and planning geared to ecosystems, these may not be good examples in that they reflect the department's earlier practices of ad hoc collaboration on projects based on the voluntary participation of people from the community.

The process of creating marine protected areas has been more systematic, but it is also peripheral to the national strategy. The Minister of Fisheries and Oceans is overseeing and co-ordinating development and implementation of the national system of marine protected areas in internal waters, the territorial sea (12 nautical miles) and the exclusive economic zone (200 nautical miles). These areas are created to provide special protection for fishery resources, endangered or threatened species, their habitats, and habitats that are unique or high in biodiversity (s.35). To promote the collaboration of interested Parties, the Department of Fisheries and Oceans in January 1997 submitted a discussion paper to public scrutiny for a 90-day period and directed Canada-wide information and discussion sessions on this document (Fisheries and Oceans Canada, 1997a). The comments received were taken into consideration when a national programme for marine protected areas was developed. So far, nine areas have been designated as "areas of interest". In keeping with the national framework developed for establishing marine protected areas, they are now subject to an assessment and a positive recommendation by the minister before the government can give them protected area status (Fisheries and Oceans Canada, 1999).

Although the most important one, the adoption of the *Oceans Act* was not the only federal initiative geared toward protecting the marine environment. In 1994 the *Canada Wildlife Act* was amended to allow specifically for the creation of marine wildlife areas.[33] This act already provided that national wildlife areas could be established in territorial waters. Since 1998, the federal government has also been trying to develop another system of marine parks in Canada. Bill C-10 entitled *An Act Respecting the National Marine Conservation Areas of Canada*[34] authorizes the Minister of Canadian Heritage to create a system of marine conservation areas that will be the equivalent of the national land. parks system. Once it is completed, this system will represent Canada's 29 marine regions in the coastal waters of the Atlantic, Arctic and Pacific oceans and in the Great Lakes.

The four marine conservation areas already created or in the negotiation process will be the first to be created and protected under this act.[35]

This overview of federal initiatives in the field of marine environmental protection illustrates that when they decide to intervene, Canada's public authorities still tend to increase specific systems or instruments and their management of environmental problems still tends to be fragmentary. There have been changes, however. To guard against the disadvantages of this scattering or fragmentation of instruments and authorities, the Minister of Fisheries and Oceans is authorized to co-ordinate certain activities of the Department of the Environment and the Department of Canadian Heritage (Fisheries and Oceans Canada, 1998b). The minister invokes these responsibilities in keeping with the *Oceans Act* terms providing for integrated management of marine protected areas. It remains to be seen whether the integrated management approach will be reduced to the integrated management of federal activities of the same nature or whether it will apply more broadly to the integration of all activities having an impact on a given marine ecosystem.

Recent legislative initiatives also illustrate changes in Canada's environmental policy with regard to protection of marine species. Better integration of environmental issues is being supported. In 1993, for example, the federal government consolidated in one regulation on marine mammals all of the legal instruments developed over the years for protecting belugas, cetaceans, narwhals, seals, and walruses.[36] Federal authorities are also using the Convention on Biological Diversity to support their conservation strategy and adoption of a federal statute on species at risk.[37] If it is passed, this law will not apply to all endangered species all over Canada – only to those species on federal lands or coming under federal jurisdiction according to the current distribution of powers within the Canadian federation. This restriction does not really affect this discussion, though, because the federal government has exclusive jurisdiction to legislate on all marine species. The bill has received a great deal of criticism. For example, ecologists criticize it for not protecting the habitats of species at risk, only their "residences," i.e. their "specific dwelling-place": "den, nest or other similar area, place or structure". They also say that subjecting the endangered species listing process to decisions of the Cabinet runs the risk of introducing political considerations into an exercise that should be purely scientific.[38]

Finally, just as it has internationally, the collapse of fish stocks has prompted numerous initiatives nationally. For example, in accordance with the *Code of Conduct for Responsible Fisheries* developed by the Food and Agriculture Organization of the United Nations (FAO), Canada's fisheries industry has given itself the *Canadian Code of Conduct for Responsible Fishing Operations*.[39] In 1999 the Department of Fisheries and Oceans began reviewing its overall policy dealing with the orientation and objectives of the Atlantic fisheries (Fisheries and Oceans Canada, 2000). This policy review is a vast public undertaking in two stages. The first aims at defining the broad orientations and strategic objectives of federal fisheries policy. The second is devoted to the development of instruments and a management framework for Canadian fisheries.

On Changes in the Normative Framework for Marine Biodiversity Protection

As shown above, the first generation of public policy developed around a series of manifest and often alarming environmental problems. The second generation of policy is geared toward chronic environmental problems stemming from pressures exerted on the environment by human activities. In addressing these problems, the international community and Canada's public authorities have been compelled to call into question the social and economic developments that have given rise to these problems and the means used until now to protect the environment and biodiversity.

Canada's policy renewal is well underway, and it has already led to significant changes. The accumulation of new initiatives and intervention systems is noticeable, but the environmental benefits are not always appreciable. In what way does the new policy help promote sustainable development and biodiversity protection? Does it offer management approaches that are more proactive than reactive and allow integration of all the decisions likely to have an impact on a given ecosystem? In fact, the pursuit of sustainable development and the conservation and sustainable use of biodiversity demand that we address problems that the new Canadian policy may not be entirely capable of resolving.

Current Development of Canadian Marine Biodiversity Policy

How can economic and social development be made compatible with the conservation of biological diversity and protection of the marine environment? This challenge is both political and methodological. It calls for a development plan that is more than a mere pile of sectoral policies: a plan that co-ordinates policies and articulates targeted sustainable development objectives. This represents a daunting challenge for Canada's public administrators because it means that they have to break with a development vision and practices that are deeply rooted. A few strengths do stand out, however. Canada now has a number of special objectives fostering marine biodiversity protection, which concern endangered species, habitat protection, responsible fishing practices, etc. Yet this new policy is not always guided by an overall plan or vision, and it does not offer many ways of reinforcing institutional integration.

Lack of an overall plan for co-ordinating federal initiatives   Canada's main response to the Convention on Biological Diversity consisted of its development of the *Canadian Biodiversity Strategy*. This was the first step that Canada took toward establishing a framework plan for biodiversity. The federal government has failed so far, however, to devise an overall plan for putting its biodiversity commitments into effect.

The commitments set out in the *Canadian Biodiversity Strategy* are very general, and very little attention is paid to marine biodiversity. The strategy does not propose many concrete measures for co-ordinating and articulating federal government initiatives directed toward the conservation and sustainable use of biodiversity.

In *Caring for Canada's Biodiversity: Canada's First National Report to the Conference of the Parties to the Convention on Biological Diversity*, submitted in 1997, the Biodiversity Convention Office outlines the federal government's progress on the implementation of the CBD (Canada, 1997)[40] as well as its shortcomings. It points out that the federal government's action plan will be based on eight sectoral reports describing plans and interventions in the sectors of wildlife diversity, protected areas, agriculture, forestry, aquatic diversity, ecological management, education, and international co-operation. (*Report*, 1997, p. 11). Of the shortcomings noted, the Office points out that one of the biggest challenges Canada faces is the rudimentary nature of its biological inventories and scientific knowledge on its biodiversity, as well as the decrease in the number of taxonomists in Canada. The report does not have a lot to say about its plans for integrating biodiversity considerations into decision-making – only that the problem is finding the resources "to continue to develop and improve these models [of integration] at the local level, as significant investments of human and financial resources are required" (*Report*, 1997, p. 22).

In 1998 and 2000, the Commissioner of the Environment and Sustainable Development also evaluated the federal government's progress in implementing its commitments under the Convention on Biological Diversity. In 1998 the commissioner noted that progress was slower than anticipated and that deadlines had not been met. For example, the eight sectoral action plans were supposed to have been completed by April 1997, but only two of them had been at the time of the commissioner's report. The commissioner concluded that the federal government would need to elaborate an overall implementation plan if it were to achieve its biodiversity goals. According to the commissioner, the eight sectoral action plans would not form an adequate overall plan if they continued to fail to specify time limits, anticipated outcomes, resources required, and performance indicators.[41] The commissioner also pointed out that for biodiversity to be managed properly, it is important for the resources assigned to biodiversity and federal-provincial co-ordination to be sufficient and for the government to be more scrupulous about measuring and communicating results.

The commissioner's audit for 2000 noted that three sectoral action plans were still missing, including the one for the aquatic diversity sector, and that the federal government still had not come up with an overall biodiversity plan. The commissioner again stressed the absence of federal-provincial co-operation on biodiversity and repeated that lack of resources remained a major problem, particularly when it came to maintaining the federal government's scientific capability.[42]

Finally, it should be pointed out that the 28 federal departments and agencies responsible for preparing and implementing a sustainable development strategy have to incorporate the conservation and sustainable use of biodiversity in this strategy and report on it annually. So far, federal authorities have been getting poor marks for their accomplishments in terms of sustainable development. The various reports of the Commissioner of the Environment and Sustainable Development emphasize the gap between the actual achievements of government departments and the commitments stated in their sustainable development strategy. The 1998 report estimated that federal authorities had only realized 11 per cent of the commitments described in their strategy and the 2000 report that they had accomplished about 20 per cent of them.

Institutional integration remains a laborious exercise Improving the performance of public policy on sustainable development and biodiversity is not only a question of better co-ordination of environmental policy but also better intergovernmental and interdepartmental articulation of environmental concerns when decisions are made. Integration of environmental concerns into economic and social decisions is an essential condition for improving public policy.

Within the Canadian federation, the concept of biodiversity transcends the division of powers between the federal, the ten provincial, and the two territorial governments and the organization of each of these governments. The sharing of legislative jurisdictions for environmental and biodiversity matters is especially complicated. These terms did not exist in 1867 at the time of the creation of the Canadian confederation, but the subjects are covered within a medley of matters assigned at the time to the different levels of government, such as navigation, fisheries, Indian reservations, and land and forestry resources. Marine biodiversity falls to the federal government, which was given jurisdiction over the sea coast and inland fisheries, navigation, international and interprovincial treaties on trade and commerce, quarantines, etc.

Canada's various levels of government need to co-operate so that biodiversity issues can be taken into account in a coherent manner everywhere in Canada. In a general way, intergovernmental co-ordination is making progress in Canada. Co-ordination agencies have been created, such as the Canadian Council of Ministers of the Environment, and working groups have led to harmonization and co-operation agreements. For instance, the signing in January 1998 of the first *Canada-wide Accord of Environmental Harmonization*, plus three sub-agreements on environmental assessment, standards, and inspections and enforcement are important new initiatives (CCME, 1998). Intergovernmental co-ordination efforts in the field of biodiversity leave much to be desired, however. Since the *Canadian*

Biodiversity Strategy was made public in 1996, departmental participation in working group meetings on biodiversity has continued to be very poor: often, only the federal government and one or two provinces are represented.[43] Additional efforts are needed to promote truly integrated initiatives on the part of the various authorities responsible for biodiversity.

Institutional integration also involves co-operation among federal departments and agencies. The existence of so many federal programmes, often designed from a specific perspective, makes co-ordination of federal authorities difficult but necessary. For example, the Department of Fisheries and Oceans counted 23 federal departments and agencies active in the oceans sector in 1997 (Fisheries and Oceans Canada, 1997b). Under the *Oceans Act*, the Department of Fisheries and Oceans is to ensure co-ordination in this sector for the purpose of developing a national oceans strategy.

Considering how split and fragmentary oceans management is, one would expect the federal government to make a real effort to concentrate its interventions in the hands of fewer authorities. This has not turned out to be the case, however. Federal authorities still prefer to divide these interventions up and scatter the activities among different agencies. The only difference now is that a special authority has the power to co-ordinate federal interventions in a given sector. The protection of marine areas is a good example of this. Federal authorities recently invested a great deal of effort in a legislative framework specifically for protecting marine ecosystems. The structure of this new normative framework is notable for its framentary nature and variety of actors. We saw earlier that with the amendments made to the *Canada Wildlife Act* (1994), the adoption of the *Oceans Act* (1996), and the tabling of *Bill C-10: An Act Respecting the National Marine Conservation Areas of Canada* (2001), the departments of the Environment, Fisheries and Oceans, and Canadian Heritage became responsible for protected marine areas, marine protected areas and marine conservation areas respectively. The *Oceans Act* conferred on the Minister of Fisheries and Oceans the power to co-ordinate federal government interventions in any matter relating to protection of marine areas. But will this piecemeal approach be effective? It would appear that the criticism made of the system ten years ago is still pertinent today. Evidently, additional efforts will be needed if federal authorities are to leave their former fragmentary approach behind and adopt more integrated intervention vis-à-vis the more global environmental objects and problems.

Implementation Measures Adopted

Although the second wave of public policy reform is not yet over, it has prompted numerous initiatives. Because of the inadequacy of the methods used in the past, Canada's public authorities have introduced new systems, and new forms of regulation in particular, that complement or replace the normative instruments already in place. What with all these new solutions, one might be tempted to believe in the many attempts to reinvent public intervention with a view to promoting a development that is sustainable. It is important, however, not to confuse the proliferation of new forms of regulation with the goal of sustainable development. For public administrators, the goal is double-edged: they must continue to thwart the specific negative effects of human activities on biodiversity while making progress towards prevention by acting on the underlying causes of problems, such as overexploitation of resources, urban sprawl, consumption, and use of toxic substances. To take up this challenge, interventions need to be measured carefully so that the more difficult of the two goals – changing paradigms – can be rapidly addressed.

Paradoxes of new forms of governance Sustainable development and biodiversity protection are not the only objectives guiding the renewal of Canada's environmental policy. Administrative documentation accompanying these reforms points out that the strategies adopted are also inspired by a search for effective, economical solutions for public administrators and citizens.[44] This concern is very commendable, but is likely to compromise the achievement of environmental goals if given precedence. Market globalization and neoliberal arguments also fuel a "deregulation" movement, which tends to shift regulatory powers to private authorities. Two examples illustrate this point.

First, there is the growing tendency to delegate certain standard development and implementation tasks, which traditionally fell to the executive branch of government, to third parties – usually the citizens themselves: self-regulation, regulation whereby standards are developed by non-government organizations, self-control of compliance with laws, etc. For the state, the goal is basically economic: reducing expenses by delegating the performance of certain tasks to citizens.[45]

The economic goal leaves much to be desired in that the federal government is not withdrawing from the sector, only changing the tasks to be done. The government must now supervise citizens at another level – studying proposed standards and checking declarations of conformity. It is undesirable, however, to leave citizens to their own devices when it comes to proposing standards or submitting information on the extent of their compliance with statutes because it places them in a conflict between their private interests and their public responsibility. The public administration bias in favour of business expertise is also worrying because it tends to eliminate ordinary citizens from the debate on environmental standards and betrays the principle of treating citizens as equals.

Another example is the development of administrative practices that would apply environmental standards with greater flexibility. These practices come in different shapes and sizes: voluntary measures, negotiation of alternative measures instead of taking offenders through the courts, exemption from and substitution of standards, etc. It is argued that flexibility will improve the instruments' effectiveness because it promotes continual harmonious co-operation between public administrators and citizens and also encourages technological innovation.

According to this reasoning, technological innovation is an important goal, and environmental protection represents a new and lucrative global market for Canadian business. In its administrative documentation, the Department of the Environment says that "intelligent regulation" of the environment can promote technological innovation by recognizing that "much of pollution can be a flaw in the production process and that environmental improvements can enhance competitiveness" (Canada, 1995, p. 5).

If these practices are not subject to any other transparency or accounting obligations, there is a risk of preferential treatment and misappropriation of the administrative process by the most powerful economic players. Besides, it is clear that these practices do not suggest any new strategies likely to reduce or indeed eliminate non-viable means of production. In fact, delegating certain tasks from the executive to business and increasing flexibility when applying standards is aimed at improving the effectiveness of former practices, whereby specific solutions were found for specific problems, and tends to accentuate the fragmentary nature of environmental management. Finally, there is a risk that the anti-pollution industry will design technology for unsustainable means of production, which should instead be replaced and even abandoned. In a more general way, there is also a risk that public authorities might become caught up with the development of these practices and neglect the development of practices that would be more likely to resolve the chronic problems that affect the environment (Atcheson, 1996).

Challenges of the ecosystem approach: new forms of solidarity Of the new forms of governance introduced in the second generation of federal environmental policy, integrated management of marine ecosystems represents the most audacious initiative and the one most likely to resolve the difficulties that reactive and fragmentary management cannot. This approach, which situates the decision-making process within the broad context of the ecosystem, has been adopted and promoted by the Conference of the Parties of the Convention on Biological Diversity as the basic principle of the Jakarta Mandate, as well as by a variety of international and national agencies.[46]

The new *Oceans Act* introduces this approach for federal management of the marine environment (s.29, 30, and 31). Application of an integrated ecosystem-based approach represents a major change of course for federal public authorities. The exercise appears to be difficult for the Department of Fisheries and Oceans in practical terms, however. Although this department and other federal departments lay claim to several integrated ecosystem management initiatives,[47] the concepts of "integrated management" and "ecosystem approach" remain vague and there is a certain amount of hesitation as to what these terms really mean. So far, the Department of Fisheries and Oceans appears to be doing things on a case-by-case basis as before, with its interventions being geared toward specific clean-up or restoration projects.

In Canada, a great deal remains to be done for this approach to become a reality in the oceans sector. I will be showing how difficulties arise when authorities attempt to apply the integrated ecosystem management approach outside the contexts of clean-up or restoration operations and voluntary initiatives. This approach tests the ability of public authorities to collaborate with each other effectively and get the various societal stakeholders to truly participate.

First, there is no one model for integrated management of marine ecosystems. Integrated management is more of an analytical and management process, and examples vary from one case to the next. This process includes several essential steps, or functions, from scientific observation to decision-making.

In an article on the governance of large marine ecosystems, Judas (1999, pp. 92-98) says that there are seven functions necessary for the implementation of an integrated management process for these ecosystems: i) determination of the ecosystem's boundaries; ii) identification of the ecosystem's resources and biological phenomena; iii) identification of human uses of the ecosystem and interactions between these uses and with the ecosystem; iv) establishment of objectives, goals, and priorities for marine resources and habitat, taking scientific and socio-economic data into consideration; v) regulation of activities that damage the ecosystem to make them compatible with objectives and priorities; vi) development of guidelines for the organizations actively involved in the achievement of objectives and priorities; vii) supervision of management activities so that ecosystem governance is constantly altered and improved.

The first step in this management, or governance, process is the geographical designation of the marine ecosystem that will become the central component in the process and its independent variable. This is a scientific exercise aimed at bringing together within the same framework the human activities and biological factors that interfere significantly with a marine environment. For example, coastal ecosystems are generally considered to include inland waters and coastal lands (OECD, 1993; *Agenda 21*, ch.17, par. 17.29).

Considering the absence of any correspondence between the geography of natural ecosystems and the geography of international and national political systems, the first function in the process is also the biggest challenge with this management approach. A marine ecosystem can concern more than one country, more than one level of government in each country, and many public or parapublic agencies or organizations with powers over the ecosystem or obligations. This is the case, for example, with the Great Lakes and the St. Lawrence River, which are bordered by the United States and Canada and by several American states and Canadian provinces.

The mismatching of marine ecosystems and national jurisdictions causes implementation problems. To eliminate them completely, one public authority would have to be able to control the entire marine ecosystem as the owner of all the seabeds and holder of all prerogatives on them. This solution is unreasonable in terms of costs and not very realistic in terms of sovereignty (Judas, 1999). The ecosystem-based approach to management offers an interesting alternative for countries and governments that share the use of the same marine environments because it integrates an ecosystem's international, regional, national, and subnational political dimensions. It offers several options, such as creation of a supranational authority, national authorities with total jurisdiction over oceans, or more modest sectoral proposals, such as that set out in the *Oceans Act*.

The integrated management proposed by the *Oceans Act* is sectoral in that the marine ecosystems affected by the act exclude inland waters and coastal lands (s.28). The act also has modest designs with respect to integration of policies, activities, and users into decision-making processes. Its integration tool is interdepartmental and intergovernmental collaboration with "affected aboriginal organizations, coastal communities and other persons and bodies, including those bodies established under land claims agreements" (s.29 and 31). The fact that they are consulted before any action is taken makes it possible to integrate social, economic, and scientific considerations that are outside the expertise of the Department of Fisheries and Oceans and to induce reflection on the direct and indirect effects of the different sectoral systems administered by the other oceans stakeholders. This type of integrated approach can be an intermediate step before more integrated management approaches are used.

Second, when it comes to implementing the ecosystem approach, public administrators face another challenge: participation of the ecosystem's users and other societal stakeholders.

In keeping with the essential components of integrated ecosystem management, the users of the ecosystem are likely to participate in two steps of the process. First, their help would appear to be needed for identifying and documenting the pressures exerted by human activities on the ecosystem (function 3). This amounts to specifying who does what (fishing, sailing, whale watching, drilling, etc.), how activities are carried out (hand-lines, nets, trawling, explosives, etc.), where exactly and why (subsistance, ancestral tradition, recreation, business, etc.). Users may also take part in the next step of the process by helping to develop management goals, objectives, and priorities for the ecosystem (function 4) – a step in which the process becomes decisional.

The integrated ecosystem management approach adopted by the *Oceans Act* is not really aimed directly at decision-making but rather at the development of a national policy and regional guidelines and programmes to orient federal initiatives and at the development of rules and regulations applicable to marine ecosystems. Also, the *Oceans Act* does not aim particularly at consulting users of marine ecosystems when policy and programmes are being developed. It targets certain categories of users, such as aboriginal organizations, coastal communities and the catch-all category of "affected...persons". At any rate, the participation of the ecosystem's users in the development of policy and programmes remains highly likely since this approach dictates that they participate in the previous step in the process, which focuses on documenting human pressures on the ecosystem.

When faced with the question of the participation of users and other societal actors, the *Oceans Act* commits sins of omission. It is stingy with details on the procedure for the participation of public authorities and other interested persons and contents itself with stating that the Department of Fisheries and Oceans must collaborate with them with a view to developing a national strategy and management programmes. *A priori*, this weakens the effectiveness of the process. It has been almost five years since the act came into force, and a national strategy has still not been developed. What is more, the absence of rules for ensuring transparency and accountability can also affect the credibility of the process, because there is good reason to fear that the people with the most resources will participate more actively in the process and be in a better position to influence its outcome. In practical terms, if the process does not ensure real and appropriate representation of users and other interested persons, this type of process runs the risk of increasing and perpetuating the influence of economic lobbies that have the most to lose from the implementation of the new forms of marine resource and environment governance.

The *Oceans Act* also fails to include people who do not have a specific interest in or are not users of the ecosystem in the collaboration exercise. This omission should be remedied if public participation and consultation are to be the prelude to the development of national and regional priorities, objectives, and goals with respect to marine resource and environment management. If not, the process will lack legitimacy. Indeed, users cannot legitimately represent the public interest because they are in a conflict of interest between their interests as users and the public interest linked to the preservation of marine biodiversity.

A final example supports theoretical reflection. On 11 March 1999, Parks Canada abandoned a marine conservation area project because a majority of the representatives of the coastal community involved opposed it. A committee had been formed, made up of professional fishers, representatives of the aquaculture and fish-processing sectors, members of economic development agencies, and residents of the community, to study the feasibility of creating the marine conservation area. They voted 12 to four to reject the project for economic reasons related to use of the area by members of the committee and community. From the viewpoint of industry representatives, the project threatened the survival of their industry; from the viewpoint of the union representative for fishing industry workers, the project could lower the standard of living of community members; and in the view of others, the creation of a marine conservation area would give rise to a new form of bureaucracy and, worse, support the cause of animal rights activists, who would attempt to limit fishing, seal hunting, and aquaculture, scaring investors away and wiping out jobs in the region.[48]

Conclusion

The renewal of Canadian policy for carrying out the commitments in the Convention on Biological Diversity is not yet finished. Despite the slowness of the process, the intervention picture is becoming clearer and new normative instruments are being put in place. All the post-Rio interventions are geared toward improving the performance of environmental protection systems in Canada. First of all, it is clear that Canada has not remained inactive in the field of biodiversity. It has applied itself to translating its commitments into actions and concrete decisions. In particular, it has complied with the various prescriptions of the CBD by developing a national strategy and action plans, making a national inventory, etc.

Canada has also introduced new mechanisms for policy development, planning, and biological resource management so that economic development, social, and environmental considerations can be integrated more effectively into the decision-making process. There is also an attempt to alleviate the fragmentary and reactive nature of public intervention by emphasizing more integrated, holistic approaches to the problems to be resolved. In this regard, the integrated approach to marine ecosystem management in the *Oceans Act* represents Canada's most innovative initiative. The ecosystem approach is directly inspired by the recommendations for marine biodiversity protection formulated by the Conference of the Parties of the Convention on Biological Diversity and known as the Jakarta Mandate on Marine and Coastal Biodiversity. The ecosystem approach appears to hold considerable promise, particularly for marine ecosystems in which habitat protection and preservation of biological and ecosystem integrity are cornerstones of the management objectives. The implementation of this approach raises a number of important challenges for Canada. There is still a certain amount of resistance, and changes are taking a great deal of time.

Some of the other means adopted are geared more toward improving earlier practices, which generated fragmentary interventions that were incapable of preventing environmental degradation and biological resource depletion. At first glance, it would appear to be a good thing to improve these practices, since integrated approaches are not meant to substitute for the regulation of specific human activities. But that line of reasoning is deceptive. Environmental goals remain ambiguous. When we look at them more closely, there is good reason to be concerned that the development of numerous instruments devoted to improving earlier practices might divert attention as well as the human and financial resources needed to perfect integrated instruments better adapted to resolving environmental and biological diversity problems. It is all a question of striking a balance. Otherwise, the environment and its biological resources will continue to suffer the same problems, and the criticism made more than ten years ago will remain just as valid.

Notes

This chapter was translated by Linda Blythe.

[1] This research was made possible by financial support from the Law Commission of Canada and the Social Sciences and Humanities Research Council of Canada. The author would like to express her gratitude to Marie-Eve Cournoyer, who carried out documentary research that was used in this study.

[2] Committee on the Status of Endangered Wildlife in Canada, *Releases Results of Species Assessment Meeting,* news releases, 3 May 2001 (http://www.ec.gc.ca/press/2001/010503-2_n_e.htm) (web page consulted on 14 June 2001).

[3] In 1996 the oceans sector produced close to $20 billion of Canada's gross domestic product (GDP). Almost one of four Canadians lives in a coastal community, and many of these people depend on the sea for their livelihood. Forty per cent of Canada's territory, i.e.

its land mass and platforms, is submerged under coastal waters (Fisheries and Oceans Canada, 2001) (web page consulted on 14 June 2001).

[4] See Convention on the International Maritime Organization (IMO), Geneva, 1948; International Convention for the Prevention of Pollution from Ships (MARPOL), London, 1973 and 1978; International Convention for the Safety of Life at Sea (SOLAS), November 1974; International Convention Relating to Intervention on the High Seas in Cases of Oil Pollution Casualties, Brussels, 1969; International Convention on Civil Liability for Oil Pollution Damage, Brussels, 1969; International Convention on the Establishment of an International Fund for Compensation for Oil Pollution Damage, Brussels, 1971; and Convention Relating to Civil Liability in the Field of Maritime Carriage of Nuclear Material, Brussels, 1971.

[5] UNEP (1985), *Montreal Guidelines for the Protection of the Marine Environment against Pollution from Land-based Sources*. These guidelines became a programme of action in 1995 with the *Declaration and Global Programme of Action for the Protection of the Marine Environment from Land-based Activities* (UNEP(OCA)/LBA/IG.2/L.3/Add., 1 November 1995).

[6] Convention for the Protection of Migratory Birds in Canada and the United States, Washington, 1916; International Convention for Regulation of Whaling, Washington, 1946.

[7] Convention on International Trade in Endangered Species of Wild Fauna and Flora (CITES), 3 March 1973, UNTS 243 (in force 1 July 1975). For example, the polar bear and walrus were listed in Schedules II and III of this Convention. Convention on Wetlands of International Importance (Ramsar), Ramsar, 1971.

[8] *Canada Shipping Act*, R.S.C. 1985, c. S-9, as am. by R.S.C. 1985, c. 6 (3rd Supp.); *Arctic Waters Pollution Prevention Act*, R.S.C. 1985, c. A-12 and its *Arctic Shipping Pollution Prevention Regulations*, C.R.C., c. 353; *Ocean Dumping Control Act*, S.C. 1974-75-76, c. 55 incorporated in *Canadian Environmental Protection Act*, R.S.C. 1985, c. 16 (4th Supp.), Schedule III. See also Juneau (1992).

[9] For example, see *Fisheries Act*, R.S.C. 1985, c. F-14; *Canada Water Act*, R.S.C. 1985, c. C-11; *Pest Control Products Act*, R.S.C. 1985, c. P-9; *Environmental Assessment and Review Process Guidelines Order*, SOR/84-457.

[10] *Migratory Birds Convention Act* R.S., c. M-12, s.1; *Fisheries Act*, R.S.C. 1985, c. F-14 and its *Narwhal Protection Regulations*, C.R.C. 1978, c. 820, *Seal Protection Regulations*, C.R.C. 1978, c. 833, *Walrus Protection Regulations*, S.O.R./80-338, *Beluga Protection Regulations*, S.O.R./80-376, *Cetacean Protection Regulations*, S.O.R./82-614, *Export and Import Act*, R.S.C. 1970, c. E-17, *Game Export Act*, R.S.C. 1985, c. G-1.

[11] *Fisheries Act*, R.S.C. 1985, c. F-14; *Territorial Sea and Fishing Zones Act*, R.S.C. 1985, c. T-8; *Act to implement the International Convention for the Northwest Atlantic Fisheries*, S.R. 1970, c. F-18; *Coastal Fisheries Protection Act*, R.S.C. 1985, c. C-33.

[12] Fathom Five in Lake Huron's Georgian Bay, see Canada Parks Service (1991).

[13] For a study of legal instruments protecting the St. Lawrence River, see Giroux (1991).

[14] *Rio Declaration on Environment and Development* (UN A/CONF.151/26, vol. I, Annexe I 1992); Convention on Biological Diversity (UN UNEP/Bio.Div/N7-INC.5/4); United Nations Framework Convention on Climate Change (UN A/AC.237/18, Part II/Add.1 and Corr.1); Non-Legally Binding Authoritative Statement of Principles for a Global Consensus on the Management, Conservation and Sustainable Development of All Types of Forests (UN A/CONF.151/26, Vol. III, Annex III); *Agenda 21*.

[15] *Rio Declaration on Environment and Development*, ibid, Principle 3.

[16] See also chapter 3 by Le Prestre in this volume.

[17] Chapter 17, "Protection of the Oceans, All Kinds of Seas, Including Enclosed and Semi-enclosed Seas, and Coastal Areas and the Protection, Rational Use and Development of their Living Resources".

[18] UN A/CONF.62/122 and Corr. 1 to 11, Part XII. The Convention obliges states to prevent several forms of pollution: pollution from dumping, pollution from ships, atmospheric pollution, transatmospheric pollution, pollution resulting from ocean-floor activities, and pollution from land-based sources.

[19] UNEP/CBD/COP/4/5 (1998). This work programme is known as the Jakarta Mandate on Marine and Coastal Biodiversity. The decision UNEP/CBD/COP/2/10 (1995) developed the proposed work programme. Since 1995, the Conference of the Parties has used the ecosystem approach as its basic principle for implementing the Convention and its programmes. See UNEP/CBD/COP/2/10, 4/1B, and 4/5. Regarding the Jakarta Mandate on Marine and Coastal Biodiversity, see Fontaubert, Downes and Agardy (1998).

[20] Official SBSTTA document at the Conference of the Parties, *Ecosystem Approach: Further Conceptual Elaboration* (UNEP/CBD/SBSTTA/5/11, p. 5). The SBSTTA also proposed 12 complementary and interdependent principles (p. 6) as well as five pieces of advice (p. 8) to be taken into consideration when using this approach.

[21] The Conference of the Parties adopted this approach as a basic principle for implementing the Convention (UNEP/CBD/COP/2/10, 4/1B, and 4/5). See also: *Agenda 21*, chapter 17; Miles (1999); Houck (1997); Canadian Council of Ministers of the Environment (1996); Brosnan (1994); Keiter (1994).

[22] *An Act to Amend the Auditor General Act*, S.C. 1995, c. 43, s.1.

[23] Commissioner of the Environment and Sustainable Development (1998), chapter 1 (web page consulted on 14 June 2001).

[24] See *Oceans Act*, S.C. 1996, c. 31; *Canadian Environmental Protection Act*, S.C. 1999, c. 33; *Parks Canada Agency Act*, S.C. 1998, c. 31; *Auditor General Act*, R.S.C. 1985, c. A-17. Bill C-10: *An Act Respecting the National Marine Conservation Areas of Canada* (37th Parl., 1st Sess., 2001, 1st reading, 20 February 2001), which expands the precautionary concept considerably by deleting the references to serious or irreversible damage, full scientific certainty, and cost-effective measures.

[25] At the national level, see Canada (1998) and Canada (1995b). Some provinces have also developed strategies and action plans for the conservation and sustainable use of biodiversity. For example, see Quebec, ministère de l'Environnement et de la Faune (1996).

[26] The federal strategy adopted two other objectives: increasing awareness of the need to conserve and use biodiversity in a sustainable fashion, and international co-operation.

[27] This was the case with amendments made to the following federal statutes: *Canada Shipping Act*, R.S.C. 1985, c. S-9 (am. S.C., c. 36); *Canadian Environmental Protection Act*, S.C. 1999, c. 33; *Canadian Environmental Assessment Act*, S.C. 1992, c. 37; *Coastal Fisheries Protection Act*, R.S.C 1985, c. C-33 (am. S.C. 1994, c. 14 and S.C. 1999, c. 19); *Canada Wildlife Act*, R.S.C. 1985, c. W-9 (am. S.C. 1994, c. 23).

[28] Canada (1995), *CEPA Review: Compilation of Comments on the Government Response "Environmental Protection Legislation Designed for the Future – A Renewed CEPA,"* part 2, chapter 1.

[29] With regard to new approaches to regulation, see Issalys (2001); Priest (1998); Baldwin (1995).

[30] See Canada (1995), chapter 14, pp. 203-235.

[31] See *Wild Animal and Plant Protection and Regulation of International and Interprovincial Trade Act*, S.C. 1992, c. 53; *Migratory Birds Convention Act*, 1994, S.C. 1994, c. 22; *Oceans Act*, S.C. 1996, c. 31; bill C-10: *An Act Respecting the National Marine Conservation Areas of Canada* (37th Parl., 1st Sess., 2001, 1st reading, 20 February 2001); and bill C-5: *An Act Respecting the Protection of Wildlife Species at Risk in Canada* (37th Parl., 1st Sess., 2001, 1st reading, 20 February 2001).

[32] Oceans Program Activity Tracking (OPAT) System (http://canoceans.dfo-mpo.gc.ca/opat_public.asp) (web page consulted on 14 June 2001).

[33] *Canada Wildlife Act*, R.S.C. 1985, c. W-9, s. 4.1 (am. S.C. 1994, c. 23, s. 8).

[34] Bill C-10: *An Act Respecting The National Marine Conservation Areas of Canada* (37th Parl., 1st Sess., 2001, 1st reading, 20 February 2001). This bill replaces two earlier bills: bill C-48 and bill C-8 were tabled in June 1998 and October 1999. They died on the Order Paper on dissolution of Parliament. The initial orientation of these bills came from the administrative review of Parks Canada policies in 1994 and the development of a national plan for the marine conservation area system. See Parks Canada (1995) and Parks Canada (1994).

[35] These four parks represent five of the 29 marine regions: Gwaii Haanas (Queen Charlotte Shelf and Hecate Strait marine regions); Fathom Five (Georgian Bay region); Lake Superior region (proposed); and Southern Strait of Georgia (proposed, Strait of Georgia region). The Saguenay-St. Lawrence Marine Park represents a sixth region (St. Lawrence estuary) but is not affected by bill C-10 because the park is governed by separate legislation passed in 1997.

[36] See regulations cited above in note 10 and the *Marine Mammal Regulations*, SOR/93-56.

[37] Bill C-5, *An Act Respecting the Protection of Wildlife Species at Risk in Canada* (37th Parl., 1st Sess., 2001, 1st reading, 2 February 2001). This bill follows two earlier proposals, bill C-33, the *Species at Risk Act*, tabled in April 2000, and bill C-65, the *Canada Endangered Species Protection Act* (CESPA), tabled in October 1996. Both earlier bills died on the Order Paper, the first in 1997 and the second in the fall of 2000, on dissolution of Parliament.

[38] Parliamentary Research Branch, *Bill C-5: The Species at Risk Act*, prepared by Kristen Douglas, Law and Government Division, 13 February 2001 (http://www.parl.gc.ca/common (web page consulted on 14 June 2001).

[39] *Canadian Code of Conduct for Responsible Fishing Operations*, consensus code, 1998 (http://www.dfo-mpo.gc.ca) (web page consulted on 14 June 2001)

[40] Canada (1997). The Biodiversity Convention Office was established by Environment Canada in September 1991 to co-ordinate Canadian involvement in the negotiations leading up to the United Nations Convention on Biological Diversity.

[41] Commissioner of the Environment and Sustainable Development (1998), chapter 4 (web page consulted on 14 June 2001).

[42] Commissioner of the Environment and Sustainable Development (2000), chapter 9 (web page consulted on 14 June 2001).

[43] Commissioner of the Environment and Sustainable Development (2000), chapter 9, section 9.57.

[44] For example, see Fisheries and Oceans Canada (2001), *Building Awareness and Capacity: An Action Plan for Continued Sustainable Development 2001-2003*, p. 13 (http://www.dfo-mpo.gc.ca/sds-sdd/index_e.htm) (web page consulted on 14 June 2001). In particular, this action plan is based on new forms of governance and shared management, which "are also inspired by the need to find more effective, less costly ways of delivering government services and programs" (Environment Canada, 1995, part 1).

[45] The influence of business on public administrations is increasing. More and more, public administrators see businesses as experts in their activity sector and consider them qualified to propose technical standards. It is also argued that as a rule, businesses will be more inclined to abide by standards that they developed themselves and that they are in a good position to ensure that their activities comply with these standards.

[46] See UNEP/CBD/COP/2/10, 4/1B, and 4/5. See also: *Agenda 21*, chapter 17; Miles (1999); Houck (1997); Canadian Council of Ministers of the Environment (1996); Brosnan (1994); Keiter (1994).

[47] Generally speaking, these have been ad hoc initiatives centred around the funding of clean-up operations or based on local volunteer initiatives. For example, see Environment Canada, *Ecosystem Initiatives* (http://www.ec.gc.ca/ecosyst/backgrounder.html) (web page consulted on 14 June 2001) and Fisheries and Oceans Canada, *Integrated Management*,

(http://www.oceansconservation.com/newenglish web page consulted on 14 June 2001).

[48] "Marine Conservation Study Axed: Move Means Bonavista and Notre Dame Bays Won't Become Specially Protected Areas," *The Telegram* (St. John's), 11 March 1999, p. 4, cited in *Bill C-8: An Act Respecting Marine Conservation Areas*, prepared by Luc Gagné, Parliamentary Research Branch, 25 October 1999, p. 13.

Chapter 13

Devoted Friends:
The Implementation of the Convention
on Biological Diversity in Madagascar

Marc Hufty and Frank Muttenzer

Introduction

The purpose of this chapter is to provide an overview of the legal, political, and practical changes induced in Madagascar by the international biodiversity regime. We will try to answer the following questions: What is the status of biological diversity[1] and of its management in Madagascar? What are the effects of the Convention on Biological Diversity (CBD) and of related norms and institutions on Madagascar's social and institutional dynamics? Does this dynamic lead to the implementation of regime norms within the domestic legal framework of this country? To answer these questions, we will develop a set of connected hypotheses.

Because of several features common to most developing countries, we think that it is possible to consider the case of Madagascar as an example of the integration of a developing country into the emerging international biological order. If we examine the environmental policies of other countries in similar situation, the Malagasy experience does appear to be generalizable. As in a majority of tropical countries, Madagascar biological diversity is associated with its forests.[2] The forest ecosystems of developing countries were of interest to the "international community" long before the advent of the Convention. The principles of conservation, regulating access to *in situ* resources, and benefit-sharing that underlie global management of biodiversity-relevant areas were already clearly stated in *Caring for the Earth* (IUCN, UNEP and WWF, 1991). This document recommended inventories of forest resources for each country in order to create permanent and legally established domains, or state lands, of natural and modified forests. These permanent domains were to be protected from deterioration with the participation of local communities in a perspective of sustainable use.

Thus, as in numerous developing countries, implementation of the standards of what we nowadays call the international biodiversity regime preceded the advent of the Convention itself. Moreover, there is a close relationship between the international biodiversity regime and the international development aid regime,[3] in particular through the use of the conditionality mechanism. In practice, dependent states have conceded an international right of inspection over their forest resources in exchange for additional development funds, which implies a loss of sovereignty. This oversight is being exercised day to day in the negotiations on the objectives and financing of Madagascar's Environmental Action Plan (EAP).

However, in other respects the Malagasy experience appears to be specific. It is therefore not a simple matter of course that our entire analysis will yield results that can be generalizable to other countries. One of these specificities is the central place given to what we describe as an ideology of biodiversity conservation in public policies. When we examine the Malagasy experience, three features appear to be essential to understanding the changes that have occurred during the past decade at the level of national policies: land-use management, the recognition of local knowledge, and the idea of governance.

The purpose of this chapter is to examine specific issues dealt with by the CBD through a case study and to develop a series of indicators for measuring the effectiveness of regime-related norms and policies. The chapter is divided into three parts. The first part offers a chronological view of environmental norms in Madagascar and tries to assess the efforts made to preserve its biological diversity. The second part, using the example of forest management, offers a network analysis of local, national, and international stakeholders. The third part places this network, as well as biodiversity-related policies in Madagascar more generally, in the context of international development aid.

The Specificity of Madagascar

Madagascar, an island the size of France (592,000 km2), is known for its biological diversity and high rate of endemism. Following its isolation from the African continent more than 100 million years ago, its ecosystems have reached original equilibriums and solutions in comparison to those of the rest of the world. It is estimated that the island has a flora of 10,000 to 12,000 vascular plant species of which 85 per cent are endemic.

However, the current state of Madagascar's natural areas is worrisome. The eroded soils are losing fertility, the hydrographic cycles are disturbed, and the ecosystems are deteriorating rapidly. Biological diversity, essentially associated with forested areas, is under extreme threat. More than 80 per cent of the original forests have disappeared,[4] mainly during the past 50 years. The causes of this environmental degradation can be grouped within two categories: direct and structural.

Table 13.1 Per Cent Endemism in Madagascar Species

Group of organisms	Known species	% Endemic species
Flowering plants	8,000-10,000	>80
Amphibians	>150	99
Reptiles	245	96
Birds	238	50
Bats	26	50
Terrestrial mammals	>70	97

Source: Jolly, A., 1980; modified by the authors

Slash-and-burn rice cropping is the most important direct cause of forest ecosystem degradation. However, clearings made for cash crops, selective harvesting of a few tree species, and firewood production also have significant consequences. Bush fires started to create pastures for cattle practised on a country-wide scale, contribute significantly as well to a loss of soil fertility.

These direct causes are amplified or caused by a series of structural factors interacting with one another. With annual demographic growth near 3 per cent, Madagascar's population, 15 million at the beginning of 2000, has doubled since 1975 and will double again by 2025.[5] Agricultural lands currently comprise only 5 per cent of the total area, and the demographic growth of a still largely rural population (71 per cent in 1999)[6] produces increased pressure on the natural environment, accelerating deforestation and reducing fallow periods.

The generalized impoverishment of the population, following political choices made in the 1970s, has brought about a drastic reduction in purchasing power, in the cities as well as in the countryside, and has had important consequences on social indicators (health, schooling, infant mortality).[7] Farmers have had to increase the production of cash crops to maintain a minimum income, and numerous salaried employees have had to return to the land to feed their families. The social structures have also felt the impact. In the countryside, mutual help mechanisms and the traditional institutions regulating the management of natural resources have lost some of their legitimacy. In addition to these problems, the country suffers from the failure of agrarian reform, the complexity and cost of inheritance formalities, as well as extremely ponderous administrative procedure for allocating public lands.

Furthermore, opening the country to external markets, promoted by international creditors and aid donors, has placed Madagascar in a fragile position of dependence. The income of small farmers depends directly on international prices for raw materials. When prices drop, living conditions, already miserable, deteriorate drastically. One example is coffee, of which Madagascar produces 65,000 tons annually, mostly of the robusta variety (92 per cent). Ranked the third export product after the production of duty-free zones and the shrimp industry,[8] it is nevertheless the first rural export associated with the country's agroforestry areas. Prices for producers have gradually decreased from 8,000 Malagasy francs per kilogram in 1995 (a relatively high price) to 1,700 in 2001.[9] Coffee is essentially produced by small farmers, self-sufficient in rice but dependent on income from coffee for the purchase of other basic necessities (soap, cooking oil, sugar, salt) but also alcohol. When coffee prices drop, they must sell rice to be able to buy these goods, thus reducing their rations of calories and protein. Children are the first to suffer from hunger.

Between 1970 and 1990, the capacities of technical services from the state were considerably weakened. Because of a lack of financial and material means, state officials have had only limited options for applying the law in rural environments or ensuring extension services to farmers to communicate ways of increasing production or improving product quality. The bare-bones forest service could not control deforestation or the poaching of precious wood species in protected areas. Government officials have reacted by inserting themselves into local economic networks, which represent considerable stakes. They collect "taxes" for tolerating charcoal production, the exploitation of precious wood species, the presence of migrants in protected areas, and illegal crops (Muttenzer, 2001). In spite of policies designed to improve and broaden the intervention of technical services put in place with the Environmental Action Plan in 1990, the response of the state remains generally weak.

The result is increasing environmental deterioration. The vegetation cover is declining in diversity and quantity. Primary forests are being gradually replaced by degraded formations,[10] open savannas are progressively being transformed into steppes. These modifications of the vegetation cover in turn cause a significant physical erosion, reducing soil fertility, and damaging irrigation systems. Forest degradation in turn prompts microclimatic variations that have important consequences for agriculture, such as rainfall deficits, and an impoverishment of the ecosystems, linked to a rapid and irreversible extinction of many species of plants and animals.

However, the problem of managing natural resources is not a new one in Madagascar. In fact, the first conservation measures date back to the period of the Malagasy kingdoms. These measures were developed again under the post-colonial regime and had become systematic as early as the 1980s under the impetus of international conservation and development aid organizations.

Natural Resource Management before 1980

Between the 16th and the 19th centuries, the Merina Kingdom (a people living in the area of Antananarivo, the Imerina) extended its influence over three-quarters of Madagascar, using a well-structured internal organization as well as diplomatic or military actions. This kingdom was based on irrigated rice cultivation, but useable lands were limited. Located in lowlands, these lands were vulnerable to silting when torrential rains caused the erosion of hillsides affected by deforestation or brush fires. In response, the kingdom established a real conservation policy. Within the limits of Imerina, mostly deforested, various regulations prohibited burning the forest and enforced severe restrictions on woodcutting. Penalties could go as far as execution of the offenders.

France conquered the country militarily between 1895 and 1900. The colonial government put in place a centralized administration originally based on ethnic divisions. It increased and diversified agricultural production through a technical extension service and the establishment of agricultural settlers. The colonial government also introduced cash crops (cloves, coffee, vanilla, pepper) and organized irrigated rice production on a larger scale.

The forests and lands without recognized owners were decreed the property of the state in 1926. Certain valuable species were overexploited to extinction, as for example the rubber-producing species. According to Boiteau (1982), of 12 million hectares of exploitable forests at the time of the conquest, a third was destroyed in the space of 50 years, whether to provide for railroad operations or for the commercial exploitation of precious wood. In the regions under economic exploitation, the colonial services tried to limit brush fires and imposed compulsory reforestation programmes, using eucalyptus and pine. On the other hand, along deforestation fronts, operators encouraged workers to cut the forests where precious species had already been harvested and turn them into agricultural land. This arrangement enabled them to keep salaries very low. Deforestation on a large scale was thus a direct consequence of the colonial economy.

The first systematic inventories of the fauna and flora were the work of a scientific community that was conscious of the biological interest of this country, described as a "naturalist's paradise". A statute and a forest service were put in place in 1927, delineating a first network of protected areas outside the colonized areas:

> French scientists who recognized Madagascar's worldwide scientific importance urged the colonial government to set aside pure wilderness reserves. They established twelve 'integral' reserves designed to preserve the endemic flora and fauna as well as two national parks open for general enjoyment. No infrastructure or upkeep was planned, since the reserves were chosen as remote, untouched areas, protected by their isolation. (Jolly, 1989, p.208)

After independence was achieved, the regime of the First Republic (1960-72) continued the colonial policy. The state, receiving a large contribution from France, maintained its rural extension service. A national middle class developed on the strength of the agricultural surplus, the per capita tax, and French aid. The level of education was then one of the highest in Africa.

The revolutionary regime that came to power in 1975, named the Second Republic, sought to break away from the neo-colonial order and to modernize society. However, as with the First Republic, it maintained the state monopoly of the management of lands and natural resources by formally excluding local populations. In reality, local populations have in specific ways developed community management schemes, including local arrangements with officials (Bertrand, 1999).

The Second Republic attempted to develop the economy through state mechanisms but rapidly collided with the limits of world economic realities, which aid from socialist countries could not overcome. The government had to borrow money to balance its budget, which forced it to accept structural adjustment measures as early as 1980. The numerous failed attempts to balance the budget deepened the financial dependency on international financing agencies and bilateral co-operation organizations. In parallel, the capacity of the state to act in the technical extension to rural regions weakened. The forest service lost its influence. Unpopular reforestation programmes were reduced, while the monitoring of brush fires, slash-and-burn cropping, and protected areas relaxed. Furthermore, internal controls on the price of rice, intended to provide low-cost food for urban populations, pushed farmers to limit their production. Madagascar lost its self-sufficiency in rice and had to import. The marked decrease in the standard of living led the country to a generalized crisis, culminating in the political events of 1991, the establishment of a Third Republic, formal political democracy, and the adoption of the liberal economic model.

The Environmental Action Plan

Having been aware of the ecological interest of this country and its environmental problems for a long time, the World Conservation Union (IUCN) and World Wide Fund for Nature (WWF) began developing their activities in Madagascar in 1980, when president Didier Ratsiraka accepted, not without reticence, the creation of a Madagascar branch of WWF International.[11] Its presence served as a catalyst for the soil and forest protection actions initiated by bilateral co-operation organizations and allowed for a larger-scale survey of the ecological specificities of the island, particularly its protected areas (Nicoll and Langrand, 1989).[12]

Alerted by these organizations about the consequences of the environmental degradation, the government adopted in 1984 the National Strategy for Conservation and Development. The following year it organized an international conference intended to help prepare a national environmental programme (Falloux and Talbot, 1992). Supported by donors and creditors, these efforts led in 1988 to the drafting of the Environmental Action Plan,[13] ratified in 1990 by parliament as the Malagasy Environmental Charter.[14] Madagascar became, two years before Rio, one of the first African states to establish an environmental action plan.[15]

Programmed over 15 years, the EAP has been divided into three "environmental programmes". The objective of the first five-year phase (1991-95), named Environmental Programme 1 (EP1), was to establish an operational structure (creation or strengthening of specialized institutions, making preliminary studies, recruiting and training of personnel) and to undertake the most urgent conservation actions.

The EP1 was given $187 million USD,[16] which represented 5 to 10 per cent of the annual budget of the country. It was composed of seven priority programmes,[17] but the "biological diversity" programme received 32 per cent of the funding and the "forest" programme received 28 per cent, a total of 60 per cent of the funding, compared to 20 per cent for the co-ordination of the programme and 20 per cent for the other programmes. Furthermore, these other programmes (co-ordination and research, mapping, land ownership) where frequently oriented toward supporting the double programme biodiversity-forests. The EP1 was thus fundamentally oriented toward the conservation of biodiversity-rich forest environments. This orientation corresponded with the priorities of the major donor to the EAP, the United States Agency for International Development (USAID), which in its annual funding request to the United States Congress justified its involvement in the following words: "Madagascar is Africa's most important biodiversity priority, and among the world's top five for species diversity and uniqueness".[18]

The result of the EP1 is considered "generally satisfactory" (World Bank, 1996b). Officially justified by a need for efficiency, three specialized implementation agencies were created: the Office national de l'environnement (ONE, or National Environmental Board), which co-ordinates the implementation of the EAP;[19] the Association nationale de gestion des aires protégés (ANGAP, or National Protected Areas Management Association), a para-statal organization the role of which is to manage protected areas; and the Association nationale d'action environnementale (ANAE, or National Environmental Action Association), responsible for soil management. In spite of significant financial and technical support from the funding agencies, they have suffered the problems common to many bureaucratic organizations in Madagascar:[20] centralization of their resources at the head office in Antananarivo, lack of co-ordination among sections, absence of a communication strategy, bureaucratic red tape, and misappropriation of resources.

According to Larson (1994), the environmental diagnostic made by the EAP is correct, but the solution it proposes is not. The main environmental problem of Madagascar is indeed closely linked to the resource-use decisions made day to day by a multitude of geographically dispersed stakeholders. However, the EAP cannot resolve this problem because it originates from a complicated set of local, national, and international dynamics over which direct managers have only limited influence.

The main management tool for protected areas was the Integrated Conservation and Development Projects (ICDP). In contrast to the "Yellowstone model," which relied on determining an area and the probability of its exploitation, such as the parks created in the colonial period, the ICDP concept added a buffer zone to the protected area, exploited under the control of the Ministry of Forests and Wildlife with the participation of adjacent populations (Wells and Brandon, 1992). By deflecting human pressures on protected areas through incentives and disincentives, these projects aimed to reach a compromise between the desire of conservationists to completely exclude populations from protected areas and the prohibitive costs of that type of measure. They tried to mobilize the population on the side of conservation by offering monetary income (hiring of local guides and redistribution of part of tourists' entrance fees to the communities) or small local development projects (access roads, schools, health stations, irrigation projects) in return for surrendering access rights to the protected area.

Promising in theory, these projects are subject to problems associated with the manner in which they were conceived and implemented. They are characterized by a mechanistic outlook that presumes that individuals living in the periphery of protected areas who commit the plundering are the main culprits in deforestation. The possibility that production channels leading to overexploitation may be centred well away from protected areas and that local development may be relatively independent of any increase in pressure on the ecosystem is neglected (Weber, 1995).

In the beginning, the ICDPs were directed by foreign biologists, who were progressively replaced by Malagasy nationals, also biologists and from the capital city. Both foreigners and nationals were not well-acquainted with local customs, were poorly informed with respect to the complexities of local social conditions, and did not speak the local dialects. Their inclination was to bind the "development" aspect to the conservation objectives, seen as a priority, and, because of their poor integration into local networks, to reinforce the principles of exclusion and subordination on which the ICDPs are ultimately based (EPB, 2000). The *faux pas* of these administrators and the priority given to conservation, obvious to local populations, have sometimes led to open conflict (Ghimire, 1991).

Furthermore, the economic alternatives proposed were limited. Ecotourism in all evidence cannot generate enough income to support the 50 or so protected areas projected for Madagascar,[21] and this income benefits only a limited and well-connected number of people.[22] Subsistence and other needs rapidly drive local populations to encroach beyond the boundaries of protected areas. The only solution remaining is repression, a guarantee of failure for projects claiming to be based on local participation.

The Environmental Programme 2

The Environmental Programme 2 (EP2), which covers the period 1997 to 2002,[23] is based on a series of evaluations of the EP1 and aimed at improving its results. The national context of this second programme is very different from that of the first: changes in government and constitution, ratification of decentralization,[24] deconcentration and economic liberalization policy, and ratification by the Malagasy state of the Convention on Biological Diversity.[25] The EP2, in symbiosis with these changes, announced its decentralization by adopting the subsidiarity principle (allocating responsibility to the lowest administrative level possible), the creation of regional representation for the EAP implementation agencies, and the increased involvement of local decision-makers in the process. The new approach, supported by the increasingly frequent use of geographic information systems (GIS), is based on a regional approach to managing zones of biological interest[26] and no longer narrowly on the relationships between protected areas and their adjacent populations. It also announced a greater consideration to "social and cultural aspects" (RdM, 1998b), which actually amounts to a reorientation of the ICDPs.

This reorientation reflects a new philosophy of foreign aid. At the beginning of the 1990s, the international community showed a sudden interest in local knowledge. This rediscovery of the "traditional" transpired during the whole discourse on biodiversity[27]: *Agenda 21*, Article 8(j) of the CBD and debates surrounding the "equitable sharing of benefits," and recognition of intellectual property rights over community knowledge associated with biodiversity (Posey, 1997). Research projects on the "commons" postulate the usefulness of customary regulations in solving problems of open access that cause deforestation (Ostrom, 1998). Although the first experiences of the Food and Agriculture Organization (FAO) with community forestry date back to the early 1980s, it was only after the Rio Earth Summit in 1992 that the transfer of renewable resources management to local communities became popular as a new administrative model. This change in perception of the role of traditional users of biodiversity will have profound consequences on national policy development in Madagascar.

Until then, the farmer was considered as the main culprit in deforestation. This is clearly expressed in the Environmental Charter, the founding text for the EAP:

> the itinerant deforestation of natural forests constitutes one of the primary factors of environmental deterioration, along with the practice of brush fires. …as long as land management will depend on the authority of Tangalamena (chiefs of customary lineages) who determine the annual tavy zones, as long as the zebu will be the centre of the civilization of an entire people, and as long as rice will be considered the only food of the Malagasy, it will be no easy task to solve the environmental problems of the Malagasy people. (RdM, 1990, p.18)

Studies on local governance in the peripheral zones of a few protected areas (Montagne d'Ambre, Zahamena, Ranomafana and Andohahela), carried out since 1991 with USAID funding, show that "efficient local traditional regulations" coexist with formal institutions and regulations (Razafindrabe, 1996; Rabesahala, 1994). Under joint funding by several agencies and following a new series of preparatory workshops,[28] these observations led to the drafting of a legal policy of "local contractual management".

According to Bill 96-025, village communities regrouped in users' associations can request concessions of exclusive use rights on the private lands of the state in a framework of negotiated management plans, a procedure known as Gelose (Gestion locale securisée or Secured Local Management).[29] By assigning a central role to the farmer and by fostering the creation of intermediate management structures, closer to the population than the *communes rurales* (decentralized local government units), this policy aims at radical changes in natural resources management.

It breaks away from the traditional state monopoly in forest management. According to its proponents, the shift to a contractual process goes far beyond "participatory" development, since it allows for the local negotiation of management rules, something that was not possible with the previous participatory approach. The goal of these contracts is to define local co-management between communities and the state. The various stakeholders concerned with renewable resources management (state, rural communities, territorial collectivities, NGOs, development or conservation projects) suddenly become partners with reciprocal obligations (Bertrand, 1999). The rapid shift from the participatory toward the negotiated depends on the establishment of operational structures, through a "common heritage approach" that recognizes the existence of local stakeholders with differing logics and interests and proposes to negotiate common objectives with respect to long-term sustainable management of resources (Babin et al., 1997). The key to this policy is the "environmental mediator," a person responsible for negotiations between the administration and the village communities on the future management rules.[30]

The common heritage approach has also led to a change in orientation of the EAP with respect to the land ownership question. During the programming of EP1, land ownership was defined exclusively in individualistic terms, sometimes against customs that forbid the transfer of lands outside kinship group. This approach had led to ineffectual surveying of agricultural lands in the peripheral zones of protected areas. Only from 1995 onwards has the individualistic approach been abandoned in favour of the common heritage approach, which accepts a plurality of stakeholders and ownership definitions.

According to proponents of the common heritage approach, the break with the previous type of resources management is important. However, no matter what approach is used, local communities and forest administration officials must subscribe to management objectives that they have not defined themselves. The government, for its part, is adapting to changes of philosophy in international development aid programmes. This is an essential point in an argument to which we will return in the third part of this chapter.

The EP1 was to put in place the EAP, while keeping in mind that its objective is "the final appropriation of the operation and of its essence by the population" (RdM, 1990, p.45). The EP2 was to increase the actions undertaken by the EP1 and progressively reduce the "logistic actions," the setting up of the institutional framework, in order to devote more resources to field actions. The EP3 (2003-2008), the last phase of the EAP, should allow a reduction of environmental deterioration through the population assuming some responsibilities. At the end of the EP3, environmental actions should occur "automatically," naturally managed and generated by the different stakeholders: collectivities at the base, government ministries, NGOs.

According to the Environmental Charter of 1990:

> this implies that:
> – the populations and collectivities at the base will have acquired the "environmental reflex" and will have appropriated the methods used to apply them on their own,
> – the structures of the State, in particular its Ministries, will have incorporated, at the level of their sectorial policies, the environmental concept in a systematic and systemic fashion,
> – the periodic national plans will have made the environment and conservation a driving force for sustainable development, and focused towards the population.
> ...at the end of this period, the environment and its preoccupations should be part of the daily conduct of collectivities and of all citizens. (RdM, 1990, p.48)

The New Forest Policy

As mentioned previously, forests are the main focus of the concerns of the international community, funding agencies, and the EAP about the conservation and management of Madagascar's biological diversity. Madagascar currently has a network of 50 protected areas totalling an area of 1,698,000 ha. This network is managed by ANGAP and comprises 11 integral natural reserves, 16 national parks, and 23 special reserves. Following the model established during the 1920s, most of these protected areas are located in regions characterized by slopes of greater than five degrees and are thus difficult to access. Their role in the preservation of the flora and fauna of Madagascar will certainly be crucial.

However, the protected areas represent only 12.8 per cent of forested areas. They are surrounded by forests on more level topography, which are much more threatened because they are more accessible. One of the findings to come out of EP1 analyses was that the majority of species and ecosystems fundamental to Madagascar's biological diversity are found outside protected areas, especially in the 158 classified forests and 99 forest reserves, covering 4,024,634 ha, managed by the Ministry of Waters and Forests, but also in the non-classified state forests (Hagen, 2000; Raharison, 2000). From a standpoint of conservation and potential commercial use of biodiversity, "conservation actions must be extended to forested areas which are subjected to the greatest deforestation, and therefore the most threatened" (Raharison, 2000, p.6).

During the EP1, a new forest policy was worked out by the administration in collaboration with the Swiss, German, and Norwegian bilateral co-operation agencies. Drafted from the work of technical working groups and regional workshops, the forest policy did not escape the eruption of conflicts of interest among the stakeholders involved in the process:

The decisional debates actually did occur at the different levels of organization (regional, national), but instead of leading to a real consensus on appropriate management rules, they exacerbated the rift between a public administration, to whom a reduction in responsibilities was imposed and a transfer of management to local communities was stipulated, and a parallel administration born of the implementation of the EAP. This open conflict benefits the major funding agencies which, as a consequence, have gained the necessary leeway to decide on their own the use of measures that were supposed to be decided in concert with national partners. (Ramamonjisoa, 2001, p.4)

According to Decree 97-120, the objectives of the new forest policy are to stop the process of forest degradation by supporting substitution practices to shift cultivation and by limiting brush fires; to better manage forest resources by implementing forest resource management plans and by rationalizing the forest system; to increase the area of protected forests and forest potential by promoting reforestation, ensuring land ownership security, and intensifying the management of watersheds; and to augment the economic performance of the sector by increasing the value of forest products. At the strategic level, the policy seeks to reconcile sustainable management of forest resources with the need for economic production, to reform the forest administration within the framework of disengagement of the state, and to encourage local and participative management of forest resources through a transfer of all or part of the management authority on certain state forests to local communities.

During the recent evolution of the concept of forest management, preoccupation has progressively moved away from technical allocation and distribution tasks toward a debate on management objectives. Nowadays, instead of defining these objectives in terms of sustained production, we define them according to the idea of common heritage as the sustainable management of forest ecosystems in a global context of land-use management (Bertrand, Babin, and Nasi, 1999). However, the implementation of management plans, which is a prerequisite to this programme, is still largely hypothetical. State forest governance remains a legal fiction established by colonial law, which the new forest policy and the national network of protected areas are only partially putting into concrete form. Although one of the implementary decrees (98-782) of the new forest law requires all forest exploitation to conform to management plans before 2001, and despite financing and support for the projects, there is to this day not a single forest exploitation in Madagascar that follows a management plan (Hagen, 2000).

A Regime with Multiple Levels of Decision-Making

The observed evolution of the norms and practices of biological diversity management in Madagascar cannot be understood without situating it in the current world context, specifically the implementation of an international biodiversity regime of which the CBD is a keystone (Hufty, 2001) and which can be defined as a set of norms, rules, and procedures that structure the behaviour and expectations of stakeholders, reduce the uncertainties facing them, and facilitate the pursuit of common objectives.

An international regime is made less out of legal documents than out of observable practices. It can be considered a process in which the texts are but an image and a benchmark at any given time. The regime can be understood as a dynamic network of decision-making and transacting,[31] articulated around the objectives sought by its stakeholders.

From this angle, two phenomena observed in Madagascar lie outside the usual perspective of international relations, where the concept of international regime originated, and deserve an explanation. On the one hand, the creation of national policies is under the continuous although diffuse influence of the conditionality mechanism. This influence is not exercised primarily on the occasion of the five-year planning of the EAP nor against the "government of Madagascar" as a distinct entity but in a continuous manner for each disbursement and in relation to each "partner" agency or ministry. On the other hand, national legislation on environmental matters has been the subject of important modifications during the past decade. These re-modellings are generally initiated, if not carried out, under the auspices of funding agencies.

How do regulations defined at the international level become operational? As pointed out in some recent research about the dynamics of negotiations on biodiversity (Thoyer, Le Goulven, and Louafi, 2001; Louafi, 2001), the difficulty is to "understand how to make the connection, for a concrete case, between the substantial objectives of the negotiations ('preserve biodiversity'), the procedural results (formulating of norms, procedure for registering questions on the political agenda, choice and influence of the stakeholders in the negotiations, etc.) and local practices in the field, in such a way as to understand what can be handled (or not) by the arrangements created by the international compromise and its mode of norm creation" (Louafi, 2001, p.3). These studies are interested in the retroaction, in terms of acquired experience and learning, between the negotiation of international norms and the results to which the application of these norms will lead. Our observations in Madagascar suggest that if such learning processes are possible, they are neither necessary nor automatic.

As a matter of fact, the regulatory base of the CBD is implemented mainly by networks of international aid. The norms and standards related to biodiversity are therefore produced before they are formalized through international negotiations, at times even despite their formalization at that level. All of the principles, norms, rules, and practices of the regime are not recorded in the Convention or other international texts, either because they represent "meta-regulations" so self-evident that they are not discussed[32] or because they have made their way into the regime little by little and are not yet formalized (Hufty, 2001, p.22), as we will show in the second part of this chapter. However, we should note that norms produced in this fashion are no less direct and discernible in their impacts than are those spelled out in the Convention and other legal texts.

We can thus perceive two distinct levels of implementation of international norms on biodiversity. We distinguish a "global" level in which norms are produced according to the standardized procedures of foreign aid and an "international" level, based on formal negotiations concerning biodiversity. Norms on biodiversity are being created at two interdependent levels, which act either as rival or as complementary spheres.

The Conditionality Mechanism

The external funding agencies of EP2 are grouped in a "multi-funding secretariat," which establishes through the Funding Committee for the Environment (FCE) a regular dialogue with the Madagascar government and the various agencies involved in the Environmental Action Plan. This structure is modelled on the roundtable system of the United Nations Development Programme (UNDP) and the World Bank in which creditors collectively enter into a "country dialogue". This dialogue is a negotiation game in which the receiving or borrowing state tries to obtain the highest level of financing for the best conditions, whereas creditors try to impose a set of payment conditions linked to their vision of the policies the receiving state should adopt. A dialogue of this type occurs regularly on the financing of the EAP. The forest policy can serve as an example of this process.

From 8 to 23 March 2001, the delegation of the Malagasy government and the donors and creditors group met in Antananarivo within the FCE framework to discuss the strategic orientation of the Environmental Action Plan up to the end of EP2 (FCE, 2001). Among the measures decided on by the FCE is an "action plan 2000-2002 to improve the efficiency and the effectiveness of the Forest Service in a framework of transparency and good governance".

This plan consists of the following measures, among others:

- a halt to all extractive activities in sensitive areas (protected areas and gazetted forests); publication of information on all currently held permits and temporary or exceptional authorizations;
- revision of the regulations and procedures for issuing exploitation permits; implementation, within a time frame of 18 months or less, of an exploitation permit delivery system by means of a call for tenders or auction; suspension of the allocation of new permits under the current procedure;
- implementation of an improved system of delivery and follow-up of authorizations for land-use conversion (agriculture on forest lands);
- reinforcement of forest control and implementation of an improved management system for infractions and for following up transactions; and

- starting the operation of the "observatory" of the forest sector, created by ministerial decree in November 2000, which is to oversee rules of good governance in the sector and the implementation of the action plan.

It is surprising to see in the annual work plan of a ministry this reaffirmation of measures that have been part of forest legislation since the beginning of the 1990s. These measures had actually not been implemented. It is equally surprising that the Ministry of Forests finally outlined its annual work plan for 2001 in May 2001, immediately after the FCE meeting. The ministry indeed had to wait until after the donor group meeting before deciding on its priorities in order to ensure the availability of the annual financing from which it benefits for the EP2 components placed under its responsibility.

In a similar context, the country-wide zoning of forests had originally been programmed at the beginning of the EP2 (to facilitate good forest management and as a prerequisite to updating the national ecological and forest survey) but had eventually received no funding from donors.

Meanwhile, at the global level, the "zoning plan" has become a central feature of exemplary management of forested areas:

> it provides the proposals for dividing these areas according to their 'vocations,' such as the density of human inhabitants and the state of the vegetation cover. The hypotheses about a linear relationship between population density and deforestation used in the zoning plan implemented in Cameroon by Canadian specialists clearly indicate that the main objective is to draw 'lines of defence' against the agricultural front. Agricultural and forest systems are put face to face in a model with dissociated areas which reflect more the western representations than the practices of the rural people of Cameroon in forested areas. (Karsenty, 1999, p.53)

In the case of Madagascar, the report of a USAID/World Bank evaluation of the management of natural forests, which was carried out prior to the 2001 meeting of the Funding Committee for the Environment, noted that "the means to achieve the objectives of the Forest Policy have not been clearly defined" and made it clear, on the basis "of the lessons acquired during the Workshop on the World Bank Strategy on forestry issues held in Washington in May 2000," that a new type of national forest management based on a zoning plan was needed, which would allow the ministry to have in its hands "elements of dialogue and follow-up with all the local entities concerned for the rational and sustainable management of forest heritage at different levels, on the one hand, and with the international technical and financial aid, on the other hand" (Hagen, 2000, pp.50-55).

Following the 2001 meeting of the Funding Committee for the Environment, a "working group on zoning" was created, bringing together the technical advisors of bilateral co-operation agencies, the conservation NGOs, and officials of the forest administration. A preliminary zoning of the country's forests should be completed, using in particular the maps of the 1996 ecological survey, to determine the zones that will be made the object of further consultation. According to the World Bank representative, the long-term vocation of the different forest expanses of the country must be determined. It is proposed, "as an example," that the nearly 12 million remaining hectares should eventually be distributed among the following four categories (FCE, 2001, p.69):

- two million hectares for protected areas;
- four million hectares for management by communities;
- four million hectares managed by the public forest administration for prevention of harvesting or for exploitation by tender; and
- two million hectares for concessions to moral or private persons, including territorial collectivities.

However, implementation of the zoning plan will eventually lead to a problem regarding the sharing of territory between the public forest administration and the village communities. To the extent to which the different categories of forests are defined in a mutually exclusive manner, public delimitation and thus the area of the potential community forest of each village will depend on its classification in the zoning plan. According to the law on local management of renewable resources, however, transfer of management can be requested for any local forest, independently of its status in the zoning plan. The risk of incoherence and jurisdictional conflicts is thus present within the recently proposed measures.

As we can see through this example, the implementation of international norms is conditioned by norm production on a global scale. Biodiversity, as an object of international relations in the traditional sense, is dealt with through multilateral environmental agreements such as the CBD. In actual practice, however, norms on biodiversity management are created and implemented through the global foreign aid regime, which has its own logic, interests, and standards. Given their great financial dependence, the networks of individuals who control a ministry, in this case the Ministry of Forests, accept adapting their roles and their policies to the agenda of foreign aid, delegating the responsibility for coherence to donors and creditors. As a result of a long practice of structural adjustment and of the progressive transformation of conditionality, developing states are splintered into different sectorial organizations that have a direct dialogue with donors. The government, although participating in the negotiation of multilateral environmental agreements, is only partially capable of ensuring a coherence between rules of international law and the day-to-day management of biodiversity on its own territory by the networks of foreign aid.

The stakes and struggles that this situation implies are underanalysed by the social sciences, primarily because these disciplines are primarily oriented by the CBD and other international agreements. It is rare to find analyses that go beyond the operational preoccupations of domestic implementation of multilateral environmental agreements and which at the same time rely on empirical analysis.

Secondly, the classical methods have problems in conceptually grasping the interactions between norm creation at the international level and norm creation at the global level.

The concept of international regime has allowed not only the inclusion of stakeholders – whose interactions are not immediately evident – into the analysis of international relations by demonstrating that their actions have significant coherence, but also the integration of practices that escape the scrutiny of traditional analyses, such as international networks. As a "bridging-concept" (Hufty, 2000), the concept of international regime can be useful for an interdisciplinary approach within which international relations, law, sociology, and political economy find a common theoretical tool. Provided that its semantic field be widened to include various forms of soft law, that is, the actual dynamics and processes that the Convention on Biological Diversity reflects, the concept of international regime appears to be operational for an analysis of domestic environmental policies.

The national conservation programmes of the South are copied on the foreign aid model. They are characterized by conditionality, programmes and projects "imposed" on the governments of weak states, technical support provided by foreign specialists, artificial creation of "local" NGOs, participatory ideology, etc. Another example of the aid regime applied to the environment is the financing mechanism for the Convention on Biological Diversity. The Global Environment Facility (GEF), created by the World Bank a year before the Rio Earth Summit, was designated, from lack of a better alternative and as a result of pressure from countries of the North, as the temporary financing mechanism for the Convention. It remains so ten years later and represents one of the major sources of financing for national conservation programmes linked to the application of the Convention. In Madagascar, the GEF has pledged to provide 25 per cent of the external funding ($20.8 million USD) for the financing plan of the EP2. Formally co-administered by the World Bank, the United Nations Development Programme and the United Nations Environment Programme, it is strongly influenced by the organizational culture of the bank and of the foreign aid regime. As one observer notes: "the GEF funds biodiversity chiefly as any other World Bank project... This means that the GEF focuses on projects rather than development paths" (Swanson, 1997, p.91).

The Effects of Development Aid: Short Circuits and Long Circuits

To analyse the domestic impacts of the norms and procedures originating from the international regime, we can borrow from recent research on the sociology of development aid. One useful concept is that of "short circuits" (Naudet, 1999), defined as the selection by development agencies of the institutions, groups, individuals, and ideas of the beneficiary society considered better suited to support their action. Concerned with succeeding in its development action, project, or programme, each agency creates a specific network of relationships with local partners who in turn need to adapt to the specificities of the planned action in order to benefit from the corresponding funding. All of these agencies are primarily concerned "with the good operation of the tools they have devised, the materialization of results that can be attributed to them and the promotion of the exemplary nature of their own style of support" (Jacob, 2000, p.24), more than with the real consequences of their actions.

Applied to the implementation of the norms on biodiversity, this analysis tool can make up for the shortcomings of a definition of the international regime that would be too restrictive if concerned only with the implementation of the regulatory base emerging from multilateral environmental agreements.

In Madagascar, the short circuits are the selections usually made by bilateral development activities, which include activities within the framework of the EAP. To continue with examples from the forest sector, within the context of support for the revision of forest policy and legislation (Polfor Project), as early as 1993 the Swiss Co-operation Agency began encouraging the elaboration of legislation based on participative and community management of forests. Enactment of a law on local management of renewable resources in 1996, prepared by the Office national de l'environnement with the assistance of French and American experts, has made the Swiss idea obsolete, because forests are its prime object. This has not prevented the drafting of a rival legal procedure called "contractualized management," inspired by Swiss technical assistance. The 2001 implementation decree of Article 24 of the forest law codifies the role of the forest administration in negotiations with village communities. These are no longer considered as legal equals with autonomous regulatory powers, but as entities to which responsibilities have been delegated unilaterally by the forest legislation prior to any negotiations. In this case, national feelings and the personal ambitions of the technical assistants coincided with the esprit de corps of forest officials. The respective advantages and disadvantages of the two management transfer procedures were recently debated during a workshop organized by the same technical assistants (Interco-opération/CI/DGEF, 2001).

There is a need to co-ordinate development and conservation actions and therefore for a national institutional framework that is coherent with the "short circuits," if only for the sake of the effectiveness of foreign aid spending. This extension of the intervention of the institutional framework can be called a "long circuit". An example comes from the Integrated Conservation and Development Projects. Each ICDP was managed by one or several distinct agencies, whose particularities determined the operational style of the ICDP supported. As a model, the ICDP tool and its participative logic represented a minimal mechanism of co-ordination among donors. Each development agency has, however, experienced the failure of this model in the field and thus the failure of its own short circuit, triggering a general demand for a change in the management model for protected areas. The official recognition of the failure of the ICDPs during the Mahajanga symposium on human inhabitation of protected areas in 1994 created the opportunity to draft a more coherent policy for areas in the periphery of protected areas (Weber, 1995). This policy later became Law 96-025 on the local management of renewable resources and the new model for common pool resource management.

Generally, there is a functional complementarity rather than a rivalry between the short circuits and the long circuits, between interventions in the field and changes in the legislative framework within which these interventions are carried out. The change in the framework reduces the tension caused by disharmony between field actions and the legal and administrative setting and is supposed to minimize transaction costs and facilitate the co-ordination of participants. However, the functional complementarity between short circuits and long circuits often operates in the opposite direction: in order to supply "scientific" proofs of the merits of administrative reorganization and the new legislative framework, EAP donors cannot do without the results of the experiments carried out by field projects.

What is the place of national institutions in this dynamic? Again using the example of the management of forests and protected areas, the Ministry of Forests remains the largest missing partner. Its staff and its financial resources are clearly insufficient to accomplish the tasks assigned to it under the legal framework despite the existence of a project to support its reorganization. Its only possibilities for action are limited to field interventions financed through the occasional support of donors. It reacts more than it anticipates and adapts to changes proposed by the agencies of the EAP or the aid regime in general.

Therefore, its adaptation remains superficial and in part deceptive. The Malagasy political elites seemingly accept adapting the country to the norms and standards that are dominant within the biodiversity regime. This acceptance manifests itself through the adoption of national laws written by technical assistants from the donor community (Gelose and new forest legislation) or through changes in the organization of state services, whether they involve the restructuring of existing administrations, as for the Ministry of Waters and Forests, or the creation of new organizations directly financed and structured by donors, such as the executive agencies of the EAP.

When external parties wish to circumvent national institutions judged to be inefficient, they may decide to duplicate them with *ex nihilo* creations. This management credo, more and more frequent in the international aid regime, advocates not worrying about existing institutional structures when they do not meet the criteria of efficiency, responsibility, and transparency. This reasoning rests on three assumptions. First, that the government of Madagascar does not have the institutional structures adapted to its needs. Second, that the ineffectiveness of these institutions is the result of a bureaucratic tradition and the informal networks that have penetrated them, networks of the exchange of favours and of corruption. The objective, therefore, is to create an unspoiled institutional situation, the new organization resting on a modern managerial base (new public management) and free of crony networks or political influence. Third, the idea that these new institutions are the spearhead of state reform and that by emulation, they will stimulate a general transformation of bureaucratic organizations.

This is how an autonomous organization was created during the first phase of the EAP, the Association nationale pour la gestion des aires protégées (ANGAP), which is in charge of managing all the protected areas and co-ordinating the various ICDPs. It is a private organization under the supervision of the state (Ministry of the Environment). Although the state remains on the face of it the only proprietor of the protected areas, the ministry charged with the supervision of ANGAP has little influence over it in reality. In contrast, the relationships between ANGAP and its donors are close. The main source of ANGAP's financing is the Grant Management Unit of USAID. Its objectives and procedures are negotiated with donors. Those in charge of its services are supported as a matter of routine by expatriate technical advisers and foreign experts who intervene punctually in the most important studies and evaluations.

However, the apparent acceptance of foreign norms and standards by the Malagasy elites hides profound conflicts, and the new institutions face significant problems. First of all, old networks are soon re-created. Traditions of reciprocity prevent individuals from isolating themselves from their entourage. Each person is linked to multiple networks (caste, geographic origin, age, schools attended) in the face of which professional loyalty is but one criterion among many. These institutions, which benefit from significant foreign funding, are artificial. They are not embedded in the historicity of the social fabric. In a logic of expecting to be "abandoned" by foreign aid, members integrate these new institutions into the historical context of the social fabric by submitting them to rules that apply to all of society. Also, the relative wealth of these new institutions and the privileges they offer evidently create resentments and antagonize the organizations that did not benefit from the funding manna. Healthy emulation is transformed into rivalry, which paralyzes their actions:

> The debate that should be focused on the management norms of the resource is but the hidden face of another on the question of the role of the stakeholders associated with decision-making. Each of the groups of stakeholders has an interest in making its situation more permanent. The parallel administration, which must disappear at the end of the Environmental Programme 3, consoles itself in its position of 'good student' when its only credibility is in complying with the rules of transparency and of conformity without any political influence from the state. This administration, which is made up of transferred personnel from the public administration, does not miss an opportunity to show that the public administration no longer has the necessary expertise to be an efficient partner in resource management. Foresters react logically to this by implementing a strategy of systematic obstruction at their level of competence: still, the right of veto is present (proposition and endorsement of legislation, powers of assent, examination and delivery of permits). (Ramamonjisoa, 2001, p.4)

It is not evident that this "right of veto" will always be tolerable for donors who wish to reduce the rate of deforestation to conserve "biodiversity". According to them, direct management of the forest domain must be defined in an institutional framework that is more "dynamic" and more efficient for meeting this objective. The forest legislation, in its Article 24, gives power to the state to delegate the management of state forests to other persons, public or private. The state could therefore delegate this responsibility to an autonomous organization charged with the conservation and the management or control of the classified or non-classified national forest domain. There is thus no impediment to removing the jurisdiction of the Ministry of Forests and Wildlife in favour of a management organization similar to ANGAP. Such an organization would be expected to ensure the prerogatives of public power, especially with regard to the application and follow-up of regulations as well as the matter of enforcement. It should also ensure dynamic technical support in order to respond efficiently to opportunities and adapt rapidly to change.

The Implementation of the CBD as an Interdisciplinary Problem

The emergence of a new international biological order is not only the work of the civil servants and international law experts who draft its norms, but also the work of ecologists, economists, political scientists and philosophers, NGOs, and of representatives of local communities and the industries of life. Each professional group casts a particular light on certain aspects of the biodiversity question, putting forward perceptions and concerns specific to its disciplinary outlook. However, these groups share a certain number of beliefs – for example, the need to conserve a universal heritage and the idea that conservation is linked to economic valuation. Their individual contributions converge in a more or less integrated whole, an "epistemic community" that gives a normative, legal, political, economic, and social basis to the new order.

This community is evidently not homogeneous. Within it exist fissures and conflicts, which can be explained in terms of differences among disciplinary viewpoints. In the ethical debates raised by the implementation of the CBD, these differences materialized at two levels. The positions adopted in the debate on intergenerational equity rest in fact on beliefs held regarding the relationship between the natural and social sciences. The manner in which a position is taken in the debate on equity *within* the same generation depends, for its part, on beliefs held regarding the relationships among the various disciplines of the social sciences, especially economics, law, and sociology.

Relationships between Humans and Nature

Problems of intergenerational equity are generally addressed from two angles. In a first perspective, generally a mechanistic conception of the natural sciences (biology, ecology) held by the proponents of conservation, we talk about "equity among species and ecosystems". Should we include this or that species on the IUCN red list? What is the importance of the endemic lemurs of Madagascar to humanity? Must we protect them for their intrinsic value or for their ecotouristic value? How many hectares of natural forests must be kept aside as protected areas? Is the network of parks implemented by the EAP sufficient to conserve biodiversity? Should we support a "zero deforestation" policy? How should we decide the "vocation" of different forest areas when it is proposed that zoning decisions be made on the scale of the entire country? Which forests should we select for "common pool resource management"?

At the origin of interventions (projects, legislation, political conditions) in support of conservation was the perception of an ecosystem disturbed by human actions. Conversely, it was expected that putting an end to human actions – ending this disturbance – would allow the ecosystem to recover its natural equilibrium. However, the conception of a management system does not rely on ecological surveys alone but essentially must develop elements and tools that involve economic, social, and political issues. The proponents of this perspective, who speak explicitly from the side of social sciences, try to show that ecosystems must be managed socially because that is the only way it can be done (Weber, 1998, p.550). If biodiversity is a social stake, it does not serve any purpose to frame the debate in terms of equity between species or ecosystems, since everything depends on humans in the end.

During the last decade of the implementation of biodiversity norms in Madagascar, perceptions seem to have evolved in this direction. The literature used in this context refers to the "tragedy of the commons," reminding us of the well-known metaphor of G. Hardin (1968) and his conclusion that we need to find appropriate rules to avoid tragedy when a resource is overexploited. Beginning in the 1980s, authors writing about common property management accused Hardin of having erred on the nature of commons. These authors asserted that the commons traditionally ensured the efficient management of renewable resources, as opposed to open access situations. The model of "common property" or "common pool resource" management is based on neo-institutionalist theses, which challenge the merits of state monopoly on property and renewable resources and propose as an alternative solution a case-by-case examination of the allocation and management rules according to type of goods considered (Ostrom, 1990).

The decentralized management of renewable resources having become the common reference in the discourse of international funding agencies and rural NGOs during the 1990s, the neo-institutional paradigm now plays a fundamental role in matters related to the sustainable management of forests and biodiversity. In recent years, this paradigm has been especially reflected in new forestry and environmental codes in developing countries planning the creation of community forests. Neo-institutionalism has become the dominant paradigm since legislative reforms have attempted to change the very structure of the local state in addition to focusing on rural development projects (communal forestry, integrated conservation and development, anti-erosion campaigns, etc.). The law on local management of 1996 (Gelose), which was to "end *de facto* situations of free access and make the management of renewable resources more coherent," established this change of paradigm in Madagascar.

The farmers, traditionally perceived as ignorant, have suddenly become the best guardians of the environment. The itinerant slash-and-burn system, which has been conclusively shown to be detrimental to the environment in Madagascar, is returning as the flavour of the day:

> The local populations, even the most 'primitive,' have management systems capable of modifying the 'natural' environment slowly but efficiently; these systems, but mostly the slash-and-burn, are multiple, original, evolving and are capable of intensification. The fallows are not abandoned to the sole reconstitution of the soil's potential but are productive spaces and can evolve, in case of need, towards different forms of forest gardens or agroforests. (Rossi, 1999, p.35)

This change in paradigm highlights one of the characteristics of the short circuits as encountered in the implementation of the EAP: their cyclic amnesia. Stakeholders suddenly reject what they had earlier promoted forcefully and with conviction, as if they were under the shock of an epistemological rupture (Jacob, 2000). Soon they will reject this new "truth" as well, convinced that they have discovered a better solution. This amnesia of the "developers" is not a shortcoming of the system but on the contrary allows for its reproduction, the capacity of pursuing a programme and its experiments, even when faced with a failure considered as temporary.

Even the most devoted conservationists now believe in the community management of forests as a solution for deforestation. The risk is great that nostalgic culturalists in search of paradise lost will be disillusioned. Under the impact of social changes (migrations, impoverishment, demographic pressure, globalization, and disintegration of traditional structures), the traditional mechanisms no longer operate. Humans have definitely transformed the ecosystems of Madagascar. Demographic growth inevitably makes sustainable slash-and-burn agriculture impossible. When "customary" rules encourage it, the problem of overexploitation remains unresolved. How then can tragedy be avoided? Certainly not without transforming these communal systems.

Of course the illusion is understandable insofar as the weak point of "Newtonian science" is indeed a misunderstanding of the interrelationships between humanity and nature. However, mysticism delays arriving at a real solution. Scientifically recorded deforestation, even from a mechanistic perspective, remains what it is: deforestation. It will not transform itself into sustainable management merely because all the parties concerned discuss it. The real ethical problem of the relationship between humanity and nature is not a question of knowing who is closest to nature (undoubtedly the farmer) but of knowing how much energy humanity as a whole can consume at the expense of other life-forms and future generations if it wants to live permanently on the planet and how this energy consumption can be shared within the current generation.

This question is related to world distribution of access to fossil fuels. If the farmers of Madagascar used modern agricultural methods and if the urban population had cheap access to gas or electricity, the forest would probably not continue to shrink at the same speed. It is not surprising, under present conditions, that forests are disappearing. To be astonished by it is to prove one's membership in the "epistemic community".

From a more removed viewpoint, it is not simply a question of choosing between the natural sciences and the social sciences in order to analyse the dilemmas of the relationship between humanity and nature and discard false solutions (a task that should be undertaken by the international biodiversity regime). To progress in this direction, it would be necessary to establish the relative autonomy of the social sciences in regard to the natural sciences, based on observable facts and not on idealistic positions.

The Sharing of Costs and Benefits

The international biodiversity regime defines the rights and responsibilities of the stakeholders involved in very diverse areas that all bear on the living. It institutionalizes them. It establishes norms for the distribution of costs and benefits associated with the use of biodiversity and influences the expectations of stakeholders. The debate on intergenerational equity, that is, future expectations, is brought to the debate on equity among the same generation. All questions concerning future generations must be decided in the present. Therefore, the causality of economic behaviour does not move from the past toward the future but from the future toward the present.

For the sake of theoretical development, regime analysis should therefore include the institutions as well as the expectations of stakeholders, and following the preceding discussion, it should be interdisciplinary. The classical institutional economy (Commons, 1934) is promising in this respect. The basic unit of this approach, the concept of transaction, defined as the "place where individual and collective actions are articulated in respect to one another" (Gislain, 1999, p.58), permits an understanding of the conflicting relationships inherent in the problem of the distribution of a rare resource, the collective action process resulting in rules that allow these conflicts to be resolved and maintain co-operation among stakeholders by creating new institutional arrangements. The transaction concept allows an integration of the viewpoints of the various social sciences disciplines: economics, through analysis of the bargaining over a rare resource; law, by seeing the transaction as an actual transfer of property and future use rights; political science, through the study of the interest groups that will influence the institutions by ensuring the authoritative distribution of the resource; sociology (and ethics), from the conditioning of these exchanges by the expectations of stakeholders.

The ethical problems associated with the sharing of benefits arising from the use of biodiversity are generally discussed as two aspects: equity among states or nations and equity within a country itself. As demonstrated by the example of bioprospecting, the concept of regime, as a unit defining new rights and responsibilities, allows for grasping transactions at different levels in a single mental sweep.[33]

Countries containing areas with rich biological diversity hope to profit from it as much as states containing oil or other natural resources. However, without the genetic engineering technology of industrialized countries, biological diversity would only entail leaves and bark (Stone, 1996, p.124). There is therefore a potential for an increase in collective wealth through co-operative activity, that is, through transactions negotiated in the market whereby a country cedes a property right (on a gene) for an immediate benefit. The question arising concerns the nature of the institutions that regulate the market and the rules they propose. Developing countries, rich in biological diversity and generally producers of raw resources, are currently at a disadvantage, a situation sanctioned by these institutions. It is in this context that the regime is evolving.

Transactions related to bioprospecting also have implications for equity within the countries themselves. Traditional knowledge about flora and fauna can be a source of information for the development of products in various sectors (especially pharmaceutical and agricultural), thanks to biotechnology. This knowledge contributes to a reduction of biotechnology research costs insofar as it increases the chances for success. As a consequence, traditional knowledge can have an important economic value.

In Madagascar, local communities affected by bioprospecting transactions can, in principle, be remunerated under the terms of contracts for the transfer of renewable resource management (Babin et al., 2001). However, we must note that the transactions studied by these authors do not bear on genetic resources. Despite the title of their study (*Methods of Rapid Appraisal for In Situ Management of Genetic Resources*), it deals with traditional non-timber forest products (*Prunus africanus*, *Centella asiatica*) from which the pharmaceutical industries of industrialized countries simply extract the active compounds.[34]

Studies of the commercial value of biodiversity suggest, in a general manner, that the matters in the dispute over a "fair sharing" are almost certainly exaggerated relative to profit potential. No immediate rush from pharmaceutical companies has yet occurred to cast doubt on this finding (Stone, 1996, p.124). One compelling example is the famous rosy periwinkle (*Catharantus roseus*, endemic to Madagascar and from which anti-cancer alkaloids are extracted), one of the rare successes of bioprospecting that can be found in all textbooks on the economy of biodiversity. Not only has this species been distributed on four continents as an ornamental plant, which makes it impossible for Madagascar to hold a commercial monopoly, but it is also cultivated on a large scale as a raw material by a capitalist sector disinclined to share its profits. Probably the toughest question is not how to divide the income – easily exaggerated – that biodiversity will produce but rather how to share the cost that the conservation of biodiversity will certainly entail.

The literature on environmental management does not sufficiently take into account the fact that the same assets must undergo distinct transactions depending on whether they are used as a biological resource or as a genetic resource. Indeed, securing transactions on genetic resources which allows for returns on investments in the life industry, is not feasible without controlling the distributive relations that have a bearing on the physical substrate of the genetic resources. However, this substrate, the biological material, still essentially has its traditional status as a biological resource so that stakeholders expecting income from genetic resources must deal with already existing rights and vested interests in the use of biological resources. These rights and interests continue to be the object of recurrent transactions in the agricultural and forestry sectors, not to mention in traditional uses of areas and resources. All of these transactions are traditionally defined by the state monopoly on land and its subdivisions (forest governance in particular) as well as by ways of evading the monopolies, which are more often the rule than the exception in developing countries.

It immediately appears that "biodiversity rent" is only very partially generated by transactions that deal with genetic resources proper but it represents in reality a composite of various types of economic anticipations.[35] Under the pretext of distributing potential benefits from genetic resources,[36] the biodiversity regime remains concerned with the renegotiation of access to biological resources. The CBD represents a compromise between opposing interest groups, which are concerned with different sets of recurrent transactions (Aubertin, Boisvert, and Vivien, 1998). According to these authors, developing countries have traded off their sovereignty over biological resources, as well as additional resources for development, for an extension of intellectual property rights to the resources and methods used by biotechnology.

However, in view of the dependency of developing countries on international aid, which allows the imposition of a resource management model by the conditionality mechanisms described above, their sovereignty over their resources can be considered limited. From a sociological point of view, the distributive relations are therefore not defined by sovereign rights of states over their resources but by the interactions of the aid regime with the results of international environmental negotiations. For the international aid community, increasing the responsibility of farmer communities in order to conserve forests is an attempt to internalize the costs of establishing control over territories and resources, given that financial means are becoming scarce (Babin and Bertrand, 1998). By making the farmer bear the cost of conservation, the current strategy of management transfer in Madagascar is part of a long tradition of indirect rule, which achieves the insertion of rural populations into the world economy.

Conclusion

During the decade of implementing international norms concerning biodiversity, actions in Madagascar have shifted from a project-based approach (the Integrated Conservation and Development Projects) toward a more integral approach using legislative and administrative reforms (local resource management, forest legislation). However, in practice, things have not evolved much. There is still a need for the equivalent of a ICDP in terms of infrastructures to negotiate the use of renewable resources as common heritage and to sign management contracts with local communities, that is, in order to apply the new legislation.

One may ask whether the new legislation did not have as an objective the facilitation of the work of development aid projects. It is certain that in spite of the shift from projects to legislation, the privileged mode of interaction between the new organizations of the regime and the existing public administration is characterized by an absence of consensus on the root of the problem and thus, at best, by "productive misunderstandings" between development agencies sure of their approaches and sectors of the administration acting according to a logic of attracting aid funding. As Lampedusa would say, everything must change on paper to make sure that nothing will change in reality. This raises questions as to whether or not the regime established by the CBD will be able to create the conditions of its own success in socio-economic settings comparable to that of Madagascar. At the present stage in the implementation of the biodiversity regime, it would seem preferable to ask good questions rather than to provide definite answers.

Currently, farmers and forest administrators refuse to engage in collective learning prompted by the international regime. These two categories of stakeholders have no reason to enter into an environmental negotiation that would challenge the existing management rules. According to informal rules, there is not necessarily a conflict of interest between farmers and the forest administration. According to the new laws, the two parties should be able to resolve their conflicts by the transfer of management from the state to the communities. However, the two parties participating in the negotiation have often previously co-operated in parallel economies organized around the exploitation of certain forest products but not ecologically viable. The idea of collective learning, therefore, should be conceived as a form of organization with the goal of rendering negotiable the rules that are not negotiable under current conditions. The learning experience is possible only if "latent" conflicts are identified and made explicit. It is also possible under the following condition: negotiation at the local level must bear effectively on the stakes that are crucial for managing the ongoing concern in question.

Ongoing concerns generated in a non-sustainable manner cannot be restructured only through negotiation at the local level. This restructuring actually poses the problem of articulating different levels of regulation by a multilevel governance (Hufty, 2001). To achieve a collective learning experience at the level of local communities, a comparable collective learning experience must occur at the national level, that is, at the level of the definition of the economic, taxation, and regulatory frameworks under which future negotiation of local management plans will take place. Ongoing research is attempting to measure the impact of these frameworks at various points in the decision-making process:

- the relationships between sectorial planning and intersectorial planning (between forest management and land-use management) and therefore between the administrations responsible for these tasks;
- the country-wide zoning of forest areas required by donors and creditors of the EAP (especially the World Bank and USAID); and
- revision of the forest taxation system and forest control in the context of the creation of the autonomous provinces.

Although it is not yet possible to delineate the boundaries of the "international biodiversity regime" without ambiguity when analysing its impacts on national policies, definitions of the normative base taken from international law are insufficient to understand its dynamics. Insofar as international funds are made available for the conservation of biodiversity (thus as investments in potential but rather elusive future benefits from genetic resources) they must be considered as part of the international biodiversity regime as a subject of study. However, the political conditionality attached to this "aid" operates outside sectorial boundaries.

For the political elite of a developing nation, it may be convenient to legislate according to the priorities of the World Bank on environmental issues in order to ensure its overall goodwill, which of course touches sectors other than biodiversity. The true stake involved is less the change in the rules for conserving genetic resources than the renegotiation of forest governance, a legacy of colonial law, without having to give up the advantages of the current use of forested areas while gaining access to additional resources in the name of their conservation. The implementation of the CBD, indeed the creation of a new international biological order capable of creating its own conditions of success, seems unlikely without a fundamental change in the delivery conditions of international aid.

Notes

This chapter was translated by Patricia Wood. The translation was revised by the authors.

[1] As opposed to most authors, we differentiate between the concepts of biological diversity (genetic, specific, and ecosystemic) and biodiversity. The latter, by being part of global environmental changes, extends beyond natural sciences. It is interdisciplinary, constructed socially around stakes that are institutional, judicial, political, economic, ethic, and cultural (Hufty, 2000).

[2] Tropical forests cover only 6 per cent of the land mass area but contain 50 per cent of living species. Edward O. Wilson (1992), *The Diversity of Life*, Harvard University Press.

[3] The relation between foreign aid and development is described by Wood (1986).

[4] Numbers vary according to their source; this number is the most often quoted.

[5] World Bank (2001), *World Development Indicators.*

[6] *Ibidem.*

[7] Between 1971 and 1996, per capita income dropped by 50 per cent (World Bank, 1996; Roubaud, 2000). Seventy-five per cent of the population was considered as being poor in 1996 (World Bank, 1996a: The poor are defined as those who are unable to purchase both the required food – 2,100 calories per day – and the minimum non-food needs).

[8] It makes up approximately 12 per cent of exportation revenues. This is an average from 1994 to 1998 but with a decreasing trend due to international prices. The Economist Intelligence Unit, Madagascar, *Country Profile 2000.*

[9] From $1.30 to 28 cents USD. *Ibidem*; and Oxfam (2001), *Bitter Coffee: How the Poor are Paying for the Slump in Coffee Prices* (http://www.oxfam.org.uk/policy/papers/coffee.htm) (25 July 2001). We must take into account a cumulated inflation of more than 100 per cent between 1995 and 2001 to fully understand the magnitude of these variations. It should be noted that the coffee tree has a high symbolic value because it implies the definite ownership of cleared land in rural areas.

[10] The statistics for the annual rate of deforestation vary among sources: between 128,000 hectares for the World Conservation Monitoring Centre (*Madagascar: Conservation of Biological Diversity*, 1998) and 200,000 to 300,000 hectares for researchers of the Institut de recherche pour le développement (*Fiche scientifique 112: Madagascar: la forêt menacée*, 2000).

[11] WWF was very active in South Africa, and the Madagascar government, because of its anti-apartheid stance, was refusing any association with organizations operating in that country. WWF was perceived as an imperialist fifth column. Interview with Barthélémy Voahita, Antananarivo, 12 July 1999.

[12] This document has had a major influence on the Madagascar biodiversity strategy, which has repeated almost verbatim the priority actions it proposes.

[13] République démocratique de Madagascar (1988), *Proposition de Plan d'action environnemental.*

[14] République démocratique de Madagascar (1990), *Charte de l'environnement* (Bill 90-033).

[15] The government of Madagascar largely repeated the EAP planning in its first *National Report on the Convention on Biological Diversity* (RdM, 1998a).

[16] Of which $181 million USD are grants and $36 million USD are loans (IDA and USAID). Of this amount, $150 million USD was spent (World Bank, 1996b). The share of the government of Madagascar was about 8 per cent of the total spent.

[17] According to funds granted (World Bank, 1996b): creation or reinforcement of a network of specialized institutions, protection of biological diversity, soil conservation, restructuring of forest management, mapping of the territory, land ownership security, research and management of marine environments.

[18] USAID, *Madagascar FY 1999 Congressional Presentation.* The same argument is repeated each year. US bilateral co-operation has provided 45 per cent of the total expenditures of the EP1 and 55 per cent of the financing of the sub-programmes biodiversity and forests.

[19] The Office concentrates on allocating funding, studies, personnel training and public education programmes, as well as administering calls for tenders. It organizes annual co-ordination meetings for the EAP.

[20] An evaluation echoed by the Antsirabe Workshop: "Some representatives of the state do not even respect the laws; fraudulent dealings and corruption are legion in the public service" (ONE, 1995, p.40). See also RdM (1998b), *Document stratégique consolidé du Programme environnemental II (PE2) par la partie malagasy*.

[21] The income for the seven protected areas most visited by tourists totalled 972 million Madagascar francs between 1992 and 1997, or approximately $140,000 USD (République de Madagascar, *Rapport national sur la diversité biologique*, 1998).

[22] According to Peters (1998), Ranomafana Park has created about 100 jobs, of which half were held by individuals coming from outside the area, for a local population of 27,000, spread among 160 villages or hamlets.

[23] The EP1 only ended in July 1997. The EP2 has been the subject of a specific legislative-programme: Bill 97-012 6 June 1997 aimed at modifying and completing the Madagascar Environmental Charter. The EP2 has funding of $152 million USD, of which $31 million USD from the government of Madagascar, $30 million USD is a loan from the World Bank, $22 million USD is a grant from USAID, and $21 million USD comes from the GEF (RdM, 1998b).

[24] Bill 93-005 of 24 February 1994 on the general orientation of the decentralization policy, modified and completed by Bill 94-039 of 3 January 1995.

[25] The Convention was sanctioned by Bill No. 95-013 of 9 August 1995 and by Decree 95-695 of 3 November 1995.

[26] An internal unit of the Office national pour l'environnement is in charge of developing the regional and spatial approach: the Regional Management and Spatial Approach Support Unit (AGERAS: Appui à la gestion régionale et à l'approche spatiale).

[27] Understood here as a concept belonging to the context of global environmental changes, at the borders of science, of the technical, of the political, and of the economy, and therefore of wider significance than the concept of biological diversity as defined in the CBD (Hufty, 2001).

[28] Workshops of Mantasoa, 1994 (local governance), Mahajunga, 1994 (human inhabitation of protected areas), Antsirabe, 1995 (local community management).

[29] For a report on Gelose after four years, see Maldidier (2000).

[30] Section 2 of Bill 96-025 and Decree 2000-028 on environmental mediators.

[31] When individual or collective actions interact while structuring themselves.

[32] The principle according to which the development of the countries of the South must occur through their incorporation into the global market is one of these meta-norms. It imposes a culturally slanted model, with institutions essential to market economics (for example, private property).

[33] See also chapter 7 by Blais in this volume.

[34] This confusion of terminology may be explained by the fact that a research project in Madagascar has, under current circumstances, a greater chance of being funded if it is presented under the label of "genetic resources" than if it is identified as a research project on non-timber forest products, which is closer to reality.

[35] See also chapter 11 by Revéret and Webster in this volume.

[36] As indicated by the restriction of the debate on access and benefit-sharing to the relatively insignificant question of bioprospecting.

Conclusion

The Long Road to a New Order

Philippe G. Le Prestre

The Convention on Biological Diversity (CBD) is a wide-ranging, ambitious, and deeply political convention. A single volume can hardly cover all its dimensions. Indeed its very scope has been seen as a weakness (e.g. Werksman, 1997). Under such circumstances, states naturally tend to favour objectives that accord better with their national priorities, the power of specific constituencies, or their own interpretation of what constitutes the core of the Convention, with the danger that implementation will be at variable speeds and asynchronic. The G-77 generally considers the three basic goals of the Convention to be linked, which is what gives the CBD its novel character in their eyes. Other Parties and stakeholders, however, would like to delink them. Activities are then promoted and supported in order to facilitate what is deemed "more feasible" in the short term, putting other issues on the back-burner and leading sometimes to an international dialogue of the deaf.

As this volume has illustrated, the scope of the CBD goes well beyond conservation to include sustainable development issues – it has even been called "the first truly and for the moment the foremost sustainable development treaty"[1]– and equity issues. It touches not only on humanity's relationship with nature and international relations but on the distribution of domestic political power as well. It involves, logically, taking into account not only the means of conserving biodiversity but also the causes of biodiversity loss and the processes that foster it, such as the structure of property rights, patterns of trade, culture, unsustainable development, and inequitable social relationships. For example, Hufty and Muttenzer, in this volume, raise the issue of external determinants of biodiversity loss and conservation in the context of Madagascar; Thomas does the same in his examination of trade and intellectual property rights issues. Likewise, Potvin et al. point to the importance of cultural variables and Guay to the social construction of biodiversity. Given the multiple dimensions of the regime, the evaluation of its effectiveness will necessarily be partial and depend on the priorities of the observer: it can be moving toward effectiveness in two or three dimensions but stalled in others.

Chapter 3 identified certain prerequisites of regime effectiveness and argued that it might be a more fruitful way of assessing the impact of the regime than focusing on outcomes, i.e. whether biodiversity loss is actually being curtailed. These prerequisites pertain to the operation of the convention governance system, or CGS (institutional development, operation, and financing), information (transparency), capacity-building (financing, national capacity-building), network-building (NGOs, co-operation with other intergovernmental organizations), the development of consensual knowledge (development of tools and indicators, role of the Subsidiary Body for Scientific, Technical and Technological Advice, or SBSTTA), legitimacy, and learning. The extent to which the CBD has made progress in strengthening these prerequisites will be addressed in the following sections which focus on the evolution and implementation of the CBD.

The Evolution of the CBD since 1992

A regime is a dynamic institution. This dynamism stems from the state of development of its learning capacity, from the nature of the Convention itself (in this case its framework character), from implementation efforts, and from its impact on the redistribution of interests and on the availability of means to pursue them. As the chapters by McGraw, Pythoud and Thomas, and Le Prestre illustrate, the regime has not – indeed could not – stand still. Some delegations, notably the United States, as related by McGraw, had even complained that the negotiations were too rushed, which meant that the final text contained too many "conceptual and drafting deficiencies" and that many gaps remained to be filled. As McGraw points out, "Because many of the most contentious issues were left unresolved at the time of the CBD's adoption, the post-agreement negotiations have proven particularly challenging". The text of the Convention established the contours of its evolution and future program of work, notably the negotiation of a protocol on biosafety and the specification of the ecosystem approach. Despite the postponement of some of the most crucial elements of negotiations (such as the nature of the financial mechanism), the CBD developed rapidly, coming into force barely 18 months after its adoption and rapidly gaining quasi-universal membership, with a few exceptions, notably that of the US.[2] The CBD of 2002 is not the same as the CBD of 1992.

Institutionally, the evolution of the CBD has been both significant and limited. On the one hand, unlike its two sister conventions, the United Nations Framework Convention on Climate Change (UNFCCC) and the United Nations Convention to Combat Desertification (UNCCD), no new subsidiary body for implementation has been created. On the other hand, a new protocol has been negotiated (two years behind the initial schedule) and institutionally incorporated into the CGS, coupled with the creation of new units. Two new subsidiary bodies were created: the Conference of the Parties (COP) responded to calls for a protocol on indigenous populations by setting up an innovative open-ended ad hoc working group on Article 8(j) (WG8J); and Decision V/26 created an ad hoc open-ended working group on access and benefit-sharing to further the third objective of the Convention. Further, the Secretariat, the SBSTTA, as well as the COP have established various panels and groups to advise them on specific matters: rosters of experts, ad hoc technical expert groups, expert panels, working groups, and liaison groups. Yet, as chapter 4 underscores, uncertainties remain regarding the proper role of the scientific subsidiary body and the role and interrelationships of the various advisory groups created by units of the CGS.

Operationally, five thematic programmes have been initiated: on marine and coastal biodiversity (the Jakarta Mandate), forest biodiversity, agricultural biodiversity, the biodiversity of inland waters, and dry and sub-humid lands (not all are funded equally, however, which limits their development). One other thematic area, mountain ecosystems, will be under consideration at COP-7. In addition, several methodological and cross-cutting issues are being addressed, such as indicators, access and benefit-sharing, the ecosystem approach, protected areas, sustainable use, invasive alien species, assessments, and traditional knowledge, with the ecosystem approach providing the primary framework for action under the Convention. Given the uncertainty of the science underlying these notions as well as their socio-political dimensions, progress has been slow and their integration into specific work programs at the international and national levels will likely be difficult. However, they are also examples of the "forcing" role of the Convention as it fosters the development and operationalization of poorly defined concepts.

Yet, given the scope of the Convention, the multiple demands put upon it, and the necessity to become rapidly operational, it was feared that the Convention might collapse under its own weigh in its early years (see McGraw, chapter 1). It had difficulties dealing with the breadth of its work programme and the expectations of the various constituencies that supported it. As discussed in chapter 4, this hampered the effectiveness of the SBSTTA, which faced an almost unworkable agenda. Consequently, the COP and SBSTTA endeavoured gradually to organize their program of work in order to focus efficiently on advancing a few issues at a time. In addition, at COP-4 the parties decided to hold an intersessional meeting in June 1999 to consider possible arrangements for improving preparations for and conduct of the meetings of the COP, which led to substantial adjustments. Decision IV/16 also adopted a programme of work for the period from COP-4 (1998) to COP-7 (2004). Thus, "a wide array of measures has been agreed upon in the context of the ongoing improvement of the operations of the Convention" (UNEP/CBD/COP/5/17), ranging from the production of a massive handbook to guide the Secretariat in the information it transmits the COP, to the establishment of additional guidelines for the interface of the COP and SBSTTA and the adoption of a strategic plan (see chapter 4). At the same time, SBSTTA undertook several internal procedural reforms to streamline its work and improve its input to the COP. An intersessional meeting on the strategic plan, national reports, and the implementation of the Convention took place in November 2001.

Finally, financing for the Secretariat and the institutions of the Convention has grown substantially, in line with the development of its programs (see tables and figures in Annex 2); this trend will continue with the implementation of the Cartagena Protocol. Financing for biodiversity by the Global Environment Facility (GEF) has also increased significantly (see Annex 2); biodiversity is now the largest portfolio of the GEF. During fiscal years 1995-2000, the GEF approved 339 projects with a total commitment of over $844 million USD. By 2001, the financial mechanism had provided support to over 130 developing countries to develop national biodiversity strategies.

Two cautionary remarks are in order, however. First, the actual level of biodiversity funding remains unclear, as is the extent to which additional resources have been forthcoming. Due to the lack of standardization in the reporting procedures of funding institutions, monitoring of these commitments through bilateral and multilateral aid programmes and private investments has proven difficult. Second, the level of voluntary contributions reflects a situation prevalent in the UN system, especially with regard to the environment, in which Parties fund pet programs, thus making planning more difficult and potentially skewing the implementation of the Convention toward issues that may be peripheral to the needs and concerns of a majority of its members.

The Convention has also developed unevenly. Some items, such as sustainable use (Article 10), have yet to receive substantial consideration by the COP (except for tourism and scattered decisions on agriculture, forests, or marine biodiversity that reflect this preoccupation). Others, such as benefit-sharing, are proving extremely complex to put into practice (see the chapter by François Blais for an elaboration of some of the conceptual difficulties involved). Still others have developed in importance to an extent that was largely unforeseen at the time of negotiation. Article 8(j), for example, has become one of the more powerful instruments that indigenous populations have had at their disposal for protecting and promoting their rights relative to those of the state and civil society at large, although Article 15 emphasizes the rights of governments over their population. The CBD has fostered international co-operation (which preceded the Convention, to be sure) and, in practice, is leading to a redefinition of biodiversity issues in socio-economic terms, a far cry from what conservationists had in mind in 1987. It remains to be seen how successfully "local populations" (whose definition is as political as it is anthropological) will use the Convention to reorder their relations with other groups and with the state and to resist globalization pressures. The CBD may represent not only an incipient biodiversity order but an incipient socio-economic one as well.

The impact of the adoption of the Cartagena Protocol on Biosafety (BP) on the evolution of the implementation of the CBD may also be profound. On the one hand, by channelling increased resources into the Convention, it could foster rapid implementation of some of its institutional (the Clearing-house Mechanism, or CHM) and policy aspects (co-operation). On the other hand, there is the danger that the management of the BP may become one of the central activities of the CGS, conditioning developed countries' priorities and the efforts and the resources of the Secretariat and other bodies devoted to its implementation at the expense of furthering other dimensions of the Convention. Indeed, considerable time was already invested in negotiation of the Protocol by the Secretariat and the parties at the expense of national and regime-level implementation of the CBD.

Normatively, the evolution has also been significant. The CBD has not only developed and disseminated new norms, it has also become a pre-eminent vehicle for norms that were initially considered secondary or that were incipient in the original agreement. Voluntary guidelines in a variety of fields are under development or are being drafted. For instance, guidelines on ecotourism are being prepared and guidelines on access and benefit-sharing aimed at improving predictability in the manner that access is granted by providers of genetic resources to users, were adopted at COP-6 in April 2002. The latter is an extremely complex exercise given the need to harmonize these norms with those governing intellectual property rights issues in other settings. Even more telling is the extent to which norms carried by the CBD have seeped into other regimes. The recent Treaty on Plant Genetic Resources for Food and Agriculture (2001), for example, shares the three objectives of the CBD[3] and recognizes the role of indigenous populations.[4]

Clearly, the CBD is not just about conservation, in practice as well as on paper; it is also about equity, about human, economic, and political rights. This importance stems in part from the uneven prior institutional development of the three areas encompassed by the triple goal of the Convention. Because a network of conservation-oriented groups, institutions, and agreements existed before the adoption of the CBD, it was able to focus on the areas where it could break new ground, such as benefit-sharing and sustainable use. To be sure, the CBD has been active in fostering co-operation, in the development of knowledge (the taxonomy initiative, the ecosystems approach, forest biodiversity[5]) and in raising awareness of several conservation issues (coral bleaching, alien invasive species, forest biodiversity), but these activities could have been undertaken equally well and with similar results in other settings, had the CBD not existed. On the other hand, the CBD has been central in the development of the ecosystem approach as well as norms associated with the other two goals (sustainable use and benefit-sharing), and although it continues to struggle with the proper balancing of its three objectives, it remains central to attempts to link these three goals into a coherent set of norms and actions.

According to more extreme interpretations of Article 8(j), for example, the concept of sovereignty, the first principle reaffirmed in the CBD, should include granting indigenous populations property rights over their cultural heritage as well as local biodiversity.[6] In part, this is intended as a way of affirming the primacy of group rights over individual rights and protecting the survival, welfare, and integrity[7] of these communities; in part, it is intended to prevent them from losing access to biodiversity resources in the name of conservation or through specific access and benefit-sharing arrangements between the state and industry. As currently contemplated, biodiversity would be "co-owned" by the state and local communities (Shiva, 1997).[8] Some representatives of these communities seek not only to control access but also the use of their knowledge and claim that the communities should be compensated for past instances of "biopiracy". In the short term, they ask for a moratorium on bioprospecting until the nature of the arrangements and the relevant rights of indigenous communities have been precisely defined, in an equitable manner.[9]

Therein lies one of the major challenges of the CBD that concerns both the North and the South, as indicated in several chapters in this volume (notably by Blais, Potvin et al., Halley, Wolf, and Hufty and Muttenzer). How will the CBD manage the contradictions that may exist among the norms intrinsic to the agreement, such as between conservation, sustainable use, and benefit-sharing or between traditional knowledge and practices and conservation (for example, the need to change traditional practices detrimental to biodiversity, on the one hand, and the need to harness local sociocultural forces through participation to protect biodiversity, on the other). In the Cartagena Protocol, advance informed agreement (AIA) aims to strike a balance among economic, social, cultural, and environmental objectives through its shared decision-making procedures. As Wolf concludes, multi-objective success will require genuine commitment to use AIA for more than trade convenience. All good things do not always go together.

The Implementation of the Convention

The number and range of obstacles to the full implementation of the regime are vast; indeed it would be fastidious and illusory to attempt to list them all and presumptuous, at this stage, to assess their relative importance. Nevertheless, we can examine a few of the more salient examples, keeping in mind that individual chapters address many others. In doing so, we will distinguish between implementation at the regime level and implementation at the national level.

Implementation at the Regime Level

As McGraw demonstrated in chapter 1, the CBD joined a crowded field, and this forced it to assert its mandate, or at least its legitimate interest, over a range of issues central to its goals. This challenge was complicated by the differing perceptions of the CBD as a "residual" or an "umbrella" convention. A case in point is the issue of forests. Although the clear role and mandate of the CBD in issues of forest biological diversity have been repeatedly confirmed by the Parties, and it is recognized within the CBD that it is vital for issues related to forests to be dealt with in a comprehensive and holistic manner, the CBD has had difficulties in playing a central role in the international debate over forests. Given the competing claims of other IGOs, such as FAO and the International Tropical Timber Organization (ITTO), the diversity of states' interests, and the reluctance to favour one set of norms (embodied by the CBD) over another (promoted by FAO) – which reflects in part the interests of different constituencies (ministries for the environment and conservation NGOs on the one hand versus ministries for agriculture and forests and the forest private sector on the other) – states have favoured discussing these issues in special international fora (such as the

Intergovernmental Panel on Forests (IPF)/Intergovernmental Forum on Forests (IFF) and the United Nations Forum on Forests (UNFF)) outside the context of a single organization. Nevertheless, at its third meeting, the Conference of the Parties requested that the Executive Secretary develop a focused work programme for forest biological diversity, and SBSTTA considered this item in November 2001. The work programme on forest biological diversity was adopted at COP-4 (Decision IV/7) and focuses on research, co-operation, and the development of technologies necessary for the conservation and sustainable use of forest biological diversity. However, at its fifth meeting the COP in Decision V/4, decided to expand the focus of the work programme from research to pratical action. The elements of this expanded work programme were proposed by an ad hoc technical expert group on forest biological diversity and adopted at the seventh meeting (November 2001) of the SBSTTA which forwarded them to the COP for consideration at its sixth meeting (April 2002).[10]

In terms of network-building, the CBD led to the emergence of several NGO-based networks largely devoted to information-sharing about convention-related activities, such as the International Liaison Group (ILG) on the Convention and Bionet (a consortium of US NGOs). Largely absent from the negotiations, NGOs have assumed an active role in implementation. The CBD strengthened existing NGOs and networks eager to promote the goals of the Convention, notably the conservation of biological resources (World Conservation Union, or IUCN), and indigenous issues. At the national level, new national biodiversity coalitions were formed and associations created. Its role in the emergence of academic and scientific networks in support of the objectives of the regime remains less clear. The Secretariat itself has worked with a limited number of well-established institutions. In general, however, its action has concentrated on co-ordination with other bodies.

Indeed, the COP and SBSTTA have repeatedly urged the Secretariat to pursue co-operation with other IGOs. The three Rio agreements advocate synergistic approaches and call for information-sharing and a division of labour to avoid duplication of efforts (Articles 16-18 of the CBD and Articles 20-22 (I) of the UNCCD). The UNCCD, for example, is also a sustainable development convention, strongly emphasizes livelihoods and ecosystems (dry lands), and attaches great relevance to local knowledge, decentralization, and community participation. The potential for operative synergies with the CBD is therefore significant, although translating these initiatives into substantive programmes of work has been slow.

Accordingly, the number of memoranda of co-operation and memoranda of understanding signed has grown steadily, but most have yet to be translated into effective action.[11] In some cases, co-operation is complicated by the newest of the Rio treaties and other agreements. When two regimes-in-the-making are trying to establish the legitimacy of their role in a given issue area, they are reluctant to negotiate a form of co-operation that may amount to a sharing of responsibilities. In other cases, one Party may be reluctant to accept what may eventually become a normative claim on its activities. It is worth noting in this regard that although the implementation of the Jakarta framework of action requires close collaboration with the United Nations Convention on the Law of the Sea (UNCLOS), no memorandum of co-operation had been signed with this organization six years after the adoption of the mandate in 1995.

Co-operation is complicated by the fact that although the CBD is only a framework convention (rather than an umbrella one), as argued by McGraw, it is dependent on co-operation with other bodies to promote and implement its provisions. Thus the question arises of the relationship between this newcomer and earlier agreements and initiatives and of the harmonization of the new principles it embodies with the norms and rules of international law found in previous agreements. Successful co-operation rests on the capacity to harmonize these different norms. Therefore, it is not surprising that the first co-ordination efforts were undertaken with the Ramsar Convention, which shares with the CBD a common ecosystem-centred perspective. As Ovejero (1999, p. 4) has pointed out, the Ramsar Convention anticipated much of the conservation approach of the CBD. It "defines wise use or sustainable utilization as 'the human use of a wetland so that it may yield the greatest continuous benefit to present generations while maintaining its potential to meet the needs and aspirations of future generations'...[and] acknowledges that wetlands constitute a resource of great economic, cultural, scientific and recreational value that should be maintained". By stating in its provisions that "listed sites do not necessarily require protected area status, provided their ecological character is maintained through a wise use management approach" the convention acknowledges that conservation of biodiversity does not necessarily mean precluding human economic activities". Thus, "[a]s early as January 1996, the Ramsar Bureau (the Secretariat of the Convention) and the CBD Secretariat prepared the ground for developing technical co-operation which is seen as a model MEAs co-operation of purely scientific nature" (Ibid, p. 5).

In contrast, although the conservation object of the Convention on International Trade in Endangered Species of Wild Fauna and Flora (CITES) and the CBD could not appear closer, co-operation is more difficult in part because of the species-centred perspective of the former, which "virtually ignores socio-economic and human development factors affecting biodiversity conservation and sustainable development" (Ibid, p. 5). Co-ordination and harmonization becomes even more difficult when one considers other regimes, such as those dealing with trade and intellectual property rights (IPR). On a number of occasions, the COP has addressed the relationship between the Convention and the Agreement on Trade-related Aspects of Intellectual Property Rights (TRIPS). In the case of trade rules, the complexity of the task is clearly made apparent in the chapters by Pythoud and Thomas on the Cartagena Protocol and by Thomas on the International Treaty on Plant Genetic Resources for Food and Agriculture (IT). It is also worth mentioning that the secretariats of the CBD and UNFCCC have not yet signed a memorandum of understanding despite numerous interlinkages between the two conventions and repeated calls by the CBD-COP (COP-5) to take biodiversity concerns into consideration in the implementation of the UNFCCC and its Kyoto Protocol. These questions of co-ordination are important for the effectiveness of the regime, a responsibility that is not solely that of the Secretariat; the other institutions of the governance system must also promote it. Not only could administrative changes be made within the Secretariat, but it is also incumbent upon the Parties themselves to overcome their tendency to compartmentalize issues (fragmentation perhaps being the price one pays for avoiding complete paralysis through endless linkages) and to realize that co-ordination begins at home.

SBSTTA was the first and remains the most important subsidiary body of the Convention. This underscores the importance negotiators originally placed on the development of scientific knowledge for biodiversity. In many ways, the absence of consensual scientific knowledge in support of the work of the Convention has been seen as one its greatest shortcomings. Scientists and many environmentalists have bemoaned the slow development of indicators of performance that would supposedly allow them to judge whether the Convention actually "works". Chapter 3 has shown why this outcome-based conception is largely misplaced, at least at this stage. Indeed, despite efforts to develop such indicators, their formulation has become embroiled in political controversy. Some groups and countries remain suspicious of an exclusive reliance on western science, of a definition of the problem largely controlled by the North, and of the possible use of such performance indicators. There are fears that these indicators would only reflect Northern priorities and could be used to determine eligibility for financial and technical assistance. This question is not new for it was at the heart of the controversies surrounding the establishment of lists of globally important species and areas during the negotiation of the Convention (see chapter 1). This initiative was ultimately abandoned despite the protests of some countries (such as France) which have since been trying to revive it in one form or another. Rather than attempting to develop scientific indicators that correspond to a definition of effectiveness in terms of outcomes (measuring the correlation between the CBD and improvement in biodiversity protection), one should first seek to emphasize indicators that reflect a political definition of effectiveness. In addition, although the ecosystem approach has been further described and developed, it needs greater operationalization and its implementation, particularly its participatory dimension, remains complex.

Chapter 4 outlined some of the problems that SBSTTA has encountered, problems again largely related to the scope of the Convention and differing conceptions of SBSTTA's role. These problems are compounded by questions related to the legitimacy of the type of knowledge being promoted (i.e. western scientific) and the type of issues addressed by this body. SBSTTA has even played a secondary role in the development of basic knowledge. Indeed, rather than scientific guidance proper, the socialization function of SBSTTA may prove more central to the promotion of the goals of the regime. The first significant scientific initiative has been the Global Taxonomy Initiative (GTI) which aims to remove taxonomic obstacles to data collection and the development of knowledge. In 2000 (Decision V/9) the COP established a Global Taxonomy Initiative co-ordination mechanism to assist the Executive Secretary in the facilitation of international co-operation and co-ordination of activities under the initiative.[12] A second significant scientific work undertaken by SBSTTA was the assessment of the status and trends of, and major threats to, forest biological diversity in 2001.

In response to initiatives by scientists, and in light of the experience of the Intergovernmental Panel on Climate Change (IPCC), attempts to improve the scientific basis of biodiversity-related decisions have been launched largely independently of the CBD, although, ultimately, they must be linked to its work. These initiatives include the *Global Biodiversity Assessment*; *The Millenium Assessment of Global Ecosystems* launched in 2001 by the World Resources Institute (WRI), United Nations Development Programme (UNDP), United Nations Environment Programme (UNEP), and the World Bank, with the support of the Food and Agriculture Organization (FAO), Global Environment Facility (GEF) and the Rockefeller Foundation;[13] and the *Global Biodiversity Information Facility*, an OECD initiative designed to promote access to existing information related to biodiversity.[14]

In one sense, these developments may be interpreted as a failure of the regime to develop the knowledge it needs, combined with an attempt to reduce the CBD to its first objective, that of conservation. But this view would be short-sighted and assume that the CBD regime can be effective or successful only if it centralizes the production of knowledge. Rather, it could also be interpreted as an outcome of the work of the CBD, which has highlighted gaps in knowledge, expressed needs for such knowledge, struggled with a lack of baseline data, and made these programmes all the more relevant because the CBD exists. Nonetheless, the CBD will have to ensure that these initiatives support the goals and approach of the Convention (by taking due account of socio-economic factors, for example) and that knowledge advances in a balanced way that addresses issues relevant to all of the Convention's objectives. It also means that SBSTTA will have to focus on its role as adviser: providing suggestions to external scientific panels and translating scientific knowledge into possible CBD actions in light of the principles and priorities of the Convention. One of the challenges will be to develop mechanisms to ensure that SBSTTA both has input into the *problématique* of these scientific initiatives and can use their results effectively.

Rather than focusing on the development of fundamental knowledge, the Convention has focused on national implementation, on raising awareness among Parties, and on the development of a set of common tools. Apart from technology transfers and additional financing, the Convention places particular emphasis on scientific co-operation, economic tools, impact assessments, participation, negotiation with relevant stakeholders (with particular emphasis on indigenous and local communities), indicators, and the development of the ecosystem approach. The development of these tools, however, has been more difficult than previously assumed. As usual, technology transfers and financial resources have remained far below expectations. The COP has often insisted on the gathering and exchange of information as a tool for developing concepts and procedures and sharing "best practices". In particular, Parties have been asked repeatedly to submit case studies to the Secretariat. Few have done so, which may be a reflection of the lack of direct impact of the CBD on national scientific research. But there has also been little appreciation of the methodological aspects of this approach: the mere collection of case studies has little value if their methodological underpinnings and the bases for comparisons and lesson-drawing are open to question. The development of the CHM (see the chapter by Reed), which is central to the implementation of the Convention, has suffered not so much from a lack of resources as from conceptual uncertainties and probably too much focus on the "hardware" and "lessons-cum-dogmas" and less on the "software" and on building a range of options derived from existing lessons learned.[15] In a similar vein, the operationalization of AIAs, as analysed by Wolf, raises practical difficulties that go beyond technical fixes and touch on fundamental issues of inequalities. Finally, as McGraw argues, the very notion of "expert knowledge" has been too narrowly defined in post-agreement negotiations, thereby resulting in, for example, insufficient support for non-programme activities on education and public awareness.

Implementation at the National Level

The CBD strengthens and expands the sovereign rights of states over their biological resources; but it contains no binding obligations. Implementation of the Convention primarily occurs at the national level, and in exchange for this recognition of their sovereign rights, "States are responsible for conserving their biological diversity and for using these biological resources in a sustainable manner". In some way, as Overejo (1999) has pointed out, this implies the application of the principle of subsidiarity whereby responsibility for the implementation of the Convention provisions is transferred to the level that can do it most efficiently. Strengthening not only national but also local capacities is thus a prerequisite to effective implementation of the Convention.[16] Although this has traditionally been defined as the capacity to respond to the expectations of the regime in terms of legal, administrative, and scientific infrastructure and the adoption of the tools identified in the Convention, it must go beyond this top-down approach to include the development of capacities to define interests and policies on the basis of local and national experience and priorities.

It is at the national level that the CBD will succeed or fail. From the outset, the COP has identified capacity-building as a priority, including human resources development and institutional development (Decision I/2). The Secretariat has worked with governments and non-state actors (IUCN, the World Bank, UNDP, UNEP, WRI) to launch a series of efforts to support the work of the CBD on capacity-building. Yet a lack of capacity in developing-country Parties remains one of the biggest constraints on the development of the principles of the CBD and their implementation. Along with Paoletto (1999), we can identify a certain number of capacity-building issues with regard to multilateral environmental agreements (MEAs) that find easy illustrations in the context of the CBD. Many of these problems affect not only developing but also industrialized countries, as the chapters on Canada and Madagascar make clear. They include:

- unco-ordinated administrative structures, divided and competing levels of administrative authority. This poses obstacles not only to the implementation of the CBD but also to the development of synergies among global conventions;
- a "brain drain" effect: after attending professional development courses, government officials can and do get promoted without fully implementing skills learned on the job or training others; in other cases, they join the local branch of international NGOs;
- uneven participation in international fora by developing country experts on MEAs: reasons range from a lack of information and networking, through limited resources for participation (often dependent on last-minute ad hoc funding from industrialized countries), to the domination of the process by a few individuals and the importance of English in international negotiating fora and in the background literature; and
- inadequate communication between stakeholders and government at local levels, which may reflect not only a lack of capacity but also political and cultural differences among countries.

Given its broad scope, it is no surprise that Parties have a long way to go to meet the expectations of the regime. Typically, Parties will have met some but not all of these expectations to varying degrees (a national strategy but no endangered species legislation for example; conservation areas but no benefit-sharing arrangements; etc.). In the case of developing countries, this situation is compounded by the failure of developed countries to abide by their own commitments. As specified in Article 20(4) of the Convention, the obligations and commitments of developing countries under the principle of common but differentiated responsibility are contingent on the developed countries' fulfilment of their commitments related to financial resources and transfer of technology.[17] In the Cartagena Protocol on Biosafety, the AIA procedure requires effective contributions from both trade initiators and recipient countries to protect biodiversity.

Assessment is made more difficult by shortcomings in national reporting, either because reports are not filed on time or because their contents differ widely, making comparisons difficult. The Secretariat and the COP have taken steps to overcome the latter problem by proposing a "model" structure that would ensure that pertinent information is included. Regarding the timeliness of filing reports, by June 2001 only two-thirds of the Parties had filed their first report, which was due in 1998, and only 22 per cent had submitted their second report on time (2001) (see Annex 2: Dimensions of the CBD). Compliance with deadlines for filing thematic reports is even worse, but due account has to be taken of the fact that these reports are not felt to be equally pertinent by all countries. On the other hand, most countries have now adopted a national strategy and action plan (Sweden and the UK as early as 1994, Canada, Japan, and Vietnam in 1995), a process, in the case of developing countries, heavily facilitated by financial support from the GEF. In certain cases, however, these strategies were only pro forma exercises. In many instances, rather than indicating national priorities, these documents were only first steps that helped identify existing policies, administrative structures, and constraints, define gaps in knowledge, and stimulate national discussion about these issues.

The complexity and scope of the Convention, its relative lack of public visibility, its political ramifications, and the underdevelopment of its key tools present significant challenges even for those developed countries, such as Canada, that have played a significant role in the negotiations and promoted the issue actively. As Halley underscores in the case of marine biodiversity (which goes for terrestrial biodiversity as well), the Canadian federal government still falls short of putting its biodiversity commitments into effect. To be sure, this sector has been characterized by substantial policy innovation. This innovation, however, was not attributable to the CBD, although its existence probably served to encourage existing trends. Despite the evolution described by Halley, problems of sectoral, federal-provincial, and interministerial co-ordination abound, which prevents the development of integrated initiatives on the part of the different authorities responsible for biodiversity. In other cases, many developing countries, such as Madagascar as analysed by Hufty and Muttenzer, are confronted with potential or actual contradictions among international norms and between these norms (or current received wisdom) and local norms and priorities. The apparent acceptance of regime norms (as evidenced by reform of national legislation and administrative structures), which was largely imposed by external donors according to these authors, masks deep conflicts within the national elite. One illustration of these difficulties, found in both Canada and Madagascar, is the challenge that public administrators face in implementing the ecosystem approach and devising appropriate, credible, and legitimate participatory structures. Insufficient attention has also been paid to potential conflicts between the goals of protecting ecosystem, species, and genetic biodiversity, of benefit-sharing, and of sustainable use, which are too often assumed to be complementary. For example, actors who expect returns on their investment in the protection and utilization of genetic resources must also come to terms with existing rights and interests that have developed around the use of biological resources.

In all likelihood, the effectiveness of the CBD will hinge as much on learning and legitimacy as on capacity-building. Learning lies at the heart of an effective system of implementation review. It is probably premature to assess the degree of learning with any precision at this stage. Moreover, such an assessment will vary according to the type of learning that one has in mind. At the national level, individual learning may have been significant, but its translation into organizational learning is more open to question. Likewise, there may be a gap between social learning (related to values) and policy learning (related to government actions) in developed countries. As far as the CGS is concerned, there are indications of some learning, as related in chapter 4 in reference to adjustments of organizational routines. This is almost inevitable, given the framework character of the Convention and the underdeveloped nature of some of the science that underlies its norms and procedures. At the level of the regime, it is likely that the speed of policy learning will be a function of the openness of the decision-making structure (see Howlett, 2001).

Strengthening the legitimacy of the CBD is even more of a challenge. On the one hand, to be sure, as Désirée McGraw mentions, the basic legitimacy of the CBD was secured during the negotiations through the multi-purpose character of the Convention itself. Industrialized states were able to focus the regime on conservation and access to genetic resources, while developing countries secured sovereignty over natural resources, differentiated responsibilities, benefit-sharing, and sustainable use. But this compromise is also, paradoxically, the source of some illegitimacy, as various constituencies question purposes they deem peripheral to their concerns and denounce the "lack of results" of the Convention, itself a function of the complexity of the biodiversity issue area and of the Convention itself. For example, many conservationists will criticize the focus on sustainable use; industry, technological transfers; indigenous populations, the hegemony of western science; some governments, the role of indigenous populations; natural scientists, the nature and operation of SBSTTA. Legitimacy will depend on the performance of the CGS in pursuing the principles and objectives on which its authority is founded and in a delicate balancing of the various objectives and concerns of the Convention. And it will lie more in the operation of the CGS than in any public awareness programme.

Toward a New Order?

The beginning of the 21st century is characterized by rival yet complementary paths toward better human welfare, each representing an incipient world order. The CBD represents such a claim through its advancement of a set of principles, priorities, and instruments that have the potential of representing a new order based on natural and human diversity, equity, respect for life, access to basic resources, and harnessing of the natural world for human welfare (conservation of aesthetic and recreational pleasure, sustainable development, exploitation of genetic resources). The philosophical and political implications of the CBD are not necessarily benign. The second decade of the CBD will demonstrate whether it was the first step toward the affirmation of new norms and a new allocation of rights, or whether other competing and no less legitimate orders will constrain it to a marginal role in defining the common good. So far, the prognosis remains guarded.

Yet the CBD has the potential to reshape the relationships between humans and nature and among states profoundly, as well as the distribution of social, cultural, political, and economic rights, responsibilities, and benefits within states. Through its preamble and articles, the CBD promotes a new relationship with nature that seeks to reconcile the intrinsic value of biodiversity with dominant utilitarian arguments. It does not posit conservation as the pillar of the relationship between societies and nature. Rather, it affirms the primacy of social and economic development. The management of this duality, conservation and sustainable use (two objectives that are not as complementary as the Convention often assumes), will be one of the greatest challenges to the implementation and acceptance of the regime.

The Convention also illustrates a general movement of enclosure or reappropriation of nature by the state and by local populations in the face of similar attempts by the market, a movement illustrated by the introduction of IPRs on living matter (see the chapter by Thomas). Biodiversity is a worldwide problem, that has local solutions. It is humanity's common concern, not its common heritage. Indeed, the Convention takes up and goes far beyond Principle 21 of the 1972 Stockholm Declaration, which declared that states have the sovereign right to exploit their natural resources in accordance with their own environmental priorities. It recognizes states' sovereignty over their genetic resources at the same time that it reaffirms the principle of open (but not free or free of rules) access to these resources. But this redistribution of rights is not limited to states, since local communities, which have shaped that biodiversity and depend on it for their cultural and economic survival, also claim a right to partake in the benefits of biodiversity and to participate in the definition of the principles that should govern its use. Thus, by creating new expectations, the CBD also creates new conflicts regarding IPRs in the context of genetic resources.

The political dynamics regarding the implementation of the CBD revolves around the nature and shape of a new international order. Some factors promote its advancement, such as the extension of the rights of states and local populations, the recognition of the interrelationship of the three goals of the Convention and attempts to give them concrete meaning, new political coalitions, the emergence of new networks, and innovative governance structures as represented by the CGS. Others work against it, such as institutional fragmentation without co-ordination, conflictual norms and contradictions within the regime itself, uncertain legitimacy, unequal power relationships at the national level, conflicts among regimes (notably between the CBD and the trade and IPR regimes), and shortcomings in national capacities. The chapters in this book indicate how sinuous, long, and rough this road will be – how many bridges will have to be built for the principles and objectives of the CBD to be given meaning and reality. The success of the journey depends on strengthening the determinants of effectiveness identified in this volume. The international community is now committed to implementing a set of principles and objectives that go far beyond the protection of life on Earth but also hold the promise of reordering fundamental relations among human communities. In truth, through the CBD, humanity has embarked on a large and uncertain political experiment.

Notes

The author would like to thank D. McGraw, A. Wolf, and especially J-P Le Danff for their helpful comments.

[1] See UN/ECOSOC (1997), Implementation of the Convention on Biological Diversity.

[2] Even though the US still has not ratified the treaty, it has taken an active part in its development.

[3] The objectives of the International Treaty "are the conservation and sustainable use of plant genetic resources for food and agriculture and the fair and equitable sharing of the benefits arising out of their use, in harmony with the Convention on Biological Diversity, for sustainable agriculture and food security".

[4] See also chapter 9 by Thomas in this volume.

[5] At it seventh meeting (November 2001), the SBSTTA undertook its first assessment of the status of and trends in forest biodiversity.

[6] "[S]overeign biodiversity property rights, embodying both biological and intellectual heritage have to be formalised and protected as existing prior to intellectual property rights. The latter can exist only where they do not infringe on the former, otherwise it becomes an infringement and violation of sovereignty" (Shiva, 1997, p. 3).

[7] In reference, for example, to the non-patenting of life. The COP has confirmed that human genetic resources are not included within the framework of the Convention (Decision II/11, par. 2).

[8] The distinction between indigenous and local communities is not always made clear in the literature.

[9] See, for example, the *Declaration of the UNDP Consultation on Indigenous Knowledge*; Indigenous Working Group of the Third Global Biodiversity Forum, Buenos Aires, Argentina, November 1996; and the Foro Internacional Indigena sobre Biodiversidad, 2-3 November 1996, Buenos Aires, Argentina.

[10] J-P. Le Danff, personal communication.

[11] The Secretariat has entered into memoranda of co-operation with the Ramsar Convention, CITES (Washington Convention), CMS (Bonn Convention), IOC, World Bank, IUCN, Cartagena Protocol on Biosafety, UNESCO, UNCTAD, UNCCD, WCMC, DIVERSITAS, CPPS, GISP, Pan-European Biological and Landscape Diversity Strategy, Bern Convention, and the Center for International Forestry Research For Scientific and Technical Co-operation.

[12] The CBD participates in the UNEP/IUCN World Conservation Monitoring Centre in Cambridge, UK, which became a UNEP centre in 2000. The WCMC is contributing significantly to the development and dissemination of knowledge and to the harmonization of procedures of biodiversity-related agreements, such as harmonization of national reporting.

[13] Its scope, however, goes well beyond that of the CBD. See http://www.milleniumassessment.org.

[14] See UNEP (1999), *Co-operation with Other Bodies* (UNEP/CBD/SBSTTA/5/2) for background information.

[15] On the evolution of the approach to capacity-building, see Paoletto (1999).

[16] In addition to lack of scientific indicators and the need to gain the co-operation of other instruments and processes, the importance of sufficient capacity at the national level was also noted by the 1998 London Workshop on the Review of the Operations of the Convention on Biological Diversity.

[17] See UN/ECOSOC (1997), *Implementation of the Convention on Biological Diversity*, (E/CN.17/1997/11). See also Table 1.2 (Negotiation trade-offs between industrialized and developing countries) in this volume.

Annex 1

Chronology of the Convention on Biological Diversity[1]

Antecedents

1971
– Ramsar Convention on Wetlands.

1972
– June 5-16, Stockholm: United Nations Conference on the Human Environment.
– November 23: Convention Concerning the Protection of the World Cultural and Natural Heritage (World Heritage Convention).

1973
–March 3, Washington DC: Convention on International Trade in Endangered Species of Wild Fauna and Flora (CITES, or Washington Convention).

1979
– June 23, Bonn: Convention on Migratory Species (Bonn Convention).

1980
– World Conservation Union (IUCN), the United Nations Organization for Educational, Scientific and Cultural (UNESCO), the Food and Agriculture Organization (FAO), and Worldwide Fund for Nature (WWF) launch the World Conservation Strategy.

1982
– October 28: UN General Assembly adopts the World Charter for Nature.

1987
– Publication by the World Commission on Environment and Development of *Our Common Future* or the Brundtland Report, which suggests studying the possibility of adopting a convention on species conservation.

Negotiations

1987
– June 8-19, Nairobi: The 14th Governing Council (GC) of the United Nations Environment Programme (UNEP) establishes two expert groups on biodiversity and biotechnologies. The GC identifies the need for an international concerted action to protect biological diversity and decides to establish an ad hoc group of experts charged with investigating "the desirability and possible form of an umbrella convention to rationalize current activities in this field."

1988
– August 29-September 1, Nairobi: first meeting of the Ad Hoc Working Group of Experts to the Executive Director of UNEP on Governing Council Decision 14/26.
– September 19-20, Nairobi: meeting of UNEP Ad Hoc Senior Advisory Panel of Experts on Biological Diversity.
– November 16-18, Geneva: first meeting of the Ad Hoc Group of Experts on Biological Diversity.

1990
– February 19-23, Geneva: second meeting of the Ad Hoc Group of Experts on Biological Diversity.
– May: UNEP establishes an Ad Hoc Group of Legal and Technical Experts on Biological Diversity (AGLTE) to prepare a new international legal instrument for the conservation and the sustainable exploitation of biological diversity. It is to study the "rationalization" of existing agreements and "the desirability and possible form of an umbrella convention."
– July 9-13, Geneva: third meeting of the Ad Hoc Group of Experts on Biological Diversity.
– November 14-16, Nairobi: Sub-Working Group on Biotechnology (SWGB).
– November 19-23, Nairobi: first meeting of the Ad Hoc Group of Legal and Technical Experts (AGLTE). This meeting would later be regarded as the first negotiating session.

1991
– February 23-March 6, Nairobi: second meeting of the AGLTE.
– May: UNEP Governing Council adopts a proposal to rename the AGLTE as the Intergovernmental Negotiating Committee for a Convention on Biodiversity (INC). It was stressed, however, that this did not have for effect to create "a *new* negotiating body nor affect the continuity of the process of elaborating the convention". Thus, combining the INC four negotiating sessions with the three previous meetings of the AGLTE, there has been seven negotiating sessions.
– June 24-July 3, Madrid: third session of the AGLTE, and first session of the INC (INC-1/3).
– September 23-October 2, Nairobi: second session of the INC (INC-2/4).
– November 25-December 4, Geneva: third session of the INC (INC-3/5).

1992
– February 6-15, Nairobi: fourth session of the INC (INC-4/6).
– May 11-21, Nairobi: fifth session of the INC (INC-5/7).
– May 22, Nairobi: adoption of the CBD (Conference for the Adoption of the Agreed Text of the CBD convened by the Executive Director of UNEP).
– June 13, Rio de Janeiro: signature of the CBD at UNCED.

Implementation

1993
– October 11-15, Geneva: first meeting of the Intergovernmental Committee for the Convention on Biological Diversity (pre-entry into force) (ICCBD)
– December 29: entry into force of the CBD.

1994
– June 20-July 1, Nairobi: second meeting of the ICCBD.
– November 28-December 9, Nassau: first Conference of the Parties (COP).

1995
– September 4-8, Paris: first meeting of the Subsidiary Body on Scientific Technical and Technological Advice (SBSTTA).
– November 6-17, Djakarta: second meeting of the COP.

1996
– The Secretariat of the CBD begins operations.
– July 22-26, Aarhus: first meeting of the Ad hoc Open Ended Working group on Biosafety (BSWG).
– September 2-6, Montreal: second meeting of the SBSTTA.
– November 4-15, Buenos Aires: third meeting of the COP.

1997
– March 8, Berlin: environment ministers adopt the Berlin Declaration on Biological Diversity and Sustainable Tourism.
– May 12-16, Montreal: second meeting of the BSWG.
– September 1-5, Montreal: third meeting of the SBSTTA.
– October 13-17, Montreal: third meeting of the BSWG.
– November 24-28, Madrid: Workshop on Traditional Knowledge.

1998
– January 5-7, London: workshop on the operations of the CBD.
– February 5-13, Montreal: fourth meeting of the BSWG.
– May 4-15, Bratislava: fourth meeting of the COP.
– August 17-28, Montreal: fifth meeting of the BSWG.

1999

– February 14-19, Cartagena: sixth meeting of the BSWG.
– February 22-23, Cartagena: first Extraordinary Meeting of the Conference of the Parties (EXCOP).
– June 21-25, Montreal: fourth meeting of the SBSTTA.
– June 28-30, Montreal: Intersessional Meeting on the Operations of the Convention (ISOC).
– October 4-8, San Jose: first meeting of the Panel of Experts on Access and Benefit-Sharing (PEABS).

2000

– January 24-28, Montreal: resumed Extraordinary Meeting (EXCOP)
– January 29, Montreal: adoption of the Cartagena Protocol on Biosafety.
– January 31- February 4, Montreal: fifth meeting of the SBSTTA.
– March 27-31, Seville: first meeting of the Ad Hoc Open Ended Intersessional Working Group on Article 8(j) and Related Provisions (WG8J).
– May 15-26, Nairobi: fifth meeting of the COP.
– December 11-15, Montpellier: first meeting of the Intergovernmental Committee for the Cartagena Protocol on Biosafety (ICCP).

2001

– March 12-16, Montreal: sixth meeting of the SBSTTA.
– March 19-22, Montreal: second meeting of the PEABS.
– October 1-5, Nairobi: second meeting of the ICCP.
– October 22-26, Bonn: first meeting of the Ad Hoc Open Ended Working Group on Access and Benefit-Sharing (WGABS).
– November 12-16, Montreal: seventh meeting of the SBSTTA.
– November 19-21, Montreal: Open Ended Intersessional Meeting on the Strategic Plan, National Reports, and Implementation of the Convention on Biological Diversity (MSP).

2002

– January 21-25, Helsinki: first meeting of the Ad Hoc Technical Expert Group on Biological Diversity and Climate Change.
– February 4-8, Montreal: second meeting of the WG8J.
– April 7-19, The Hague: sixth meeting of the COP.
– April 22-26, The Hague: third meeting of the Intergovernmental Committee for the Cartagena Protocol on Biosafety (ICCP).

Notes

[1] Compiled by D. M. McGraw and J. Crowley.

Annex 2

Dimensions of the CBD

List of Tables

List of Figures

Table A-1 Number of Signatures and Ratifications of the Convention on Biological Diversity and the Cartagena Protocol on Biosafety

Agreement	State[1]		Signature		Ratification, Accessions, Acceptance or Approval	
	193		Yes	No	Yes	No
Convention on Biological Diversity	Parties[2]	Non Parties[3]	168	25	181	12 (6 signed)
	181	12				
Cartagena Protocol on Biosafety	Parties	Non Parties	103	90	5[4]	188 (100 signed)
	5	188				

[1]"State" excludes Holy See, Palestinian Authorities and non sovereign territories, except for Cook Islands (New Zealand), and includes European Union.
[2]"Parties" are states that have ratified the CBD (including Cook Islands and European Union)
[3]Afghanistan, Andorra, Bosnia and Herzegovina, Brunei Darussalam, Iraq, Kuwait, Saudi Arabia, Somalia, Thailand, Tuvalu, United States of America and Yugoslavia
[4]Bulgaria, Fiji, Norway, Trinidad and Tobago and Saint Kitts and Nevis

Source: Secretariat of the CBD (10 June 2001)

Table A-2 National and Thematic Reports by Region (2001)

Region	Total	First national report (1998)			Second national report (2001)			Thematic report on alien species (2000)	Thematic report on benefit-sharing (2000)	Thematic report on forest ecosystems (2001)
		Int[1]	Fin[2]	%	Int[1]	Fin[2]	%			
Africa	51	14[3]	22	43	-	13	25	10	1	7
Asia	28	2	17	61	-	3	11	10	2	2
Middle East	10	1	5	50	-	1	10	3	-	1
Europe	45	1	31	69	-	12	27	19	6	13
Caribbean	14	5	3	21	-	1	7	2	1	-
North America	2	-	2	100	-	1	50	1	-	1
Central America	7	2	2	29	-	-	0	2	1	1
South America	12	2	6	50	-	3	25	3	-	1
Oceania	15	1	5	33	-	6	40	2	1	3
Total			119			40		52	12	29
%			65.75			22.10		28.73	6.63	16.02

[1] Interim
[2] Final
[3] Guinea held a draft

Table A-3 Participation in CBD Negotiations (1988-1992)

	Phase I				Phase II				Phase III		
Meeting No.	**1**	**2**	**3**	**4**	**5**	**6**	**7**	**8**	**9**	**10**	**T**
No. of Governments	*20*	*32*	*47*	*49*	*52*	*53*	*55*	*53*	*57*	*59*	
No. of IGOs/NGOs	*5*	*3*	*3*	*4*	*5*	*5*	*5*	*5*	*5*	*6*	
Argentina	-	-	X	X	X	X	X	X	X	X	8
Australia	X	X	X	X	X	X	X	X	X	X	10
Austria	X	X	X	X	X	X	X	X	X	X	10
Bahamas	-	-	X	X	X	X	X	X	X	X	8
Belgium	-	-	-	X	X	X	X	X	X	X	7
Brazil	X	X	X	X	X	X	X	X	X	X	10
Bulgaria	-	-	-	-	-	-	X	X	X	X	4
Canada	-	X	X	X	X	X	X	X	X	X	9
Chile	-	-	X	X	X	X	X	X	X	X	8
China	X	X	X	X	X	X	X	X	X	X	10
Colombia	-	-	X	X	X	X	X	X	X	X	8
Costa Rica	-	-	-	-	X	X	X	X	X	X	6
Cyprus	-	-	-	-	X	-	-	-	-	-	1
Czech Rep.	-	-	-	-	X	-	X	X	X	X	5
Denmark	X	X	X	X	X	X	X	X	X	X	10
Egypt	X	X	X	X	X	X	X	X	X	X	10
Ethiopia	-	-	X	X	X	-	X	X	X	X	7
Finland	-	X	X	X	X	X	X	X	X	X	9
France	X	X	X	X	X	X	X	X	X	X	10
Gambia	-	-	X	X	X	X	X	-	X	X	7
Germany	-	X	X	X	X	X	X	X	X	X	9
Ghana	-	-	X	X	X	X	X	X	X	X	8
Greece	-	X	X	X	X	X	X	X	X	X	9
Guinea	-	-	X	X	X	X	X	X	X	X	8
Guyana	-	-	X	X	X	X	X	X	X	X	8
Hungary	-	-	-	-	-	-	-	-	-	X	1
India	-	X	X	X	X	X	X	X	X	X	9
Indonesia	X	X	X	X	X	X	X	X	X	X	10
Ireland	-	-	-	-	-	-	-	-	-	X	1
Israel	-	-	-	-	X	-	-	-	-	-	1
Italy	-	-	-	-	-	X	X	X	X	X	5
Japan	-	X	X	X	X	X	X	X	X	X	9
Jordan	-	X	X	-	-	-	-	-	X	X	4
Kenya	X	X	X	X	X	X	X	X	X	X	10
Malaysia	X	X	X	X	X	X	X	X	X	X	10

Table A-3 Concluded

Malawi	-	-	X	X	X	X	X	X	X	X	8
Malta	-	X	X	X	-	-	-	-	X	X	5
Mauritius	-	-	-	-	-	X	X	X	X	X	5
Mexico	X	X	X	X	X	X	X	X	X	X	10
Netherlands	X	X	X	X	X	X	X	X	X	X	10
New Zealand	-	X	X	-	-	X	-	-	X	X	5
Nigeria	-	X	X	X	X	X	X	-	X	X	8
Norway	X	X	X	X	X	X	X	X	X	X	10
Pakistan	-	-	X	-	X	X	X	X	X	X	7
Peru	-	X	X	X	-	X	X	X	X	X	8
Poland	-	-	-	-	X	X	X	X	X	X	6
Portugal	-	-	-	X	X	X	X	X	X	X	7
Romania	-	-	-	X	X	X	X	X	X	X	7
Russian Fed.	X	X	X	X	X	X	X	X	X	X	10
Spain	X	X	X	X	X	X	X	X	X	X	10
Sweden	X	X	X	X	X	X	X	X	X	X	10
Switzerland	X	X	X	X	X	X	X	X	X	X	10
Tanzania	-	-	-	X	X	X	X	X	X	X	7
Thailand	X	X	X	X	-	X	X	X	X	X	9
Turkey	-	-	-	X	X	X	X	X	X	X	7
Uganda	-	-	X	X	X	X	X	X	X	X	8
UK	X	X	X	X	X	X	X	X	X	X	10
Uruguay			X	X	X	X	X	X	X	X	8
US	X	X	X	X	X	X	X	X	X	X	10
Venezuela	X	X	X	X	X	X	X	X	X	X	10
Zambia			X	X	X	X	X	X	X	X	8
Zimbabwe	X	X	X	X	X	X	X	X	-	X	9
EU	X	-	-	X	X	X	X	X	X	X	8
FAO	X	X	X	X	X	X	X	X	X	X	10
UNESCO	X	X	-	X	X	X	X	X	X	X	8
IUCN	X	X	X	-	X	X	X	X	X	X	8
WWF	X	-	X	X	X	X	X	X	X	X	8
GREENPEACE	-	-	-	-	-	-	-	-	-	X	1

Source : Adapted by D. M. McGraw from Koester 1997

Note: Table A-3 presents the participation frequency of 62 countries and six organizations in the 10 meetings leading to the adoption of the CBD. It includes 20 industrialized countries, 42 developing countries, six countries with economies in transition, and five IGOs/NGOs. See: Box 1.2 and Annex 1 – Chronology for the specific the meetings covered by each phase.

Table A-4 Number of Employees of the Secretariat of the Convention on Biological Diversity

Year	CBD
1992	-
1993[2]	-
1994[3]	-
1995[3]	-
1996[4]	6
1997[5]	28
1998[6]	34
1999[7]	50
2000[8]	55
2001[9]	56

[1] Doesn't include short-term professionals and consultants hired for events like SBSTTA or COP meetings.

[2] The interim Secretariat has been implemented in October 1993 in Geneva (Switzerland), (UNEP/CBD/COP/2/15, p. 2).

[3] The interim Secretariat was managed by UNEP's employees. *Report on the administration of the Convention,* September 1995, pp. 2-3 (UNEP/CBD/COP/2/15).

[4] Relocation of the Secretariat from Geneva to Montreal took place in 1996. The transition between the interim and the permanent phase of the Secretariat and the recruitement of a new team began in 1996. *Administration of the Convention on Biological Diversity,* September 1996, pp. 4-6 (UNEP/CBD/COP/3/32).

[5] *Quarterly report 1*, May 1997.

[6] *Quarterly report 3*, November 1998.

[7] *Quarterly report 7*, January 2000.

[8] *Quarterly report 11*, January 2001.

[9] Recruitment is currently in progress for many positions (April 2001).

Source: Secretariat of the Convention on Biological Diversity

Table A-5 GEF Support for National Focal Points' Clearing-House Mechanism add-on Modules[1]

CHM			
Country	*Amount*	*Agency*	*CEO Approval Date*
Africa			
Algeria	14,000.00	UNDP	17/11/1998
Benin	13,950.00	UNDP	27/06/1998
Burkina Faso	13,984.00	UNDP	23/04/1998
Burundi	11,085.00	UNDP	13/08/1999
Cameroon	13,000.00	UNEP	11/02/1998
Cape Verde	14,000.00	UNDP	04/03/1998
Central African Republic	13,600.00	UNDP	13/08/1999
Chad	13,970.00	UNDP	12/07/1998
Congo	13,500.00	UNDP	26/10/1998
Côte d'Ivoire	13,800.00	UNEP	19/05/1998
Democratic Republic of Congo	12,710.00	UNDP	18/11/1998
Egypt	14,000.00	UNEP	09/01/1998
Gabon	12,750.00	UNDP	19/05/1998
Gambia	13,950.00	UNEP	16/04/1998
Guinea	13,450.00	UNDP	16/12/1998
Madagascar	10,000.00	UNEP	10/11/1997
Malawi	11,000.00	UNEP	10/11/1997
Mali	13,140.00	UNDP	08/05/1998
Mauritania	14,000.00	UNEP	16/04/1998
Mauritius	12,300.00	UNEP	23/04/1998
Morocco	14,000.00	UNEP	05/06/1998
Mozambique	13,300.00	UNEP	10/11/1997
Niger	11,338.00	UNDP	10/11/1997
Rwanda	13,950.00	UNDP	24/06/1998
Senegal	11,300.00	UNDP	15/02/1998
Seychelles	10,100.00	UNEP	29/10/1997
South Africa	13,500.00	UNDP	26/08/1998
Sudan	14,000.00	UNDP	26/08/1998
Swaziland	14,000.00	UNDP	03/02/2000
Asia-Middle East-Oceania			
Fiji	11,150.00	UNDP	14/07/1998
Indonesia	10,300.00	World Bank	18/11/1998

Table A-5 Concluded

Jordan	12,500.00	UNDP	10/07/1998
Kiribati	12,800.00	UNDP	02/05/2000
Lebanon	9,500.00	UNDP	02/07/1998
Maldives	12,206.00	UNDP	19/07/1999
Mongolia	8,050.00	UNDP	17/11/1998
Nepal	13,200.00	UNDP	17/06/1999
Niue	14,000.00	UNDP	06/09/2000
Samoa	14,000.00	UNDP	06/09/2000
Solomon Islands	8,580.00	UNEP	29/09/1998
Sri Lanka	8,250.00	UNDP	09/02/2000
Syrian Arab Republic	14,000.00	UNDP	18/02/2000
Vanuatu	13,100.00	UNEP	10/06/1998
Yemen	14,000.00	UNDP	26/06/1998
Europe			
Albania	14,000.00	World Bank	12/08/1999
Hungary	7,000.00	UNEP	29/10/1997
Poland	11,000.00	UNEP	09/01/1998
Ukraine	14,000.00	World Bank	08/05/1998
America-Caribbean			
Antigua and Barbuda	14,000.00	UNDP	19/07/1999
Bahamas	14,000.00	UNEP	16/04/1998
Belize	7,000.00	UNDP	07/12/1998
Dominica	7,150.00	UNDP	23/11/1998
Panama	14,000.00	UNEP	09/01/1998
Peru	9,250.00	UNDP	30/06/1998
Uruguay	13,837.00	UNDP	15/03/1999
Total	**678,550.00**		
Average	**12,337.27**		

[1] Add-on to GEF's enabling activity projects. As of November 2000.

Source Secretariat of the CBD (http://www.biodiv.org/chm/chm-gef.asp) (2000).

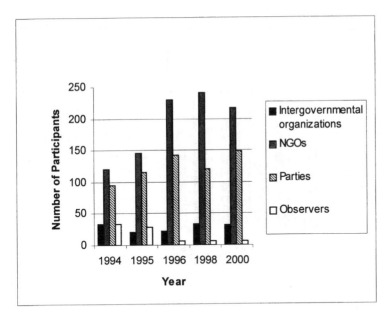

Figure A-1 Evolution of Participation by Category of Participant at CBD–COP Meetings (1994-2000)

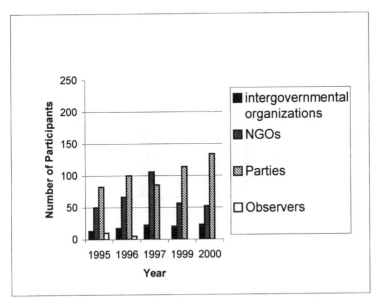

Figure A-2 : Evolution of Participation by Category of Participant at CBD-SBSTTA Meetings (1995-2000)

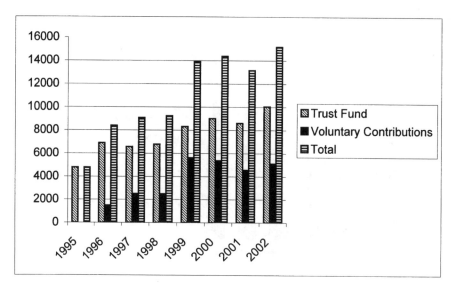

Source: Secretariat of the CBD

Figure A-3 Budget of the Secretariat of the CBD (in $1,000 USD)

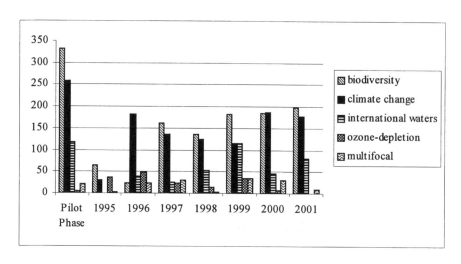

Note: Data for 2001 are provisional.

Source: GEF Annual Reports

Figure A-4 GEF Allocations to Work Programs (1995-2001) (in $million USD)

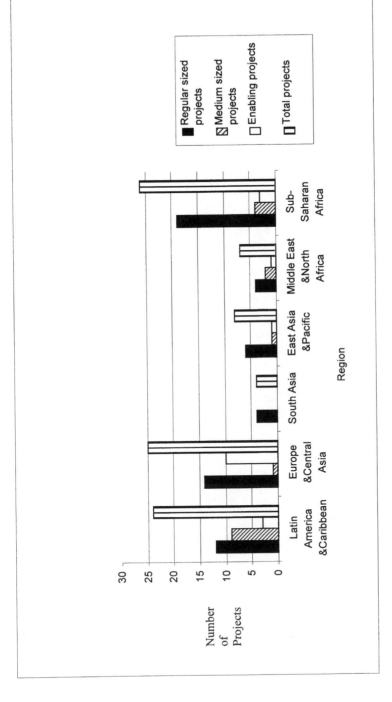

Figure A-5 GEF Projects by Region (Fiscal Year 1992-1999)

Annex 3

The Convention on Biological Diversity

Preamble

The Contracting Parties,

Conscious of the intrinsic value of biological diversity and of the ecological, genetic, social, economic, scientific, educational, cultural, recreational and aesthetic values of biological diversity and its components,

Conscious also of the importance of biological diversity for evolution and for maintaining life sustaining systems of the biosphere,

Affirming that the conservation of biological diversity is a common concern of humankind,

Reaffirming that States have sovereign rights over their own biological resources,

Reaffirming also that States are responsible for conserving their biological diversity and for using their biological resources in a sustainable manner,

Concerned that biological diversity is being significantly reduced by certain human activities,

Aware of the general lack of information and knowledge regarding biological diversity and of the urgent need to develop scientific, technical and institutional capacities to provide the basic understanding upon which to plan and implement appropriate measures,

Noting that it is vital to anticipate, prevent and attack the causes of significant reduction or loss of biological diversity at source,

Noting also that where there is a threat of significant reduction or loss of biological diversity, lack of full scientific certainty should not be used as a reason for postponing measures to avoid or minimize such a threat,

Noting further that the fundamental requirement for the conservation of biological diversity is the in situ conservation of ecosystems and natural habitats and the maintenance and recovery of viable populations of species in their natural surroundings,

Noting further that ex situ measures, preferably in the country of origin, also have an important role to play,

Recognizing the close and traditional dependence of many indigenous and local communities embodying traditional lifestyles on biological resources, and the desirability of sharing equitably benefits arising from the use of traditional knowledge, innovations and practices relevant to the conservation of biological diversity and the sustainable use of its components,

Recognizing also the vital role that women play in the conservation and sustainable use of biological diversity and affirming the need for the full participation of women at all levels of policy-making and implementation for biological diversity conservation,

Stressing the importance of, and the need to promote, international, regional and global co-operation among States and intergovernmental organizations and the non-governmental sector for the conservation of biological diversity and the sustainable use of its components,

Acknowledging that the provision of new and additional financial resources and appropriate access to relevant technologies can be expected to make a substantial difference in the world's ability to address the loss of biological diversity,

Acknowledging further that special provision is required to meet the needs of developing countries, including the provision of new and additional financial resources and appropriate access to relevant technologies,

Noting in this regard the special conditions of the least developed countries and small island States,

Acknowledging that substantial investments are required to conserve biological diversity and that there is the expectation of a broad range of environmental, economic and social benefits from those investments,

Recognizing that economic and social development and poverty eradication are the first and overriding priorities of developing countries,

Aware that conservation and sustainable use of biological diversity is of critical importance for meeting the food, health and other needs of the growing world population, for which purpose access to and sharing of both genetic resources and technologies are essential,

Noting that, ultimately, the conservation and sustainable use of biological diversity will strengthen friendly relations among States and contribute to peace for humankind,

Desiring to enhance and complement existing international arrangements for the conservation of biological diversity and sustainable use of its components, and

Determined to conserve and sustainably use biological diversity for the benefit of present and future generations,

Have agreed as follows:

Article 1. Objectives

The objectives of this Convention, to be pursued in accordance with its relevant provisions, are the conservation of biological diversity, the sustainable use of its components and the fair and equitable sharing of the benefits arising out of the utilization of genetic resources, including by appropriate access to genetic resources and by appropriate transfer of relevant technologies, taking into account all rights over those resources and to technologies, and by appropriate funding.

Article 2. Use of Terms

For the purposes of this Convention:

"Biological diversity" means the variability among living organisms from all sources including, inter alia, terrestrial, marine and other aquatic ecosystems and the ecological complexes of which they are part; this includes diversity within species, between species and of ecosystems."

"Biological resources" includes genetic resources, organisms or parts thereof, populations, or any other biotic component of ecosystems with actual or potential use or value for humanity.

"Biotechnology" means any technological application that uses biological systems, living organisms, or derivatives thereof, to make or modify products or processes for specific use.

"Country of origin of genetic resources" means the country which possesses those genetic resources in in situ conditions.

"Country providing genetic resources" means the country supplying genetic resources collected from in situ sources, including populations of both wild and domesticated species, or taken from ex situ sources, which may or may not have originated in that country.

"Domesticated or cultivated species" means species in which the evolutionary process has been influenced by humans to meet their needs.

"Ecosystem" means a dynamic complex of plant, animal and micro-organism communities and their non-living environment interacting as a functional unit.

"Ex situ conservation" means the conservation of components of biological diversity outside their natural habitats.

"Genetic material" means any material of plant, animal, microbial or other origin containing functional units of heredity.

"Genetic resources" means genetic material of actual or potential value.

"Habitat" means the place or type of site where an organism or population naturally occurs.

"In situ conditions" means conditions where genetic resources exist within ecosystems and natural habitats, and, in the case of domesticated or cultivated species, in the surroundings where they have developed their distinctive properties.

"In situ conservation" means the conservation of ecosystems and natural habitats and the maintenance and recovery of viable populations of species in their natural surroundings and, in the case of domesticated or cultivated species, in the surroundings where they have developed their distinctive properties.

"Protected area" means a geographically defined area which is designated or regulated and managed to achieve specific conservation objectives.

"Regional economic integration organization" means an organization constituted by sovereign States of a given region, to which its member States have transferred competence in respect of matters governed by this Convention and which has been duly authorized, in accordance with its internal procedures, to sign, ratify, accept, approve or accede to it.

"Sustainable use" means the use of components of biological diversity in a way and at a rate that does not lead to the long-term decline of biological diversity, thereby maintaining its potential to meet the needs and aspirations of present and future generations.

"Technology" includes biotechnology.

Article 3. Principle

States have, in accordance with the Charter of the United Nations and the principles of international law, the sovereign right to exploit their own resources pursuant to their own environmental policies, and the responsibility to ensure that activities within their jurisdiction or control do not cause damage to the environment of other States or of areas beyond the limits of national jurisdiction.

Article 4. Jurisdictional Scope

Subject to the rights of other States, and except as otherwise expressly provided in this Convention, the provisions of this Convention apply, in relation to each Contracting Party:

(a) In the case of components of biological diversity, in areas within the limits of its national jurisdiction; and

(b) In the case of processes and activities, regardless of where their effects occur, carried out under its jurisdiction or control, within the area of its national jurisdiction or beyond the limits of national jurisdiction.

Article 5. Co-operation

Each Contracting Party shall, as far as possible and as appropriate, co-operate with other Contracting Parties, directly or, where appropriate, through competent international organizations, in respect of areas beyond national jurisdiction and on other matters of mutual interest, for the conservation and sustainable use of biological diversity.

Article 6. General Measures for Conservation and Sustainable Use

Each Contracting Party shall, in accordance with its particular conditions and capabilities:

(a) Develop national strategies, plans or programmes for the conservation and sustainable use of biological diversity or adapt for this purpose existing strategies, plans or programmes which shall reflect, inter alia, the measures set out in this Convention relevant to the Contracting Party concerned; and

(b) Integrate, as far as possible and as appropriate, the conservation and sustainable use of biological diversity into relevant sectoral or cross-sectoral plans, programmes and policies.

Article 7. Identification and Monitoring

Each Contracting Party shall, as far as possible and as appropriate, in particular for the purposes of Articles 8 to 10:

(a) Identify components of biological diversity important for its conservation and sustainable use having regard to the indicative list of categories set down in Annex I;

(b) Monitor, through sampling and other techniques, the components of biological diversity identified pursuant to subparagraph (a) above, paying particular attention to those requiring urgent conservation measures and those which offer the greatest potential for sustainable use;

(c) Identify processes and categories of activities which have or are likely to have significant adverse impacts on the conservation and sustainable use of biological diversity, and monitor their effects through sampling and other techniques; and

(d) Maintain and organize, by any mechanism data, derived from identification and monitoring activities pursuant to subparagraphs (a), (b) and (c) above.

Article 8. In Situ Conservation

Each Contracting Party shall, as far as possible and as appropriate:

(a) Establish a system of protected areas or areas where special measures need to be taken to conserve biological diversity;

(b) Develop, where necessary, guidelines for the selection, establishment and management of protected areas or areas where special measures need to be taken to conserve biological diversity;

(c) Regulate or manage biological resources important for the conservation of biological diversity whether within or outside protected areas, with a view to ensuring their conservation and sustainable use;

(d) Promote the protection of ecosystems, natural habitats and the maintenance of viable populations of species in natural surroundings;

(e) Promote environmentally sound and sustainable development in areas adjacent to protected areas with a view to furthering protection of these areas;

(f) Rehabilitate and restore degraded ecosystems and promote the recovery of threatened species, inter alia, through the development and implementation of plans or other management strategies;

(g) Establish or maintain means to regulate, manage or control the risks associated with the use and release of living modified organisms resulting from biotechnology which are likely to have adverse environmental impacts that could affect the conservation and sustainable use of biological diversity, taking also into account the risks to human health;

(h) Prevent the introduction of, control or eradicate those alien species which threaten ecosystems, habitats or species;

(i) Endeavour to provide the conditions needed for compatibility between present uses and the conservation of biological diversity and the sustainable use of its components;

(j) Subject to its national legislation, respect, preserve and maintain knowledge, innovations and practices of indigenous and local communities embodying traditional lifestyles relevant for the conservation and sustainable use of biological diversity and promote their wider application with the approval and involvement of the holders of such knowledge, innovations and practices and encourage the equitable sharing of the benefits arising from the utilization of such knowledge, innovations and practices;

(k) Develop or maintain necessary legislation and/or other regulatory provisions for the protection of threatened species and populations;

(l)   Where a significant adverse effect on biological diversity has been determined pursuant to Article 7, regulate or manage the relevant processes and categories of activities; and

(m) Co-operate in providing financial and other support for in situ conservation outlined in subparagraphs (a) to (l) above, particularly to developing countries.

Article 9. Ex Situ Conservation

Each Contracting Party shall, as far as possible and as appropriate, and predominantly for the purpose of complementing in situ measures:

(a) Adopt measures for the ex situ conservation of components of biological diversity, preferably in the country of origin of such components;

(b) Establish and maintain facilities for ex situ conservation of and research on plants, animals and micro-organisms, preferably in the country of origin of genetic resources;

(c) Adopt measures for the recovery and rehabilitation of threatened species and for their reintroduction into their natural habitats under appropriate conditions;

(d) Regulate and manage collection of biological resources from natural habitats for ex situ conservation purposes so as not to threaten ecosystems and in situ populations of species, except where special temporary ex situ measures are required under subparagraph (c) above; and

(e) Co-operate in providing financial and other support for ex situ conservation outlined in subparagraphs (a) to (d) above and in the establishment and maintenance of ex situ conservation facilities in developing countries.

Article 10. Sustainable Use of Components of Biological Diversity

Each Contracting Party shall, as far as possible and as appropriate:

(a) Integrate consideration of the conservation and sustainable use of biological resources into national decision-making;

(b) Adopt measures relating to the use of biological resources to avoid or minimize adverse impacts on biological diversity;

(c) Protect and encourage customary use of biological resources in accordance with traditional cultural practices that are compatible with conservation or sustainable use requirements;

(d) Support local populations to develop and implement remedial action in degraded areas where biological diversity has been reduced; and

(e) Encourage co-operation between its governmental authorities and its private sector in developing methods for sustainable use of biological resources.

Article 11. Incentive Measures

Each Contracting Party shall, as far as possible and as appropriate, adopt economically and socially sound measures that act as incentives for the conservation and sustainable use of components of biological diversity.

Article 12. Research and Training

The Contracting Parties, taking into account the special needs of developing countries, shall:

(a) Establish and maintain programmes for scientific and technical education and training in measures for the identification, conservation and sustainable use of biological diversity and its components and provide support for such education and training for the specific needs of developing countries;

(b) Promote and encourage research which contributes to the conservation and sustainable use of biological diversity, particularly in developing countries, inter alia, in accordance with decisions of the Conference of the Parties taken in consequence of recommendations of the Subsidiary Body on Scientific, Technical and Technological Advice; and

(c) In keeping with the provisions of Articles 16, 18 and 20, promote and co-operate in the use of scientific advances in biological diversity research in developing methods for conservation and sustainable use of biological resources.

Article 13. Public Education and Awareness

The Contracting Parties shall:

(a) Promote and encourage understanding of the importance of, and the measures required for, the conservation of biological diversity, as well as its propagation through media, and the inclusion of these topics in educational programmes; and

(b) Co-operate, as appropriate, with other States and international organizations in developing educational and public awareness programmes, with respect to conservation and sustainable use of biological diversity.

Article 14. Impact Assessment and Minimizing Adverse Impacts

1.   Each Contracting Party, as far as possible and as appropriate, shall:

(a) Introduce appropriate procedures requiring environmental impact assessment of its proposed projects that are likely to have significant adverse effects on biological diversity with a view to avoiding or minimizing such effects and, where appropriate, allow for public participation in such procedures;

(b) Introduce appropriate arrangements to ensure that the environmental consequences of its programmes and policies that are likely to have significant adverse impacts on biological diversity are duly taken into account;

(c) Promote, on the basis of reciprocity, notification, exchange of information and consultation on activities under their jurisdiction or control which are likely to significantly affect adversely the biological diversity of other States or areas beyond the limits of national jurisdiction, by encouraging the conclusion of bilateral, regional or multilateral arrangements, as appropriate;

(d) In the case of imminent or grave danger or damage, originating under its jurisdiction or control, to biological diversity within the area under jurisdiction of other States or in areas beyond the limits of national jurisdiction, notify immediately the potentially affected States of such danger or damage, as well as initiate action to prevent or minimize such danger or damage; and

(e) Promote national arrangements for emergency responses to activities or events, whether caused naturally or otherwise, which present a grave and imminent danger to biological diversity and encourage international co-operation to supplement such national efforts and, where appropriate and agreed by the States or regional economic integration organizations concerned, to establish joint contingency plans.

2.   The Conference of the Parties shall examine, on the basis of studies to be carried out, the issue of liability and redress, including restoration and compensation, for damage to biological diversity, except where such liability is a purely internal matter.

Article 15. Access to Genetic Resources

1.   Recognizing the sovereign rights of States over their natural resources, the authority to determine access to genetic resources rests with the national governments and is subject to national legislation.

2.   Each Contracting Party shall endeavour to create conditions to facilitate access to genetic resources for environmentally sound uses by other Contracting Parties and not to impose restrictions that run counter to the objectives of this Convention.

3.   For the purpose of this Convention, the genetic resources being provided by a Contracting Party, as referred to in this Article and Articles 16 and 19, are only those that are provided by Contracting Parties that are countries of origin of such resources or by the Parties that have acquired the genetic resources in accordance with this Convention.

4.   Access, where granted, shall be on mutually agreed terms and subject to the provisions of this Article.

5.   Access to genetic resources shall be subject to prior informed consent of the Contracting Party providing such resources, unless otherwise determined by that Party.

6.   Each Contracting Party shall endeavour to develop and carry out scientific research based on genetic resources provided by other Contracting Parties with the full participation of, and where possible in, such Contracting

Parties.

7.   Each Contracting Party shall take legislative, administrative or policy measures, as appropriate, and in accordance with Articles 16 and 19 and, where necessary, through the financial mechanism established by Articles 20 and 21 with the aim of sharing in a fair and equitable way the results of research and development and the benefits arising from the commercial and other utilization of genetic resources with the Contracting Party providing such resources. Such sharing shall be upon mutually agreed terms.

Article 16. Access to and Transfer of Technology

1.   Each Contracting Party, recognizing that technology includes biotechnology, and that both access to and transfer of technology among Contracting Parties are essential elements for the attainment of the objectives of this Convention, undertakes subject to the provisions of this Article to provide and/or facilitate access for and transfer to other Contracting Parties of technologies that are relevant to the conservation and sustainable use of biological diversity or make use of genetic resources and do not cause significant damage to the environment.

2.   Access to and transfer of technology referred to in paragraph 1 above to developing countries shall be provided and/or facilitated under fair and most favourable terms, including on concessional and preferential terms where mutually agreed, and, where necessary, in accordance with the financial mechanism established by Articles 20 and 21. In the case of technology subject to patents and other intellectual property rights, such access and transfer shall be provided on terms which recognize and are consistent with the adequate and effective protection of intellectual property rights. The application of this paragraph shall be consistent with paragraphs 3, 4 and 5 below.

3.   Each Contracting Party shall take legislative, administrative or policy measures, as appropriate, with the aim that Contracting Parties, in particular those that are developing countries, which provide genetic resources are provided access to and transfer of technology which makes use of those resources, on mutually agreed terms, including technology protected by patents and other intellectual property rights, where necessary, through the provisions of Articles 20 and 21 and in accordance with international law and consistent with paragraphs 4 and 5 below.

4.   Each Contracting Party shall take legislative, administrative or policy measures, as appropriate, with the aim that the private sector facilitates access to, joint development and transfer of technology referred to in paragraph 1 above

for the benefit of both governmental institutions and the private sector of developing countries and in this regard shall abide by the obligations included in paragraphs 1, 2 and 3 above.

5.   The Contracting Parties, recognizing that patents and other intellectual property rights may have an influence on the implementation of this Convention, shall co-operate in this regard subject to national legislation and international law in order to ensure that such rights are supportive of and do not run counter to its objectives.

Article 17. Exchange of Information

1.   The Contracting Parties shall facilitate the exchange of information, from all publicly available sources, relevant to the conservation and sustainable use of biological diversity, taking into account the special needs of developing countries.

2.   Such exchange of information shall include exchange of results of technical, scientific and socio-economic research, as well as information on training and surveying programmes, specialized knowledge, indigenous and traditional knowledge as such and in combination with the technologies referred to in Article 16, paragraph 1. It shall also, where feasible, include repatriation of information.

Article 18. Technical and Scientific Co-operation

1.   The Contracting Parties shall promote international technical and scientific co-operation in the field of conservation and sustainable use of biological diversity, where necessary, through the appropriate international and national institutions.

2.   Each Contracting Party shall promote technical and scientific co-operation with other Contracting Parties, in particular developing countries, in implementing this Convention, inter alia, through the development and implementation of national policies. In promoting such co-operation, special attention should be given to the development and strengthening of national capabilities, by means of human resources development and institution building.

3.   The Conference of the Parties, at its first meeting, shall determine how to establish a clearing-house mechanism to promote and facilitate technical and scientific co-operation.

4.   The Contracting Parties shall, in accordance with national legislation and policies, encourage and develop methods of co-operation for the development and use of technologies, including indigenous and traditional technologies, in pursuance of the objectives of this Convention.   For this purpose, the Contracting Parties shall also promote co-operation in the training of personnel and exchange of experts.

5.   The Contracting Parties shall, subject to mutual agreement, promote the establishment of joint research programmes and joint ventures for the development of technologies relevant to the objectives of this Convention.

Article 19. Handling of Biotechnology and Distribution of its Benefits

1.   Each Contracting Party shall take legislative, administrative or policy measures, as appropriate, to provide for the effective participation in biotechnological research activities by those Contracting Parties, especially developing countries, which provide the genetic resources for such research, and where feasible in such Contracting Parties.

2.   Each Contracting Party shall take all practicable measures to promote and advance priority access on a fair and equitable basis by Contracting Parties, especially developing countries, to the results and benefits arising from biotechnologies based upon genetic resources provided by those Contracting Parties. Such access shall be on mutually agreed terms.

3.   The Parties shall consider the need for and modalities of a protocol setting out appropriate procedures, including, in particular, advance informed agreement, in the field of the safe transfer, handling and use of any living modified organism resulting from biotechnology that may have adverse effect on the conservation and sustainable use of biological diversity.

4.   Each Contracting Party shall, directly or by requiring any natural or legal person under its jurisdiction providing the organisms referred to in paragraph 3 above, provide any available information about the use and safety regulations required by that Contracting Party in handling such organisms, as well as any available information on the potential adverse impact of the specific organisms concerned to the Contracting Party into which those organisms are to be introduced.

Article 20. Financial Resources

1.   Each Contracting Party undertakes to provide, in accordance with its capabilities, financial support and incentives in respect of those national activities which are intended to achieve the objectives of this Convention, in accordance with its national plans, priorities and programmes.

2.   The developed country Parties shall provide new and additional financial resources to enable developing country Parties to meet the agreed full incremental costs to them of implementing measures which fulfil the obligations of this Convention and to benefit from its provisions and which costs are agreed between a developing country Party and the institutional structure referred to in Article 21, in accordance with policy, strategy, programme priorities and eligibility criteria and an indicative list of incremental costs established by the Conference of the Parties. Other Parties, including countries undergoing the process of transition to a market economy, may voluntarily assume the obligations of the developed country Parties. For the purpose of this Article, the Conference of the Parties, shall at its first meeting establish a list of developed country Parties and other Parties which voluntarily assume the obligations of the developed country Parties. The Conference of the Parties shall periodically review and if necessary amend the list. Contributions from other countries and sources on a voluntary basis would also be encouraged. The implementation of these commitments shall take into account the need for adequacy, predictability and timely flow of funds and the importance of burden-sharing among the contributing Parties included in the list.

3.   The developed country Parties may also provide, and developing country Parties avail themselves of, financial resources related to the implementation of this Convention through bilateral, regional and other multilateral channels.

4.   The extent to which developing country Parties will effectively implement their commitments under this Convention will depend on the effective implementation by developed country Parties of their commitments under this Convention related to financial resources and transfer of technology and will take fully into account the fact that economic and social development and eradication of poverty are the first and overriding priorities of the developing country Parties.

5.   The Parties shall take full account of the specific needs and special situation of least developed countries in their actions with regard to funding and transfer of technology.

6.   The Contracting Parties shall also take into consideration the special conditions resulting from the dependence on, distribution and location of, biological diversity within developing country Parties, in particular small island States.

7.   Consideration shall also be given to the special situation of developing countries, including those that are most environmentally vulnerable, such as those with arid and semi-arid zones, coastal and mountainous areas.

Article 21. Financial Mechanism

1.   There shall be a mechanism for the provision of financial resources to developing country Parties for purposes of this Convention on a grant or concessional basis the essential elements of which are described in this Article. The mechanism shall function under the authority and guidance of, and be accountable to, the Conference of the Parties for purposes of this Convention. The operations of the mechanism shall be carried out by such institutional structure as may be decided upon by the Conference of the Parties at its first meeting. For purposes of this Convention, the Conference of the Parties shall determine the policy, strategy, programme priorities and eligibility criteria relating to the access to and utilization of such resources. The contributions shall be such as to take into account the need for predictability, adequacy and timely flow of funds referred to in Article 20 in accordance with the amount of resources needed to be decided periodically by the Conference of the Parties and the importance of burden-sharing among the contributing Parties included in the list referred to in Article 20, paragraph 2. Voluntary contributions may also be made by the developed country Parties and by other countries and sources. The mechanism shall operate within a democratic and transparent system of governance.

2.   Pursuant to the objectives of this Convention, the Conference of the Parties shall at its first meeting determine the policy, strategy and programme priorities, as well as detailed criteria and guidelines for eligibility for access to and utilization of the financial resources including monitoring and evaluation on a regular basis of such utilization. The Conference of the Parties shall decide on the arrangements to give effect to paragraph 1 above after consultation with the institutional structure entrusted with the operation of the financial mechanism.

3.   The Conference of the Parties shall review the effectiveness of the mechanism established under this Article, including the criteria and guidelines referred to in paragraph 2 above, not less than two years after the entry into force of this Convention and thereafter on a regular basis. Based on such review, it shall take appropriate action to improve the effectiveness of the mechanism if

necessary.

4.   The Contracting Parties shall consider strengthening existing financial institutions to provide financial resources for the conservation and sustainable use of biological diversity.

Article 22. Relationship with Other International Conventions

1.   The provisions of this Convention shall not affect the rights and obligations of any Contracting Party deriving from any existing international agreement, except where the exercise of those rights and obligations would cause a serious damage or threat to biological diversity.

2.   Contracting Parties shall implement this Convention with respect to the marine environment consistently with the rights and obligations of States under the law of the sea.

Article 23. Conference of the Parties

1.   A Conference of the Parties is hereby established. The first meeting of the Conference of the Parties shall be convened by the Executive Director of the United Nations Environment Programme not later than one year after the entry into force of this Convention. Thereafter, ordinary meetings of the Conference of the Parties shall be held at regular intervals to be determined by the Conference at its first meeting.

2.   Extraordinary meetings of the Conference of the Parties shall be held at such other times as may be deemed necessary by the Conference, or at the written request of any Party, provided that, within six months of the request being communicated to them by the Secretariat, it is supported by at least one third of the Parties.

3.   The Conference of the Parties shall by consensus agree upon and adopt rules of procedure for itself and for any subsidiary body it may establish, as well as financial rules governing the funding of the Secretariat. At each ordinary meeting, it shall adopt a budget for the financial period until the next ordinary meeting.

4.   The Conference of the Parties shall keep under review the implementation of this Convention, and, for this purpose, shall:

(a) Establish the form and the intervals for transmitting the information to be submitted in accordance with Article 26 and consider such information as well as reports submitted by any subsidiary body;

(b) Review scientific, technical and technological advice on biological diversity provided in accordance with Article 25;

(c) Consider and adopt, as required, protocols in accordance with Article 28;

(d) Consider and adopt, as required, in accordance with Articles 29 and 30, amendments to this Convention and its annexes;

(e) Consider amendments to any protocol, as well as to any annexes thereto, and, if so decided, recommend their adoption to the parties to the protocol concerned;

(f) Consider and adopt, as required, in accordance with Article 30, additional annexes to this Convention;

(g) Establish such subsidiary bodies, particularly to provide scientific and technical advice, as are deemed necessary for the implementation of this Convention;

(h) Contact, through the Secretariat, the executive bodies of conventions dealing with matters covered by this Convention with a view to establishing appropriate forms of co-operation with them; and

(i) Consider and undertake any additional action that may be required for the achievement of the purposes of this Convention in the light of experience gained in its operation.

5.   The United Nations, its specialized agencies and the International Atomic Energy Agency, as well as any State not Party to this Convention, may be represented as observers at meetings of the Conference of the Parties. Any other body or agency, whether governmental or non-governmental, qualified in fields relating to conservation and sustainable use of biological diversity, which has informed the Secretariat of its wish to be represented as an observer at a meeting of the Conference of the Parties, may be admitted unless at least one third of the Parties present object. The admission and participation of observers shall be subject to the rules of procedure adopted by the Conference of the Parties.

Article 24. Secretariat

1.   A secretariat is hereby established. Its functions shall be:

(a) To arrange for and service meetings of the Conference of the Parties provided for in Article 23;

(b) To perform the functions assigned to it by any protocol;

(c) To prepare reports on the execution of its functions under this Convention and present them to the Conference of the Parties;

(d) To co-ordinate with other relevant international bodies and, in particular to enter into such administrative and contractual arrangements as may be required for the effective discharge of its functions; and

(e) To perform such other functions as may be determined by the Conference of the Parties.

2.   At its first ordinary meeting, the Conference of the Parties shall designate the secretariat from amongst those existing competent international organizations which have signified their willingness to carry out the secretariat functions under this Convention.

Article 25. Subsidiary Body on Scientific, Technical and Technological Advice

1.   A subsidiary body for the provision of scientific, technical and technological advice is hereby established to provide the Conference of the Parties and, as appropriate, its other subsidiary bodies with timely advice relating to the implementation of this Convention. This body shall be open to participation by all Parties and shall be multidisciplinary. It shall comprise government representatives competent in the relevant field of expertise. It shall report regularly to the Conference of the Parties on all aspects of its work.

2.   Under the authority of and in accordance with guidelines laid down by the Conference of the Parties, and upon its request, this body shall:

(a) Provide scientific and technical assessments of the status of biological diversity;

(b) Prepare scientific and technical assessments of the effects of types of measures taken in accordance with the provisions of this Convention;

(c) Identify innovative, efficient and state-of-the-art technologies and know-how relating to the conservation and sustainable use of biological diversity and advise on the ways and means of promoting development and/or transferring such technologies;

(d) Provide advice on scientific programmes and international co-operation in research and development related to conservation and sustainable use of biological diversity; and

(e) Respond to scientific, technical, technological and methodological questions that the Conference of the Parties and its subsidiary bodies may put to the body.

3.   The functions, terms of reference, organization and operation of this body may be further elaborated by the Conference of the Parties.

Article 26. Reports

Each Contracting Party shall, at intervals to be determined by the Conference of the Parties, present to the Conference of the Parties, reports on measures which it has taken for the implementation of the provisions of this Convention and their effectiveness in meeting the objectives of this Convention.

Article 27. Settlement of Disputes

1.   In the event of a dispute between Contracting Parties concerning the interpretation or application of this Convention, the parties concerned shall seek solution by negotiation.

2.   If the parties concerned cannot reach agreement by negotiation, they may jointly seek the good offices of, or request mediation by, a third party.

3.   When ratifying, accepting, approving or acceding to this Convention, or at any time thereafter, a State or regional economic integration organization may declare in writing to the Depositary that for a dispute not resolved in accordance with paragraph 1 or paragraph 2 above, it accepts one or both of the following means of dispute settlement as compulsory:

(a) Arbitration in accordance with the procedure laid down in Part 1 of Annex II;

(b) Submission of the dispute to the International Court of Justice.

4.   If the parties to the dispute have not, in accordance with paragraph 3 above, accepted the same or any procedure, the dispute shall be submitted to conciliation in accordance with Part 2 of Annex II unless the parties otherwise agree.

5.   The provisions of this Article shall apply with respect to any protocol except as otherwise provided in the protocol concerned.

Article 28. Adoption of Protocols

1.   The Contracting Parties shall co-operate in the formulation and adoption of protocols to this Convention.

2.   Protocols shall be adopted at a meeting of the Conference of the Parties.

3.   The text of any proposed protocol shall be communicated to the Contracting Parties by the Secretariat at least six months before such a meeting.

Article 29. Amendment of the Convention or Protocols

1.   Amendments to this Convention may be proposed by any Contracting Party. Amendments to any protocol may be proposed by any Party to that protocol.

2.   Amendments to this Convention shall be adopted at a meeting of the Conference of the Parties. Amendments to any protocol shall be adopted at a meeting of the Parties to the Protocol in question. The text of any proposed amendment to this Convention or to any protocol, except as may otherwise be provided in such protocol, shall be communicated to the Parties to the instrument in question by the secretariat at least six months before the meeting at which it is proposed for adoption. The secretariat shall also communicate proposed amendments to the signatories to this Convention for information.

3.   The Parties shall make every effort to reach agreement on any proposed amendment to this Convention or to any protocol by consensus. If all efforts at consensus have been exhausted, and no agreement reached, the amendment shall as a last resort be adopted by a two-third majority vote of the Parties to the instrument in question present and voting at the meeting, and shall be submitted by the Depositary to all Parties for ratification, acceptance or approval.

4.   Ratification, acceptance or approval of amendments shall be notified to the Depositary in writing. Amendments adopted in accordance with paragraph 3 above shall enter into force among Parties having accepted them on the ninetieth day after the deposit of instruments of ratification, acceptance or approval by at least two thirds of the Contracting Parties to this Convention or of the Parties to the protocol concerned, except as may otherwise be provided in such protocol. Thereafter the amendments shall enter into force for any other Party on the ninetieth day after that Party deposits its instrument of ratification, acceptance or approval of the amendments.

5.   For the purposes of this Article, "Parties present and voting" means Parties present and casting an affirmative or negative vote.

Article 30. Adoption and Amendment of Annexes

1.   The annexes to this Convention or to any protocol shall form an integral part of the Convention or of such protocol, as the case may be, and, unless expressly provided otherwise, a reference to this Convention or its protocols constitutes at the same time a reference to any annexes thereto. Such annexes shall be restricted to procedural, scientific, technical and administrative matters.

2.   Except as may be otherwise provided in any protocol with respect to its annexes, the following procedure shall apply to the proposal, adoption and entry into force of additional annexes to this Convention or of annexes to any protocol:

    (a) Annexes to this Convention or to any protocol shall be proposed and adopted according to the procedure laid down in Article 29;

    (b) Any Party that is unable to approve an additional annex to this Convention or an annex to any protocol to which it is Party shall so notify the Depositary, in writing, within one year from the date of the communication of the adoption by the Depositary. The Depositary shall without delay notify all Parties of any such notification received. A Party may at any time withdraw a previous declaration of objection and the annexes shall thereupon enter into force for that Party subject to subparagraph (c) below;

    (c) On the expiry of one year from the date of the communication of the adoption by the Depositary, the annex shall enter into force for all Parties to this Convention or to any protocol concerned which have not submitted a notification in accordance with the provisions of subparagraph (b) above.

3.   The proposal, adoption and entry into force of amendments to annexes to

this Convention or to any protocol shall be subject to the same procedure as for the proposal, adoption and entry into force of annexes to the Convention or annexes to any protocol.

4.   If an additional annex or an amendment to an annex is related to an amendment to this Convention or to any protocol, the additional annex or amendment shall not enter into force until such time as the amendment to the Convention or to the protocol concerned enters into force.

Article 31. Right to Vote

1.   Except as provided for in paragraph 2 below, each Contracting Party to this Convention or to any protocol shall have one vote.

2.   Regional economic integration organizations, in matters within their competence, shall exercise their right to vote with a number of votes equal to the number of their member States which are Contracting Parties to this Convention or the relevant protocol. Such organizations shall not exercise their right to vote if their member States exercise theirs, and vice versa.

Article 32. Relationship between this Convention and its Protocols

1.   A State or a regional economic integration organization may not become a Party to a protocol unless it is, or becomes at the same time, a Contracting Party to this Convention.

2.   Decisions under any protocol shall be taken only by the Parties to the protocol concerned. Any Contracting Party that has not ratified, accepted or approved a protocol may participate as an observer in any meeting of the parties to that protocol.

Article 33. Signature

This Convention shall be open for signature at Rio de Janeiro by all States and any regional economic integration organization from 5 June 1992 until 14 June 1992, and at the United Nations Headquarters in New York from 15 June 1992 to 4 June 1993.

Article 34. Ratification, Acceptance or Approval

1.   This Convention and any protocol shall be subject to ratification, acceptance or approval by States and by regional economic integration organizations. Instruments of ratification, acceptance or approval shall be deposited with the Depositary.

2.   Any organization referred to in paragraph 1 above which becomes a Contracting Party to this Convention or any protocol without any of its member States being a Contracting Party shall be bound by all the obligations under the Convention or the protocol, as the case may be. In the case of such organizations, one or more of whose member States is a Contracting Party to this Convention or relevant protocol, the organization and its member States shall decide on their respective responsibilities for the performance of their obligations under the Convention or protocol, as the case may be. In such cases, the organization and the member States shall not be entitled to exercise rights under the Convention or relevant protocol concurrently.

3.   In their instruments of ratification, acceptance or approval, the organizations referred to in paragraph 1 above shall declare the extent of their competence with respect to the matters governed by the Convention or the relevant protocol. These organizations shall also inform the Depositary of any relevant modification in the extent of their competence.

Article 35. Accession

1.   This Convention and any protocol shall be open for accession by States and by regional economic integration organizations from the date on which the Convention or the protocol concerned is closed for signature. The instruments of accession shall be deposited with the Depositary.

2.   In their instruments of accession, the organizations referred to in paragraph 1 above shall declare the extent of their competence with respect to the matters governed by the Convention or the relevant protocol. These organizations shall also inform the Depositary of any relevant modification in the extent of their competence.

3.   The provisions of Article 34, paragraph 2, shall apply to regional economic integration organizations which accede to this Convention or any protocol.

Article 36. Entry Into Force

1.   This Convention shall enter into force on the ninetieth day after the date of deposit of the thirtieth instrument of ratification, acceptance, approval or accession.

2.   Any protocol shall enter into force on the ninetieth day after the date of deposit of the number of instruments of ratification, acceptance, approval or accession, specified in that protocol, has been deposited.

3.   For each Contracting Party which ratifies, accepts or approves this Convention or accedes thereto after the deposit of the thirtieth instrument of ratification, acceptance, approval or accession, it shall enter into force on the ninetieth day after the date of deposit by such Contracting Party of its instrument of ratification, acceptance, approval or accession.

4.   Any protocol, except as otherwise provided in such protocol, shall enter into force for a Contracting Party that ratifies, accepts or approves that protocol or accedes thereto after its entry into force pursuant to paragraph 2 above, on the ninetieth day after the date on which that Contracting Party deposits its instrument of ratification, acceptance, approval or accession, or on the date on which this Convention enters into force for that Contracting Party, whichever shall be the later.

5.   For the purposes of paragraphs 1 and 2 above, any instrument deposited by a regional economic integration organization shall not be counted as additional to those deposited by member States of such organization.

Article 37. Reservations

No reservations may be made to this Convention.

Article 38. Withdrawals

1.   At any time after two years from the date on which this Convention has entered into force for a Contracting Party, that Contracting Party may withdraw from the Convention by giving written notification to the Depositary.

2.   Any such withdrawal shall take place upon expiry of one year after the date of its receipt by the Depositary, or on such later date as may be specified in the notification of the withdrawal.

3.   Any Contracting Party which withdraws from this Convention shall be considered as also having withdrawn from any protocol to which it is party.

Article 39. Financial Interim Arrangements

Provided that it has been fully restructured in accordance with the requirements of Article 21, the Global Environment Facility of the United Nations Development Programme, the United Nations Environment Programme and the International Bank for Reconstruction and Development shall be the institutional structure referred to in Article 21 on an interim basis, for the period between the entry into force of this Convention and the first meeting of the Conference of the Parties or until the Conference of the Parties decides which institutional structure will be designated in accordance with Article 21.

Article 40. Secretariat Interim Arrangements

The secretariat to be provided by the Executive Director of the United Nations Environment Programme shall be the secretariat referred to in Article 24, paragraph 2, on an interim basis for the period between the entry into force of this Convention and the first meeting of the Conference of the Parties.

Article 41. Depositary

The Secretary-General of the United Nations shall assume the functions of Depositary of this Convention and any protocols.

Article 42. Authentic Texts

The original of this Convention, of which the Arabic, Chinese, English, French, Russian and Spanish texts are equally authentic, shall be deposited with the Secretary-General of the United Nations.

IN WITNESS WHEREOF the undersigned, being duly authorized to that effect, have signed this Convention.

Done at Rio de Janeiro on this fifth day of June, one thousand nine hundred and ninety-two.

Bibliography

Acot, P. (1988), *Histoire de l'écologie*, PUF, Paris.

African Centre for Technology Studies (ACTS) (1996), *East African Sub-Regional Forum on the Convention on Biological Diversity: national opportunities and responsibilities*, African Centre for Technology Studies, Nairobi.

Alderson, P. and Goodey, C. (1998), "Theories of Consent", *British Medical Journal*, November 7, pp. 1313-1316.

Alter, K. J. (2000), "Regime Design Matters: Designing International Legal Systems for Maximum or Minimum Effectiveness", International Studies Association Annual Meeting.

ANGAP (1999), *Plan stratégique du Réseau des aires protégées de Madagascar.*

Andersen, S. and Sjærseth, J. B. (1999), "Can International Environmental Secretariats Promote Effective Co-operation?", in United Nations University's International Conference on Synergies and Co-ordination Between Multilateral Environmental Agreements (Interlinkages_99), July 14-16, Tokyo.

Atcheson, J. (1996), "Can We Trust Verification?", *The Environmental Forum*, vol. 13, no. 4, pp. 15-21.

Aubertin, C. (2000), "L'ascension fulgurante d'un concept flou", *La Recherche*, vol. 333, pp. 84-87.

Aubertin, C. et al. (1998), "La construction sociale de la question de la biodiversité", *Natures, Sciences et Sociétés*, vol. 6, pp. 7-19.

Aubertin, C. and Vivien, F-D. (1998), *Les enjeux de la biodiversité*, Economica, Paris.

Aubertin, C., Boisvert, V., and Vivien, F-D. (1998), "La construction sociale de la question de la biodiversité", *Natures, Sciences, Sociétés*, vol. 6, no. 1, pp. 7-19.

Ayling, J. (1997), "Serving Many Voices: Progressing Calls for an International Environmental Organization", *Journal of Environmental Law*, vol. 9, no. 2, pp. 343-370.

Babin, D. and Bertrand, A. (1998), "Comment gérer le pluralisme: subsidiarité et médiation patrimoniale", *Unasylva*, vol. 49, no. 194, pp. 19-25.

Babin, D., Bertrand, A., Weber, J., and Antona, M. (1997), "Patrimonial mediation and management subsidiarity: managing pluralism for sustainable forestry and rural development", in *Pluralism and Sustainable Forestry and Rural Development*, Proceedings of an International Workshop, FAO, IUFRO, and CIRAD, Rome, pp. 277-303.

Babin, D. et al. (2001), "Methods of Rapid appraisal for *In Situ* Management of Genetic Resources: A Malagasy Set of Tools", submitted in *Genetics, Selection, Evolution.*

Baldwin, R. (1995), *Rules and Government*, Oxford, Clarendon Press.

Banque mondiale (1990), *Rapport d'évaluation: République démocratique de Madagascar, Programme environnemental*, Report No. 8348-MAG, IBRD, Washington.

Barbier, E. B. (1996), "Ecological Economics, Uncertainty and Implications for Policy Settings Priorities for Biodiversity Conservation", presented at OECD International Conference on Incentive Measures for Biodiversity Conservation and Sustainable Use, Australia, 25-28 March 1996.

Barnes, T. and Burgiel, S. (2001), "Negotiations on the International Treaty on Plant Genetic Resources for Food and Agriculture", *Earth Negotiations Bulletin*, vol. 9, no. 213, 5 November 2001 (www.iisd.ca).

Barnes T., Burgiel, S. and Le Goulven, K. (2000), "Fourth Intersessional Meeting of the IUCG-4 in Neuchâtel, Switzerland, 12-17 November", *Environmental Negotiations Bulletin*, vol. 9, no. 167, 20 November 2000 (http://www.iisd.ca).

Baskin, Y. (1997), *The Works of Nature. How the Diversity of Life Sustains Us*, Island Press, Washington DC.

Bell, D. E. (1993), "The 1992 Convention on Biological Diversity: The continuing significance of U.S. objections at the Earth Summit", *George Washington Journal of International Law and Economics*, vol. 26, pp. 479-537.

Benedick, R. (1991), *Ozone Diplomacy*, Harvard University Press, Cambridge, Massachusetts.

Berkes, F., Feeny D., McCay B. J., and Acheson, J. M. (1989), "The Benefits of the Commons", *Nature*, vol. 340.

Bernauer, T. (1995), "The Effects of International Environmental Institutions: How We Might Learn More", *International Organization*, vol. 49, no. 2, pp. 351-377.

Bertrand, A. (1999), "La gestion contractuelle, pluraliste et subsidiaire des ressources renouvelables à Madagascar (1994-1998)", *African Studies Quarterly*, vol. 3, no. 2 (http://web.africa.ufl.edu/asq/v3/v3i2.htm).

Bertrand, A., Babin, D., and Nasi, R. (1999), "L'aménagement forestier. Mais où est donc cette gestion forestière durable que chacun cherche désespérément des tropiques humides aux zones sèches?", *Bois et forêts des tropiques*, no. 260(2), pp. 33-40.

Beurier, J-P. (1996), "Le droit de la biodiversité", *Revue juridique de l'environnement*, vol. 1, no. 2, pp. 5-28.

Bilderbeek, S. (1992), *Biodiversity and International Law: The Effectiveness of International Environmental Law*, IOS Press, Washington DC.

Bingham, G. et al. (1995), "Issues in ecosystem valuation: improving information for decision making", *Ecological Economics*, vol. 14, no. 2, pp.73-90.

Blowers, A. and Glasbergen, P. (eds.) (1996), *Environmental Policy in an International Context: Prospects for Environmental Change*, Arnold, London.

Boehmer-Christiansen, S. (1993), "Science, Policy, the IPCC and the Climate Change Convention: The Codification of a Global Research Agenda", *Energy and Environment*, vol. 4, pp. 362-407.

Bohman, J. (1999), "International Regimes and Democratic Governance: Political Equality and Influence in Global Institutions", *International Affairs*, vol. 75, no. 3, pp. 499-513.

Boiteau, P. (1982), *Contribution à l'histoire de la nation malgache*, Editions Sociales, Paris.

Bowman, M. (1996), "The Nature, Development and Philosophical Foundations of the Biodiversity Concept in International Law", in M. Bowman and C. Redgewell (eds.), *International Law and the Conservation of Biological Diversity*, Kluwer International Law, London, pp. 5-31.

Bragdon, S. H. (1992), "National Sovereignty and Global Environmental Responsibility: Can the Tension Be Reconciled for the Conservation of Biological Diversity?", *Harvard International Law Journal*, vol. 33, no. 2, pp. 381-392.

Bramble, B. J. and Porter, G. (1992), "Non-governmental Organizations and the Making of US International Environmental Policy", in A. Hurrell and B. Kingsbury (eds.), *The International Politics of the Environment: Actors, Interests, and Institution*, Clarendon, Oxford, pp. 313-353.

Brenton, T. (1994), "Biodiversity", in T. Brenton (ed.), *The Greening of Machiavelli: The Evolution of International Environmental Politics*, Earthscan and the Royal Institute of International Affairs, London, pp. 197-204.

Brosnan, D. M. (1994), "Ecosystem Management: An Ecological Perspective for Environmental Lawyers", *University of Baltimore Journal of Environmental Law*, vol. 4, pp.135-153.

Brown, E. Weiss. (1998), "The Five International Treaties: A Living History", in E. Brown Weiss and H. K. Jacobson (eds.), *Engaging Countries: Strengthening Compliance with International Environmental Accords*, MIT Press, Cambridge and London, pp. 89-172.

Brown, M. (1995), *A History of Madagascar*, Ipswich Book.

Brown, M. and Wyckoff-Baird, B. (1992), *Designing Integrated Conservation and Development Projects*, World Wildlife Fund, Washington DC.

Burgenmeier, B, *La Socio-économie*, Économica, Paris.

Burhenne-Guilmin, F. and Glowka, L. (1994), "An Introduction to the Convention on Biological Diversity", in A. F. Krattiger et al. (eds.), *Widening Perspectives on Biodiversity*, World Conservation Union and International Academy of the Environment, Cambridge and Gland, pp. 14-18.

Busby, J. R. (1997), "Management of Information to Support Conservation Decision-Making", in D. L. Hawksworth, P. M. Kirk and S. D. Clarke (eds.), *Biodiversity Information: Needs and Options*, Cab International, Londres, pp. 105-114.

Cameron, J., Werksman, J., Roderick P. et al. (1996), *Improving Compliance with International Environmental Law*, Earthscan, London.

Canada (1995a), *L'examen de la LCPE: Réponse du Gouvernement. Mesures législatives sur la protection de l'environnement conçues pour l'avenir – Une LCPE renouvelée*, Public Works and Government Services Canada, Ottawa.

Canada (1995b), *Canadian Biodiversity Strategy. Canada's Response to the Convention on Biological Diversity*, Public Works and Government Services Canada, Ottawa.

Canada (1997), *Caring for Canada's Biodiversity:Canada's First National Report to the Conference of the Parties to the Convention on Biological Diversity (and Annex)*, Public Works and Government Services Canada, Ottawa.

Canada House of Commons (1995), *Report of the House of Commons Standing Committee en Environment and Sustainable Development, It's about our Health! Toward Pollution Prevention* (CEPA), Public Works and Government Services Canada, Ottawa.

Canada Parks Service (1991), *State of the Parks 1990 Report*, Minister of Supply and Services Canada, Ottawa.

Canadian Council of Ministers of the Environment (1996), *A Framework for Developing Ecosystem Health Goals, Objectives, and Indicators: Tools for Ecosystem-Based Management*, Manitoba Statutory Publications, Winnipeg.

Canadian Council of Ministers of the Environment (1998), *Canada-wide Accord of Environmental Harmonization; Sub-agreement on Environmental Assessment; Sub-agreement on Inspections and enforcement; Canada-wide Environmental Standards Sub-agreement*, 29 January 1998 (www.ccme.ca/3e_priorities/3e.)

Cannabrava, F. (2001), "TRIPS and the CBD: what Language for the Ministerial Declaration?", *Bridges*, vol. 5, no. 8, October 2001, pp. 7 and 10.

Cansari, R. (2001), "The Scientific Community and the Indigenous Embéra Community of Panama", in C. Potvin, M. Kraenzel, and G. Seutin (eds.), *Protecting Biological Diversity: Roles and Responsibilities*, McGill-Queen's University Press, Montreal and Toronto, pp. 26-40.

Chandler, M. (1993), "The Biodiversity Convention: Selected Issues of Interest to the International Lawyer", *Colorado Journal of International Environmental Law and Policy*, vol. 4, pp. 141-175.

Chapin, F. S. III, Zavaleta, E. S., and Eviners, V. T. (2000), "Review article: Consequences of changing biodiversity", *Nature*, vol. 405, pp. 234-242.

Charnovitz, S. (1992), "GATT and the Environment: Examining the Issues", *International Environmental Affairs*, vol. 4, no. 3, Summer, pp. 203-234.

Charnovitz, S. (1995), "Improving Environmental and Trade Governance", *International Environmental Affairs*, vol. 7, no. 1, Winter, pp. 59-92.

Charnovitz, S. (2000), "World Trade and the Environment: A Review of the New WTO Report", *Georgetown International Environmental Law Review*, Winter, pp. 523-541.

Chayes, A. and Chayes, A. H. (1991), "Adjustment and Compliance Process in International Regulatory Regimes", in Mathews, J. T. (ed.), *Preserving the Global Environment: The Challenge of Shared Leadership*, W.W. Norton and Co, New York, pp. 280-308.

Chayes, A. and Chayes, A. H. (1995), *The New Sovereignty. Compliance with International Regulatory Agreements*, Harvard University Press, Cambridge, United Kingdom and Massachusetts.

Chayes, A., Chayes, A. H., and Mitchell, R. B. (1998), "Managing Compliance: A Comparative Perspective", in E. Brown Weiss and H. K. Jacobson (eds.), *Engaging Countries: Strengthening Compliance with International Environmental Accords*, MIT Press, Cambridge, Massachusetts, pp. 39-62.

Chevassus-au-Louis, N. (2000), "L'industrie aime bien, sans plus", *La Recherche*, vol. 333, pp. 92-95.

Chiappetta, V. (2000), "The Desirability of Agreeing to Disagree: The WTO, TRIPS, International IPR Exhaustion, and a Few Other Things", *Michigan Journal of International Law*, vol. 21, Spring, pp. 333-392.

Chichilnisky, G. (1997), *Towards an International Bank for Ecological Settlements (IBES)*, World Bank, UNDP, UNESCO.

Comité de fonds pour l'environnement (2001), *Procès verbal des conclusions communes sur les orientations stratégiques du PE2*, prepared by the Comité de négociations malagasy and the Groupe des bailleurs de fonds, Antananarivo. (www.ksurf.net/~smb-mad/new.htm).

Commission on Global Governance (1995), *Our Global Neighborhood: The Report of the Commission on Global Governance*, Oxford University Press, New York.

Commissioner of the Environment and Sustainable Development (1998), *Report of the Commissioner of the Environment and Sustainable Development (1998)*, chapter 1 (http://www.oag-bvg.gc.ca/domino/reports.nsf/html/c801me.html).

Commissioner of the Environment and Sustainable Development (1998), "Canada's Biodiversity Clock is Ticking", in *Report of the Commissioner of the Environment and Sustainable Development (1998)*, chapter 4 (http://www.oag-bvg.gc.ca/domino/reports.nsf/html/c8menu_e.html).

Commissioner of the Environment and Sustainable Development (1999), *Moving Up the Learning Curve. The Second Generation of Sustainable Development Strategies*, Office of the Auditor General of Canada (http://www.oag-bvg.gc.ca/domino/cesd_cedd.nsf/html/c9dec_e.html).

Commissioner of the Environment and Sustainable Development (2000), "Follow-up of Previous Audits: More Action Needed", in *Report of the Commissioner of the Environment and Sustainable Development, 2000*, chapter 9 (http://www.oag-bvg.gc.ca/domino/reports.nsf/html/c0menu_e.html).

Commons, J. R. (1934), *Institutional Economics. Its Place in Political Economy*, Macmillan, New York.

Convention on the Prior Informed Consent Procedure for Certain Hazardous Chemicals and Pesticides in International Trade (1998), Rotterdam, (http://www.fao.org/ag/agp/agpp/pesticid/pic/finact.htm).

Coomes, O. T. (1995), "A Century of Rain forest Use in Western Amazonia: Lessons for Extraction-based Conservation of Tropical Forest Resources", *Forest & Conservation History*, vol. 39, pp. 108-120.

Cooper, D. (1993), "The International Undertaking on Plant Genetic Resources", *Plant Genetic Resources*, vol. 2, no. 2, pp. 158-167.

Correa, C. M. (2000), *Intellectual Property Rights, the WTO and Developing Countries – theTRIPS Agreement and Policy Options*, Third World Network, Penang, Malaysia.

Cosbey, A. and Burgiel, S. (2000), "The Cartagena Protocol on Biosafety: An Analysis of Results", briefing note, International Institute for Sustainable Development, Winnipeg, Canada (ww.iisd.ca).

Cottier, T, (1998), "The Protection of Genetic Resources and Traditional Knowledge: towards more Specific Rights and Obligations in World Trade Law", *Journal of International Economic Law*, vol. 1, no. 4, pp. 555-584.

Cracraft, J. and Grifo, F. T. (eds.) (1999), *The Living Planet in Crisis: Biodiversity Science and Policy*, Columbia University Press, New York.

Cullet, P. (1999), "Revision of the TRIPS Agreement Concerning the Protection of Plant Varieties – Lessons from India", *Journal of World Intellectual Property*, vol. 2, no. 4, pp. 617-657.

Cullet, P. (2001a), "Property Rights over Biological Resources: India's Proposed Legislative Framework", *Journal of World Intellectual Property*, vol. 4, no. 2, pp. 211-231.

Cullet, P. (2001b), "Plant Variety Protection in Africa: toward Compliance with the TRIPS Agreement", *Biopolicy International Series*, vol. 23, African Centre for Technology Studies, Nairobi.

Dalle, S. P. and Potvin, C. (2001a), "Conservation of Useful Plants: An Evaluation of Local Priorities from Two Indigenous Communities in Eastern Panama", submitted to *Conservation Biology*.

Dalle, S. P. and Potvin, C. (2001b), "Conservation Status of Traditional Plant Resources on Indigenous Territories: A Quantitative Evaluation from Two Communities in Eastern Panama", submitted to *Conservation Biology*.

Dalle, S. P. et al. (2001), "Spatial Distribution and Habitats of Useful Plants. an Initial Assessment for Conservation on an Indigenous Territory, Darien (Panama)", in press *Biological Conservation*.

Davenport, D. S. and Bertrand, T. L. (2000), "Failure as Success: toward an Evaluation and Explanation of Ineffective International Environmental Agreements", International Studies Association Annual Meeting.

Davis, S. and Wali, A. (1994), "Indigenous Land Tenure and Tropical Forest Management in Latin America", *Ambio*, vol. 23, no. 8, pp. 485-490.

De Klemm, C. (1982), "Conservation of Species: The Need for a New Approach", *Environmental Policy and Law*, vol. 9, no. 4, pp. 118-128.

De Klemm, C. (1985), "Le Patrimoine naturel de l'humanité", colloque "L'Avenir du droit international de l'environnement" (1984), Martinus Nijhoff Publishers, Dodrecht, pp. 117-150.

De Klemm, C and Shine, C. (1993), *Biological Diversity Conservation and the Law: Legal Mechanisms for Conserving Species and Ecosystems*, IUCN, Bonn, Germany.

Deléage, J-P. (1992), *Histoire de l'écologie*, La Découverte, Paris.

De Montgolfier, J. and Natali, J. M. (1987), *Le Patrimoine du futur: des outils pour une gestion patrimoniale*, Economica, Paris.

Deschamps, H. (1972), *Histoire de Madagascar*, Berger-Levrault, Paris.

DeSombre, E. R. (2000), *Domestic Sources of International Environmental Policy: Industry, Environmentalists, and U.S. Power*, MIT Press, Cambridge, Massachusetts.

Deutz, A. M. (1997), *Institutionalized Review Processes of the Adequacy of Commitments in International Environmental Agreements*, unpublished doctoral dissertation, Tufts University.

Diamond, P. and Hausman, J. (1994), "Contingent Valuation: Is Some Number Better Than No Number?", *Journal of Economics Perspectives*, vol. 8, pp. 45-54.

Dobson, A. P. (1996), *Conservation and Biodiversity*, Scientific American Library, New York.

Douglas, M. (1971), "De la souillure: essai sur les notions de pollution et de tabou", translation of "Purity and Danger" by Anne Guérin (1967), François Maspéro, Bibliothèque d'Anthropologie, Paris.

Downes, D. (1995), "The Convention on Biological Diversity and the GATT", in R. Housman, D. Goldberg, B. Van Dyke, and Z. Durwood (eds.), *The Use of Trade Measures in Select Multilateral Environmental Agreements*, United Nations Environment Programme, pp. 197-251.

Downs, G. W., Rocke, D. M., and Barsoom, P. N. (1996), "Is the Good News about Compliance Good News about Co-operation?", *International Organization*, vol. 50, no. 3, pp. 379-406.

Drouin, J-M. (1991), *Réinventer la nature. L'Écologie et son histoire*, Desclée de Brouwer, Paris.

Dutfield, G. (2000), *Intellectual Property Rights, Trade and Biodiversity*, Earthscan and IUCN, London.

Dutfield, Graham (2001), "Biotechnology and Patents: What Can Developing Countries Do About Article 27.3 (b)?", *Bridges*, vol. 5, no. 9, November-December, pp. 17-18.

Dyoulgerov, M. F. (2000), "Global Legal Instruments on the Marine Environment at the Year 2000", in C. Sheppard (ed.), *Seas at the Millennium: An Environmental Evaluation*, Elsevier Science Ltd., New York, pp. 331-348.

Dyson, F. (1999), *The Sun, the Genome, the Internet*, Oxford University Press, Oxford.

Environnement Canada (1995), *Mesures législatives sur la protection de l'environnement conçues pour l'avenir – Une LCPE renouvelée*, ministre des Approvisionnements et Services Canada, Ottawa.

EPB (2000), *Projet écologie politique et biodiversité: requête de subside auprès du Fonds national suisse pour la recherche scientifique pour la phase de d'engagement*, Geneva.

Faden, R. R. and Beauchamp, T. L. (1986), *A History and Theory of Informed*

Consent, Oxford University Press, New York.

Falkner, R. (2000), "Regulating Biotech Trade: The Cartagena Protocol on Biosafety", *International Affairs*, vol. 76, no. 2, April, pp. 299-313.

Falloux, F. and Talbot, L. (1992), *Crise et opportunité*, Maisonneuve et Larose, Paris.

Faucheux, S. and Froger, G. (1993), "Le revenu national soutenable; indicateur de soutenabilité ou indicateur du coût de la soutenabilité", Cinquième colloque de comptabilité nationale, 12-14 December 1993, Paris.

Faucheux, S. and Noël, J. F. (1995), *Économie des ressources naturelles et de l'environnement*, Armand Colin Éditeur, Paris.

Faucheux, S. and O'Connor, M. (2000), "Technosphère et écosphère. Choix technologiques et menaces environnementales: signaux faibles, controverses et décisions", *Futuribles*, vol. 251, pp. 29-55.

Fearon, J. D. (1991), "Counterfactuals and Hypothesis-Testing in Political Science", *World Politics*, vol. 43, pp. 169-195.

Finnemore, M. (1996), *National Interests in International Society*, Cornell University Press, Ithaca.

Fisher, D. I. (1990), *Prior Consent to International Direct Satellite Broadcasting*, Martinus Nijhoff Publishers, Dordrecht.

Fisheries and Oceans Canada (1997a), *An Approach to the Establishment and Management of Marine Protected Areas Under the Oceans Act*, Discussion Paper, January 1997.

Fisheries and Oceans Canada (1997b), *Rôle du gouvernement fédéral dans le secteur des océans*, ministre des Travaux publics et Services gouvernementaux Canada, Ottawa.

Fisheries and Oceans Canada (1998), *Integrated Management of Activities in Canada's Coastal and Ocean Waters*, Backgrounder, December 1998.

Fisheries and Oceans Canada (1999), *National Framework for Establishing and Managing Marine Protected Areas*, Working Document, March 1999.

Fisheries and Oceans Canada, *Working Together for Marine Protected Areas. A National Approach.*

Fisheries and Oceans Canada, *Atlantic Fisheries Policy Review.*

Fontaubert, A. C., Downes, D. R., and Agardy, T. S. (1998), "Biodiversity in the Seas: Implementing the Convention on Biological Diversity in Marine and Coastal Habitats", *Georgetown International Environmental Law Review*, vol. 10, pp. 753-854.

Fowler, C. (1995), "Biotechnology, Patents and the Third World", in V. Shiva and I. Moser (eds.), *Biopolitics. A Feminist and Ecological Reader on Biotechnology*, Zed Books Ltd, London and New Jersey.

Frank, D. J. (1997), "Science, Nature, and the Globalization of the Environment, 1879-1990", *Social Forces*, vol. 76, pp. 409-437.

Frank, D. J. et al. (2000), "The Nation-State and the Natural Environment over the Twentieth Century", *American Sociological Review*, vol. 65, pp. 96-116.

Freeman, C. and Soete, L. (1997), *The Economics of Industrial Innovation*, MIT Press, Cambridge, Massachusetts.

Frei, B., Sticher O., and Heinrich, M. (2000), "Zapotec and Mixe Use of Tropical Habitats for Securing Medicinal Plants in Mexico", *Economic Botany*, vol. 54, no. 1, pp. 73-81.

Fuller, S. (2000), *Thomas Kuhn. A Philosophical History of our Times*, University of Chicago Press, Chicago.

Funtowicz, S. et al. (2000), "Science and Governance in the European Union: A Contribution to the Debate", *Science and Public Policy*, vol. 27, pp. 327-336.

Funtowicz, S. and Ravetz, J. R. (1994), "Emergent Complex Systems", *Futures*, vol. 26, pp. 568-582.

Gadgil, M., Berkes, F., and Folke, C. (1993), "Indigenous Knowledge for Biodiversity Conservation", *Ambio*, vol. 22, no. 2-3, pp. 151-156.

Gardner Brown Jr., Wes H. (1989), *The Economic Value of Elephants*, IIED/UCL, London Environmental Economics Centre, LEEC Paper 89-12.

Gaston, K. J. (2000), "Review Article: Global Patterns in Biodiversity", *Nature*, vol. 405, pp. 220-227.

GEF (1995), *Annual Report 1995*, GEF, Washington DC.

GEF (1996), *Quarterly Operational Report, March 1996*, GEF, Washington DC.

GEF (1996), *Quarterly Operational Report, June 1996*, GEF, Washington DC.

GEF (1996), *Quarterly Operational Report, October 1996*, GEF, Washington DC.

GEF (1997), *Quarterly Operational Report, March 1997*, GEF, Washington DC.

GEF (1997), *Quarterly Operational Report, June 1997*, GEF, Washington DC.

Gehring, T. (1990), "International Environmental Regimes: Dynamic Sectoral Legal Systems", *Yearbook of International Environmental Law*, vol. 1, pp. 35-56.

Gehring, T. (1994), *Dynamic International Regimes: Institutions for International Environmental Governance*, Peter Lang, Frankfurt and Main.

Georgescu-Roegen, N. (1979), *Demain la décroissance*, Favre, Paris.

Ghirime, K. B. (1991), *Parks and People: Livelihood issues in National Parks Management in Thailand and Madagascar*, Discussion Paper (29), UNRISD, Geneva.

Gibbons, M. et al. (1994), *The New Production of Knowledge*, Sage, London.

Giddens, A. (1984), *The Constitution of Society*, University of California Press, Berkley.

Gilruth, P. T., Marsh, S. E., and Itami, R. (1995), "A Dynamic Spatial Model of Shifting Cultivation in the Highlands of Guinea, West Africa", *Ecological Modelling*, vol. 79, pp. 179-197.

Giroux, L. (1991), "La protection juridique du fleuve St-Laurent", *Les Cahiers de Droit*, vol. 32, pp. 1027-1072.

Gislain, J-J. (1999), "Les conceptions évolutionnaires de T. Veblen et J. R. Commons", *Economies et sociétés*, vol. 35, no. 1, pp. 49-65.

Global Environmental Change Project of the United Kingdom (GECP-UK) (1999), *Who governs the global environment?*, (http://www.gecko.ac.uk).

Glowka, L., Burhenne-Guilmin, F., and Synge, H. in collaboration with McNeely, J. A., and Gündling, L. (1994), *A Guide to the Convention on Biological Diversity*, IUCN, Gland, Switzerland.

Godard, O. (1989), "Jeux de nature: quand le débat sur l'efficacité des politiques publiques contient la question de leur légitimité", in N. Mathieu and M. Jolivet (eds.), *Du rural à l'environnement. La question de la nature aujourd'hui*, L'Harmattan, Paris.

Godard, O. (1999), "De l'usage du principe de précaution en univers controversé", *Futuribles*, February-March, pp. 37-59.

Groombridge, B. (1992), *Global Biodiversity. Status of the Earth's Living Resources*, Chapman et al.

Guay, L. (1999), "Constructing a Response to Ecological Problems under Scientific Uncertainty: A Comparison of Acid Rain and Climate Change in Canada", *Energy and Environment*, vol. 10, pp. 597-616.

Guillaud, Y. (1998), "Gestion durable des ressources naturelles et partage des bénéfices liés à la bio-prospection: le cas Biodivalor", studies prepared for OECD Experts Group on the Economics of Biodiversity, (ENV/EPOC/GEEI/BIO(98)4), OECD, Paris.

Gupta, A. (2000a), "Creating a Global Biosafety Regime", *International Journal of Biotechnology*, vol. 2, no. 1, 2 and 3, pp. 205-230.

Gupta, A. (2000b), "Governing Trade in Genetically Modified Organisms – The Cartagena Protocol on Biosafety", *Environment*, May, pp. 22-34.

Hagen, R. (2000), *Évaluation des projets pilotes d'aménagement des forêts naturelles à Madagascar*, USAID Madagascar, Antananarivo.

Haas, E. (1990), *When Knowledge is Power: Three Models of Change in International Organizations*, University of California Press, Berkeley.

Haas, P. M. (1990), *Saving the Mediterranean. The Politics of International Environmental Co-operation*, Columbia University Press, New York.

Haas, P. M. (1992), "Introduction: Epistemic Communities and International Policy Co-ordination", *International Organization*, vol. 46, pp. 1-35.

Haas, P. M. (1998), "Compliance with EU Directives: Insights from International Relations and Comparative Politics", *Journal of European Public Policy*, vol. 5, no. 1, pp. 17-37.

Haas, E. and Haas, P. M. (1995), "Learning to Learn: Improving International Governance", *Global Governance*, vol. 1, no. 3.

Haas, P. M., Keohane, R. O., and Levy, M. A. (1993), *Institutions for the Earth: Sources of Effective International Environmental Protection*, MIT Press, Cambridge MA.

Haeuber, R. (1996), "Setting the Environmental Policy Agenda: The Case of Ecosystem Management", *Natural Resources Journal*, vol. 36, pp. 1-28.

Haggard, S. and Simmons, B. A. (1987), "Theories of International Regimes", *International Organization*, vol. 41, pp. 491-517.

Hall, M. A. (1997), "A Theory of Economic Informed Consent", *Georgia Law Review*, vol. 31, pp. 511-586.

Halley, P. (1998), "Les ententes portant immunité de poursuite et substitution de norme en droit de l'environnement québécois", *Cahiers de droit*, vol. 39, pp. 3-50.

Halweil, P. (2000), "Where Have All the Farmers Gone?" *World Watch*, vol. 13, no. 5, pp. 12-30.

Hampicke, U. (1999), "The Limits to Economic Valuation of Biodiversity", *International Journal of Social Economics*, vol. 26, no. 1, 2 and 3, pp. 158-173.

Hannigan, J. A. (1995), *Environmental Sociology: A Social Constructionist Perspective*, Routledge, London.

Hardin, G. (1968), "The tragedy of the Commons", *Science*, vol. 162, pp. 1243-1248.

Hasenclever, A., Mayer, P., and Rittberger, V. (1997), *Theories of International Regimes*, Cambridge University Press, Cambridge.

Hawksworth, D. L. (1997), "The Response of the International Scientific Community to the Challenge of Biodiversity", in P. H. Raven and T. Williams (eds.), *Nature and Human Society*, National Academy Press, Washington DC, pp. 347-357.

Hays, S. P. (1959), *Conservation and the Gospel of Efficiency*, Atheneum, New York.

Hays, S. P. (1987), *Beauty, Health and Permanence: Environmental Politics in the United States: 1955-1985*, Cambridge University Press, Cambridge.

Hempel, L. C. (1996), *Environmental Governance*, Island Press, Washington DC.

Herzog, D. (1989), *Happy Slaves: A Critique of Consent*, University of Chicago Press, Chicago.

Heywood, V. H. (ed.) (1995), *Global Biodiversity Assessment*, Cambridge University Press, Cambridge.

Hoberg, G. (1997), "Governing the Environment: Comparing Canada and the United States", in K. Banting, G. Hoberg, and R. Simon (eds.), *Degrees of Freedom: Canada and the United States in a Changing World*, McGill-Queen's University Press, Montreal, pp. 341-388.

Hobbelink, H. (1995), "Biotechnology and the Future of Agriculture", in V. Shiva and I. Moser (eds.), *Biopolitics. A Feminist and Ecological Reader on Biotechnology*, Zed Books Ltd., London and New Jersey.

Homer-Dixon, T. (1996), "Strategies for Studying Causation in Complex Ecological-Political Systems", *Journal of Environment and Development*, vol. 5, no. 2, pp. 132-148.

Houghton, J. T. et al. (eds.) (1995), *Climate Change 1995. The Science of Climate Change*, Cambridge University Press, Cambridge.

Houck, O. A. (1997), "On the Law of Biodiversity and Ecosystem Management", *Minnesota Law Review*, vol. 81, pp. 869-979.

Howlett, M. (2001), "Complex Network Management and the Governance of the Environment: Prospects for Policy Change and Policy Stability", in E. A. Parson (ed.), *Governing the Environment: Persistent Challenges, Uncertain Innovations*, McGill-Queen's University Press, Montreal and Kingston, pp. 303-344.

Hufty, M. (2000), "Normes, transactions et action collective dans la gestion environnementale. Contribution à une méthodologie interdisciplinaire et réaliste", colloque "Observer, décrire, interpréter", en l'honneur de Raymond Quivy, FUCAM, Mons, 30-31 October 2000.

Hufty, M. (2001), "La gouvernance internationale de la biodiversité", *Etudes internationales*, vol. 32, no. 1, pp. 5-29.

Hufty, M., Chollet, M., and Razakamanantsoa, A. (1995), "Biodiversité et Plan d'action environnemental à Madagascar: conservationnisme ou néo-colonialisme vert?", in F. Sabelli (ed.), *Ecologie contre nature: développement et politiques d'ingérence*, Nouveaux Cahiers de l'IUED, IUED/PUF, pp. 143-148.

Hufty, M., Chollet, M., and Razakamanantsoa, A. (1997), *Le programme d'action environnemental à Madagascar: conservation et néo-colonialisme*, Série Documents de travail EPB, vol. 1, December.

Hughes, J., Daily, G. C., and Ehrlich, P.R. (1997), "The Loss of Population Diversity and Why It Matters", in P. H. Raven and T. Williams (eds.), *Nature and Human Society*, National Academy Press, Washington DC, pp. 71-83.

Huntington, H. P. (2000), "Using Traditional Ecological Knowledge in Science: Methods and Applications", *Ecological Applications*, vol. 10, pp. 1270-1274.

Huot, M. (1993), *Liste des espèces de la faune vertébrée susceptible d'être désignées menacées ou vulnérables*, Bibliothèque nationale du Québec.

Hurlbut, D. (1994), "Fixing the Biodiversity Convention: toward a Special Protocol for Related Intellectual Property", *Natural Resources Journal*, vol. 34, no. 2, pp. 379-409.

Intercoopération/CI/DGEF (2001), *Les premiers pas de la gestion contractualisée des forêts à Madagascar*, workshop report, Mantasoa, 28-30 November 2000, Antananarivo.

Issalys, P. (2001), *Répartir les normes – Le choix entre les formes d'action étatique*, Société de l'assurance automobile du Québec, Quebec.

IUCN (1996), "Guide to the Convention on Biological Diversity", *Environmental Policy and Law Paper*, (030).

IUCN, UNEP, and WWF (1991), *Caring for the Earth*, Gland.

Jacob, J-P. (2000), "Connaissance et développement en Afrique" in J-P. Jacob (ed.), *Sciences sociales et coopération en Afrique: les rendez-vous manqués*, Nouveaux Cahiers de l'IUED, IUED/PUF, Paris and Geneva, vol. 10, pp. 11-30.

Jacob, J-P. and Charmillot, M. (2000), "Approches de la connaissance et de l'ignorance selon quelques ouvrages consacrés au développement", in J.-P. Jacob (ed.), *Sciences sociales et coopération en Afrique: les rendez-vous manqués*, Nouveaux Cahiers de l'IUED, IUED/PUF, Paris and Geneva, vol. 10, pp. 225-244.

Jacobson, H. K., and Weiss, E. B. (1998), "Assessing the Record and Designing Strategies to Engage Countries", in E. Brown Weiss and H. K. Jacobson (eds.), *Engaging Countries: Strengthening Compliance with International Environmental Accords*, MIT Press, Cambridge Massachusetts, pp. 511-554.

Jasanoff, S. (1990), *The Fifth Branch: Science Advisers as Policy-Makers*, Harvard University Press, Cambridge, Massachusetts.

Johnson, N. (1995), *Biodiversity in the Balance: Approaches to Setting Geographic Conservation Priorities*, Biodiversity Support Program, Washington DC.

Johnston, S. (1995), "Sustainability, Biodiversity and International Law" in C. Redgwell and M. Bowman (eds.), *International Law and the Conservation of Biological Diversity*, Kluwer Law International, London, pp. 51-69.

Johnston, S. (1997), "The Convention on Biological Diversity: The next phase", *RECIEL*, vol. 6, no. 3, pp. 219-230.

Jolly, A. (1980), *A World Like our Own*, Yale University Press, New Haven.

Joyal, E. (1996), "The Palm Has its Time: An Ethnoecology of *Sabal uresana* in Sonora, Mexico", *Economic Botany*, vol. 50, no. 4, pp. 446-462.

Judas, L. (1999), "Considering in Developing a Functional Approach to the Governance of Large Marine Ecosystems", *Ocean Development and International Law*, vol. 30, no. 2, pp. 89-125.

Juillet, L. (1998), "Les politiques environnementales canadiennes", in M. Tremblay (ed.), *Les politiques publiques canadiennes*, Presses de l'Université Laval, Sainte-Foy, pp. 161-204.

Juma, C. (1999), "Intellectual Property Rights and Globalization: Implications for Developing Countries", *Center for International Development*, Discussion Paper No. 4, Harvard University, Boston.

Juma, C, (forthcoming), "International Trade and Environment – Toward Integrative Responsibility", in *Global Connections: Globalism, Environments and Environmentalism*, Oxford University Press, Oxford.

Juma, C. and Henne, G. (1997), "Science and Technology in the Convention on Biological Diversity", in P. H. Raven and T. Williams (eds.), *Nature and Human Society*, National Academy Press, Washington DC, pp. 387-397.

Juneau, P. (1992), "Le Canada et la protection de l'environnement marin en droit international", *Revue Juridique Thémis*, vol. 26, pp. 43-85.

Karr, J. R. (1991), "Biological Integrity: A Long-neglected Aspect of Water Resource Management", *Ecological Application*, vol. 1, pp. 66-84.

Karsenty, A. (1999), "Vers la fin de l'Etat forestier? Appropriation des espaces et partage de la rente forestière au Cameroun", *Politique africaine*, vol. 75, October, pp. 147-161.

Keiter, R. B. (1994), "Beyond the Boundary Line: Constructing a Law of Ecosystem Management", *University of Colorado Law Review*, vol. 65, pp. 293-333.

Kellow, A. (1999), *International Toxic Risk Management: Ideals, Interests and Implementation*, Cambridge University Press, Cambridge.

Keohane, R. O. (1984), *After Hegemony: Co-operation and Discord in the World Political Economy*, Princeton University Press, Princeton.

Keohane, R. O. (1989), "Neoliberal Institutionalism: A Perspective on World Politics", in R. O. Keohane (ed.), *International Institutions and State Power: Essays in International Relations Theory*, Westview Press, Boulder.

Keohane, R. O. (1993), "The Analysis of International Regimes: towards a European-American Research Programme", in V. Rittberger (ed.), *Regime Theory and International Relations*, Clarendon Press, Oxford, pp. 23-48.

Keohane, R. O. (1996), "Analyzing the Effectiveness of International Environmental Institutions", in R. O. Keohane and M. A. Levy (eds.), *Institutions for Environmental Aid: Pitfalls and Promises*, MIT Press, Cambridge Massachusetts, pp. 3-27.

Keohane, R. O., Haas, P. M., and Levy, M. A. (1993), "The Effectiveness of International Environmental Institutions", in P. M. Haas, R. O. Keohane, and M. A. Levy (eds.), *Institutions for the Earth. Sources of Effective International Environmental Protection*, MIT Press, Cambridge Massachusetts, pp. 3-24.

Keohane, R. O. and Levy, M. A. (1996), *Institutions for Environmental Aid: Pitfalls and Promise*, MIT Press, Cambridge Massachusetts.

Kerr, J. T., Sugarand, A., and Packer, L. (2000), "Indicator Taxa, Rapid Biodiversity Assessment, and Nestedness in an Endangered Ecosystem", *Conservation Biology*, vol. 14, pp. 1726-1734.

Kimball, L. A. (1997), "Institutional Linkages Between the Convention on Biological Diversity and other International Conventions", *RECIEL*, vol. 6, no. 3, pp. 239-248.

Kimmel, A. J. (1988), *Ethics and Values in Applied Social Research*, Sage, Newbury Park.

Kiss, A. C. (1976), *Survey of Current Developments in International Environmental Law*, IUCN, Gland.

Kiss, A. C. (1993), "Les traités-cadres: une technique juridique caractéristique du droit international de l'environnement", *Annuaire français de droit international*, vol. 39.

Knill, C. and Lenschow, A. (2000), "New Concepts – Old Problems? The Institutional Constraints for the Effective Implementation of EU Environmental Policy", International Studies Association Annual Meeting.

Knudsen, A. J. (1995), "Reinventing the Commons: New Metaphor or New Methodology?", paper presented at the 5th Annual Common Property Conference of the International Association for the Study of Common Property, 24-28 May 1995, Bodoe.

Koester, V. (1997), "The Biodiversity Convention Negotiation Process – and some Comments on the Outcome", *Environmental Policy and Law*, pp. 175-192 (also in E. M. Basse (ed.), *Environmental Law: From International to National Law*, Gad Jura, Copenhagen, pp. 205-258).

Kokotsis, E. and Kirton, J. (1997), "National Compliance with Environmental Regimes: The Case of the G7, 1988-1995", International Studies Association Annual Meeting.

Kothari, A. and Anuradha, R. V. (1999), "Biodiversity and Intellectual Property Rights: Can the Two Co-Exist?", *Journal of International Wildlife Law and Policy*, vol. 2, no. 2, pp. 337-359.

Krasner, S. D. (1982), "Structural Causes and Regimes Consequences: Regimes as Intervening Variables", *International Organization*, vol. 36, no. 2, pp. 185-205.

Krasner, S. D. (1983), *International Regimes*, Cornell University Press, Ithaca.

Krattiger, A. F. et al. (1994), *Widening Perspectives on Biodiversity, World Conservation Union and International Academy of the Environment*, Cambridge and Gland.

Kratochwil, F. and Ruggie J. G. (1986), "International Organizations: A State of the Art or an Art of the State", *International Organization*, vol. 40, no. 4, pp. 753-775.

Krause, J. H. (1999), "Reconceptualizing Informed Consent in an Era of Health Care Cost Containment", *Iowa Law Review*, vol. 85, no. 1, pp. 261-386.

Kremen, C., Colwell, R. K., Erwin, T. L., Murphy, D. D., Noss, R. F., and Sanjayan, M. A. (1993), "Terrestrial Arthropod Assemblages: Their Use in Conservation Planning", *Conservation Biology*, vol. 7, pp. 796-808.

Krimsky, S. and Golding, D. (eds.) (1992), *Social Theories of Risk*, Praeger, Westport.

Krueger, J. (2000), *Information in International Environmental Governance: The Prior Informed Consent Procedure for Trade in Hazardous Chemicals and Pesticides*, Belfer Center for Science and International Affairs, Harvard University, Boston.

Kuhn, T. (1970), *The Structure of Scientific Revolutions*, University of Chicago Press, Chicago.

Kütting, G. (2000), *Environment, Society and International Relations: Towards More Effective International Environmental Agreements*, Routledge, New York and London.

Laird, S. A., and E. Lisinge (1998), "Benefit-Sharing Case-Studies: Ancistrocladus korupensis and Prunus africana", submitted by the United Nations Environment Programme for the fourth meeting of the COP of the CBD (UNEP/CBD/COP/4/Inf.25).

Lang, W. (1992), "Diplomacy and Environmental Law Making: Some Observations", *Yearbook of International Environmental Law*, vol. 3, pp. 108-162.

Lang, W. (1993), "International Environmental Co-operation", in G. Sjöstedt and U. Svedin (eds.), *International Environmental Negotiations: Process, Issues and Contexts*, Swedish Institute of International Affairs, Stockholm, pp. 15-21.

Larson, B. (1994), "Changing the Economics of Environmental Degradation in Madagascar: Lessons from the National Action Plan Process", *World Development*, vol. 22, no. 5, pp. 671-689.

Larson, P. and Seslar Srendsen, D. (1996), *Participatory Monitoring and Evaluation: A Practical Guide to Successful ICDPs*, World Wildlife Fund, Washington DC.

Lebow, R. N. (2000), "What's So Different about a Counterfactual?", *World Politics*, vol. 52, no. 4.

Legendre, P. and Legendre, L. (1998), *Numerical Ecology*, Elsevier, Amsterdam.

Le Prestre, P. G. (1997), *Ecopolitique internationale*, Guérin Universitaire, Montreal.

Le Prestre, P. G. (1999), "Vers un nouvel ordre biologique international?", *Natures , Sciences, Sociétés*, vol. 7, no. 1, pp. 64-71.

Le Prestre, P. G., Reid, J. R., and Morehouse, E. T. (eds.) (1998), *Protecting the Ozone Layer: Lessons, Models and Prospects*, Kluwer, Boston.

Le Roy, E. (1993), "Les recherches sur le droit interne des pays en développement. Du droit du développement à la définition pluraliste de l'État de droit" in C. Choquet, O. Dollfuss, E. Le Roy, and M. Vernières (eds.), *État des savoirs sur le développement, trois décennies de sciences sociales en langue française*, Karthala, Paris, pp. 75-86.

Lescuyer, G. (2000), *Évaluation économique et gestion viable de la forêt tropicale: Réflexion sur un mode de coordination des usages d'une forêt de l'est-Cameroun*, Ph.D. thesis, École des Hautes études en Sciences Sociales, Paris.

Leskien, D. and Flitner, M. (1998), "The TRIPS Agreement and Intellectual Property Rights for Plant Varieties", in *Signposts to* sui generis *Rights*, Grain, Barcelona.

Lévêque, C. (1997), *La biodiversité*, Que-Sais-Je?, PUF, Paris.

Lévêque, C. (1998), "La biodiversité: un avis d'écologue", *Natures, Sciences, Sociétés*, vol. 6, pp. 37-40.

Levy, M. A., Young, O. R., and Zürn, M. (1995), "The Study of International Regimes", *European Journal of International Relations*, vol. 1, no. 3, pp. 267-330.

Limoges, C. et al. (1993), "Les risques associés au largage dans l'environnement d'organismes génétiquement modifiés: analyse d'une controverse", *Cahiers de recherche sociologique*, vol. 21, pp. 17-51.

Lin, L. L. (2000), "Biosafety Talks End on Mixed Note", *Third World Resurgence*, vol. 114-115, February-March, pp. 6-11(www.twnside.org.sg/title/note/htm).

Ling, C. Y. (2000), "The Vienna Setting: Towards more Transparent and Democratic Global Negotiations", *Third World Resurgence*, vol. 114-115, February-March, pp. 27-30 (http://www.twnside.org.sg/bio_1.htm).

Litfin, K. (1994), *Ozone Discourses. Science and Politics in Global Environment Co-operation*, Columbia University Press, New York.

Louafi, S. (2001), "Négociation sur la biodiversité et procéduralisation contextuelle", communication à l'atelier de recherche "Biodiversité, de l'action collective à la gouvernance", 5-7 March 2001, IUED, Geneva.

Loureiro, W. (1996), *Ecological Incentive toward Biodiversity Conservation, a Successful Experience in Brazil. WWF*, paper presented at the Global Biodiversity Forum, September 1996, Montreal.

Lyster, S.(1985), *International Wildlife Law: An Analysis of International Treaties Concerned with the Conservation of Wildlife*, Grotius Pubns, Cambridge.

MacNeill, J., Winsemius, P., and Yakushiji, T. (1991), *Beyond Interdependence - The Meshing of the World's Economy and the Earth's Ecology*, Oxford University Press, Oxford, (32).

MacPhee, R. D. E. (1999), *Extinctions in Near Time: Causes, Contexts, and Consequences*, Plenum Press, New York.

MacPhee, R. D. E. and Flemming, C. (1999), "*Requiem Aeternam*: The Last Five Hundred Years of Mammalian Species Extinctions", in J. Cracraft and F. T. Grifo (eds.), *The Living Planet in Crisis: Biodiversity Science and Policy*, Columbia University Press, New York, pp. 73-124.

Maldidier, C. (2000), *La décentralisation de la gestion des ressources renouvelables à Madagascar: les premiers enseignements sur les processus en cours et les méthodes d'intervention*, Antananarivo (www.ksurf.net/~smb-mad/new.htm).

Maljean-Dubois, S. (2000), "Biodiversité, biotechnologies, biosécurité: le droit international désarticulé", *Journal du droit international*, vol. 127, no. 4, October.-November, pp. 949-997.

Marcussen, H. S. (2000), "Burkina Faso: systèmes de (mé)connaissance et politiques environnementales", *Sciences sociales et coopération en Afrique*, pp. 147-165.

Marshall, L. P. (2000), "Canada's Implementation of the Convention on International Trade in Endangered Species of Wild Fauna and Flora (CITES): The Effect of the Biodiversity Focus of International Environmental Law", *Journal of Environmental Law and Practice*, vol. 9, pp. 31-54.

Martin, C, (2001), "The Relationship Between Trade and Environment Regimes: What Needs to Change?", in G. Sampson (ed.) (2000), op. cit., pp. 137-155.

Martin, R. B. (2000), "Biological Diversity. Divergent Views on Its Status and Diverging Approaches to Its Conservation", in R. Bailey (ed.), *Earth Report 2000*, McGraw-Hill, New York, pp. 208-236.

Mayr, E. (1982), *The Growth of Biological Thought. Diversity, Evolution, and Inheritance*, Harvard University Press, Cambridge, Massachusetts.

McConnell, F. (1996), *The Biodiversity Convention. A Negotiating History*, Kluwer Law International, London.

McCormick, J. (1989), *The Global Environmental Movement*, Belhaven, London.

McGraw, D. (2000), "Multilateral Environmental Treaty-Making", in Boutin et al. (eds.), *Innovations in Global Governance – ACUNS Policy Brief*, Academic Council of the United Nations System and American Society of International Law, p.7 (http://www.yale.edu/acuns/publications/Policy_Brief/index.html).

McGraw, D. (2001), *Options for Improving Co-ordination and Coherence among Multilateral Environmental Agreements*, International Policy and Co-operation Branch, Environment Canada.

McGraw, D. (2002), "Negotiating the Biodiversity Convention: A Case Study in International Regime Formation", unpublished thesis submitted in partial fulfillment of the requirements for the Ph.D. degree in the Faculty of Economics of the University of London (London School of Economics and Political Science).

McNeill, J. R. (2000), *Something New Under the Sun. An Environmental History of the Twentieth-Century World*, Norton, New York.

Michael, M. A. (1995), "International Justice and Wilderness Preservation", *Social Theory and Practice*, vol. 21, no. 2, pp. 149-176.

Miles, E. L. (1999), "The Concept of Ocean Governance: Evolution Toward the 21st Century and the Principle of Sustainable Ocean Use", *Coastal Management*, vol. 27, pp. 1-30.

Miller, C. A. (2000), "The Dynamics of Framing Environmental Values and Policy: Four Models of Societal Process", *Environmental Values*, vol. 9, pp. 211-233.

Miller, K., Allegretti, M. H., Johnson, N. and Jonnon, B. (1995), "Measures for Conservation of Biodiversity and Sustainable Use of its Components", in V. H. Heywood and R. T. Watson (eds.), *Global Biodiversity Assessment*, Cambridge University Press, Cambridge. pp. 915-1063.

Miller, M. A. L. (1995), *The Third World in Global Environmental Politics*, Lynne Rienner Publishers, Boulder.

Miller, M. D. (1997), "The Informed-Consent Policy of the International Conference on Harmonization of Technical Requirements for Registration of Pharmaceuticals for Human Use: Knowledge is the Best Medicine", *Cornell International Law Journal*, vol. 30, pp. 203-44.

Milon, J. W. (1995), "Implications of Alternative Concepts of Sustainability for Total Valuation of Environmental Resources", *Economie appliquée*, tome XLVIII, vol. 2, pp. 59-73.

Ministère de l'Aménagement du territoire et de la Ville, (1999), *Compte-rendu de l'Atelier sur le Foncier à Madagascar du 8 et 9 avril 1999, Ambohimanambola*, DGDSF, Antananarivo.

Mishra, J. P. (2001), "Intellectual Property Rights and Food Security", *Journal of World Intellectual Property*, vol. 4, no. 1, pp. 5-26.

Mitchell, R. B. (1994a), *Intentional Oil Pollution at Sea: Environmental Policy and Treaty Compliance*, MIT Press, Cambridge, Massachusetts.

Mitchell, R. B. (1994b), "Compliance Theory: A Synthesis." *RECIEL*, vol. 2, no. 4, pp. 327-334.

Mitchell, R. B. (1998), "Sources of Transparency: Information Systems in International Regimes", *International Studies Quarterly*, vol. 42, pp. 109-130.

Mitchell, R. B. (2000), "Transparency's Three Paths of Influence", International Studies Association.

Mitchell, R. C. and Carson, R. T. (1989), *Using Survey to Value Public Goods: The Contingent Valuation Method*, Resources for the Future, Washington DC.

Mittermeier, R. and Werner, T. (1990), "Wealth of Plants and Animal Unites Megadiversity Countries", *Tropicus*, vol. 4, pp. 4-5.

Monagle, C. (2001), "Biodiversity and Intellectual Property Rights", joint discussion paper WWF International, and Center for International Environmental Law, Gland and Geneva.

Mooney, H. A. (1999), "On the Road to Global Ecology", *Annual Review of Energy and Environment*, vol. 24, pp. 1-31.

Moran, K. (1998), "Mechanisms for Benefit-Sharing: Nigerian Case-Study for the Convention on Biological Diversity", study submitted to the Secretariat of the CBD by Healing Forest Conservancy, Washington DC.

Moravcsik, A. (1997), "Taking Preferences Seriously: A Liberal Theory of International Politics", *International Organization*, vol. 51, no. 4, pp. 513-553.

Muller, F. G. (2000), "Does the Convention on Biodiversity Safeguard Biological Diversity?", *Environmental Values*, vol. 9, pp. 55-80.

Muttenzer, F. (2001), "La mise en œuvre de l'aménagement forestier négocié, ou l'introuvable gouvernance de la biodiversité à Madagascar", communication à l'atelier de recherche "Biodiversité, de l'action collective à la gouvernance", 5-7 March 2001, IUED, Geneva.

Myers, N. (1988), "Threatened Biotas: 'Hot Spots' in Tropical Forests", *The Environmentalist*, vol. 8, pp.187-208.

Myers, O. (1992), "The Management of Transboundary Stocks: Atlantic Salmon and Northern Shrimp", in V. Zwaag (ed.), *Canadian Ocean Law and Policy*, Butterworths, Toronto, pp. 91-114.

National Intelligence Council (United States) (2000), "Global Trends 2015: A Dialogue About the Future With Nongovernment Experts", *NIC*, vol. 2, December.

Naudet, J-D. (1999), *Trouver des problèmes aux solutions. Vingt ans d'aide au Sahel*, Club du Sahel/OECD, Paris.

Nelson, D. and Stern, M. (1997), "Endowing the Environment: Multilateral Development Banks and Environmental Lending in Latin America", in G. J. MacDonald, D. Nelson and M. A. Stern (eds.) (1997), *Latin American Environmental Policy in International Perspective*, Westview Press, Boulder, pp. 130-155.

Nicoll, M. E. and Langrand, O. (1989), *Madagascar: Revue de la conservation et des aires protégées*, WWF International, Gland.

Nolan-Haley, J. M. (1999), "Informed Consent in Mediation: A Guiding Principle for Truly Educated Decision-Making", *Notre Dame Law Review*, vol. 74, pp. 775-840.

Norton, B. G. (1995), "Evaluating Ecosystem States: Two Competing Paradigms", *Ecological Economics*, vol. 14, no. 2, pp. 113-127.

Norton, B. G. (2001), "Conservation Biology and Environmental Values: Can there Be an Universal Earth Ethic?", in C. Potvin, M. Kraenzel and G. Seutin (eds.) (2001), *Protecting Biological Diversity: Roles and Responsibilities*, McGill-Queen's University Press, Montreal, pp. 71-102.

Nordström, H. and Vaughn, S. (1999), "Trade and Environment", *WTO Special study 4*, WTO, Geneva.

Noss, R. F. (1990), "Indicators for Monitoring Biodiversity: A Hierarchical Approach", *Conservation Biology*, vol. 4, pp. 355-364.

Nowotny, H., Scott, P. and Gibbons, M. (2001), *Rethinking Science: Knowledge and the Public in an Age of Uncertainty*, Polity Press, Oxford.

Obser, A. (1999), "Institutional Choice in International Secretariats: Nested Governance Arrangements in the Administration of Global Change", International Studies Association.

Office national de l'environnement (1995), *Résultat du Colloque national sur la gestion locale communautaire des ressources renouvelables, Antsirabe, 8-12 Mai*, OSIPD.

Okowa, P. N. (1997), "Procedural Obligations in International Environmental Agreements", in *British Yearbook of International Environmental Law 1996*, Clarendon Press, Oxford, pp. 275-336.

Okun, A. M. (1975), *Equality and Efficiency: The Big Tradeoff*, Brookings Institution, Washington DC.

Oliver, I. and Beattie, A. J. (1993), "A Possible Method for Rapid Assessment of Biodiversity", *Conservation Biology*, vol. 7, pp. 562-568.

Ollagnon, H. (1989), "Une approche patrimoniale de la qualité du milieu naturel", in N. Mathieu and M. Jollivet (eds.), *Du rural à l'environnement. La question de la nature aujourd'hui*, L'Harmattan, Paris.

Organisation de coopération et de développement économique (OCDE) (1999), *Aspects économiques du partage des avantages: concepts et expériences pratiques, Groupe de travail sur l'intégration des politiques économiques et de l'environnement – Sous-groupe sur les aspects économiques de la biodiversité*.

OECD (1993), *Coastal Zone Management Integrated Policies*, OECD, Paris.

OECD (1996), *Préserver la diversité biologique, les incitations économiques*, OECD, Paris.

Ortiz Quinjano, R. (1996), *Latin American Biodiversity Forum: Summary Report*, Fundación Pro-Sierra Nevada de Santa Marta, Columbia.

Ostrom, E. (1990), *Governing the Commons. The Evolution of Institutions for Collective Action*, Cambridge University Press, Cambridge.

Ostrom, E. (1998), "Self-Governance and Forest Resources", presentation for the International CBNRM Workshop, Washington DC, 10-14 May.

Ovejero, J. (1999), "The Contribution of Biodiversity-Related Multilateral Environmental Agreements to Sustainable Development: A Discussion of some the Issues", prepared for Inter-Linkages – International Conference on Synergies and Co-ordination Between Multilateral Environmental Agreements, United Nations University, 14, 15 and 16 July, Tokyo.

Paarlberg, R. L. (1994), "Managing Pesticides Use in Developing Countries", in P. M. Haas, R. O. Keohane and M. A. Levy (eds.), *Institutions for the Earth*, MIT, Cambridge, Massachusetts, pp.309-350.

Pallemaerts, M. (1988), "Development in International Pesticide Regulation", *Environmental Policy and Law*, vol. 18, no. 3, pp. 62-68.

Pallemaerts, M. (1995), "Conférence de Rio: grandeur et décadence du droit international de l'environnement", *Revue belge de droit international*, vol. 28, no. 1, pp. 175-223.

Panjabi, R. K. L. (1997), *The Earth Summit at Rio. Politics, Economics, and the Environment*, Northeastern University Press, Boston.

Paoletto, G. (1999), "Capacity Building Systems for Inter-Linkages", prepared for Inter-Linkages – International Conference on Synergies and Co-ordination Between Multilateral Environmental Agreements, United Nations University, 14, 15 and 16 July, Tokyo.

Parizeau, M-H. (1997), *La Biodiversité: tout conserver ou tout exploiter?*, DeBoeck, Bruxelles.

Parks Canada, Department of Canadian Heritage (1994), *Guiding Principles and Operational Policies*, Minister of Supply and Services Canada, Ottawa.

Parks Canada, Department of Canadian Heritage (1995), *Sea to Sea to Sea: Canada's National Marine Conservation Areas System Plan*, Ministry of Supply and Services Canada, Ottawa.

Parsons, T. (1951), *The Social System*, Free Press, New York.

Pateman, C. (1970), *Participation and Democratic Theory*, Cambridge University Press, Cambridge.

Patenaude, G. (2000), *Perspective d'une communauté indigène panaméenne sur les priorités de conservation faunique: Quelles complémentarités avec les priorités exprimées par la CITES et l'IUCN?* Mémoire de maîtrise en sciences de l'environnement, Université du Québec à Montréal.

Pearce, D. (1996), "Economic Valuation and Ecological Economics", plenary address to the European Ecological Economics Inaugural International Conference, Université de Versailles, 23-25 May 1996.

Pearce, D., Markandya, A. and Barbier, E. D. (1989), *Blueprint for a green economy*, Earthscan, London.

Pearce, D. and Turner, R. K. (1990), *Economics of Natural Resources and the Environment*, Johns Hopkins University Press, Baltimore.

Pearce, D. W. and Warford, J. J. (1993), *World Without End: Economics, Environment, and Sustainable Development*, Oxford University Press, New York.

Perrez, F. X. (2000), "The Cartagena Protocol on Biosafety and the Relationship Between the Multilateral Trading System and MEAs", in L. Boisson de Chazournes and U. P. Thomas (eds.), "The Biosafety Protocol: Regulatory Innovation and Emerging Trends", *Swiss Review of International and European Law*, vol. 10, no. 4, pp. 518-528.

Perrings, C., Folke C. and Mäler, K. G. (1992), "The Ecology and Economics of Biodiversity Loss: The Research Agenda", *Ambio*, vol. 21, no. 3, pp. 201-211.

Peters, J. (1998), "Transforming the Integrated Conservation and Development Projects (ICDP) Approach: Observations from the Ranomafana National Park Project, Madagascar", *Journal of Agricultural and Environmental Ethics*, vol. 11, no. 1, pp. 17-48.

Peterson, M. J. (1998), "Organising for Effective Environmental Co-operation", *Global Governance*, vol. 4, no. 4, pp. 415-38.

Phillips, P. W. B. and Kerr, W. A. (2000), "Alternative Paradigms: The WTO Versus the Biosafety Protocol", *Journal of World Trade*, vol. 34, no. 4, pp. 63-76.

Polfor-Miray (1998), *Aménagement et gestion participative des forêts*, report of Antananarivo Workshop Intercoopération et conservation internationales, 14, 15 and 16 October 1998, Antananarivo.

Posey, D. (1997), *Traditional Resource Rights: International Instruments for Protection and Compensation for Indigenous Peoples and Local Communities*, IUCN, Gland.

Posey, D. A. and Balée, W. (eds.) (1989), *Resource Management in Amazonia: Indigenous and Folk Strategies*, New York Botanical Garden, The Bronx.

Potvin, C. (1997), "La biodiversité pour le biologiste: 'protéger' ou 'conserver' la nature?", in M-H. Parizeau (ed.), *La biodiversité. Tout préserver ou tout cultiver?*, DeBoeck, Bruxelles, pp. 37-46.

Priest, M. (1998), "The Privatization of Regulation: Five Models of Self-Regulation", *Revue de droit Ottawa*, vol. 29, pp. 233-302.

Puchala, D. J. and Hopkins, R. F. (1983), "International Regimes: Lessons from Inductive Analysis", in S. D. Krasner (ed.), *International Regimes*, Cornell University Press, Ithaca, pp. 61-91.

Purdue, D. A. (2000), *Anti-GenetiX: The Emergence of the Anti-GM Movement*, Ashgate, Aldershot.

Purvis, A. and Hector, A. (2000), "Review Article: Getting the Measure of Biodiversity", *Nature*, vol. 405, pp. 212-9.

Putnam, R. D. and Bayne, N. (1987), *Hanging Together: Co-operation and Conflicts in the Seven-Power Summit*, Harvard University Press, Cambridge Massachusetts.

Pythoud, F. (1996), "Biotechnology and Biosafety in the CBD", BINAS (UNIDO) News 2/1, pp. 2-4.

Pythoud, F. (2000), "Le Protocole de Cartagena sur la prévention des risques biotechnologiques: les enjeux principaux des négociations", in L. Boisson de Chazournes and U. P. Thomas (eds.), "The Biosafety Protocol: Regulatory Innovation and Emerging Trends", *Swiss Review of International and European Law*, vol. 10, no. 4, pp. 528-536.

Pythoud, F. (forthcoming 2002), "Commodities", in C. Bail, R. Falkner and H. Marquard (eds.), *The Cartagena Protocol on Biosafety: Reconciling Trade in Biotechnology with Environment and Development?*, Royal Institute of International Affairs/Earthscan, London.

Ministère de l'Environnement et de la Faune du Québec (1996), *Stratégie de mise en œuvre de la Convention sur la diversité biologique*.

Ministère de l'Environnement et de la Faune du Québec (1996), *Plan d'action québécois sur la diversité biologique*.

Rabesahala, N. et al. (1994*), Rapport sur les recherches relatives à la gouvernance locale à Madagascar*, DFM-ARD, USAID/KEPEM.

Raharison, R. (2000), *Contexte institutionnel de la conservation des forêts à Madagascar, Série Etudes sur la politique de conservation des ressources forestières à Madagascar*, Conservation internationale et Direction générale des Eaux et Forêts, Antananarivo.

Ramakrishna, K. (1992), "North-South Issues, the Common Heritage of Mankind and Global Environmental Change", in I. H. Rowland and M. Green, (eds.), *Global Environmental Change and International Relations*, Macmillan, London.

Ramamonjisoa, B. S. (2000), *Soutien informationnel aux politiques de gestion des ressources naturelles à Madagascar*, Centre technique de coopération agricole et rurale (CTA), Wageningen.

Ramamonjisoa, B. S. (2001), "Stratégie nationale de la biodiversité et politique forestière: une étude comparative", communication à l'atelier de recherche "Biodiversité, de l'action collective à la gouvernance", 5-7 March, IUED, Geneva.

Raustiala, K. and Victor, D. G. (1996), "Biodiversity since Rio: The Future of the Convention on Biological Diversity", *Environment*, vol. 38, pp. 37-45.

Raven, P. H. and Williams, T. (eds.) (1997), *Nature and Human Society*, National Academy Press, Washington, DC.

Ravetz, J. R. (1993), "The Sin of Science. Ignorance of Ignorance", *Knowledge*, vol. 15, pp. 157-165.

Razafindrabe, M. (1996), "Étude sur le cas de Madagascar", proceedings from the Workshop on Capacity Development in Environment, Rome, 4-6 December, DAC/OECD.

Redford, K. H. and Padoch, C. (eds.) (1992), *Conservation of Neotropical Forests: Working from Traditional Resource Use*, Colombia University Press, New York.

Regens, J. L. and Rycroft, R. W. (1988), *The Acid Rain Controversy*, University of Pittsburg Press, Pittsburg.

Reinicke, W. (1998), *Global Public Policy: Governing Without Government*, Brookings Institution, Washington DC.

Republic of Madagascar (1990), *Charte de l'Environnement*.

Republic of Madagascar (1998a), *Rapport national sur la Convention sur la diversité biologique*.

Republic of Madagascar (1998b), *Document stratégique consolidé du Programme environnemental II (PE2) par la partie malagasy*.

Revéret, J-P., Pelletier, J., Chabot, A., and Bibeault, J. F. (1990*), La mesure économique des bénéfices et des dommages environnementaux*, ministère de l'Environnement du Québec, Quebec.

Revéret, J-P. (1991), *La pratique des pêches: comment gérer une ressource renouvelable?* L'Harmattan, Paris.

Rich, B. (1994), *Mortgaging The Earth: The World Bank, Environmental Impoverishment And The Crisis Of Development*, Earthscan, London.

Rodrigues, J P., Pearson, D. L., and Barrera, R. (1998), "A Test for the Adequacy of Bioindicator Taxa: Are Tiger Beatles (Coleoptera: Cicindelidae) Appropriate Indicators for Monitoring the Degradation of Tropical Forests in Venezuela?", *Biological Conservation*, vol. 83, pp. 69-76.

Rohlf, D. (1994), "Six Biological Reasons Why the Endangered Species Act Doesn't Work – and What to Do about It", in R. E. Grumbine (ed.), *Environmental Policy and Biodiversity*, Island Press, Washington, pp. 181-200.

Rolston III, H. (1995), "Environmental Protection and an Equitable International Order: Ethics after the Earth Summit", *Business Ethics Quarterly*, vol. 5, no. 4, pp. 735-752.

Rosenau, J. N. and Czempiel, E. O. (1992), *Governance Without Government: Order and Change in World Politics*, Cambridge University Press, New York.

Rosendal, K. (1994), "Implications of the US 'No' in Rio", in V. Sanchez, and C. Juma (eds.), *Biodiplomacy: Genetic Resources and International Relations*, African Centre for Technology Studies (ACTS) Press, Nairobi, pp. 87-105.

Rosendal. K. (1999), *Implementing International Environmental Agreements in Developing Countries: The Creation and Impact of the Convention on Biological Diversity*, University of Oslo in co-operation with Unipub forlag, Akademika AS, Oslo.

Rossi, G. (1999), "Forêts tropicales entre mythes et réalités", *Nature, Sciences, Sociétés*, vol. 7, no. 3, pp. 22-37.

Roubaud, F. (2000), *Identités et transition démocratique: l'exception malgache?*, L'Harmattan, Paris.

Ruivo, B. (1994), "Phases or Paradigms of Science Policy?", *Science and Public Policy*, vol. 21, pp. 157-164.

Russell, A. M. (1988), *The Biotechnology Revolution. An International Perspective*, St. Martin's Press, New York.

Sachs, W. (ed.) (1993), *Global Ecology: A New Area of Political Conflict*, Zed Books, London.

Sage, W. (1999), "Regulating Through Information: Disclosure Laws and American Health Care", *Colorado Law Review*, vol. 99, no. 7, pp. 1701-1829.

Sagoff, M. (1998), "On the Uses of Biodiversity", in L. D. Guruswamy and J. A. McNeely (eds.), *Protection of Global Biodiversity*, Duke University Press, Durham North Carolina, pp. 265-284.

Sahai, S. (2001), "India's Plant Variety Protection and Farmer's Rights Act", *Bridges*, vol. 5, no. 8, 11-12 October.

Salter, L. (1988), *Mandated Science: Science and Scientists in the Making of Standards*, Kluwer Academic, Dordrecht.

Sampson, G. P. (ed.) (2001), *The Role of the World Trade Organization in Global Governance*, UN University Press, Tokyo.

Sampson, G. P. and Bradnee Chambers, W. (eds.) (1999), *Trade, Environment and the Millennium*, UN University Press, Tokyo.

Sanchez, V. and Juma, C. (eds.) (1994), *Biodiplomacy: Genetic Resources and International Relations*, African Centre for Technology Studies (ACTS) Press, Nairobi.

Sand, P. H. (1991), "International Co-operation: The Environmental Experience", in Mathews, J. T. (ed.), *Preserving the Global Environment: The Challenge of Shared Leadership*, W.W. Norton and Co, New York, pp. 236-79.

Sand, P. H. (ed.) (1992), *The Effectiveness of International Environmental Agreements: A Survey of Existing Legal Instruments*, Grotius, Cambridge.

Sands, P. (1995), *Principles of International Environmental Law 1: Frameworks, Standards, and Implementation*, Manchester University Press, Manchester.

Sandford, R. (1994), "International Environmental Treaty Secretariats: Stage-Hands or Actors?", in H. O. Bergesen and G. Parmann (eds.), *Green Globe Yearbook of International Co-operation on Environment and Development*, Oxford University Press for the Fridtjof Nansen Institute, London, pp. 17-29.

Saksena, J. (2000), "The Unintended Consequences of Regimes: A Theoretical Appraisal", International Studies Association Annual Meeting.

Schäfer, W. (ed.) (1983), *Finalization in Science*, Reidel, Dordrecht.

Shackley, S. and Wynne, B. (1995), "Integrating Knowledges for Climate Change: Pyramids, Nets and Uncertainties", *Global Environmental Change*, vol. 5, pp. 113-126.

Shackley, S. and Wynne, B. (1996), "Representing Uncertainty in Global Climate Change Science and Policy: Boundary-Ordering Devices and Authority", *Science, Technology and Human Values*, vol. 21, no. 3, Summer, pp. 275-302.

Shiva, V. and Holla-Bhar, R. (1993), "Intellectual Piracy and the Neem Tree", *The Ecologist*, vol. 23, no. 6, pp. 223-227.

Shiva, V. (1995), "Biotechnological Development and the Conservation of Biodiversity", in V. Shiva and I. Moser (eds.), *Biopolitics. A Feminist and Ecological Reader on Biotechnology*, Zed Books, London/New Jersey, pp. 193-213.

Shiva, V. (1997), "The Draft Biological Diversity Legislation: An Anti-National, Anti-People law", *Mimeo*, November.

Simmons, I. G. (1993), *Environmental History*, Blackwell, Oxford.

Simmons, I. G. (1996), "Representing Uncertainty in Global Climate Change Science and Policy: Boundary-Ordering Devices and Authority", *Science, Technology and Human Values*, vol. 21, pp. 275-302.

Smets, H. (1991), "The Right for Information on the Risks Created by Hazardous Installations at the National and International Levels", in F. Francioni and T. Scovazzi (eds.), *International Responsibility for Environmental Harm*, Graham and Trotman, London, pp. 449-472.

Snidal, D. (1985), "Co-ordination versus Prisoner's Dilemma: Implications for International Co-operation and Regimes", *American Political Science Review*, vol. 79, pp. 923-942.

Spielmann, P. J. (1992), "White House has Serious Problems with UN Species-Saving Accord", *Associated Press*, 8 May 1992.

Sprinz, D. (1998), "Measuring the Effectiveness of International Environmental Regimes," APSA Annual Meetings.

Stenson, A. J. and Gray, T. S. (1999), "An Autonomy-Based Justification for Intellectual Property Rights of Indigenous Communities", *Environmental Ethics*, vol. 21, no. 2, pp. 176-190.

Sterne, P. and Zagon, S. (1997), *Public Consultation Guide: Changing the Relationship Between Government and Canadians*, Canadian Centre for Management Development, (www.ccmd-ccg.gc.ca/documents/research/Intro Res Doc.).

Stilwell, M. and Turk, E. (1999), "Trade Measures and MEAs – Resolving WTO Uncertainty", paper prepared for WWF International, Center for International Environmental Law, Geneva.

Stone, C. D. (1996), "La convention de Rio de 1992 sur la diversité biologique", in I. Rens (ed.), *Le droit international face à l'éthique et à la politique de l'environnement*, Georg, Geneva, pp. 119-133.

Stone, C. D. (1997), "Stemming the Loss of Biological Diversity: The Institutional and Ethical Contours", *RECIEL*, vol. 6, no. 3, pp. 231-238.

Susskind, L. E. (1994), *Environmental Diplomacy. Negotiating More Effective Global Agreements*, Oxford University Press, New York.

Svatos, M. (1996), "Biotechnology and the Utilitarian Argument for Patents", *Social Philosophy and Policy*, vol. 13, no. 2, pp. 113-144.

Svensson, U. (1993), "The Convention on Biodiversity: A New Approach" in G. Sjöstedt and U. Svedin (eds.), *International Environmental Negotiations: Process, Issues and Contexts*, Swedish Institute of International Affairs, Stockholm, pp. 164-191.

Swanson, T. (1995), *Intellectual Property Rights and Biodiversity Conservation*, Cambridge University Press, Cambridge.

Swanson, T. (1997), *Global Action for Biodiversity: An International Framework for Implementing the Convention on Biological Diversity*, Earthscan, London.

Swanson, T. (1999), "Why Is There a Biodiversity Convention? The International Interest in Centralized Development Planning", *International Affairs*, vol 75, no. 2, pp. 307-331.

Talafré, J. (2001), *Systèmes de suivi de la mise en œuvre et efficacité des régimes environnementaux: le cas de la Convention sur la lutte contre la désertification*, Mémoire de maîtrise, Institut des sciences de l'environnement, Université du Québec à Montréal.

Takacs, D. (1996), *The Idea of Biodiversity. Philosophies of Paradise*, Johns Hopkins University Press, Baltimore.

Tansey, G. (1999), *Commerce, propriété intellectuelle, alimentation et diversité biologique*, en association avec le bureau Quaker auprès des Nations Unies (Geneva) avec l'appui financier du Department of International Development (UK).

ten Kate, K. and Lasén Diaz, C. (1997), "The Undertaking Revisited", *Plant Genetic Resources*, vol. 6, no. 3, pp. 284-293.

ten Kate, K. and Laird, S. A. (1999), *The Commercial Use of Biodiversity: Access to Genetic Resources and Benefit-Sharing*, report prepared for the European Commission by Royal Botanic Gardens, Earthscan, London.

Theys, J. (1993), "Le savant, le technicien et le politique", in D. Bourg (ed.), *La nature en politique ou l'enjeu philosophique de l'écologie*, L'Harmattan, Paris, pp. 49-65.

Theys, J. (1999), "L'environnement au XXIe siècle. Entre continuités et ruptures", *Futuribles*, vol. 239-240, pp. 5-22.

Thomas, W. L. (ed.) (1956), *Man's Role in Changing the Face of the Earth*, University of Chicago Press, Chicago.

Thomas, U. P. (1997), "UN Reform and Global Ecopolitical Forces.", in R. Wheeler and H. McConnell (eds.), *Swords and Plowshares*, Canadian Scholars Press, Toronto, pp. 229-243.

Thomas, U. P. (2000), "Civil Society and its Role in the Negotiation of the Biosafety Protocol", in L. Boisson de Chazournes and U. P. Thomas (eds.), "The Biosafety Protocol: Regulatory Innovation and Emerging Trends", *Swiss Review of International and European Law*, vol. 10, no. 4, pp. 550-558.

Thoyer, S., Le Goulven, K., and Louafi, S. (2001), "La nature des conflits dans les négociations environnementales internationales: l'exemple de la biodiversité", communication à l'atelier de recherche "Biodiversité, de l'action collective à la gouvernance", 5-7 March 2001, IUED, Geneva.

Thoyer, S. and Tubiana, L. (2001), "Economie politique des négociations internationales sur la biodiversité: acteurs, institutions et gouvernance globale", *Economie et Société*, Série développement, 1st Semester.

Ticktin, T. (2000), *Ethnoecology of Aechmea magdalenae (Bromeliaceae): A Participatory Investigation into the Sustainable Harvest and Conservation of a Non-Timber Forest Product*, Ph.D. thesis, McGill University.

Tilman, D. (2000), "Overview: Causes, Consequences and Ethics of Biodiversity", *Nature*, vol. 405, pp. 208-211.

Tinker, C. (1995), "A 'New Breed' of Treaty: The United Nations Convention on Biological Diversity", *Pace Environmental Law Review*, vol. 12, no. 2, Spring, pp. 191-218.

Tolba, M. and Rummel-Bulska, I. (1998), *Global Environmental Diplomacy: Negotiating Environmental Agreements for the World, 1973-1992*, MIT Press, Cambridge Massachusetts.

Trumbore, P. F. (1997), "A Seat at the Bargaining Table: Public Opinion as a Domestic Constraints in Two-Level International Negotiations", International Studies Association Annual Meeting.

Turner, B. L. (ed.) (1990), *The Earth as Transformed by Human Action. Global and Regional Change in the Biosphere over the Past 300 Years*, Cambridge University Press, New York.

Tuxill, J. (1999), "Appreciating the Benefits of Plant Biodiversity", in L. Brown et al. (eds.) (1999), *State of the World 1999*, Norton/Worldwatch Institute, New York, pp. 96-114.

Tuxill, J. (2000), "The Biodiversity that People Made.", *World Watch*, vol. 13, no. 3, May, pp. 24-36.

Underdal, A. (1992), "The Concept of Regime Effectiveness", *Co-operation and Conflict*, vol. 27, no. 3, pp. 227-240.

UNEP/BioDiv.1/Inf.2, *Proceedings of the Ad Hoc Working Group on the Work of its First Session*, 16-18 November 1988.

UNEP/BioDiv.2/2, *Note by the Executive Director to the Second Session of the Ad Hoc Group of Experts on Biological Diversity*, 19-23 February 1990.

UNEP/BioDiv.3/12, *Report of the Ad Hoc Group of Experts on Biological Diversity on the Work of its Third Session in Preparation for a Legal Instrument on Biological Diversity of the Planet*, 9-13 July 1990.

UNEP/Bio.Div./SWGB.1/3, *Ad Hoc Group of Experts on Biological Diversity. Biotechnology and Biodiversity*, 14 November 1990.

UNEP/IGM/1/INF/1, *Open-Ended Intergovernmental Group of Ministers or Their Representatives on International Environmental Governance. Multilateral Environmental Agreements: A Summary*, 30 March 2001.

UNEP/CBD/MSP/2, *Note by the Executive Secretary on the Strategic Plan for the Convention on Biological Diversity to the Open-Ended Inter-Sessional Meeting on the Strategic Plan, National Reports and Implementation of the CBD*, 19-21 November 2001.

UNEP Internal Memorandum from A. Timoshenko and S. Bragdon to M. Tolba, *Comments on Climate Change Documents as they pertain to Biological Diversity Negotiations*, 23 April 1992.

UNEP Executive Director Letter to Governments Concerning Convening a Meeting in Nairobi, 19 September 1990.

US House Judiciary Resolution 648, 100th Congress, 2nd Session, 1988.

UNEP (1992), *Convention on Biological Diversity: Texts and Annexes*, Secretariat of Convention on Biological Diversity, Geneva.

UNEP (1994), *Decisions and Ministerial Statement from the First Meeting of the Conference of the Parties to the Convention on Biological Diversity*, Secretariat of the Convention on Biological Diversity, Montreal.

UNEP (1995a), *Establishment of the Clearing-House Mechanism to Promote and Facilitate Technical and Scientific Co-operation*, Secretariat of the Convention on Biological Diversity, Montreal.

UNEP (1995b), *Report of the Conference of the Parties to the Convention on Biological Diversity, First Meeting, Nassau, 28 November-9 December 1994*, Secretariat of the Convention on Biological Diversity, Montreal.

UNEP (1995c), *Report of the Conference of the Parties to the Convention on Biological Diversity, Second Meeting, Jakarta, 6-17 November 1995*, Secretariat of the Convention on Biological Diversity, Montreal.

UNEP (1996a), *A Call to Action: Decisions and Ministerial Statement from the Second Meeting of the Conference of the Parties to the Convention on Biological Diversity*, Secretariat of the Convention on Biological Diversity, Montreal.

UNEP (1996b), *Operation of the Clearing-House Mechanism to Promote and Facilitate Technical and Scientific Co-operation: Report by the Executive Secretary*, Secretariat of the Convention on Biological Diversity, Montreal.

UNEP (1997a), *Conference of the Parties to the Convention on Biological Diversity, Third Meeting, 4-15 November 1996, Buenos Aires, Argentina*, Secretariat of the Convention on Biological Diversity, Montreal.

UNEP (1997b), *Decisions and Ministerial Statement from the Third Meeting of the Conference of the Parties to the Convention on Biological Diversity*, Secretariat of the Convention on Biological Diversity, Montreal.

UNEP (1997c), *Report of the Workshop on Traditional Knowledge and Biological Diversity, Madrid, Spain, 24-28 November, 1997*, Secretariat of the Convention on Biological Diversity, Montreal.

UNEP (1997d), *The Biodiversity Agenda: Decisions from the Third Meeting of the Conference of the Parties to the Convention on Biological Diversity*, Secretariat of the Convention on Biological Diversity, Montreal.

UNEP (1997e), *Workshop on Traditional Knowledge and Biological Diversity, Madrid, Spain, 24-28 November, 1997*, Secretariat of the Convention on Biological Diversity, Montreal.

UNEP (1998a), *Country Reports: Belize; Cape Verde; Congo; Costa Rica; Lesotho; Mexico; Mozambique; Niger; Panama; Senegal; Swaziland; Togo; Uruguay; Zambia*; Secretariat of the Convention on Biological Diversity, Geneva.

UNEP (1998b), *Decisions and Ministerial Statement from the Fourth Meeting of the Conference of the Parties to the Convention on Biological Diversity*, Secretariat of the Convention on Biological Diversity, Montreal.

UNEP (1998c), *Implementation of Article 8j and Related Provisions: Note by the Executive Secretary*, Secretariat of the Convention on Biological Diversity, Montreal.

UNEP (1998d), *Implementation of the Pilot Phase of the Clearing-House Mechanism: Report of the Executive Secretary*, Secretariat of the Convention on Biological Diversity, Montreal.

UNEP (1998e), *Final Report on the Regional Workshops on the Clearing-House Mechanism*, Secretariat of the Convention on Biological Diversity, Montreal.

UNEP (1998f), *Review of National, Regional and Sectoral Measures and Guidelines for the Implementation of Article 15*, Note for the Conference of the Parties, Montreal.

UNEP (1999a), *Report of the Independant Review of the Pilot Phase of the Clearing-House Mechanism*, Secretariat of the Convention on Biological Diversity, Montreal.

UNEP (1999b), *Co-operation with Other Bodies*, Secretariat of the Convention on Biological Diversity, Montreal.

UNEP (1999c), *Global Environmental Outlook*, Earthscan, London.

UNEP (2000a), *Cartagena Protocol on Biosafety to the Convention on Biological Diversity (Biosafety Protocol)*, Secretariat of the Convention on Biological Diversity, Montreal.

UNEP (2000b), *Decision-Making Procedures (Article 10, Para 7), Intergovernmental Committee for the Cartagena Protocol on Biosafety*, Note by the Executive Secretary, Montreal.

UNEP (2000c), *Handbook of the Convention on Biological Diversity*, Secretariat of the Convention on Biological Diversity, Montreal.

United Kingdom – *Global Environmental Change Project* (GECP-UK) (1999).

United Nations Economic and Social Council (1997), *Implementation of the Convention on Biological Diversity. A Report by the Executive Secretary*, United Nations, New York.

United Nations University (1999), International Conference on Synergies and Co-ordination Between Multilateral Environmental Agreements (Interlinkages_99), July 14-16, Tokyo.

United States. Agency for International Development (USAID) (1994), *USAID/Madagascar Environment Program*, Antananarivo.

United States. National Intelligence Council (2000), *Global Trends 2015: A Dialogue About the Future With Non-government Experts*, NIC2000-02.

Vaillancourt, J-G. (1995), "Penser et concrétiser le développement durable", *Ecodécision*, Winter, pp. 24-29.

Vanderzwaag, D. (1995), *Canada and Marine Environmental Protection. Charting a Legal Course Towards Sustainable Development*, Kluwer Law International, London.

Velasquez Runk, J. (1998), "Productivity and Sustainability of a Vegetable Ivory Palm (Phytelephas aequatorialis, Arecaceae) under Three Management Regimes in Northwestern Ecuador", *Economic Botany*, vol. 52, no. 2, pp. 168-182.

Ventocilla, J., Núñez, V., Herrera, F., Herrera, H,. and Chapin, M. (1995), "Los indígenas kunas y la conservación ambiental", *Mesoamérica*, vol. 29, pp. 95-124.

Verdeaux, F. (1981), L'aizi Pluriel, chronique d'une ethnie lagunaire de Côte d'Ivoire, Office de la recherche scientifique et technique outre-mer, Centre ORSTOM de petit Bassam, Abidjan.

Victor, P. (1994), "How Strong is Weak Sustainability?", Actes du colloque "Modèles de développement soutenable: des approches exclusives ou complémentaires de la soutenabilité", Université Panthéon-Sorbonne, Paris, pp. 93-114.

Victor, D. (1998), "External Enforcement of International Agreements", International Studies Association Annual Meeting.

Victor, D. (1999), "The Market for International Environmental Protection Services and the Perils of Co-ordination", in International Conference on Synergies and Co-ordination Between Multilateral Environmental Agreements (Interlinkages_99), 14-16 July, Tokyo.

Victor, D., Raustiala, K., and Skolnikoff, E. B. (eds.) (1998), *The Implementation and Effectiveness of International Commitments: Theory and Practice*, MIT Press/IIASA, Cambridge Massachusetts.

Vining, A. R. and Weimer, D. L. (1988), "Information Asymmetry Favoring Sellers: A Policy Framework", *Policy Sciences*, vol. 21, pp. 281-303.

Vogler, J. (1995), *The Global Commons: A Regime Analysis*, John Wiley and Sons, Chichester.

Vogler, J. and McGraw, D. (2000), "An International Environmental Regime for Biotechnology? The Case of the Cartagena Protocol on Biosafety", in J. Vogler, and A. Russell (eds.), *The International Politics of Biotechnology: Investigating Global Futures*, Manchester University Press, Manchester, pp. 123-141.

Von Weizsäcker, C. (1993), "Competing Notion of Biodiversity", in W. Sachs (ed.), *Global Ecology. A New Arena of Political Conflict*, Zed Books, London.

Walker, S. (2001), *The TRIPS Agreement, Sustainable Development and the Public Interest*, IUCN and World Conservation Union, Gland/Geneva.

WCED (1987), *Our Common Future: The Report of the World Commission on Environment and Development*, Oxford University Press, New York.

Weber, J. (1995), "L'occupation humaine des aires protégées à Madagascar: diagnostic et éléments pour une gestion viable", *Natures, sciences, sociétés*, vol. 3, no. 2, pp. 157- 164.

Weber, J. (1996), "Conservation, développement et coordination: Peut-on gérer biologiquement le social?", Colloque Panafricain Gestion communautaire des ressources naturelles renouvelables et développement durable, 24-27 June 1996, Harare.

Weber, J. (1998), "Perspectives de gestion patrimoniale des ressources renouvelables", in P. Lavigne Delville (ed.), *Quelles politiques foncières pour l'Afrique rurale ? Réconcilier pratiques, légitimité et légalité*, Karthala and Coopération française, Paris, pp. 534-552.

Weber, J. and Bailly, D. (1989), "Prévoir, c'est gouverner", *Nature, Sciences, Sociétés*, vol. 1, no. 1 (http://www.elsevier.fr/html/detrevue.cfm?code=NS).

Weber, J. and Revéret, J-P. (1993), *Biens communs: les leurres de la privatisation*, Savoirs *Le monde diplomatique*, Paris.

Weeks, P., Packard, J., and Martínez-Velarde, M. (2001), "Cultural Lenses and Reflexibility in Conservation Biology", in C. Potvin, M. Kraenzel and G. Seutin (eds.), *Protecting Biological Diversity: Roles and Responsibilities*, McGill-Queen's University Press, Montreal, pp. 41-57.

Wells, M. and Brandon, K. (1993), "The Principles and Practice of Buffer Zones and Local Participation in Biodiversity Conservation", *Ambio*, vol. 22, no. 2-3.

Wells, M., Brandon, K., and Hannah, L. (1992), *People and Parks: Linking Protected Area Management with Local Communities*, IBRD/WWF/USAID.

Werksman, J. (ed.) (1996), *Greening International Institutions*, Earthscan, London.

Werksman, J. (1997), "Five MEAs, Five Years Since Rio: Recent Lessons on the Effectiveness of Multilateral Environmental Agreements", Foundation for International Environmental Law & Development (FIELD), United Kingdom.

Western, D., Wright, M., and Strum, S. C. (eds.) (1994), *Natural Connections: Perspectives in Community-Based Conservation*, Island Press, Washington DC.

Wettestad, J. (1999), *Designing Effective Environmental Regimes: The Key Conditions*, Edward Elgar, Cheltenham United Kingdom/Northampton Massachusetts.

Wettestad, J. and Andersen, S. (1991), *The Effectiveness of International Resource Co-operation: Some Preliminary Findings*, Report No. R:007, Fridtjof Nansen Institute, Lysaker.

Whitley, R. (1984), *The Intellectual and Social Organization of the Sciences*, Clarendon Press, Oxford.

Williams, R. (2000), "A Modern Earth Narrative: What Will Be the Fate of the Biosphere?", *Technology in Society*, vol. 22, pp. 303-339.

Willinger, M. (1996), "La méthode d'évaluation contingente: de l'observation à la construction des valeurs de préservation", *Nature, Sciences, Sociétés*, vol. 4, pp. 6-22.

Wilson, E. O. (1993), *The Diversity of Life*, Belknap Press, Cambridge Massachusetts.

Wilson, E. and Peters, F. M. (eds.) (1988), *Biodiversity*, National Academy Press, Washington DC.

Wold, C. (1995), *The Biodiversity Convention and Existing International Agreements: Opportunities for Synergy*, Humane Society of United States and Humane Society International, Washington DC.

Wold, C. (1998), "The Futility, Utility, and Future of the Biodiversity Convention", *Colorado Journal of International Environmental Law and Policy*, vol. 9, no. 1, pp. 1-42.

Wolf, A. (2000), "Informed Consent: A Negotiated Formula for Trade in Risky Organisms and Chemicals", *International Negotiation*, vol. 5, no. 3, pp. 485-521.

Wood, R. E. (1986), *From Marshall Plan to Debt Crisis: Foreign Aid and Development Choices in the World Economy*, University of California Press, Berkeley.

Wood, P. M. (2000), *Biodiversity and Democracy: Rethinking Society and Nature*, UBC Press, Vancouver.

World Bank (1992), *World Development Report*, Oxford University Press, New York.

World Bank (1996a), *Madagascar Poverty Assessment*, Report No. 14044-MAG, IBRD, Washington DC.

World Bank (1996b), *Staff Appraisal Report. Madagascar Second Environment Program*, Report No. 15952-MAG, IBRD, Washington DC.

World Commission on Environment and Development (WCED) (1987), *Our Common Future*, Oxford University Press, Oxford.

World Resources Institute (2000), *World Resources 2000-2001: People and Ecosystems*, World Resources Institute, Washington DC.

WTO (1994), *The Results of the Uruguay Round of Multilateral Trade Negotiations – The Legal Texts*, World Trade Organization, Geneva.

WTO Secretariat (1999), *Guide to the Uruguay Round Agreements*, WTO and Kluwer Law International, The Hague.

Worldwide Fund for Nature (1996), *Endangered Spaces. Progress Report 1994-1995*.

Yamin, F. (1995), "Biodiversity, Ethics and International Law", *International Affairs*, vol. 71, no. 3, pp. 529-546.

Young, O. R. (1989a), *International Co-operation: Building Regimes for Natural Resources and the Environment*, Cornell University Press, Ithaca.

Young, O. R. (1989b), "The Politics of International Regime Formation: Managing Natural Resources and the Environment", *International Organization*, vol. 43, pp. 349-376.

Young, O. R. (1992), "The Effectiveness of International Institutions: Hard Cases and Critical Variables", in J. N. Rosenau and E. O. Czempiel (eds.), *Governance without Government: Change and Order in World Politics*, Cambridge University Press, New York, pp. 160-194.

Young, O. R. (1994), *International Governance: Protecting the Environment in a Stateless Society*, Cornell University Press, Ithaca.

Young, O. R. (1996), "Introduction: The Effectiveness of International Governance", in O. R. Young, G. J. Demko and K. Ramakrishna (eds.), *Global Environmental Change and International Governance*, University Press of New England, Hanover and London, pp. 1-27.

Young, O. R. (1997), "Global Governance: Toward a Theory of Decentralized World Order", in O. R. Young (ed.), *Global Governance: Drawing Insights from the Environmental Experience*, MIT Press, Cambridge, Massachusetts pp. 273-299.

Young, O. R. (ed.) (1999), *The Effectiveness of International Environmental Regimes: Causal Connections and Behavioral Mechanisms*, MIT Press, Cambridge, Massachusetts.

Young, O. R. (2001), "Inferences and Indices: Evaluating the Effectiveness of International Environmental Regimes", International Studies Association Annual Meeting.

Zarrilli, S. (2000), "International Trade in GMOs: Developing Country Concerns and Possible Options", in L. Boisson de Chazournes and U. P. Thomas (eds.), "The Biosafety Protocol: Regulatory Innovation and Emerging Trends", *Swiss Review of International and European Law*, vol. 10, no. 4, pp. 543-550.

Index